THE OBSERVER OBSERVED

1791   1991

THE
OBSERVER
OBSERVED

◆

200 YEARS OF
DISTINGUISHED
WRITING FROM
ONE OF THE
WORLD'S GREAT
NEWSPAPERS

◆

Edited by
Joanna Anstey and John Silverlight

BARRIE & JENKINS
LONDON

First published in Great Britain in 1991 by Barrie & Jenkins Ltd,
20 Vauxhall Bridge Road, London SW1V 2SA

Picture Editor: Jenny de Gex

Typeset by SX Composing Ltd, Rayleigh, Essex
Colour separation by Chroma Graphics, Singapore
Printed and bound in Portugal by Printer Portuguesa

A catalogue record for this book is available
from the British Library.

ISBN 0-7126-4699-X

The editors wish to thank
Rhona Drummond, Publisher, Observer Communications;
and Jeffrey Care, the Observer Librarian, and
his colleagues, for all their help and encouragement
in preparing this book.

CONTENTS

A range of The Observer's *photography.*
Top left: Tottenham Hotspur's goalkeeper, John Hollowbread, White Hart Lane, London, 1964. Top right: jubilant villagers greet Patriotic Front fighters during the Rhodesian elections in 1980. Middle left: the funeral of a young Romanian student, killed by a Securitate sniper's bullet during the Romanian revolution. Middle right: Peter O'Toole as MacBeth. Bottom left: Champion jockey Lester Piggott. Bottom right: the turf flies at a Newbury national hunt meeting.

INTRODUCTION

Since 1908 *The Observer* has had only three editors: J.L. Garvin, David Astor and Donald Trelford. (Between 1942 and 1948, when David Astor was mainly abroad on active service, Ivor Brown was Acting Editor.) The paper's founder, in 1791, was W.S. Bourne; the next proprietor, William Innell Clement. Between about 1807 and 1908 there were five editors: Lewis Doxat, Joseph Snowe, Edward Dicey, Austin Harrison and H.D. Traill. That is not a vast number either, but large enough to make for variety of style. There is certainly that, but there are remarkable consistencies.

One is readability. Perhaps I am prejudiced: someone who has spent three-quarters of his working life more or less happily on a newspaper is unlikely to be objective about it. For evidence, however, see the account of Marie Antoinette's execution (11 November 1793) and Sir Len Hutton's obituary (9 September 1990).

Other persistent themes are concern for the underprivileged and support for reform. It is difficult to glance cursorily at current issues without noticing a major piece, if not two or three, about people in need of special care – the old, the handicapped, the very young, not to mention the poor who are always with us – who are being overlooked. The third item in this collection (12 February 1792) is about 'a poor little sweep-chimney, not above seven years of age', who 'was almost smothered to death by the remaining effluvia of charcoal, in the chimney of a house . . . in Austin-friars'. There was sympathetic reporting on the Luddites and on Peterloo. An early piece on juvenile delinquency (14 September 1817) ends: '. . . the severity of penal law; and the frequency of capital punishment, are evidences little creditable to the system of which such evils are the result.'

From 1832 onwards the paper consistently backed the extension of the franchise. On the California Gold Rush it commented: 'It is a matter of congratulation that England has not discovered this immense mine of gold; and why? because she would have assigned it exclusively to the privileged classes – who, Heaven knows! are privileged too much already.' (31 December 1848.) In the American Civil War the British upper classes and much of the Press were pro-South. The lower and middle classes were anti-slavery and pro-North. So was *The Observer*, to its cost in circulation and revenue (cf. Suez, 4 November 1956).

The third example of consistency goes to the heart of what journalism is about. Our task, which makes us at least as important as doctors, soldiers, lawyers, perhaps any group except priests and poets and other artists, is to expose to the light what should be exposed. Journalists should not pry into private grief, should not be prurient, should not endanger the State. But they must pick up the stones and look under them. Otherwise corruption breeds. In 1820 the Lord Chief Justice forbade reporting of the Cato Street Conspiracy trial. *The Observer* did report it (6 March and 1 May 1820). The proprietor was summoned before the court. Clement refused to appear and was fined the immense sum in those days of £500. He never paid. That double act of defiance helped to re-establish the freedom of crime reporting. I was reminded of this when re-reading our leading article on the Spycatcher case (16 October 1988), in which *The Observer* played a leading part right up to a hearing in the European Court.

In 1905 Lord Northcliffe, then Sir Alfred Harmsworth, acquired *The Observer*, describing it, a bit unfairly, as 'lying in the Fleet ditch'. (He sold it in 1911 to the first Viscount Astor, who gave it to his son Waldorf in 1915.) In 1908 Northcliffe appointed J.L. (for James Louis) Garvin as editor. Almost immediately Garvin gave the paper a dominant position among journals of opinion.

He differed sharply from his predecessors and successors in his approach to journalism. His interest was high politics, in which he wished to play a part. Thanks to a powerful pen and powerful friends (e.g. 'Jackie' Fisher, First Sea Lord; Balfour, Tory leader; Alexander Murray, the Master of Elibank, Chief Liberal Whip), he succeeded. John Grigg, in his *Lloyd George: the People's Champion*, describes Garvin's role in Opposition politics at that time as 'almost the equivalent to that of a parliamentary leader'. The historian John Stubbs has written that *The Observer* of that period is 'remembered for Garvin's unique political writing. The successful campaign for a more rapid development of a modern navy had given it unequalled authority' (see 2 February 1908).

Two years later, Edward VII died unexpectedly. Fierce controversy was raging over economic reform and Irish Home Rule. On 8 May 1910 Garvin called for a 'Truce of God', a suspension of political dispute in which leaders of both parties could consult each other 'before any prerogative of the Crown is made a direct issue in an almost unquenchable conflagration of party passions.' A five-month 'truce' duly followed.

That was Garvin's peak. To quote John Grigg again, this time reviewing David Ayerst's *Garvin of The Observer*, his influence was 'of a kind that few journalists have ever rivalled. At that time he was not merely an authoritative commentator, but a key participant in high politics. Afterwards he remained indeed formidable but was never again so influential.' Roy Jenkins, reviewing A.M. Gollin's *The Observer and J.L. Garvin*, writes: 'After reading Dr Gollin's expertly marshalled evidence, my view is that this faltering in the paper's performance (in 1912 and 1913) was due to Garvin having exhausted his initial momentum.'

Garvin's momentum did not fully return. There was the fine 'Dragon's Teeth' leading article on 11 May 1919 attacking the Versailles Treaty, but as Garvin's political contacts died or lost influence, so his writing lost some of its primal force, though the paper remained a highly respected journal, with its excellent Arts reviewers, who included Percy Scholes and, latterly, William Glock (music); Ivor Brown and St John Irvine (theatre); and C.A. Lejeune, the best cinema critic of her time.

Waldorf Astor had his differences with Garvin but was fond of him. Garvin was a frequent visitor to Cliveden, the Astor country seat. (He lived nearby, in Beaconsfield – his house, Gregories, was once owned by Burke – where he edited *The Observer* with secretaries shuttling to and from London, and his Rolls rushing proofs to him on Saturdays.)

David, Waldorf's second son, did not share his father's regard for Garvin. Nor was he particularly interested in journalism at first, though he had a spell in 1936 on the *Yorkshire Post*, which was edited by Waldorf's friend Arthur Mann. The coming of war changed all that. David's close friend at Oxford had been the German Rhodes scholar Adam von Trott, who was executed in 1944 for his part in the July Plot against Hitler. Young Astor – he was born in 1912 – saw the war not as just a repeat of 1914,

an old-fashioned nationalist conflict, but as a civil war between two ideologies, democracy and totalitarianism, with many Germans such as von Trott on the same side as ourselves.

Although only a junior officer in the Royal Marines, he also had ideas on how the war should be fought. In 1941 he drew up a list of issues which the Government should be thinking about and wasn't, and which *The Observer* should be writing about and wasn't. They included: the study of guerrilla warfare; propaganda; a proper political party truce, not just a group of party figureheads grouped around one warlord (he turned down an offer from Anthony Eden of what would have been a safe Tory seat); post-war economics in this country and the rest of Europe; how to improve Anglo-Russian relations.

And he had in mind the writers he wanted. Another Rhodes scholar friend was E.F. Schumacher, author of *Small is Beautiful* (29 August 1965). Astor also knew Michael Foot, then editing Beaverbrook's *Evening Standard*, and Stafford Cripps – like von Trott, Cripps' son John was with Astor at Balliol. Cripps introduced him to Barbara Ward (later Lady Ward Jackson) and Geoffrey (later Lord) Crowther, both on the *Economist*; so was the historian Isaac Deutscher. Another German refugee friend was Sebastian Haffner (real name Raimund Pretzel); he and Deutscher both became important voices on the David Astor *Observer*. Through Cyril Connolly, editor of *Horizon* (he too joined the paper briefly), he met Arthur Koestler and George Orwell.

The result of all this was 'The Forum', a 'medium of free expression by various writers', as a footnote described the column when it appeared on the paper's leader page, where Garvin had been persuaded to give up some space. It was, in effect, the David Astor *Observer* in the making, articles on subjects that mattered by people qualified to write them, including Astor himself. It was a 'Forum' piece that led to Garvin's departure.

Lord Astor too was becoming restive about Garvin, especially his editing the paper twenty-odd miles from Whitehall, Westminster and, as important, clubland. There was also Garvin's age, seventy-three. Negotiations went on for months to persuade him to accept an Associate Editor who would run the paper while he remained Editor-in-Chief. Items of 15 and 22 February 1942 tell how the break came.

David was now liaising with the Press for

Lord Louis (as he then was) Mountbatten, Chief of Combined Operations. Somehow he found time, and energy, to keep in touch with the tiny staff who continued to bring out the paper (see March 1942); to meet the News Editor-cum-Production Editor at Boodles, where they read proofs and discussed production problems; to discuss leaders every week with the stand-in leader writer, G.M. Young, the historian, at the Athenaeum.

Things became less hectic when John Beavan (later, editor of the *Daily Herald* and now Lord Ardwick) came in as 'a sort of Managing Editor', as he has put it. Ivor Brown, the drama critic, was appointed Acting Editor (the word 'acting' was never used publicly, though Waldorf made it clear that David would be taking over after the war). Donald Tyerman, another *Economist* writer, became in effect Brown's deputy and chief leader writer. *The Observer* was a proper newspaper at last, noticeably better than under Garvin: the first profile (Stafford Cripps) appeared a fortnight after Garvin's departure.

Soon after D-Day Astor took part in a Special Operations Executive air-drop in France and was wounded – being ready to go on raids was part of his job at Combined Ops (he was awarded the Croix de Guerre). He became Foreign Editor in 1946 and Editor in 1948. The next years were exciting: the Greek civil war; Israel; China; Korea; Africa – the last, so said the wags, was created journalistically by *The Observer*, which early on began giving warning of the latent dangers in colonialism generally and, above all, racialism, as manifested in apartheid. Talent pressed to join, notably when the late Kenneth Tynan, already becoming the most notable post-war theatre critic, applied to be Number Three under Ivor Brown and J.C. Trewin if that was the only way of getting on the paper.

Good as they were, *Observer* journalists were of course mere mortals, but to me when I joined, in 1960, they were gods. To name individuals would be invidious, but three can be picked out with less risk of that since they moved on from journalism and are dead. Alastair Buchan, the Diplomatic Correspondent, left to become the first Director of the International Institute for Strategic Studies, and later Montague Professor of International Relations at Oxford. William Clark, whose jobs on the paper had included being Diplomatic Correspondent and Our Man in Washington,

became the first Director of the Overseas Development Institute. He then went to work for Robert McNamara at the World Bank, became president of the Institute for Environment and Development, and later became an independent director of *The Observer*. Andrew Shonfield (who was knighted later), the Economics Correspondent and Business Editor, who had transformed the financial pages, went to the Royal Institute of International Relations (otherwise Chatham House) first as Director of Studies, then as Director. He later became Professor of Economics at the European Institute in Florence. (Waldorf Astor was Chairman of Chatham House from 1935 to 1949.)

Of those who stayed with *The Observer* throughout their careers and, through their editing, helped shape its character in the third quarter of the century, three select themselves. Ken Obank joined *The Observer* during the war and became the strongest influence in the presentation of news and a dominant office 'presence'. Terence Kilmartin, who had met Astor on that SOE war-time parachute drop, had a parallel influence on the newspaper's Arts sections. Michael Davie, who had originally joined *The Observer* from Oxford in the unlikely role of religious affairs correspondent after admiring an article from China by Patrick O'Donovan, occupied a series of key positions in this period: News Editor, Sports Editor, the first Colour Magazine Editor, Deputy Editor, with constant interest in the United States and a late-flowering career as an award-winning columnist.

People talk of a distinctive *Observer* 'style' in the post-war period. Some attribute its origins to Ivor Brown, others to Orwell. If there was such a thing (and readers may judge this for themselves in the pages that follow) Kilmartin's team of book reviewers, led by Malcolm Muggeridge, Philip Toynbee and A.J.P. Taylor, and critics like Tynan, Penelope Gilliatt, Peter Heyworth and Nigel Gosling must have contributed strongly to it, as did foreign correspondents such as Dennis Bloodworth, Cyril Dunn and Gavin Young. At home there were John Gale, Edward Crankshaw, Anthony Sampson and the stylist's stylist himself, Patrick O'Donovan.

The 'style', if such it was, entered the political pages through Hugh Massingham, who invented a new genre of political columns that is represented today by Alan Watkins. It can be detected in the women's pages in the writing of

Anne Scott-James, Alison Settle and Katharine Whitehorn, in Eric Newby's travel writing and in a whole group of sports writers led by Hugh McIlvanney and Christopher Brasher. Most of these names are represented in the following pages. Others, perhaps equally deserving, are not: cutting 200 years to about 300 pages can be a cruel business.

By the early 1960s, economic clouds were beginning to gather around *The Observer*. The great struggle among the quality Sundays was beginning. The *Sunday Telegraph* was launched in 1961. The *Sunday Times* started its colour magazine in 1962. (Ours started in 1964 and paid off handsomely in advertising revenue and circulation. Particularly successful were three series: *Who Killed Jesus*, by Colin Cross; Piers Paul Reid's *Alive*, an account of survival after an aircrash in the Andes thanks to cannibalism; and *French Cookery School*.)

At the end of 1975 David Astor retired as editor and was succeeded by his thirty-eight-year-old deputy, Donald Trelford. From school in Coventry he had joined the RAF (where he acquired an interest in flying that saw him in the cockpit of a Tornado over the age of 50) before taking up an exhibition at Selwyn College (where he was a contemporary of Richard Harries, now Bishop of Oxford, and John Gummer, the Minister of Agriculture). At Cambridge he excelled in English, at cricket and rugby, and in student journalism. He worked as a reporter and sub-editor for newspapers in Coventry and Sheffield, and was then sent out by the Thomson group at the age of 25 to edit a paper in newly-independent Malawi.

While there he also covered Ian Smith's UDI in Rhodesia and civil wars in Nigeria and the Congo for *The Observer*, *The Times* and the BBC. When he answered an *Observer* advertisement in 1966 seeking an assistant news editor, he flew home at his own expense and got the job. Soon he was exercising far more influence than the title suggested. The Thomson group tried to buy him back, offering him a management job at three times his *Observer* salary. Astor told him, 'I can't match their offer. But you're a journalist. You won't be happy in management.' He stayed, with a modest rise. Two years later, Astor made him his deputy. Eight years later he became editor.

There were six contenders. Before appointing Trelford the Observer Trustees (see box on page 108) canvassed the whole editorial staff, though they would not necessarily have been bound by the result. Trelford was the emphatic choice of a large majority. On the basis of that poll the Trustees decided that he was the most eligible.

It was a critical time to take over. The cost of newsprint had been going up inexorably. More damaging still was the grip of the production unions, who clung to restrictive practices, resisted the introduction of new technology and readily sacrificed publication of the newspaper to enforce extravagant wage demands. Money was running out fast and inflation was rising. The Trust, organised by the Astor family, to which the paper's ownership had been transferred, was a fine, a noble concept. It was similar in intent to the one set up by the *Manchester Guardian*, but it lacked the built-in inflation factor enjoyed by the *Guardian* in the shape of the *Manchester Evening News* and its other media investments.

The Trustees decided to make new financial arrangements and cast around for a suitable proprietor. At one point Rupert Murdoch came on the scene, but withdrew after opposition from the staff. Satisfactory arrangements were soon made with another candidate, the American oil firm Atlantic Richfield chaired by Robert O. Anderson. In 1981 they sold *The Observer* to Lonrho (see page 251) which agreed, after a contested hearing at the Monopolies and Mergers Commission, to include on the board five independent directors to settle possible disputes between proprietor and editor, an arrangement that has worked well. Lonrho has made a substantial investment in the paper over the past decade, without which it could not have survived. This has allowed expansion of the newspaper's editorial coverage in a number of areas, including the introduction of a separate Business section.

The Observer has remained *The Observer*, in spirit as in name. Evidence of this are the Press awards which the paper has taken for granted ever since they started, and still does. Hugh McIlvanney is the most 'decorated' journalist, with more than a dozen major awards. In 1989 Jonathan Mirsky was named International Reporter of the Year for his eye-witness coverage of the Tiananmen Square massacre. That is gratifying. Far more important is the fact that Donald Trelford, like David Astor, is dedicated to journalism at its finest and most responsible, and has acquired an international reputation as a defender of press freedom.

He has often quoted a passage from J.M.

Keynes as summing up his view of his calling. Though it was written with politics in mind, it will do for journalism too: 'The events of the coming year will not be shaped by the deliberate acts of statesmen, but by the hidden currents flowing continually beneath the surface of political history, of which no one can predict the outcome. In one way only can we influence these hidden currents – by setting in motion those forces of instruction and imagination which change opinion. The assertion of truth, the unveiling of illusion, the dissipation of hate, the enlargement and instruction of men's hearts and minds, must be the means.'

What continuity does all this have with a paper founded for another age, in the year of Mozart's *Magic Flute*? Trelford does indeed see continuity. In an article in January to mark our bicentenary he wrote: 'Part of the consistency is trying to look at things anew and not being a slave to what was said before, even by us; trying not to "con" readers that all problems have easy solutions, and that we know what they are; being reasonable even if we can't always be right; giving off a strong whiff of idealism that attracts some people and irritates others; trying harder than some to be open-minded; not recoiling from the awkward truth when we see it; being, in Orwell's phrase, the enemies of nonsense, especially our own.

'If this sometimes makes for what Conor Cruise O'Brien has called "muzziness, our besetting sin", one can only say that there are worse faults for a newspaper to have, like being untruthful, prejudiced or boring, which we hope we are not – except, perhaps, when we go on too long about ourselves.'

John Silverlight

Jane Bown's view of Prime Minister Hugh Gaitskell, and Aneurin Bevan at a Labour Party Conference in Brighton.

ADDRESS TO THE PUBLIC.

AT a period, eminently diftinguifhed for the moft bold and mafterly productions of Genius; *for the moft polifhed refinements in* Art; *and for the moft majeftic expanfions of* Science, *little encouragement can be expected, to inftitutions of any kind, which have not, for their* animating principles,

THE MORAL AND RELIGIOUS ADVANTAGES

OF SOCIETY.

Without *the irrefiftible vigour of fuch principles, publications, embellifhed by all the brilliancy of genius, become dangerous—they* allure, *to the fubverfion of* fentiment, *and they* fafcinate, *to the abatement of* intellecutal purity.

Confcious of thefe important truths, the Proprietors *of the* OBSERVER *have determined upon a variety of Arrangements, which from their* intrinfic *qualities, as well as from their adventitious importance, they flatter themselves, will not fail to attach,* in preference to any fimilar publication, *the approbation of a people, not lefs eminent for their liberal rewards of merit than for their ample powers of difcrimination.*

The prefent extraordinary era, which opens upon an aftonifhed World, views for paft ages undifcovered, and unthought of, affords a noble opportunity for the contemplation of wifdom, and, in the improvement *of* legiflative *and* political *eftablifhments, for the exercife of human ability. Thofe* grand, *thofe* awful objects! *are at prefent feen but in a crude and difproportionate array—they* claim *the affiftance of afpiring capacity; the modulation of* truth, *of* justice, *of* indifpenfable fubordination, *of* neceffary obedience, *and of* equitable right—*They* invite the fons *of* Virtue; *the call is* imperative, *and the* OBSERVER, *with all its energies,* obedient.

The particular objects *next in succeffion to thofe great* univerfal attainments, *is the colonial and domeftic profperity of the*

BRITISH EMPIRE,

to restore to the conftitution *and the* Laws *their* original fpirit, *to preferve them from* vifionary emendations, *and to fupport every meafure which* Reason *dictates for their improvement and perfection in* Church *and* State.

In aid of this truly patriotic duty, *fome of the beft informed men, and the moft able and impartial pens, have already pledged themfelves, and it is the intention of the Proprietors to induce, by every liberal means, the further affiftance of knowledge and observation.*

But, although they intend to apply the ftricteft attention and care to those greater *objects of general concern, it is by no means their intention to lofe fight of others, which, though lefs confequental in the abftract, are yet materially effential in the detail of public convenience and felicity. — The* fine Arts—*emanations of* Science—*the* Tragic *and the* Comic Mufe—*the* National Police—Fafhion, *and* fafhionable Follies; *and trufting to the underftandings, and enlightened fpirit of* Britifh Juries—*a free communication of* truth, *however* dignified *the* characters, *and however* marked *the circumftances which may involve them.*

TO CONCLUDE——

From the certainty *of a fyftematic and* unerring *regulation, the Merchant, Manufacturer, Tradefman, Broker, Artift, and, in fhort, al clasffes, whofe intereft occasionally depends upon* public information, *may rely upon having their feveral* Advertifements *difperfed to the remoteft parts of the three kingdoms—Servants also, as the Observer cannot fail of becoming a favourite family Paper, will find it their peculiar intereft to give it their decided perference.*

Thus, then, to every rank and order will the OBSERVER *have its feparate recommendation; to the wifeft and moft exalted, as the vehicle of rational amufement; to the middling lines conveying fafe and grounded information, and rendering, even to the very loweft, the moft effential fervices; whilft it breathes, invariably, towards all, the fpirit of enlightened* Freedom, decent Toleration, *and* univerfal Benevolence.

An 'Address to the Public' which appeared in the first issue of
The Observer, *Sunday 4 December 1791.*

THE
EARLY
YEARS

1791-1907

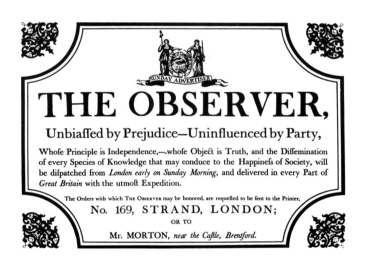

The Observer *was launched by an impecunious but resourceful young Irishman, W.S. Bourne, with an initial investment of £100. His stated intentions were high-principled and inspiring. He also hoped the paper would make his fortune.*

*   The Observer *first appeared in London on Sunday, 4 December 1791. It is now the world's oldest Sunday newspaper.*

MR WILBERFORCE

William Wilberforce, born in 1759, an MP at 21, became leader of the anti-slavery movement in 1787. The trade was abolished in British colonies in 1807, slavery itself in 1833, the year he died.

25 December 1791

With every argument in support of humanity, with every argument in support of trade and commerce; with every argument in support of national honour; of abstract improvement; and of individual advantage; Mr. Wilberforce brings forward his religious, moral, and Politic Bill for the abolition of the *odious* slave trade, early in the ensuing session of Parliament. That just; that merciful; that benignant great Being; whose creatures of every colour, and of every nation, are equally dear, will, surely, support this true patriot in a measure of so sublime a nature; will, surely, inspire him with zeal, and eloquence, to prostrate the opinions and sophistry of men, who, slaves themselves to temporary interest, would persecute, torment, and entail perpetual slavery, on others. Should the divine Power, for the purpose of trying the virtue of a favoured nation, suffer the intentions of this illustrious senator, to be delayed, can there be a doubt, but associations will form in every part, and a great majority unite in abstaining from the use of rum and sugar, until the object is accomplished.

DIED

25 December 1791

Friday morning, suddenly, at the Crown Inn, Slough, in his way to his seat at Hurley, Berks, Joseph Wilcocks, Esq. son of the late Bishop of Rochester.

At Maestricht, on the 13th instant, General Comte de Maillebois.

On the 5th inst. at Vienna, Wolfgang Mozart, the celebrated German composer.

Sunday se'nnight, at Osbaldwick, near York, aged 103, James Sampler. He has left a widow, to whom he had been married 70 years. He had never been confined a day to his bed till that of his death.

COUNTRY NEWS

25 December 1791

Shrewsbury. A couple from Pudsey were married on Tuesday last at Cheverley Church; immediately after the ceremony, the bride was taken in labour, and in less than an hour presented her husband with a fine boy.

POOR INFANTS

12 February 1792

A few days ago, a poor little sweep-chimney, not above seven years of age, was almost smothered to death by the remaining effluvia of charcoal, in the chimney of a house in Queen Ann-street West. Some time before, an infant of this profession, oppressed by fatigue, fell asleep in the chimney of a house in Austin-friars, and, notwithstanding, every effort to wake him, continued his nap for more than three full hours.

EXECUTION OF THE QUEEN OF FRANCE

10 November 1793

Her Majesty had been confined in the prison of the Conciergerie since the 1st of August last, in a room twelve feet long, eight feet broad, four feet under ground, and with a grated window on a level with it. Her food was of the coarsest kind, and she was constantly kept in sight by a female prisoner and two light-horse men. On Wednesday morning she was brought into the Court to hear her sentence. Being asked if she had anything to offer against it, she answered 'Nothing'. Her hands were tied behind her with cords, and she was conveyed to the tumbril that waited for her. The tying her hands behind her previous to her ascending the scaffold was also a peculiar act of cruelty, not even practised on Charlotte Corday. Beside her, sat the priest and executioner. Her head was bare: the hand of the hangman had already cut off those once fair tresses. Thus attended in this constrained and painful attitude, amidst two ranks of insulting and applauding ruffians, over a rugged pavement for near a mile, passed the mother, daughter, sister, and wife of Emperors and Kings; the offspring of Maria Theresa, the descendant of the Caesars!

The procession lasted near an hour and a half; during this whole time no murmur, no sign of indignation, anger or complaint, escaped her; she looked round her with a calm and dignified air. When she mounted the scaffold, the same applauses and bravoes were heard again. She smiled. The executioners bound their victim to the plank which bowed her to the axe, and terminated all her sufferings.

David's drawing of Marie Antoinette on the way to her death.

By 1794 W.S. Bourne, owner of The Observer, *was in dire financial trouble. He had tried and failed to sell the paper to an anti-government group in London.*

In 1794 his more prosperous, and more conformative, elder brother put up £1600 to keep the paper alive. He in turn tried, and failed, to sell it, this time to the Government. Although this attempt, too, failed the paper retained links with the Government until at least the middle 1800s: Vincent George Dowling, its first and most famous early reporter was in the pay of the Home Office; and Lord Palmerston paid The Observer *from Secret Service funds and wrote editorials for the paper supporting his foreign policy.*

DANGER OF RISING IN IRELAND

Ireland in the 1780s was relatively prosperous (not the peasantry). Repression of Catholics had eased; so had discontent. Then came the French Revolution and new stirrings of revolt. Only bad weather foiled a French landing in 1796. The Observer *was worried. (Unnecessarily. The 1798 Great Rebellion, even with a French landing, failed utterly.)*

16 July 1797

We have long and uniformly stated an apprehension, founded on documents strong and exclusive, that many of the Militia of Ireland, though not to be surpassed for bravery or appearance by any soldiers in the world, were not, whilst in Ireland, to be depended on; they will suppress a petty tumult; they would have fought, on its first arrival, an invading army; but they feel themselves a part of that people who in murmurs proclaim that they are wretched and oppressed; and they have recently been taught, however fallaciously, to look to France as the medium of deliverance.

A strong force in Ireland is at present, but we trust will not long continue, essential to its peace. That Government cannot be permanent which exists by terror. We tremble at the consequences of continued coercion. The strength of Government is doubtless superior to the spirit of internal discontent; but a knowledge of that spirit may incite our enemies to a continuance of war, in the hope of some months hence evading the vigilance of our navy, when the loss of Ireland would be, we fear, inevitable.

ROBERT BURNS

31 July 1796

Robert Burns, the Scotch poet, died, on the 21st inst. at Dumfries. He was literally, a ploughman, and latterly, an exciseman, at a salary of something less than 50l. per annum: he was the pupil of nature, the poet of inspiration, and possessed in a distinguished degree, the powers and the failings of genius: he was much addicted to liquor: and though he died at any early age, his mind was previously exhausted.

COURTSHIP OF 50 YEARS

26 February 1797

After a courtship of fifty years, John Brown, Esq. of Stratford upon Avon, was married to Miss Ancon, at Charlecote, in Warwickshire. This sober, cautious couple have furnished an admirable instance of constancy, and proved that reflection does not always damp the ardour of love.

WIFE SOLD IN-CHILD

23 July 1797

A Blacksmith, in the Cliffe, near Leeds, sold his wife, a smart young woman, with-child, to one of his journeymen, for two guineas, agreeably to an engagement drawn up by an attorney for that purpose. The blacksmith is persuaded he disposed of the child to the *real father.*

COW-POX

28 July 1799

In some of our former numbers we mentioned numberless experiments and observations on this malady; made by Dr. Jenner of Berkley, and others. A letter from Dr. Pearson, of Leicester Square is now before us. After stating that between the 20th of January and the 12th of March last he and Dr. Woodville inoculated *one hundred and sixty* patients, from two weeks to 40 years of age, with the Cow Pox, he observes that of the entire number not one died.

BATTLE OF MARENGO

Marengo (4 June 1800) was one of the victories Napoleon took most pride in. French casualties included General Desaix – 'the generous Desaix', one historian calls him – but for whom it could have been defeat.

29 June 1800

The Bulletin of the Army of Reserve, June 15, treating of the eventful Battle of Marengo: 'The General in Chief had his clothes pierced like a sieve with balls.' When the death of Desaix was communicated to Bonaparte, in the midst of a most furious fire, the following words were all that escaped from him: 'Why is it not permitted me to weep?'

A Bulletin dated Milan, June 17, relates the death of the French General Watrin, at the battle of Marengo. It adds, 'At Paris as at Vienna, in France as in Germany, in the French Army as in the Austrian, every body is desirous of Peace.'

SOMERSET ASSIZES

22 April 1801

At the Somerset assizes, two men, convicted of rioting, and taking fifteen loaves from a baker's shop, to distribute among the mob, were sentenced to be hanged, and have been left for execution.

A woman engaged in the late riots at Chorley has been sentenced to seven years transportation: four others are ordered to be imprisoned in solitary cells.

COUNTRY INTELLIGENCE

5 July 1801

A Blacksmith, near Beverley, lately sold his wife to a neighbouring bachelor, and delivered her in the customary manner on such occasions, with a halter round her neck, at the Market-cross.

3 April 1803

The press continues very strong at Plymouth: on Wednesday evening the Boadicea boarded the whole flotilla of trawl-boats off the Eddystone, and took two men from each.

31 July 1803

Two fellows, named Denny and Allen, stood in the pillory at Norwich, a few days since, for preferring a detestable charge against F. Latham, Esq. with a view to extort money. After their conviction, they confessed that they knew Mr. L. only by name. The populace were so enraged, that they pelted Denny, who had before been guilty of similar practices, in the most violent manner with potatoes, &c. till he fainted, and was taken from the pillory before the expiration of his time. This wretch is 30 years old, and has been thirteen years in different prisons.

7 August 1803

A press-gang was lately attacked in Marsh-street, Bristol, by a number of women, who, by throwing stones, bricks, &c. compelled the gang to leave some men whom it had impressed.

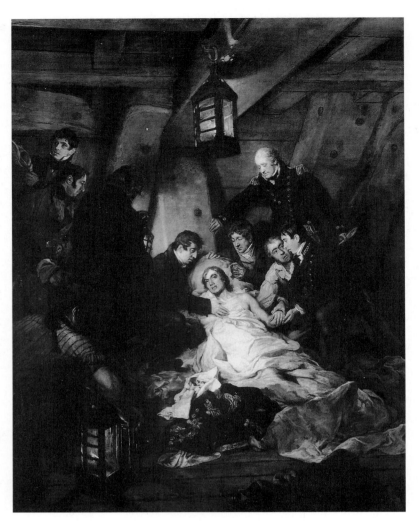

Devis's famous painting of the dying Nelson in the orlop deck of the Victory.

FURTHER PARTICULARS OF LORD NELSON'S VICTORY

17 November 1805

As soon as Lord Nelson was convinced that he had it in his power to bring the enemy to action, on the 21st, he caused it to be understood on board every ship, 'That England expected every man to do his duty'. There was, however, little necessity for the intimation; every man seemed to partake of the ardour of the Commander in Chief, and burned with impatience to commence the action.

It was about two o'clock, when the battle was at the hottest, that the gallant Nelson fell. The surgeons pronounced the wound mortal. His Lordship received the intelligence with firmness and pious resignation. He immediately sent an Officer to Admiral Collingwood, the second in command, with instructions for continuing the action. A few minutes before he expired, he sent for Capt. Hardy; and inquired how many of the enemy's ships had struck; the Captain replied, that, as nearly as he could ascertain, fifteen sail of the line had struck their colours. His Lordship then, fervently returned thanks to the Almighty; then turning to Capt. Hardy, he said, 'I know I'm dying. I could have wished to survive to breathe my last upon

British ground; but the will of God be done.' In a few moments he expired!

It is remarkable that his Lordship had a strong presentiment of his fate. The date before he left town, he called on his undertaker, who has the coffin which was made from the main-mast of Admiral Brueys's ship that blew up at Aboukir, and told him to get it ready, as he apprehended he should want it on his return. His constant salutation to his crew, previous to an action, was 'Now my lads, victory or Westminster Abbey.'

DISPATCHES FROM CORUNNA

29 January 1809

Our readers will, we are persuaded, be deeply affected by the perusal of the dispatches from Lieut.-Gen. Hope, containing the particulars of the Battle of Corunna, with the death of the gallant and amiable Sir John Moore, in the flower of his age, and at the moment of Victory. After being struck by the cannon-ball, which in a few hours terminated his honourable life, he retained the full use of his faculties.

He gave his orders with coolness, and heard the victory of his troops with the satisfaction of a patriot. Sir J. Moore, we understand, was buried in his clothes, and without a coffin, in a grave dug by the hands of the officers of his staff.

He expressed the strongest satisfaction that he had fallen in the cause of his country and particularly that the army under his command was about to return home in honour and triumph.

The cannon-ball carried away his right breast and arm.

THE RIOTS AT NOTTINGHAM

'Luddite', nearly two centuries after its appearance, is probably still the dirtiest word in industrial relations. As this account of a Luddite incident makes clear, Luddism was a despairing protest against loss of work and resulting destitution. Messages were often left behind signed 'General (or Captain) Lud'. The origin of the name is obscure.

24 November 1811

The riots of Nottingham were of a more serious and alarming nature, than from the first accounts we were led to believe. Their origin is thus stated. For some time past, the wholesale hosiers in the metropolis and in other large towns, who have stocking weaving establishments at Nottingham, have been obliged to curtail their hands, by which the journeymen were reduced almost to a state of starvation. They murmured; but were pacified by representation that importations of silk would give them employment.

Their riotous spirit was, however, roused a second time by the trade having brought into use a certain wide frame for the manufacture of stockings and gaiters, by which was produced a considerable saving in manual labour, tending still further to the decrease of the hands employed. On Sunday the 10th inst. this being generally known, a number of weavers assembled at different places in the vicinity of Nottingham, and commenced their career of outrage and riot, by forcibly entering the houses of such persons as had in use those frames, so obnoxious to them.

At Bullwell, a master weaver, named Hollingworth, having been threatened by the rioters, armed all his men, and barricaded his house. On Monday evening they made their appearance, broke open the door, and would have put the whole family to death, had not they made their escape out of the back door. They then proceeded to gut the house and burnt the contents.

A LETTER FROM 'GENERAL LUD'

9 February 1812

The men that had the things weir entire strangers to my borders or they *never* dworst nor have tuch'd one thinck but they have been punished for their vileny for one of them have been hanged for 3 Menet and then Let down agane I ham a friend of the pore and Distrest and an enemy to the opressers thron.
General Lud

In 1814 The Observer was bought by William Innell Clement, the most important press magnate of his time. As proprietor of four major London newspapers – The Observer, The Morning Chronicle, Bell's Life in London and The Englishman – Clement, who was a newsvendor before selling out to W.H. Smith, estimated that in 1828 he controlled 10 per cent of all newspapers published in England. He lavished money on making The Observer a popular and influential journal. Editor and manager until 1857 was Lewis Doxat. Doxat prided himself on never writing 'an article on any subject under any circumstances whatever'. This was part of the tradition of the great managing editors of the nineteenth century.

Under Clement and Doxat, The Observer began to blossom. With new, well-paid and well-informed staff the content improved; with new papers and new typography, so did the appearance. Woodcut illustrations made a dramatic impact at the time of the Cato Street conspiracy and Clement's courageous stand at the time of the conspirators. Circulation doubled.

ST HELENA

17 December 1815

During the passage to St. Helena, Buonaparte, in one of those intervals when he was induced to talk upon recent events, was asked whether he really mistook Bulow's corps, that advanced at the close of the battle of Waterloo, for Grouchy's? He replied in the negative, but that he thought Grouchy's corps was so close in the rear of it, that it would soon be able to occupy the whole attention of Bulow. The firmness, perseverance, and impetuosity of the British troops astonished him. Night coming on, he had no longer the power of making himself visible to his troops, and of thus improving the advantages he had gained! When the Northumberland reached St. Helena, Buonaparte was employed two hours in surveying it through a glass: he was observed to be very restless during the survey.

JUVENILE OFFENDERS

14 September 1817

*From the House of Commons
New Police Report*

Your Committee remark that the greater part of Juvenile Offenders, some of them infants of 9, 10 and 11 years of age, are mixed indiscriminately with old offenders of all ages, and all of them with boys of the ages of 15 or 16, many of whom have been long practised in the commission of various acts of fraud and crime . . . Your Committee feel it their duty to observe, that the tendency which the young and the ignorant have to fall into the snares and allurements which are spread around them by the guilty and designing; the severity of penal law; and the frequency of capital punishment, are evidences little creditable to the system of which such evils are the result.

◆

The island of St Helena as Napoleon Bonaparte saw it on beginning his exile.

EXECUTION FOR HORRID MURDER

23 February 1818

At an early hour this morning a great concourse of spectators assembled in the Old Bailey, for the purpose of witnessing the execution of David Evans, who was on Friday convicted of the wilful murder of Elizabeth Evans his wife. The unhappy malefactor has since his condemnation conducted himself with the greatest propriety and resignation, and has been unremitting in his devotions to the Being from whom alone forgiveness can be expected. He admitted the justice of his sentence, and although he could not tell with any degree of accuracy the cause which led to the perpetration of the horrid deed, yet he believed he was infuriated at being told of his wife's infidelity, and in a paroxysm of irritation, he must have struck the blows which terminated the existence of the unfortunate woman.

He was extremely feeble and debilitated, but continued in fervent prayer until he was brought upon the platform. The executioner having completed all the necessary arrangements, the unhappy delinquent was launched into eternity. At nine o'clock his body was cut down.

The body of the murderer and suicide, Haitch, will be drawn from Newgate in a cart, to-morrow morning, to the bottom of Newgate-street, at eight o'clock, where he will be buried; and a stake will be driven through his body, agreeable to the usual custom.

CHANGE OF CLIMATE

8 June 1818

There are reasons for believing that, previously to the fifteenth century, England enjoyed a warmer summer climate than since that period. It is sufficiently apparent that at one time vineyards were very common in England; and that wine, in very considerable quantity, was made from them – the Isle of Ely was named, in the times of the Normans, '*Ile de Vignes*', the bishop of which received three or four tons of wine yearly for his tenth.

But wine is known to have been made in England at a much more recent period. Among the MS notes of the late Peter Collinson (to whom the European world is indebted for the introduction of some of its choicest plants) is the following memorandum: 'Oct. 18th 1765. I went to see Mr Roger's vineyard, at Parson's-green, all of Burgundy grapes, and seemingly all perfectly ripe. I did not see a green half-ripe grape in all this great quantity. He does not expect to make less than fourteen hogs-heads of wine. The branches and fruit are remarkably large, and the vines very strong.' These facts set aside the idea that the vineyards of England are apple orchards, and that the wine was cider.

But a prospect far more gloomy than the mere loss of wine had begun to present itself by the increase chilliness of our summer months. It is too well known that there was not sufficient warmth in the summer of 1816 to ripen the grain; and it is generally thought, that if the ten or twelve days of hot weather at the end of June last had not occurred, most of the corn must have perished. It was sufficiently alarming to be told that on ground where the clustering vine once flourished, the apple has, of late years, scarcely ripened, and that it is now sixteen years since the orchards have afforded a plentiful crop, that our posterity may be in the same situation in regard to cider that we are now placed in with respect to wine; when the apple tree, like the vine will only afford a penurious supply of sour fruit and will be cultivated in forcing houses to supply the tables of the rich.

The warm and settled appearance of the weather at this early period of the season, leads us to hope that an agreeable change is about to take place in our planet; and that we shall not, as for many past years, have to deplore the deficiency of that solar heat, which is so necessary to ripen the productions of the earth.

ACCOUNT OF RIOTS AT MANCHESTER

On 16 August 80,000 people gathered in St Peter's Field, Manchester (now the site of the Free Trade Hall), to demonstrate for parliamentary reform and against the Corn Laws. The magistrates sent in the yeomanry to arrest the chief speaker, Henry ('Orator') Hunt. Eleven people were killed and five hundred injured, a hundred of them women and children. Hunt was jailed for three years. Peterloo, as it came to be called with savage sardonicism, was a moral victory. Such force was never again used against a peaceful crowd in this country.

22 August 1819

Moderate men universally concluded, that the meeting would be allowed to go off peacefully, provided no breach of the peace was committed by the people. None of the military had been seen in the streets, though it was known that the Manchester and Salford Yeomanry Cavalry were concealed in Messrs. Pickfords' (the carriers') yard. On his mounting the hustings Mr. Hunt exhorted the people to be firm, but peaceable. 'And', said, he, 'if any man makes the slightest attempt to break the peace, put him down and keep him down.' Just as he had uttered those words, the Manchester and Salford Yeomanry Cavalry came galloping down Mosley-street and Peter-street, and ranged themselves in front of a row of houses on the south side of the area where the meeting was, in one of which the magistrates were assembled.

The greater part of the persons instantly ran away; but the main body remained compact and firm, and finding the soldiers halt under the houses, faced round to and cheered them. But a few moments had elapsed, when some orders were given to the troops, and they instantly dashed at full gallop amongst the people, actually hacking their way up to the hustings. A comparatively undisciplined body, led on by officers who had never had any experience in military affairs, and probably all under the influence both of personal fear and considerable political feeling of hostility, could not be expected to act either with coolness or discrimination; and accordingly, men, women and children – constables and Reformers were all equally exposed to their attacks. Numbers were trampled down; and numbers were cut down.

When they arrived at the hustings, the standards were torn or cut from the hands of those who held them. Hunt was taken along by the constables to the house where the magistrates were sitting, crying out 'Murder' as he was every instant struck by the bludgeons of numbers of constables who surrounded him.

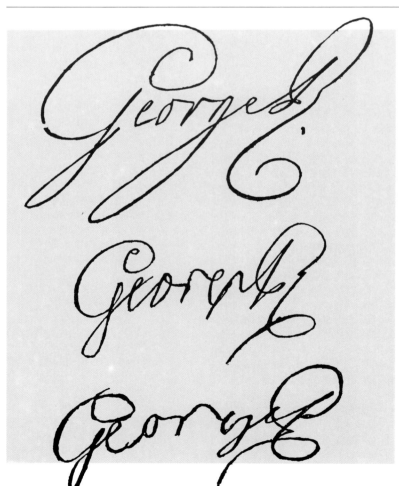

FACSIMILES OF THE LATE KING'S SIGN MANUAL

27 February 1820

In previous numbers of *The Observer* we gave the fullest particulars respecting his late Majesty George the Third [who died on 29 January] that it was in our power to collect in so short a period; and it was our intention to have accompanied them with facsimiles of our late venerable Sovereign's handwriting; but the illness of the artist to whose execution they were entrusted has delayed its insertion until the present number. The facsimiles are the sign manual of the late King, and were written at the periods specified at the head of each.

◆

The 'periods specified' were: after his accession (top); after his recovery from his first illness (middle); after his eyesight became impaired.

THE CATO STREET CONSPIRACY

The decade 1810-1820 was not happy: war until 1815 – as in most of the previous two decades; bad harvests; the Luddites; Peterloo. Lack-lustre governments whose only reaction to rising discontent was more and more repression, culminating in the Six Acts of 1819, one of which forbade meetings of more than fifty people unless six days' notice was given to a magistrate. Ultra-radicals planned to assassinate Cabinet Ministers on 23 February 1820 as they dined in Grosvenor Square. The plot was revealed and the conspirators were seized at a stable in Cato Street, in Marylebone. A policeman was shot by the ringleader, Arthur Thistlewood. He and four others were hanged. Five more were transported for life.

Woodcut reconstructions of the arrest of the conspirators. Above, the killing of the policeman Smithers by the ringleader, Arthur Thistlewood.

6 March 1820

The interest excited by the discovery of the diabolical conspiracy to assassinate his Majesty's Ministers has, throughout the last week, continued with unabated force. Every thing which tended to throw a light upon the subject was read with avidity; and the most trifling anecdote connected either with the progress of the conspiracy, the history of the conspirators, or the occurrences attending their arrest, was sought for with the utmost anxiety. The premises in Cato-street, which will be ever memorable for the events of which they were the scene, was visited by several thousand persons. Among whom were many individuals of the highest rank. The blood of poor Smithers was still visible on the floor, and seemed to be avoided with a sort of reverential awe. Among others attracted to the spot, we remarked several of the fair sex, who braved the inconvenience of the difficult ascent to the loft for the gratification of their curiosity.

Thistlewood trying to escape and firing at the policeman Westcoate. Right, another conspirator trying to escape from the stable.

REPORT OF THE TRIAL: THE OBSERVER FINED

Lord Chief Justice Abbott, probably without precedent, forbade all reporting of the Cato Street conspiracy trial until sentence had been passed. The Observer defied the order. Clement was summoned before the court but refused to appear. He was fined £500, which he never paid. His defiance helped to re-establish the freedom of crime reporting and no similar restrictive orders have been invoked since.

1 May 1820

Our readers will observe that, for the step which we took on Sunday last, in publishing a correct and impartial report of the trials of Arthur Thistlewood and James Ings, we have subjected ourselves to what we cannot help thinking as unmerited severity on the part of the Commissioners – who have ordered us to pay 'a fine to the King of *Five Hundred Pounds!*' Upon the right of the learned Judges to make this order, or to enforce its execution, we cannot at present say anything. It is a question which we trust will not be ultimately decided without that deliberation which the interests of the press, as well as the interests of the public at large, imperiously demand.

We cannot abstain from stating, however, that their Lordships' order is characterised by an undue degree of harshness; first, because there was no proof that Mr. Clement, the proprietor of this paper, ever received their Lordships' summons to attend at their bar to explain or justify his conduct; and, secondly, because the offence, if any, with which he was charged, had already been committed by the journals of the sister kingdom (the *Dublin Evening Post*, and two Cork papers) with perfect impunity, and in a manner much more reprehensible, because they only contained a partial statement of the charges against the prisoners, without the arguments which were urged in their favour .... We have not published an ex parte or a partial report, we have done justice to all sides. We have, as we apprehend we had a right to do, published the proceedings of a public court of justice, and we submit, with humble deference to our judges, and our jurors, under circumstances of no respect calculated 'to prejudice the course of public justice' – 'to mislead the minds of British jurymen,' or 'improperly to inform the minds of honest witnesses.'

MOZART POISONED

19 April 1824

A journal speaks of the poisoning of Mozart, by Salieri, as a certain fact, but the following account of this matter, from Vienna, by a gentleman who frequently sees the illustrious Composer places it in a proper point of view:- 'We have been much astonished to read in several Journals that Salieri had cut his throat in an hospital in Vienna. This patriarch is still living, and in the midst of his family, by whom he is both loved and cherished.

But age has weakened his powers, of which the following is a proof. He has the practice of taking all his acquaintance aside and to say to them with a smiling countenance – 'I have a little secret to confide to you. I poisoned Mozart out of jealousy; but I have never felt the least remorse, for it has never prevented me making good music!' All those, to whom he makes this strange avowal, see in it only an act of second childishness. There is nothing in his life consistent with such a crime.

That he might have been jealous of the sublime author of *Don Juan* may be easily believed, but betwixt jealousy and assassination there is a wide difference. Salieri has always had the reputation of uprightness and mildness of character.

DEATH OF BYRON

17 May 1824

The following is a translation of the Proclamation which was issued by the Greek Authorities at Missolonghi to the grief of its inhabitants, who were thus arrested in the celebration of their Easter festivities:

The present days of festivity are converted into days of bitter lamentation for all – Lord Byron departed this life to-day, about eleven o'clock in the evening, in consequence of a rheumatic inflammatory fever, which had lasted for ten days. During the time of his illness your general anxiety evinced the profound sorrow that pervaded your hearts. All classes, without distinction of sex or age, oppressed by grief, entirely forgot the days of Easter. The death of this illustrious personage is certainly a most calamitous event for all Greece, and still more lamentable for this city, to which he was eminently partial, of which he became a citizen.

Tomorrow, by sun-rise, thirty-seven minute guns shall be fired from the batteries of this town, equal to the number of years of the deceased personage.

A general mourning shall take place for twenty-one days.

Funeral ceremonies shall be performed in all the churches.

A. Mavrocordato
Giorgio Praidi, Secretary

Portrait of the youthful Byron in Albanian costume, painted by Thomas Smith in 1813.

EXHIBITION OF THE ROYAL ACADEMY

9 May 1825

Harbour of Dieppe (J.M.W. Turner R.A.). A picture of great merit, but one that, with less ambition of effect, would have been more magnificent: nothing can be finer than the distance view, and the enchanting softness and purity of the aerial perspective – it reminds us of the splendid view of the port of Genoa, by Berghem, but the latter artist did not, like Mr. Turner, attempt impossibilities, and we hold it an impossibility to represent the direct noon-day effulgence of the unclouded sun. The greatest of the ancient masters in producing brilliant effects of light, such as Claude, Rembrandt, Cuyp, &c. rather expressed the fervour of the sun by reflexion of the objects which it illuminated, than by its direct radiance.

The water in Mr. Turner's picture is very clear and transparent, but he has thrown such a variety of party-coloured reflections upon it as create too gaudy an effect. Nevertheless the shipping is well drawn, and the numerous figures are painted with great spirit and character.

Landscape (J. Constable). A scene on a canal; a boat towed by a horse, which is in the act of springing over a bar laid across the path to prevent the passage of carriages. The composition has all the pleasing peculiarities of this artist's style, who describes aquatic scenery with the minute and picturesque fidelity of Crabbe.

Taking a Buck (E. Landseer). The murderous onset of the dogs; the despairing energy of the buck, and the wild vigour of the huntsman's action, are powerfully represented. There is, however, no depth in the execution: it equals Sneyders in every thing but the charm of his colouring.

BEETHOVEN

22 April 1827

Ludwig van Beethoven died on 26 March, aged 56

We find, in Russell's *Tour in Germany*, the following account of the celebrated musical composer, Beethoven, whose recent death in circumstances of poverty and distress, alleviated only by English charity, has attracted much notice. The author seems to have met him in 1822:– 'Beethoven is the most celebrated of living composers in Vienna. Though not an old man, he is lost to society, in consequence of his extreme deafness, which has rendered him almost unsocial. Even among his oldest friends he must be humoured like a wayward child.

I have heard him play, but to bring him so far required some management, so great is his horror of being any thing like exhibited. Had he been plainly asked to do the company that favour, he would have flatly refused; he had to be cheated into it. Every person left the room, except Beethoven and the master of the house, one of his most intimate acquaintances. The gentleman, as if by chance, struck the keys of the open piano beside which they were sitting, gradually began to run over one of Beethoven's own compositions, made a thousand errors, and speedily blundered one passage so thoroughly, that the composer condescended to stretch out his hand and put him right. It was enough; the hand was on the piano; his companion immediately left him. Beethoven, left alone, seated himself at the piano. At first he only struck new and then a few hurried and interrupted notes, as if afraid of being detected in a crime; but gradually he forgot every thing else, and ran on during half an hour, in a phantasy, in a style extremely varied, and marked, above all; by the most abrupt transitions. The amateurs were enraptured; to the initiated, it was more interesting to observe how the music of the man's soul passed over his countenance. The muscles of the face swell, and its veins start out; the wild eye rolls doubly wild. Beethoven looks like a wizard, overpowered by the demons, whom he himself has called up.

DEATH OF GEORGE THE FOURTH

27 June 1830

Much as we may be disposed to speak of the qualities of His Majesty in private life, it is with regret we must admit that we can find little in his public or political life to satisfy our feeling of what was demanded from him, to justify an opinion that he was a wise Sovereign, or to induce us to point out his course as worthy of the imitation of a successor. No disguise or cant can conceal the truth, that all reforms, and all meritorious public exertions, were forced on him by the progress of the age, not adopted from an ardent wish to signalise his reign. Although a scholar, a gentleman, and a patron of arts, our Sovereign, however worthy of being regretted, was neither a great King, an enlightened statesman, nor a national benefactor.

OPENING OF MANCHESTER TO LIVERPOOL RAILWAY

George Stephenson (1781-1848) paid for night-school lessons from his earnings as a fireman. He built his first locomotive in 1814 and was in charge of the construction of the Stockton-Darlington Railway and then of the Manchester and Liverpool Railway, on which his improved locomotive, the 'Rocket', made its trial trip. The Duke of Wellington and the Liberal statesman William Huskisson were among guests at the opening, which was marked by pomp – and tragedy.

19 September 1830

This great national work was opened to the public on Wednesday last. As early as seven o'clock, the people of Liverpool were seen flocking in crowds to the Tunnel, in order to secure god places for a view of the procession . . . Eight of the Company's beautiful locomotive engines were brought down to the mouth of the Tunnel. . . . While these masterly productions of human intellect were being paraded up and down on the road with the same ease and under as much command as a small pony, we could hardly persuade ourselves that we were not looking on animal life. The steam flowed from them with a curiously sharp noise, and considerably heightened the delusion. A person who has not seen it can have no idea of the graceful and easy movement of one of these machines, and the power with which they perform their work is really surprising even in these days of mechanical improvement.

The Duke of Wellington arrived about ten, and his arrival was greeted with considerable enthusiasm. A cannon was fired and we regret to say that a man who was standing on the opposite side of the railway had his eye blown out by a splinter of wood which was supposed to be a part of the ramrod. The military band played 'See, the conquering hero comes!' and in a few minutes the Duke was drawn from the tunnel. He was almost surrounded by ladies in the carriage, and was loudly cheered by all the spectators.

At Park Side the Northumbrian, or Royal Car, in which the Duke and all the principal persons of the party were seated, stopped first. Several of the passengers got out to walk on the railway, and among them was Mr. Huskisson. He was discoursing with Mr. J. Sandars, one of the principal originators and promoters of this rail-road, when he was called away to speak with some other gentlemen.

The gentlemen detained him some time, and whilst he was standing with them, the Rocket engine came slowly up, and as the engineer had been for some time checking its velocity, so silently that it was almost upon the group before they observed it. In the hurry of the moment all attempted to get out of the way. Mr. Huskisson hesitated, staggered a little, as if not knowing what to do, then attempted again to get into the car. As he took hold of the door to do this, he must have thrown his gravity too much upon it, for on its suddenly turning on its hinges, on being seized by him, the motion threw him off his balance, and before he could recover he was thrown down directly in the path of the Rocket, as that engine came opposite the Duke's car. Mrs. Huskisson, who, along with several other ladies, witnessed the accident, uttered a shriek of agony, which none who heard will ever forget.

The unfortunate gentleman died last night.

DENUNCIATION OF PARLIAMENTARY REFORM

On 2 November 1830 the Duke of Wellington, the Prime Minister, declared that he would always feel it his duty to resist proposals for parliamentary reform.

7 November 1830

The speech from the Throne is silent on that all-important and all-engrossing subject – parliamentary reform – while the Premier, with a degree of impolicy and want of tact, which no man could have supposed possible, has satisfied the country that the omission must be construed into hostility, by the positive declaration that in his time, and while he holds power, no reform will be granted.

The Duke has laid aside the mask; he has avowed the course to which he is pledged. There is, however, an extremely curious question connected with this declaration. Does the Sovereign, the liberal popular, free-thinking, free-spoken William the Fourth countenance this denunciation against Reform?

The great manufacturing and commercial towns must have representatives. Their claims are too strong to be resisted. We think, indeed, that if the Duke of Wellington remains at the head of the Treasury, and is permitted to adhere to his declarations, the character of William the Fourth will suffer in the eyes of his people, and the throne become unpopular, in an exact ratio with the extravagant expectations which have been recently excited by the expressions of its new possessor.

RECEPTION OF THEIR MAJESTIES BY THE PEOPLE IN LONDON

Wellington fell from power. Earl Grey formed a Whig Ministry and asked the King to create fifty peers and so get a Reform Bill through the House of Lords. William refused.

13 May 1832

The Court Circular having announced that their Majesties would come to town on Saturday, the popular feeling had an opportunity presented for displaying itself, which was seized with extraordinary avidity. At a quarter-past twelve o'clock, the royal carriage in which their Majesties were seated, without attendants, reached the village of Hounslow. The postillions passed on at a rapid rate till they entered the town of Brentford; where the people, who had assembled in great numbers, expressed, by groans, hisses, and exclamation, their disapprobation of his Majesty's conduct with respect to the Administration. The escort kept close together, and it is probable that they protected their Majesties from insult, as it alleged that pieces of mud were flung towards the carriage.

Along the whole of the road to London the people continued to express their feelings of dissatisfaction. When the carriage entered the park, it proceeded at a very rapid rate towards the palace, amidst the hisses, mingled with a few occasional cheers, of the crowds assembled to receive it.

The Duke of Wellington had entered the palace in full uniform about a quarter of an hour before their Majesties, and had been assailed by the people with groans, hisses and other marks of disapprobation. The Duke retired about a quarter-past four, after more than three hours, amidst groans and hisses even more vehement than when he arrived.

William IV with leading characters in the 'Great Question of Reform'. 'Political Memento' distributed with Bell's Messenger.

THE REFORM BILL

10 June 1832

House of Lords, Monday 4 June: the Third Reading of the Reform Bill

The Earl of Winchilsea begged to say a few words on this closing scene of the tragedy which had been of late enacting the parliament. It was a daring and atrocious policy which had produced such a disastrous result. The noble earl opposite [Grey] had delivered himself over to the radical, revolutionary, and infidel spirit of the age.

Earl Grey: The constitution of this country is admirable: it has stood the test of time (Opposition cheers). Yes, but it has also proved the humanity of its origin by yielding to the influence of time, the great innovator, time, which generates abuses, against which it is the duty of those to whom are intrusted the affairs of state to provide a remedy.

The question 'that this Bill do pass,' was then put and agreed to. A number of noble lords immediately surrounded Earl Grey, and appeared to be congratulating him on the successful termination of his arduous labours.

THE HOPE OF ENGLAND

1 July 1838

In celebration of Queen Victoria's coronation all persons confined in her Majesty's Gaol of Newgate, of whatever degree, were supplied by the Sheriffs with a pound of beef, a pound of potatoes, a pound of white bread, and a pint of strong beer, and prisoners doomed to solitude were allowed to mingle for a short space with their fellow men.

She is the Hope of England, and up to the present moment all that she has done and all that she has said appear to justify that hope, and to promise its most happy realisation. One of our contemporaries had designated her 'an institution', and accounts for the enthusiasm with which she was received by that designation. Her sex awoke the gallantry – her manners, her disposition as manifested in her behaviour, have won the affection – of her subjects.

The little incident which occurred in the Abbey of her sympathetically springing from her seat on the Throne to assist an aged nobleman who had stumbled and fallen in approaching to perform the ceremony of the homage, will endear her to all.

DANGERS OF SMOKING

18 October 1846

The wide-spread habit of smoking has not yet had due medical attention paid to its consequences. It is only by two or three years' observations that Dr. Laycock had become fully aware of the varied and obscure forms of disease to which especially excessive smoking gave origin. The action of the heart and lungs is impaired by the influence of the narcotic on the nervous system; but a morbid state of the larynx, trachea, and lungs results from the direct action of the smoke. The patient hardly ever had the pipe out of his mouth.

SHOCKING AFFAIR OF LOLA MONTEZ

14 March 1847

The affair lately noticed as having taken place at Munich, relating to the well-known Spanish *danseuse* Lola Montez, has, it seems assumed a more serious character than that of a passing *amour* of the monarch of Bavaria. A letter in the *Journal des Débats* of Friday week, corrects the rumour of the expulsion of the lady from Munich, and makes the following remarks on the resignation of Ministers: 'All Europe is aware at present, of the high favour enjoyed by the too-well-known *danseuse*, and how her royal protector, rather than give her up, has accepted the resignation of his ministers. It is an unheard-of occurrence, and must have greatly surprised every one.'

Signora Lola Montez's first appearance, and notoriety which she thereby gained, caused, about three years ago, a disgusting correspondence in almost all the leading London papers. Her adventures afterwards at Berlin, Warsaw, and Paris are too notorious to deserve any notice. Finally, she made her appearance at Munich in November last, and, applied to the manager of the Royal Theatre for an engagement as a *danseuse*. It seems that before any engagement is entered into with a female performer the *Débutantes* have first to perform before his Majesty in private. To this Lola Montez had to submit likewise, and the consequences was that her application for an engagement was refused, but that she nevertheless remained at Munich, and purchased a few weeks afterwards a handsome house magnificently furnished, where she immediately commenced an establishment calculated only for a lady of great wealth.

Lola Montez: Not just the king's passing amour.

REVOLUTION IN FRANCE

27 February 1848

For the magnitude of its movements the revolution of the third week of February 1848 may view with the last week of July 1830. According to the most authentic recent accounts received from Paris it was the battalion of troops posted in the Foreign Office that commenced the first fusillade upon the crowd; an act which was as atrocious as it was treacherous. The soldiery fired upon their fellow-citizens from behind stone walls; and fifty-two human beings were in a moment hurried into eternity . . . In the meanwhile pretenders to the crown of France have sprung up like mushrooms in a night; and one and all are now eagerly engaged in advancing their pretensions. Already it is on record that Louis Napoleon Bonaparte has proceeded to Paris. The infant grandson of the late Sovereign (Louis Philippe) has his pretensions also, poor child!

This demonstration at Kennington, near the Oval, marked the last outburst of Chartism.

REVOLUTION IN PRUSSIA

26 March 1848

A revolution in Prussia was, perhaps the most unexpected event that could occur. The whole country was a military camp; and the King thereof sat in the midst of his vassals, doling out so much of the light of liberty as he deemed good for the people. He had learned to dread and condemn the constitutional system, as worked in England and in France; and he considered himself called upon to preserve a system far more solid in which the royal power should preserve the great initiative and high intellectual influence.

But in an hour this fine edifice fell and the King became, instead of the political and religious dictator of Germany, the tearful, humble, abject suppliant of his people.

From that day and henceforward the 'sovereignty of the people' is henceforth the common law of Europe for the old dogmas of power, consisting in wealth, in knowledge, in hereditary rights, in loyal armies, or in passive obedience, have been swept away when the population of a city, numbering scarcely 300,000 souls, overcame an army like the Prussian, unlimited in numbers, in equipment, and unflinching in loyalty and devotion to their sovereign.

THE GREAT CHARTIST DEMONSTRATION

Coinciding with the general unrest throughout Europe was the rise of Chartism – that 'cry of rage on the part of the suffering wage-earner' (G.M. Trevelyan in his History of England*). It fizzled out after its last outburst described here, but its 'ominous shadow in the background' (Trevelyan again) accelerated such reforms as the Factory Acts and Mines Acts. Feargus O'Connor was one of its founders.*

16 April 1848

The metropolis presented on Monday a scene of unusual excitement and alarm. The determination of the Chartist National Convention to hold their meeting and procession in defiance of the law; the military preparations to put down any insurrectionary attempts; and the remarkable unanimity with which the middle and higher classes placed their services at the disposal of the Government, had each in turn contributed to increase the general feeling of undefined apprehension with which the intentions of the Chartists were regarded. The weather was exceedingly favourable; no obstruction was offered by the police; and yet, instead of the 300,000 persons who, we were told would assemble on Kennington Common the most liberal estimate of the number of persons within view at one time does not reach 50,000.

Mr. O'Connor presented himself, and was vociferously cheered. He said: 'My children, we have succeeded in holding our meeting today; but I must tell you that the Government has taken possession of all the bridges. I have always been a man of determination, as you know, and a man of courage too; but how should I rest in my bed tonight if, through any incautious advice or expression of mine I made any of your wives widows? Therefore we should not attempt to cross the bridges. The huge petition which you have prepared will be taken down to the House of Commons and I shall be there ready to present it. You have by your conduct today more than repaid me for all I have done for you, and I will go on conquering until you have the land and the People's Charter becomes the law of the land' (loud and long-continued cheers, in the midst of which the hon. and learned gentleman, who was evidently labouring under severe indisposition, sank exhausted on the shoulder of a private friend).

REVOLUTION IN VIENNA

22 October 1848

Even while these lines are penning, the fate of the House of Habsburg may be decided, and its greatness set for ever; or the beautiful city of Vienna may be a heap of smoking ashes, its inhabitants slaughtered or fled. The night of Tuesday, the 10th inst., was unquestionably the most disturbed which Vienna had witnessed since its bombardment by Napoleon in 1809. In the streets nothing was seen but armed men. Every now and then single shots were fired. Behind and upon the barricades armed men in blouses were gathered round the watchfires, and among them women and girls of not very respectable exterior were scattered, some sleeping upon heaps of stones, others laughing and diverting themselves. The ramparts and bastions of the city in particular had a most animated appearance; watchfire joined watchfire, each surrounded by a motley group; legionaries, workmen and National Guards. Above the gates were mounted cannons besides them were burning torches borne by the burgher Artillery, scattered academicians, or common workmen. Close by were ranged whole companies, armed with every kind of weapon, whose patrols marched up and down, each keeping guard with a musket or a rifle, with a carabine or pike.

Meanwhile the Diet, the Communal Council, the Central Committee of the Democratic Union, and the Supreme Command of the National Guard, remained in permanence. The attention of all was fixed upon the military camp in the Schwarzenberg Garden, from whence a sudden attack on the city was apprehended.

THE GOLD REGION OF CALIFORNIA

31 December 1848

Now that the existence of gold in almost incredible quantities in California has been attested by the Message of the President to Congress, the official reports of the Government officers in California, and the concurrent statements of private persons at present in that country, it becomes a question, what will be the influence of this discovery upon what is termed 'civilization'.

There are one or two circumstances, however, connected with this great discovery that cannot fail to gratify every well-wisher of man's common humanity. In the first place it is that the untold wealth of the world has fallen into the hands of a free commercial people. In the second place, it is a matter of congratulation that England has not discovered this immense mine of gold; and why? because she would have assigned it exclusively to the privileged classes – who, Heaven knows! are privileged too much already.

THE GREAT EXHIBITION

4 May 1851

On Thursday, May 1st, at twelve o'clock, the Great Exhibition of the Industry of all Nations was inaugurated by her Majesty the Queen. The whole world, invited to a vast competition in the power of conceiving and perfecting works of art and industry; examples of such works forwarded from every clime, and collected in a structure itself so novel, so ingenious and so graceful as only not to surpass in interest the congregated wonders of its contents; this display of marvels inaugurated by the most powerful Monarch of the earth presented a scene not often recorded in the annals of the world.

As the Exhibition will attract, probably, the greatest assemblage ever collected on one small spot of the earth's surface, so it will likewise determine the exact degree to which, in the middle of the 19th century, the skill and ingenuity of man have arrived.

Victoria opening the Exhibition at Crystal Palace: 'So novel, so ingenious, so graceful'.

NEGRO LIFE IN THE UNITED STATES

5 September 1852

Uncle Tom's Cabin: or Negro Life in the United States of America (Harriet Beecher Stowe). Negro slavery is the blot upon North America. America may be powerful and populous, rich and progressive, but so long as slavery is one of her *institutions* she must ever be the morally despised among nations – next to Russia. The book now under notice hits this blot in the national character of America; laying bare that canker in the Columbian wreath of freedom – negro slavery.

MR GLADSTONE'S BENEVOLENCE

15 May 1853

A correspondent of a morning journal makes the following statement on the subject of Mr. Gladstone's benevolence a' nights to 'unprotected females' in distress.

Two young women are passing by the top of the Haymarket about eleven o'clock in the evening. A man asks one of the girls some questions. The answers she gives increase the interest he at first felt for her. Upon his wishing her to go home, she says she durst not unless she takes some money with her. He gives her the sum she names, puts her into a cab, and sends her home. He next day makes inquiries respecting her, and finds that everything she told him was true. From that time he

has been a kind, and, moreover, a disinterested friend to that girl. The gentleman of whom I am now speaking was Mr. Gladstone. To account for the interest he took in her I must refer to the girl's story.

Her father keeps an inn on the seacoast in Sussex. A lady took her into her service as maid and companion to herself. She remained with this lady about four years. Towards the close of this time the nephew of a clergyman, a lieutenant in the navy, came home from sea and gained the affections of the lady's companion, then under 18 years of age, and seduced her. He returned to sea, where he still remains. As for the poor girl, she

proved pregnant, had to leave her situation, and become the mother of a child.

Her own mother was dead, and her father had remarried – therefore that door was closed. Need it excite surprise, then, that she took what seemed to her to be the only course to save herself from starvation? She took it, and there, three months afterwards, Mr. Gladstone found her. His great difficulty has been with the girl. She dreads the world's opinion, and, when he has offered to place her in some way of obtaining a respectable livelihood, she has always objected on the ground of the scorn and reproaches to which she would be certain to be subjected.

29

ATTEMPTED ENCLOSURE OF HAMPSTEAD HEATH

29 May 1853

Considerable sensation has been created during the past week among the copyholders and leaseholders in Hampstead, consequent on a renewed attempt on the part of the Lord of the Manor of Hampstead, Sir Thomas Maryon Wilson, Bart., to get an act smuggled through the House of Lords, empowering him to grant building leases, or in other words to enclose and destroy the beautiful scenery of Hampstead Heath. At a period when London is extending on every side, and when building operations have brought the metropolis to the very verge of the Hampstead hills, any attempt to enclose or destroy that most healthful and beautiful suburb, Hampstead Heath, is viewed with the greatest alarm, not merely by the wealthy class bankers, merchants, and others who have laid out vast sums of money in the erection of villa residences in its vicinity, but by the more humble classes, who have, from its proximity to London, been enabled to enjoy the fine scenery which surrounds it as well as its salubrity of atmosphere.

THE RIGHTS OF MARRIED WOMEN

Before 1882 a woman's property became her husband's at marriage – a strange contrast to the groom's words in the Book of Common Prayer, 'with all my worldly goods I thee endow'. Despite the Attorney-General's pledge reported here it took twenty-five years for the Married Women's Property Act to be passed.

15 June 1856

The movement of Sir C. Perry in favour of the separate property of married women has ended in a compromise. He accepted the pledge of the Attorney-General that Government would bring forward next session a measure for removing the admitted anomalies of the existing law. Sir Alexander Cockburn admitted that the rules of the common law affecting the property of married women are in many respects odious, unjust, and altogether inapplicable to the existing state of society in this country.

That the Chancery lawyers should be disposed to take the other side is not to be wondered at. Their apprehension naturally is that if the general rule of law on this subject were rendered equitable and just, there would be comparatively little occasion to introduce those particular conventions between married people which, under the familiar name of marriage settlements, now provide so lucrative a branch of business to practitioners in equity.

ELIZABETH MARTHA BROWN

17 August 1856

The following confession was made by Elizabeth Martha Brown, just previous to her execution.

'My husband, John Anthony Brown, deceased, came home on Sunday morning, the 6th of July, at two o'clock, in liquor and was sick. He had no hat on. I asked him what he had done with his hat. He abused me and said 'What is it to you, — — you?' He then asked for some cold tea. I said that I had none, but would make some warm. He replied, 'Drink that yourself and be — —.' I then said, 'What makes you so cross? Have you been at Mary Davis's?' He then kicked out the bottom of the chair on which I had been sitting. We continued quarrelling until three o'clock, when he struck me a severe blow on the side of my head, which confused me so much that I was obliged to sit down. Supper was on the table, and he said 'Eat it yourself and be — —.' At the same time he reached down from the mantelpiece a heavy horsewhip with a plaited end, and struck me across the shoulders with it three times. Each time I screamed out. I said, 'If you strike me again I will cry murder,' He retorted, 'If you do, I will knock your brains out through the window.' He also added, 'I hope I shall find you dead in the morning.' He then kicked me on the left side, which caused me much pain, and he immediately stooped down to untie his boots. I was much enraged, and in an ungovernable passion, on being so abused and struck, I directly seized a hatchet which was lying close to where I sat, and which I had been using to break coal with to keep up the fire and keep his supper warm, and with it (the hatchet) I struck him several violent blows on the head, I could not say how many.

He fell at the first blow on his head, with his face towards the fireplace. He never spoke or moved afterwards. As soon as I had done it I wished I had not, and would have given the world not to have done it. I had never struck him before, after all his ill-treatment; but, when he hit me so hard at this time, I was almost out of my senses, and hardly knew what I was doing.'

THE BATHING AT RAMSGATE AND MARGATE: ENGLISH DECORUM

24 August 1856

For years the manner in which bathing is carried on has been severely commented upon, but this year it is worse than ever. The following is a specimen of what may be witnessed continually: the beach is so crowded with ladies and gentlemen that it is difficult to walk through the throng. The water is black with bathers; should the sea be rather rough the females do not venture beyond the surf, and lay themselves on their backs, waiting for the coming waves, with their bathing dresses in a most *dégagée* style. The waves come and carry their dresses up to their neck, so that, as far as decency is concerned, they might as well be without any dresses at all. Then follows a series of antics, with a running accompaniment of screaming that might do very well in an Eastern harem, but which is certainly anything but creditable to English women. And all this takes place in the presence of thousands of spectators. In fact, it is looked upon much as a scene at a play would be, as the gentlemen are there with their opera glasses, bandying criticisms as if they were in Fop's Alley in the Opera House.

But this is not all. If the gentlemen come to look at the ladies bathing, it is equally the fact that ladies pay as much attention to the performances of the gentlemen. The portion of the beach allotted to the men is crowded with well-dressed females, or, in other words, ladies, who calmly look on without a blush or even a giggle and seem much amused by what is going on. How is that ladies who are so very delicate in London, should, when they arrive at Ramsgate, throw off all pretentions to modesty and decency, as they do their shawls and wrappers? The authorities cannot, perhaps, prevent them from carrying on their antics in the water. But this they can and ought to do; they ought to compel gentlemen to wear, as in France, *caleçons*, and the ladies' dresses should at least be so constructed as to prevent a wholesale exposure of their natural perfections or imperfections as now momentarily takes place.

William Clement died in 1852, as did Dowling his star reporter. Lewis Doxat retired in 1857. The new editor was Joseph Snowe and he championed the cause of the North in the American Civil War, contrary to the views of the British Government. Probably as a result of this, circulation dropped and The Observer *went into a decline which lasted until at least 1870.*

THE PLAGUE SORE OF MODERN SOCIETY

15 February 1857

It is a terrible incident of our social existence that the resources for gaining a livelihood left open to women are so few. Struggle as they will – with the exception of those who may be employed in factories – it is with them, stitch, stitch, stitch. Far on, into the cheerless night the poor seamstress plies her allotted task; too thankful if she can save herself from pollution and from pinching hunger by her incessant and monotonous toil. To be sure, there are thousands upon thousands of poor women throughout the country who have taken upon themselves the office of wife and mother without much prospect of being able to find raiment, shelter, and food for themselves and for the miserable creatures whom they may bring into the world; but what could they do? The alternative was a cadetship in the army of the needle.

At present, the language practically held by modern society to destitute women may be resolved into 'Marry – Stitch – Die – or Do worse!' The first command implies well-nigh incessant toil, the anguish without the joys of maternity – too often submission to the drunken freaks of a ruffian, and patient toleration of his violence. The second means toil still more incessant, ungladdened by any ray of human sympathy – toil for sixteen hours of each day, carried out in some chill attic. It means the hectic flush, the hard, dry cough, and, at last, despair. The third alternative we will pass over, for it is not for us to say what compensation may be reserved elsewhere for the poor creatures who have drawn so sad a number in the lottery of life. Of the fourth command it is enough to add that it is too commonly obeyed, as is known to all men who frequent the thoroughfares of our great towns at certain hours of the night. It is, indeed, obeyed so well that all vestige of the Divine stamp is at length obliterated from the medal which was intended to be worn next the heart of one, and only one, but which has been too roughly and too frequently passed from hand to hand. The resources then open to women are few indeed, and at the head of these stand the Needle.

UNEXPECTED CONVERT TO THE FRANCHISE

The failure of the 1832 Reform Act to enfranchise working men was one of the chief causes of Chartism. Only one in eighteen of the urban population had the vote.

2 June 1857

The Duke of Cleveland [is] 'far from holding that an extension of the suffrage in counties would be injurious,' provided, that is, that the extension is made in the way it ought to be, namely, that the influence enjoyed by the landed interest, is not interfered with. He would enfranchise 'the village curates, almost every village schoolmaster, clerks in mercantile offices, banks, and railways, and others.' Not so bad; and we should not dispute with His Grace that 'all these persons ought to have the franchise.' But he dreads the admission of £10 householders, whom he somewhat strangely identifies with journeymen carpenters and masons of migratory habits. Contemplating the bare possibility of a proposal to extend the suffrage to that point, he foresees, in such an event, 'that the landed interest in every county of England is extinguished for ever.'

INSURRECTION OF THE INDIAN ARMY

The deep-rooted cause of the Indian Mutiny in 1857 was the resentment among the higher castes against the westernisation of the country's social and legal systems. Its immediate occasion was the attempt by English officers to enforce the use in the army of cartridges which had been greased with a mixture of pork and beef fat. The ends of the cartridges had to be bitten off, which the sepoys, Hindu and Muslim alike, regarded as defilement. The chief result of the Mutiny was the transfer of government from the East India Company to the Crown.

2 August 1857

A Proclamation. 'Be it known to all the Hindoos and Mohammedans, the subjects and servants on the part of the officers of the English forces stationed at Delhi and Meerut, that all the Europeans are united in this point – first, to deprive the army of their religion, and then by the force of strong measures to Christianise all the subjects.

In fact it is the absolute orders of the Governor-General to serve out cartridges made up with swine and beef fat. For this reason we have merely for the sake of the faith concerted with all the subjects, and have not left one infidel of this place alive.'

REPORTS OF ATROCITIES

6 September 1857

Chinsurah, July. Were I to write you an account of the awful deeds the mutineers have perpetrated you would not, could not, believe it. The truth is so awful that the newspapers dare not publish it. The soldiers are furious, and whenever they get at the mutineers depend upon it the revenge will be commensurate with the outrages that caused it. I will only disgust you with two instances; but, alas! there are only too many similar ones: An officer and his wife were tied to trees, their children tortured to death before them, and portions of their flesh crammed down the parents' throats; the wife was then violated before her husband – he mutilated in a manner too horrible to relate – then both were burnt to death. Two young ladies named (very pretty) were seized at Delhi, stripped naked, tied on a cart, taken to the Bazaar, and there violated. Luckily for them they soon died from the effects of the brutal treatment they received. Can you wonder that, with stories like the foregoing (and there are plenty such), we feel more like fiends than men?

THE TRAGEDY OF INDIA

11 October 1857

A great sorrow has come to almost every home, and mingled with the sense of a public calamity and peril, to induce the mass of the community to join in contrition for sins committed, and duties unperformed . . . The duty of an alien Government towards a subject people of different religion to their own must not be confounded with our duty as individual Christians to propagate a knowledge of our faith amongst the heathen. The part of the Government in India is to act with perfect tolerance towards all the races and religions amongst their subjects. The only safe and just rule is for the Government to avoid all appearance of proselytising. On no other tenure can it be possible for us, a mere handful of strangers, as with all our Anglo-Saxon energy and power we must ever be amongst the myriads that people the Indian peninsula, to preserve and perpetuate our reign over them.

END OF THE EAST INDIA COMPANY

11 June 1858

The India Bill was read a third time and passed in the House of Commons on Thursday night. No opposition is expected in the Lords, and therefore the measure will in a few days become law. So ends the great East India Company. It is impossible to contemplate the extinction of so mighty and historical a corporation without a feeling similar to that with which Gibbon heard the monks chanting in the Flavian Amphitheatre, and beheld the cows feeding in the Roman Forum. For good or evil, a power has passed away from the earth.

THE LIONS FOR THE NELSON COLUMN

15 August 1858

The construction of the lions for the Nelson Pillar have been given by the Government to Sir Edwin Landseer. As Sir Edwin is a painter, and not a sculptor, it seems strange that a national work such as this should be confided to what must be held to be unskilled hands. Michelangelo was, no doubt, equally great as a painter and a sculptor, but Sir Edwin Landseer is not a Michelangelo, great artist though he be, and the world has yet to learn that he has ever mastered even the rudiments of sculpture.

THE ROYAL ACADEMY

1 May 1859

The ninety-first annual exhibition of the Royal Academy of Arts was opened to private view on Friday. *The Vale of Rest,* by J.E. Millais, R.A., is one of those dreary pictures which this erratic artist occasionally exhibits – dreary in point of subject, and dreary in colour. It represents the garden of a nunnery, with one nun digging a grave, and another nun, in all the agony of fear or piety or remorse, squatted beside it. The digger is commonplace enough; but the witness – if such the second nun may be designated – is extraordinary for her contortions of countenance, and for her ridiculous attitude. The picture is scarcely worthy the name the painter has acquired; and indicates retrocession rather than advancement in art.

Landseer at work on his lions. Unskilled hands? Had he mastered even the rudiments of sculpture?

THE WAR IN AMERICA

The American Civil War broke out on 12 April 1861. The British upper classes were pro-South, as were sections of the Press, notably The Times. *The lower and middle classes were anti-slavery. So, to its cost in circulation and revenue, was* The Observer.

11 August 1861

All our sympathies are necessarily with the North. We should deplore, in common with all friends of humanity, the result of any struggle, long or short, that would end in leaving four millions of dusky brothers in hopeless and confirmed servitude. But we may yet hope that this may not be, unpromising as it looks just now. Our course, however, is strictly neutral, and must continue to be so whatever circumstances may arise. We do not believe that the North has gone into this war for the sake of the abolition of negro slavery.

They have never exhibited the proper degree of interest or zeal in the cause, or allowed themselves to incur any risk of their commerce or their wealth to uphold it. But in the struggle that now promises to be protracted, some most beneficial results may arise in the long run.

THE NUISANCE OF INCOME TAX

14 August 1864

With the exception of the window-tax, we believe that since the days of Wat Tyler there has been no impost so universally unpopular as the income-tax. Unequally distributed amongst the different classes of society, it levies its blackmail upon the produce of the brain or the result of energy, hard labour, and thrift on the same terms as upon dividends and rents. The more industrious and economical the professional man may be, the more he has to pay from his increased prosperity. Every additional hundred produced from his talent or his labour must pay its quota to the demand of the tax-gatherer. Unpleasant and perhaps unfair as all this undoubtedly is, it fails on that ground to justify the evasion and fraud that are too evidently practised in rendering the periodical returns of income.

We know that the income-tax is a nuisance; that more than twenty years ago it was introduced for a brief time only, and that since its introduction it has been frequently expiring but as constantly revived and resuscitated, until now it promises to become a permanent thorn in the irritable side of the British lion.

MPs in New Move on Franchise

The most powerful group in the movement for further parliamentary reform was the Reform Group, which included ex-Chartists, trade union leaders and middle-class radicals such as Edmund Beales.

19 February 1865

Within the last few months there has been an awakening of the people in several of the large cities and towns of the kingdom on the question of Parliamentary Reform and the Extension of the Franchise.

Negotiations have been afoot between members of Parliament and others, and several of the leaders amongst the working classes, for the purpose of ascertaining whether the working men are really desirous of obtaining the franchise. Amongst other gentlemen who have taken a deep interest in this movement, may be enumerated the following members of Parliament:– Messrs. Cobden, Bright, Stansfeld, P. Taylor, Seely, Forster, White, &c., and also several well-known public men, such as Mr. Samuel Morley, Mr. E. Beales, Mr. T.B. Potter, Mr. Mason Jones, &c.

These gentlemen state that they are prepared, if they see the working classes themselves moving earnestly in the matter, to put down a sum of £5,000 to carry on the agitation.

Assassination of President Lincoln

In 1862 Lincoln proclaimed the emancipation of slaves. The battle of Gettysburg (1-3 July 1863) where General Robert E. Lee was defeated and Lincoln made his immortal Address, one of the great passages of English prose, was the turning point of the war. Lee surrendered at Appomattox on 9 April 1865. On 14 April President and Mrs Lincoln went to Ford's Theatre in Washington to see The American Cousin.

30 April 1865

The theatre was densely crowded, and everybody seemed delighted with the scene before them. During the third act a sharp report of a pistol was heard, which merely attracted attention, but suggested nothing serious, until a man rushed to the front of the President's box, waving a long dagger in his right hand, and exclaiming, 'Sic semper tryannis!' and immediately leaped from the box to the stage beneath, and across to the opposite side, making his escape amid the bewilderment of the audience from the rear of the theatre, and, mounting a horse, fled.

The screams of Mrs. Lincoln first disclosed the fact to the audience that the President had been shot, when all present rose to their feet and rushed towards the stage, many exclaiming, 'Hang him! Hang him!'. There was a rush towards the President's box, when cries were heard to 'Stand back, and give him air!' On a hasty examination it was found that the President had been shot through the head above and below the temporal bone, and that some of the brain was oozing out. He was removed to a private house opposite to the theatre, and the Surgeon-General of the army and other surgeons were sent for to attend to his condition.

Intense sorrow is depicted in all countenances; the grief of all good men is apparent everywhere. No flags were hoisted this morning [15 April] until the state of the President was known, when they were all placed at half-mast.

The Reform League

7 May 1865

The following address to the working classes has just been issued by the executive committee of the League: Fellow Workmen: The working classes of our country, the producers of its wealth, are in a degraded and humiliating position. We are denied those inherent rights which the working men of other countries possess, or are in a fair way to acquire. England has now become stationary, if not retrogressive. The working classes pay the great bulk of the taxes, but they are pertinaciously refused all share in the election of those who impose the taxes. The working classes obey the laws, but are allowed no voice in electing the men who make the laws.

Let us, therefore – the entire body of unrepresented men in the three kingdoms – league ourselves together to carry into effect that fundamental principle of all genuine reform and self-government – manhood suffrage. Take courage from the triumphs of our brethren in America, and let us emulate their virtues and resolution, while constitutionally battling for our rights.

Edmund Beales, President

COMPOSITION OF THE HOUSE OF COMMONS

18 February 1866

The *Spectator* finds that the members of the present House of Commons are sons, brothers, uncles, nephews, sons-in-law, or brothers-in-law of the present heads of the 31 houses known in its columns as the great governing families of England. The landed interests are further represented by 170 near relatives of peers, 15 of them heirs-apparent or presumptive, not included in the 31 families, and 60 baronets.

Real Necessity for Extensive Reform of Parliament

21 October 1866

The disclosures of the commissions of inquiry into corrupt practices at several boroughs have deeply affected the public mind, and it will no longer be possible to leave a large portion of the representation of the country in the hands of small and corrupt constituencies. It is equally clear that the time has come when the working classes must be effectually represented in the House of Commons.

That there are drunken, idle, and profligate individuals amongst the working classes is perfectly true; but so there are, and probably in much the same proportion, in every other class. Nothing could be more admirable than the bearing of the working men during the cotton famine; and those who know them best will bear witness to the independence and manly spirit which animate them at all times.

The aristocratical and wealthy classes have it all their own way in the present Parliament. They have not misused their power; on the contrary, it is remarkable how wisely and liberally they have dealt by the general public. Still, people are tired of seeing others legislate for them; they think they can do better for themselves, and that certain admitted abuses will stand a better chance of being removed. In these days, when everything progresses so rapidly, it would be strange if, after so long an interval of time, no alteration could be beneficially made in the representation of the people.

Dagger in hand, John Wilkes Booth rushes across the stage shouting, 'Sic semper tyrannis,' and making his escape from Ford's Theatre after shooting Abraham Lincoln.

NATIONAL EDUCATION

The 1870 Education Act set up a system of free compulsory elementary education. By 1876 the numbers of children in all elementary schools had more than doubled.

1 March 1868

If there is one question of the day upon which there is a general unanimity of opinion it is that of the want of a more extended education among the people. It has been established that 22 per cent of the adult male population of the country are unable to write their names; that one in three of our criminals can neither read nor write; and that there are nearly half a million children who are all but without any education, and who are growing up in the most abject ignorance.

'THE GREAT UNWASHED'

The Second Reform Act, described here as a 'leap in the dark', gave the vote to male urban workers but not agricultural workers or miners, let alone women.

11 October 1868

The Great Unwashed (by the Journeyman Engineer).

It is at all times well that the different classes of society should be acquainted with the habits and feelings of their fellow-citizens; but more particularly at the present time, when, as Lord Derby has announced, a great 'leap in the dark' has been taken, has such knowledge become necessary, especially to those who have hitherto been deemed the ruling classes. This volume is divided into two parts. The first describes 'the great unwashed in their public relations,' under which the writer treats of working men, working-men's homes and wives, working men and politics, the working classes and the Church, and trade unionism. The second part describes the inner life of working men. The writer gives vivid descriptions of life at home, life in the clubs, very cheap literature, and other matters, from which, did space allow, we should gladly give extracts. As it is, we must content ourselves with the following remarks of the writer on the feelings of the working classes towards the Church: 'The surroundings of life make working men look at things in a practical light, and they will never be brought to believe in the real christianity of a Church which, with ample revenues, displays the disgraceful spectacle of a bishop with thousands a year preaching a charity sermon for the benefit of poor clergymen, the said poor clergymen being meanwhile the real workers in the vineyard.'

*J*ulius Beer bought The Observer *in 1870. Beer, born in Frankfurt, had made a considerable fortune on the London Stock Exchange. He bought* The Observer *more as a rich man's toy and an occasional mouthpiece for his views on foreign affairs than as a profit-making venture. He appointed his close friend Edward Dicey as editor.*

Dicey had come to The Observer *in 1870. His unusual knowledge of foreign affairs gave the paper a new authority in that field, and his use of able writers re-invigorated earlier standards of critical comment in the world of the arts.*

CHARLES DICKENS

12 June 1870
Dickens died on 9 June, aged 58.

If ever in the annals of our literature there was a man whose name was, in very truth, a household word to all English speaking men it was Charles Dickens. To all of us, to young and old, to rich and poor, the tidings, which saddened England on Friday, came home like the news of a friend's death. The chords he struck vibrated somehow through all our hearts. At the time that *Dombey and Son* was being published an eminent reviewer summed up his criticism of the work with the comment that it was hard to judge of it fairly when a whole nation was 'in tears for the death of little Paul.'

There have been within our day writers of fiction with subtler insight into the working of human passions, with more varied knowledge of society, with greater constructive faculty, with higher faculty of diction, but there is none who, like him, could make his characters live, move, and be.

No doubt something of Dickens's wide-spread popularity was due to the circumstances of his time. In our days the reading public has reached dimensions which our forefathers would have deemed impossible, while the facilities of communication between all parts of the globe enable the written word to circulate with a rapidity rivalling that of the telegraph itself. But still, the like facilities were open to all writers of our time; and yet it was Dickens, and Dickens only, who made his works quoted through the length and breadth of every one of those vast regions where the English tongue rules supreme.

THE OPENING OF THE ALBERT HALL

2 April 1871

The Albert Hall was opened with much pomp on Wednesday. There may be two opinions about the architectural value of the building, and we do not venture to say whether those are right who compare the edifice to a gardener's gigantic forcing cover. There may be two opinions also about the necessity of the Hall, and, of course, some allege that the building would be faultless if it were not useless. It may still be dreaded that the echo will disturb future performances. 'Praise undeserved is scandal in disguise;' and until the building has been adequately tested, it would be premature to praise the building without reserve. But the scenic success of the opening there is no denying. Why cannot one order so many princes, princesses, and maharajahs to grace the opening of every public building?

DENIAL OF TOBACCO BEFORE HANGING

15 December 1872

The other morning a wretched man was executed at Newgate for shooting a woman. It was not a very shocking murder, as times go: having had a quarrel with her, in a moment of frenzy he merely shot both her and himself with a revolver. Unfortunately she died, and he recovered. He was tried for murder and found guilty, with a half-and-half recommendation to mercy by the jury.

When visited in his cell by the sheriffs and the Governor a short time before his execution, he asked, it is stated, for two glasses of brandy; he also begged permission to smoke for a short time, but this request was denied. It is difficult to understand what possible objection there can be to permitting a man on the brink of death to smoke a pipe if he is so inclined. Why should he be allowed brandy, and not tobacco? In every other country but this a condemned criminal is allowed to walk to the place of execution with a pipe or cigar in his mouth. Who can tell how much the strain on the nerves in the agonising minutes that precede death may be lessened by a few whiffs of tobacco? And even the British Anti-Tobacco Association would hardly have the heart to take the pipe out of the hands of the condemned criminal at the foot of the gallows; but officialism in England cannot relax its rules even on the edge of the grave.

The opening of the Albert Hall. 'There may be two opinions about the architectural value of the building . . . Some compare it to a gardener's gigantic forcing cover'.

CRICKET

20 August 1876

Gloucestershire v. Yorkshire. Played on the ground in front of Cheltenham College, on Thursday and Friday, and concluded yesterday (Saturday), the match, as was generally expected, terminating in a draw. Gloucestershire scored 528 in their first innings, Mr. W.G. Grace making no less than 318 runs.

DANGER OF BICYCLISTS

3 September 1876

Bicycling may be a very enjoyable and healthful exercise, but there can be no two opinions as to the extreme danger caused by velocipedes when used in public thoroughfares. Although there can be no excuse for the brutal conduct of the riders on the St. Albans coach towards a bicyclist the other day, it is only what might be expected to result from the haphazard manner in which bicycle riders dash all over the roads, making horses restive and giving great annoyance to drivers. It is peculiarly unfortunate for bicyclists that this incident should have occurred just when they are endeavouring to obtain a wider range for their exercise by getting permission to practice in the parks. In our suburban districts these noiseless machines, flying along at night, here, there, and everywhere, have become quite a dangerous nuisance, and if they were allowed in the parks accidents could not be avoided. If it be thought advisable, there is no reason why a special space should not be set aside for bicycling, much in the same way as Rotten Row is for equestrians. But it is most desirable that the parks should be kept free from these machines. If bicyclists are wise they will let well alone.

ITALIAN CHILDREN SLAVES TO ORGAN GRINDERS

8 October 1876

The unfortunate condition of Italian children who are employed by organ grinders in the London streets has often given rise to severe comment on the part of the press. It is an undoubted disgrace to any civilised country that such a system of slavery as exists with regard to these children should be allowed to continue, but it is by no means easy to suggest an effective remedy. It would be impossible to prohibit street music altogether. Although to a large number of persons organ grinders are a nuisance, they are popular with the masses, and it is impossible to prevent even that portion of the public who do not appreciate the beauties of street music from obeying the dictates of charity, and giving occasional pence to these itinerant musicians.

In many cases the organ men themselves are as much the slaves of the padrones from whom they hire their organs as the children who accompany them to excite charity, and it is quite time some legislative measure was adopted to suppress, in as far as possible, the kidnapping of children to be brought up to mendicancy. Much good might be effected by introducing a system of licenses for all children who are employed by street musicians. A register should also be kept of their names and addresses, and it should be made compulsory for them to keep the police informed as to their places of residence, under pain of forfeiting their licenses. The adoption of such a system could not fail to prevent, in a great measure, the kidnapping of children, and the cruel treatment to which they are now subjected.

HER MAJESTY EMPRESS OF INDIA: A MISTAKE

Queen Victoria was declared Empress of India on 1 May 1876

7 January 1877

The ceremony which has just taken place at Delhi is scarcely one on which we can congratulate ourselves. The Delhi ceremonial was one which necessarily owed the greater part of its scenic splendour to those who were in reality the subordinate actors in the drama – the native princes themselves. The mood of the native prince seems, on the whole, to be best described as indifference tempered by ill humour. One of the most important of the body was offended at not getting something more substantial than barren honours. And we cannot learn that the commemorative medals, the strings of titles, the accolades of knighthood, and the honorary military appointments, evoked anything approaching to enthusiasm or even satisfaction from their various recipients.

We can scarcely suppose that the tranquillity of our Indian Empire can be thus easily secured, and if this is the only point in which the Delhi ceremonial has made any impression on the native princes its results, we fear, have been infinitesimal. Indeed, we are strongly of opinion that in its fundamental conception the whole affair was a mistake. For a native prince to have a commemorative medal hung round his neck in token – for it amounts to that – of his vassalage to the Imperial Power in India, could hardly be supposed to give him acute pleasure; and the banners, complimentary speeches, honorary titles, and other adjuncts of the occasion do not appear likely to have added materially to his satisfaction.

The 1877 Durbar. 'In its fundamental conception the whole affair was a mistake. The mood of the native prince seems, on the whole, to be described as indifference tempered by ill-humour.'

THE TRAFFIC AT HYDE PARK CORNER

18 February 1877

As regularly as the season comes round, loud and general complaints are made with regard to the want of greater accommodation for the traffic which centres at Hyde Park Corner. It is not for us to attempt to point out which of the various suggestions which have lately been made for relieving the traffic at this point is the best, although Mr. Edward M. Barry's scheme for constructing a subway, or sunken road, from Hamilton place into Constitution Hill, so that the east to west traffic should pass over that going north and south, seems to be the most effective. Public convenience and safety demand that immediate steps should be taken to make some improvement. There has been time enough wasted in talking about it.

THE SEWAGE OF LONDON

16 December 1877

After great trouble and almost infinite expense, it would seem that the main drainage works have left London and its neighbourhood very much where it was before. Sixty years ago the sewage of the metropolis was carefully stored in cesspools, out of which it from time to time bubbled up, producing epidemics of typhoid, dyphtheria, cholera, and other such malignant plagues. Then came an attempted improvement. The whole of the sewers of London were opened into the Thames, and it was fondly hoped by the ratepayers that the river would save them the expense of a proper system of sewerage. This expectation was falsified by the inevitable operation of the laws of nature. The Thames became nothing less than a vast tidal cesspool. The next step was the construction of the main drainage works, by which the sewage of the metropolis, instead of being emptied into the river between the London Bridge, is poured into it at Barking. It now appears that we have simply carried the nuisance some few miles lower down. The flood tide is stronger than the ebb, and the whole bulk of the filth which London daily pours into the Thames at Erith, floats up and down between tide and tide, depositing itself on the bed and shores of the river in a foul mass, which day by day creeps nearer and nearer to London. The great problem, What is to be done with the sewage of London? remains as unanswered as ever. Meantime, it must be remembered that sewage in itself is a substance of considerable mercantile value.

RIGHTS OF THE PRESS AT EXECUTIONS

3 August 1879

Without reflecting in any way upon the arrangements for the carrying out of the execution of Kate Webster at the Wandsworth Goal, it is desirable that steps should be taken to prevent the Press being excluded from executions. Most people agree with the abolition of public executions. The notion of such sights acting as a deterrent to crime has long been given up as a mistake, but so long as capital punishment is allowed all executions should be carried out in the presence of independent witnesses. It is not enough that the newspapers should receive official accounts of such proceedings. There is no doubt, in case of any important personage being hung, rumours would get about that the law had been evaded, and the criminal allowed to escape. Such rumours might be unfounded, but every precaution should be taken to prevent their arising, and the best possible means of maintaining the public faith in the carrying out of such sentences is to admit the Press. All sensational reports of executions are to be deprecated, and every effort made to discourage them; but every leading newspaper should have the distinct right of sending its reporter to give the public an impartial account of the proceedings.

THE BOERS AND THE TRANSVAAL

18 January 1880

We are certainly in a dilemma in the Transvaal. The Boers are very much in earnest in their determination to get rid of us. Some people are of opinion that the best thing we can do is to abandon the country, and leave the Boers to the full enjoyment of the anarchy which would inevitably ensue. Such a step, however, is strongly to be deprecated, for the Transvaal is so situated that its independence would give rise to constant difficulties with frontier tribes, the effects of which would disturb the peace and prosperity of our South African possession. We *must* maintain order in the Transvaal, in our own interests. The Boers are quite incapable of improvement, and are notoriously dishonest and aggressive, and cruel to all natives with whom they come into contact. But even in the Transvaal itself the Boers are in a minority. There are the Kaffirs, who are entitled to some consideration. It is, therefore, in the interest of an overwhelming majority in the Transvaal that we are bound to maintain our rule.

STATE OF IRELAND: THE BOYCOTT EXPEDITION

The Land League was formed in 1879 to protect Irish tenant farmers against rack-renting and eviction. Members refused to work for landlords or their agents and generally ostracised them. One such campaign, against an agent in County Mayo, gave a new word not only to English but other languages, including French and German.

14 November 1880

Cong. Saturday. The northern labourers [brought in from Ulster] began ploughing out Captain Boycott's potatoes at ten this morning. A strong police escort surrounded them while working, and a cavalry vedette and policemen were stationed all around. The Land League are working strenuously to prevent any offence being shown to the northerners. Their view is that any collision between the northerners and the residents would prevent the hoped-for accession of Orange farmers to the League. Captain Boycott intends to leave the neighbourhood immediately his crops are saved. He and his wife will sojourn abroad for some months; but he expresses himself firmly determined to return. The soldiers encamped on Captain Boycott's demesne last night killed and ate his sheep, and two of his ducks were stolen. It is alleged that a countrywoman, who keeps a huckster shop, and sold groceries to Captain Boycott's party, was carded.

At Castlebar the authorities evidently imagine a reign of terror generally prevails throughout the entire of Mayo, as the ammunition arriving for the military this morning was escorted from the railway station by a formidable guard with fixed bayonets.

DEATH OF CHARLES DARWIN

23 April 1882

Darwin died on 19 April, aged 73

Where previous thinkers had merely thrown out gleams of light, Darwin, with untiring patience and with infinite toil, constructed a clear and broad road. To Charles Darwin, and to him alone we owe the universal recognition of the fact that the various existent modes of life are not distinct, but fluent; and that their changes and imitations depend upon a struggle for existence, in the course of which, by an inexorable rule of fate, the weakest go to the wall and the strongest survive. The doctrine is one of those immense generalisations which reduce a mass of recorded facts to a coherent scientific unity.

When the *Origin of Species* first appeared it passed through every stage of opposition. It is an old saying that, when a new and strange truth is promulgated, we are at once told that it is wicked and irreligious. This difficulty surmounted, we are gravely assured that on scientific grounds it is inaccurate. Lastly, rushes in the unworthy crowd of scientific place-hunters loudly crying that there is nothing new in the discovery, and, indeed, that it has always been known, recognised, and acted upon.

Darwin must many times have laughed at the folly and arrogance of the ignorant. Theologians cursed him. Zoologists of eminence gravely decided that the whole thing was a vast delusion, and that its author was a dilettante country gentleman. Lord Beaconsfield, then Mr. Disraeli, went down to Oxford to tell a crowd of country parsons and Conservative squires that he at least, for one, was 'on the side of the angels,' and declined to believe himself the lineal descendant of a monkey.

Peerages and decorations are conferred upon men who successfully conduct negotiations in the sugar trade, or wage wars with the Martini-Henry rifle against naked savages. Darwin, we believe enjoyed no such distinction. His whole life was one continued worship of truth for its own sake. He was incapable of jealousy, ambition, or self-seeking, and – though he himself knew it not – the moral lesson of his life is perhaps even more valuable than is the grand discovery which he has stamped on the world's history.

Darwin as seen by a cartoonist in an 1874 issue of the London Sketch Book.

MURDER OF THE CHIEF SECRETARY FOR IRELAND

7 May 1882

On the eve of going to press we have received with feelings of utmost regret, the intelligence of the murder in Dublin of the Chief Secretary of State for Ireland, and of the Assistant Secretary, Mr. Burke. Lord Frederick Cavendish had only arrived in Dublin yesterday morning. We have had too many crimes in Ireland which have remained too long unpunished and unrepressed.

BOMBARDMENT OF ALEXANDRIA

In 1875 an Egyptian financial crisis enabled Disraeli to buy a forty-four per cent holding in the Suez Canal Company. This gave us what amounted to a leasehold over the whole country. Nationalist feeling was aroused, rioting broke out in Alexandria, lives were lost and the Royal Navy bombarded the city. Troops were landed. Egyptian army officers revolted, led by Ahmet Arabi, who was defeated by General Sir Garnet Wolseley at Tel-el-Kebir.

16 July 1882

At last the authority of Great Britain in Egypt has been asserted by force of arms. Deeply as we deplore the results of the recent bombardment, we yet do not hesitate to say that in our judgment it is better both for Egypt and for England that Alexandria should have been reduced to ruins, than that the military tyranny of Araby and his fellow-conspirators should have been allowed to endure.

On the other hand, it would not be right to conceal our conviction that Egypt would never have fallen into her present plight if England and France, the two Powers who had made themselves responsible for the good administration of the country, had restored order at once, the occasion for the bombardment would not have arisen.

41

JINGOISM AND THE EMPIRE

29 October 1882

For the last few years we have been protesting to the world that we had had enough of empire. We assured others, and we assured ourselves, that the enthusiasm which greeted the annexation of Cyprus was merely a passing ebullition of transient sentiment. We were never tired of proclaiming our conversion from Jingoism, and repudiating the old-fashioned creed of which *Rule Britannia* may be said to be the embodiment in verse. But the moment an attempt was made to count upon our forbearance and encroach upon our interests, it was found that our abnegation of Imperialism was skin-deep only. The heartfelt approval with which our intervention in Egypt has been received shows how very little hold the doctrines of the anti-Imperialist school have ever had upon the mass of the English people.

For our own part, we have always thought that the Liberal outcry against Jingoism was a mistake, because, after all, Jingoism was only the vulgar manifestation of the sentiments which have made England what she is. All we wish is to lay down the truth; that, whether under a Conservative or a Liberal administration, the dominant instincts of England as an Imperial power remain the same. Our past compels us. We have got to to forward or to go backwards. The time has not yet come when England is prepared to abdicate the Imperial power won by a series of adventures of which that conducted by Sir Garnet Wolseley is the last and not the least.

DEATH OF CAPTAIN WEBB IN NIAGARA WHIRLPOOL

29 July 1883

The death of Captain Matthew Webb in a foolhardy attempt to swim the rapids of Niagara has excited universal regret. It does not appear that anything except the desire of fame, and a determination that, as he had stated in writing he would swim Niagara, swim he would, induced him to make this more than hazardous experiment. For bulldog strength and courage, however, he was unequalled, and these qualities which were displayed, not only in his famous swim across the Straits of Dover in 1875 but in saving more than one life in mid ocean. They were also accompanied by the attraction of rare personal modesty.

After all, these characteristics, if not the highest gifts of all, have yet been among the chief factors in determining the character and history of our race; and as Englishmen we cannot but mourn that one who possessed them in so pre-eminent a degree should have thus idly thrown his life away.

NEW SALVATION ARMY A PUBLIC NUISANCE

1 June 1884

Whether the proceedings of the Salvation Army tend to reduce the prevalence of intoxication or to improve the moral condition generally of the classes to whom its supporters apply their endeavours is a question which, like all religious arguments, remains where it commenced; but one thing is certain, good or bad, Salvationism is rendering itself a public nuisance and a public danger. The old idea of a quiet English Sunday, be it good or bad, is a thing of the past. From early morning till late in the evening ragged processions, accompanied by screeching cornets, big drums, and concertinas, parade some of the principal thoroughfares, frightening horses, and generally disturbing the great bulk of the residents. The right of public procession is one which no one would wish to see interfered with, but the law which allows such processions never contemplated a body of dancing and shrieking fanatics marching about the streets upon a Sunday endangering life and limb and seriously annoying the majority of the community. If there exists no law to stop these unseemly exhibitions it is quite time measures were taken to pass an Act for the special purpose.

UNTIMELY DEATH OF JUMBO

20 September 1885

The untimely death of Jumbo, the huge African elephant, who was sold by the Zoological Society some few years ago to Mr. Barnum, will be matter of regret in two continents. He was sold by the society because it was alleged that he was getting old, and becoming *must*, or dangerous; and we pointed out strongly at the time that there was absolutely no foundation whatever for this assertion, and that all that the animal really needed was active exercise and plenty of it. If he had been allowed to remain where he was, in the Regent's Park, he would almost certainly have been alive to this day.

VINDICTIVE PUNISHMENT
OF YOUNG WOMEN

25 October 1885

Sarah Guest, aged thirty-nine, and Margaret Tickett, aged thirty-eight, both married, have been sentenced by the learned Chairman of the Surrey Sessions to ten years' penal servitude for 'shop-lifting,' the article stolen being a piece of cotton of the value of two shillings. It is fair to state that there were other charges against them. Let us even admit that they were 'notorious thieves.' Even so, however, the sentence seems terribly severe. It will not deter others from the same offence, for the poor creatures who feel tempted to steal a yard of flannel or a roll of ribbon on the moment's impulse do not usually read the Surrey Sessions reports. And it is out of all proportion to the character of the offence itself, unless we are to regard a previous conviction as making any one of the Queen's subjects a *caput lupinum*, to be hunted down ever afterwards. Ten years' penal servitude is virtual death. It is fitting punishment – perhaps – for a garotter, or for a burglar who has added violence to theft; but it is simply a vindictive punishment for such an offence as the petty larceny of a piece of draper's stuff worth twenty-four pence.

Julius Beer had died suddenly in 1880, leaving The Observer *to his son Frederick, who was plagued by continual ill health. In 1887 he married Rachel Sassoon, a rich heiress with a strong character. She was far more interested in* The Observer *than her ailing husband was – both Dicey and Traill, who took over as editor in 1889, complained of her interference. In 1891, the year Traill retired, she virtually became editor: she described herself in* Who's Who *as 'assistant editor and sometime editor of* The Observer'. *(In 1893 she was to buy the* Sunday Times *and edited that too.) Whatever her talents or failings – and the paper certainly went into decline towards the end of the century – she was much involved in one of the great scoops in journalistic history: the revelation that the document that had led to the conviction of Dreyfus for high treason was a forgery by his fellow officer Esterhazy.*

Rachel Beer: Rich, handsome, directress and 'sometime editor of The Observer'.

RETIREMENT OF THE GERMAN CHANCELLOR

23 April 1890

'The old order changeth, giving place to new,' and such a change it is that is heralded by the retirement of the German Chancellor. In form it is but the substitution of General von Caprivi for Fürst von Bismarck, but in fact the new Chancellor is the Emperor himself. Europe understood the old Chancellor's policy: Germany and her gains safe – by fair means if possible, if not by foul; but now that the twenty-years pilot of the Empire has surrendered the tiller into the impulsive hands of the Kaiser, who shall say what is in store for us? It is alike hopeless and unprofitable to try to discover why this particular moment for retiring was fixed upon. Undoubtedly the clearness of the political sky had something to do with it. So good a patriot as the Chancellor would scarcely have taken such a step under other conditions; and if his retirement has not caused the slightest panic anywhere, it is because the peace of the world is felt to be assured for the moment, though for the moment only.

'Bodices should fit easily, the sleeves being sufficiently loose to allow of free action'.

STATE PENSIONS

Charles Booth, author of the paper discussed here, was a statistician, ship-owner, social reformer, Privy Councillor, Fellow of the Royal Society and, from 1892 to 1894, President of the Royal Statistical Society.

20 December 1891

Mr. Charles Booth's paper on State pensions for the aged poor proves that the pauperism which it most probable is not, as we have all been taught, due to drunkenness, vice, and laziness, but to other causes, which should excite compassion rather than contempt. Not more than 12 per cent. of the pauperism of the London parishes he investigated is directly, and not more than 13 per cent. is indirectly, due to drink. The percentage traceable to vice and laziness is microscopic, and about 4½ per cent, is caused by want of work.

Sickness and old age – these, and not drunkenness, laziness and vice, are, according to Mr. Booth's unimpeachable figures, the chief cause of poverty in London. Indeed, old age alone is responsible for about one-third of the pauperism in England and Wales. The logical deduction therefore is that sixty-five is the right age at which pensions, if they are to be given at all, should begin.

In these circumstances we turn to various pension schemes. All these plans, however, vanish in the solvent of Mr. Booth's destructive criticism, and he startled the world by contending that the simplest manner of dealing with destitution in old age is to give an inalienable State pension of 5s. a week as a matter of right to every man and woman above the age of sixty-five, quite irrespective of rank or riches.

GOLF AND GOLFING GOWNS

25 September 1892

No game has in so comparatively short a period made such rapid strides in popular opinion as golf. Twenty years ago one could count on the fingers of both hands the number of links in the whole of the United Kingdom. To-day no fewer than five hundred and twenty are in existence. Nowhere does a woman neatly turned out – *bien chaussée et bien gantée* – appear to greater advantage. That skirts must be made to clear the ground goes without saying. Bodices, too, should fit easily, the sleeves being sufficiently loose to allow of free action for the arms. Blouses are undoubtedly the most comfortable garments to play in, and now that the weather is getting too cold to wear cotton some smart flannel ones are to be seen. Only the other day I met with a very neat frock which had been prepared for a fair golfer. It was made of dark grey Scotch cheviot.

Indeed, enthusiastic golf-players have their dresses made of water-proof tweed or serge, so as to be prepared for all weathers, for the idea of wearing a cloak or mackintosh is not be thought of.

THE LAST OF OUR POET LAUREATES?

9 October 1892

Alfred Tennyson died on 6 October

In our opinion, there is one way, and one way only, in which the loss sustained by English literature through the death of Lord Tennyson can be adequately recognised. The question has already been raised in many quarters as to who is the most fitting successor for the post rendered vacant by the Laureate's demise. We all feel that it would be something of a slight to the dead man's memory if the office he has filled so long and so worthily were given into hands unequal to the honour. It may be said that a like difficulty occurs whenever a great statesman or a great soldier dies. But men who have made their mark in the camp or the council leave of necessity work behind them which must be carried on. The man is dead but the country lives on, and someone must step in to fill the breach. In the case of the Poet Laureateship no such necessity exists. The post is practically a sinecure, and now that Lord Tennyson is dead we may fairly say that the existence of such an office is an anachronism. Odes on the births, deaths, and marriages of Royal personages are not in harmony with the taste of the day. There would be a singular appropriateness if the line of Poets Laureate which

began with John Dryden should come to an end with Alfred Tennyson.

THE DEGRADATION OF CAPTAIN DREYFUS

6 January 1895

The degradation of Captain Alfred Dreyfus, who was lately condemned by court-martial to confinement for life in a fortress, having communicated military secrets to a foreign Government, took place at nine o'clock this morning at the Ecole Militaire. The commander of the troops, General Darras, occupied the centre of the quadrangle with his staff. Dreyfus, who was escorted by four artillerymen in command of a corporal, was led across the square. The prisoner, who was pale and flushed by turns, marched with a firm step. He appeared to be greatly excited and moved. At a sign from General Darras an official read aloud the sentence of the court-martial, and then the General pronounced the following words: 'Alfred Dreyfus, you are adjudged unworthy to bear arms, and in the name of the French people we degrade you.' The command to begin the act of degradation was then given. As the officer approached to carry out the sentence, Dreyfus started back, and cried out loudly: 'I am innocent! I swear it. Long live France!' The first act was the tearing off the epaulettes, next the lace on the tunic and the other distinctions marking the officer's grade were taken off, and finally the sword was unbuckled, drawn from the scabbard, and broken in two, the fragments being thrown at the feet of the condemned man. As his sword was being broken Dreyfus again uttered his despairing cry of '*Je suis innocent! Vive la France!*'

The degraded officer had then to march bareheaded round the

entire square in front of the troops. He preserved his fortitude in an extraordinary degree, and never seemed to falter. As he passed the place where the journalists were posted, he turned to them and said in loud, firm tones, 'Tell the whole of France that I am innocent!' Some officers retorted with the words, 'Down with Judas! Silence, traitor!' Two gendarmes took possession of the ex-officer, handcuffed him, and took him to the prison in which convicts are placed before beginning their sentence.

THE DREYFUS AFFAIR: WILD SCENE IN THE CHAMBER

Dreyfus was sent to Devil's Island where he spent more than four years in solitary confinement largely on the strength of le bordereau, *a memorandum destined for German Military Intelligence, which fell into the hands of the French counter-espionage service. It contained information about French artillery (the arm in which Dreyfus served) and the handwriting resembled his. However, an officer in French Military Intelligence, Picquart, decided that it was a forgery and that the actual writer was probably a penniless French officer named Esterhazy. The military did not want to know. Esterhazy was court-martialled and acquitted. Picquart was shunted off to Tunisia.*

Anti-semitism was already virulent enough; now a great wave swept the country. But a pro-Dreyfus movement was growing, led by politicians such as Jaurès and Clemenceau, and the writer Emile Zola, with his open letter to the President of France, J'accuse.

23 January 1898

Never was there such a scene in the Chamber as that which took place this afternoon ... An inkpot, aimed at the Comte de Bernis by Socialist deputy Deville, hit an usher, but the contents fell on a Conservative deputy, whose face was smothered in blood and ink. One deputy fainted in the corridor from loss of blood and excitement. The Mussulman deputy, Grenier, whose turban had been knocked off in the scrimmage, was seen to be praying aloud with upraised arms. In the editors' gallery a fight was going on between the editor of the *Paix* and M. de Claye of the *Gaulois*. The President put on his hat and suspended the sitting, and a guard of infantry lined up in the lobbies, where the quarrel was continued with extreme violence.

M. Méline then ascended the tribune, and said that the campaign which had been carried on regarding the Dreyfus affair was deplorable (applause). An illustrious writer [Zola] had used his pen to dishonour the army. M. Jaurès protested against the attempt to create a diversion against the Socialists. He accused the Conservatives of driving the Government along the path of reaction. M. de Bernis (Conservative) here exclaimed that M. Jaurès was acting as counsel for the Dreyfus syndicate, to which the former replied, 'You are a scoundrel and a coward!' M. de Bernis made a rush for the tribune, but several Socialist deputies started from their seats and intercepted him. A series of hand-to-hand encounters now took place, and blows were freely exchanged. In the midst of the tumult, M. de Bernis forced his way through the deputies surrounding him, reached the tribune, and succeeded in striking M. Jaurès. Conservatives and Socialists went to the assistance of their friends, and around the tribune the *mêlee* became general.

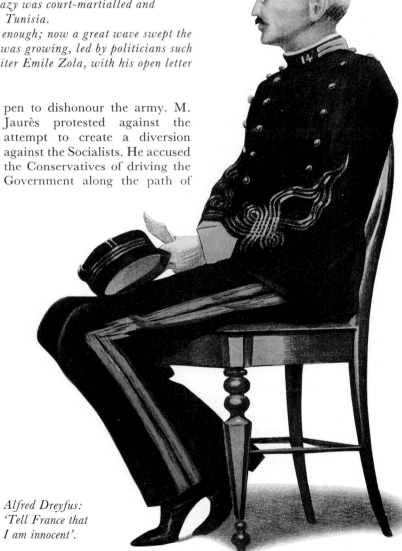

Alfred Dreyfus: 'Tell France that I am innocent'.

ESTERHAZY'S REPEATED CONFESSION

In September 1898 Esterhazy was in London where, so The Observer *reported, he confessed to being the author of the* bordereau. *He made the confession to Mrs. Rachel Beer, 'the directress of* The Observer*', as its Paris correspondent, Rowland Strong, who was present, described her. After the publication of the story Esterhazy retracted it, threatened a libel action and managed to get £500. In the following June, Strong's magnificent scoop was confirmed.*

4 June 1899

Esterhazy has informed a correspondent of the *Matin* that it was indeed he (Esterhazy) who wrote the *bordereau*. '*Oui, c'est moi qui ai fait le bordereau,*' are the precise words attributed to him. 'I wrote it,' he continued, 'at the invitation of Colonel Sandherr, my superior officer, my chief, and my friend.'

He explained further to the *Matin* correspondent that he kept his secret so long as he was a soldier, for then it was no business of his; he executed orders. It was the business of his chiefs.

'I now speak spontaneously and for nothing. I reveal the secret which nobody has been able, even for gold, to hear from me.'

This confirms what Esterhazy himself told me: that both De Bois-andré and Gaston Mény, of the Libre *Parole*, knew that he was the author of the *bordereau*.

All this is merely a repetition in brief of a portion of the revelations which Esterhazy made to me, and which were published in *The Observer* on Sept. 25 of last year. In spite of his subsequent contradiction, he now confirms absolutely his original confession.

With regard to myself, I may be permitted to say that, in spite of the grotesque insults of the Anti-Dreyfus Press, and of one nameless cur, an Englishman who disgraces his nationality, it has always been a matter of the utmost satisfaction to me that I was able in the columns of *The Observer* to first throw positive light on the true authorship of the *bordereau*, the unique document upon which the conviction of Dreyfus stands or falls. I have always felt confident that, in spite of his contradictions, Esterhazy would reiterate the confession which he first made to myself and Mrs. Rachel Beer.

Esterhazy: 'I now reveal the secret nobody, even for gold, has been able to hear from me'.

OFF TO THE CAPE

The Boer War broke out in 1899 and lasted until 1902. The Transvaal and Orange Free State were incorporated into the British Empire.

17 September 1899

At last! Yesterday the first instalment of the troops who are to bring Mr. Kruger to reason by dint of the mailed fist, if other and more pacific methods fail, quitted the shores of Old England for South Africa ... One glance at Tommy Atkins' face showed the frame of mind he was in. Whatever regret he may have felt on account of the girl he was leaving behind him was obviously swallowed up in his delight at going out once more on what promises to be active service. Jokes, and chaff, and laughter were the order of the day.

THE 'PARDON'

*In that month too the Court of Cassation quashed the 1894 verdict and ordered a new court martial. Incredibly, in view of Esterhazy's public admission, Dreyfus was again found guilty, although 'with extenuating circumstances' and sentenced to ten years' imprisonment (*The Observer *headline was '*FRANCE'S SHAME*'). This time, however, the public outcry could not be withstood, and he was pardoned.*

17 September 1899

To pardon the innocent is an eccentric proceeding, especially after a trial which was a mockery of justice; but any sign of returning grace in France is welcome. It is only the first step, for nobody can seriously believe that a pardon will end the 'Affaire.' Dreyfus will still be under a legal stigma; moreover, he will be deprived of all civil and political rights. To a man of his dauntless spirit that must be intolerable. To be free, but not a citizen; to have liberty without honour; to bequeath to his children a name under the ban of the law, and the worst reproach that can fall upon a patriot and a soldier! Such a compromise would aggravate the original injustice.

A PATRIOTIC AUDIENCE

MAFEKING

1 October 1899

An extraordinary demonstration of patriotic feeling burst into life last night at the Queen's Hall promenade concert. The 'selection', which always begins the second part of the concert, was the familiar fantasia on English airs. The fantasia ends, in most assertive fashion, with the melody of 'Rule Britannia,' and in this the Queen's Hall audience quickly saw an opportunity for the expression of their feelings on the political situation. The final bars of the tune were scarcely audible through the hurricane of cheers that rose from all parts of the hall, and the tempest continued till Mr. Henry J. Wood, realising the position, signalled for a repetition of the melody.

This time Mr. Wood turned towards the audience, and in a couple of seconds 'Rule Britannia' was being sung by some 2,000 people to the accompaniment of England's finest orchestra ... Then an enthusiast in the gallery called for 'Three cheers for Chamberlain' – which were given with deafening unanimity. Not satisfied, he demanded 'Groans for Kruger' – and the sounds which followed would have shamed a second-hand bassoon.

This gave opportunity for a striking manifestation of the level-headedness and command of self which so distinguished the Anglo-Saxon. Realising that dignity was in danger, all further demonstration was sternly repressed, the huge audience resuming their attitude as interested hearers of a concert as quickly as they had adopted the role of political enthusiasts.

Mafeking withstood a siege of 217 days; the garrison commander was Colonel Baden-Powell. When the siege ended, the country went mad – a new word entered the language: 'to maffick', to celebrate uproariously. On 21 May the Pall Mall Gazette *wrote: 'We trust that Cape Town will "maffick" today, if we may coin a word.'*

20 May 1900

While life lasts no man or woman of English blood will forget the first thirty-six hours after the news arrived of the relief of Mafeking. A passion of joy has swept over the country and the Empire. The nation has rejoiced, and is rejoicing, not nearly so much over the defeat of an enterprise prosecuted by the Boers with remarkable persistence, despite the menacing advance of

the British armies upon the Transvaal, as over the deliverance of a band of men and women who, under the inspiring and resourceful leadership of Colonel Baden-Powell, have borne themselves with perfect courage and endurance amid long-protracted dangers and privations. Whatever anyone thought about the origin of the war, or the blunders of the War Office, or the failures of certain Generals, or the aims and methods of Mr. Rhodes, there could be no two opinions with regard to the commander and the garrison of the little open town on the Bechuanaland border, who kept the British flag flying against heavy odds in numbers and artillery, for seven long months on end.

———————◆———————

Crowds 'mafficking' in Piccadilly to mark the end of the siege.

DEATH OF A GREAT ARTIST

19 July 1903

By the death of James McNeill Whistler the world of Art and the world of Letters are both made poorer. A great artist and a quaint and original, if not considerable, humorist have passed away in him.

The note of his work as an artist was the subtlety of it. The cachet of his literary production was the surprise of it. These are marks of genius. In art he was, moreover, a pioneer, having been one of the earliest and, to the end, one of the finest exponents of what has been neatly defined as the higher Impressionism.

Above all he was a master of colour as well as a skilled interpreter of its value in black and white. There are, indeed, those who contend that he was the greatest of all as an etcher. Take such a thing as *The Path in the Sea to Torcello*, with its luminous atmosphere and wide dimpling water.

The economy of means is marvellous, yet none the less is it impeccably and completely finished by the magic of suggestion. Still, it is mainly as a colourist that the painter of *The Portrait of my Mother* – for all that it is a study in black and grey – will take his place among the immortals. Last, let us say of the man whom we knew, that, for all his passion for paradox, for all his strident iconoclasm, for all his unconcealed delight in affronting prejudice and making enemies he was a charming and sympathetic companion.

ANNEXATION BY REVOLUTION

In 1903 the Province of Panama seceded from Colombia with American support and formed an independent republic. The Canal Zone came under American military government. U.S. Army engineers completed the canal and it was opened in 1914.

8 November 1903

The revolution in Panama has produced a curious situation; but it was an event long and surely expected. The Americans are an inventive people, and they have invented a new thing – annexation by revolution. Purists in international morals may object; but the world will not take a harsh view, and unquestionably the enterprise which shattered the fortune and broke the heart of Lesseps will now at length be carried out. The Panama Canal will be made.

*F*rederick Beer had died in 1901. The Observer *had been in the hands of Beer's trustees since 1903. Its fortunes were in decline.*
In 1905 it was bought by Sir Alfred Harmsworth, later Lord Northcliffe, proprietor of the Daily Mail, *who was looking for a vehicle for his political influence.*
His first editor was Austin Harrison who started to build up The Observer *again, and edited it with distinction until J.L. Garvin took over in 1908.*

MAJOR DREYFUS AND THE ARMY

The 1894 verdict against Dreyfus was quashed in 1906. He fought in World War I, was awarded the Legion of Honour in 1919 and died in 1935.

15 July 1906

'I am an officer now and cannot possibly allow myself to be interviewed.' This is the remark that Captain Dreyfus makes to the journalists who knock at his door in the Boulevard Malesherbes to obtain his view of the acquittal. The ex-prisoner of Devil's Island occupies a pleasant flat, modestly furnished, and here he has lived quietly with his family for some years past. His hair has gone quite grey, and he wears the look of a man who has suffered much. It is stated to be the intention of the Government to reinstate Dreyfus in the army with a certain ceremony. He will be promoted to the rank of major. There is no regiment of artillery in Paris, Versailles being the nearest point. It is probable, therefore, that he will join a regiment in the royal town. The circumstance that the ceremony does not take place in Paris robs it of much of the danger of a hostile demonstration.

MOTOR SEASON SUPPLEMENT BY H. MASSAC BUIST.

SUNDAY, JUNE 23, 1907.

HUMBER CARS
BEESTON (NOTTS) & COVENTRY.

The Observer was pro-motor car from early days. It praised Edward VII for a 'flying visit to Windsor on automobile'. Above is Page 1 of one of the colour supplements the paper published in that period.

◆

These Humber cars, clockwise from below, are: 20 HP Beeston; 30 HP Beeston landaulette; 10-12 HP Coventry.

THE
GARVIN
YEARS

1908-1942

Lord Northcliffe appointed James Louis Garvin as editor of The Observer *in 1908; he remained editor for thirty-four years. Garvin was supremely confident of his own judgment of men and events and week after week he presented that judgment to readers in signed articles that often filled five or six columns.*

THE NAVY AND THE NATION

On 12 January 1908 The Observer *carried this item on Page 1: 'Mr J. L. Garvin, late editor of the* Outlook, *will assume the editorship of* The Observer.'

James Louis Garvin, had close contacts in high places, notably the First Sea Lord 'Jackie' Fisher. A key issue, in view of the growing German threat, was the Navy: Fisher wanted to modernise it with Dreadnoughts and concentrate it in the North Sea. Bitterly opposing him was the Home Fleet C.-in-C., Lord Charles Beresford, whose supporters called for an 'Enquiry'. To set one up would have suggested Governments mistrust of Fisher, who fed Garvin secret Cabinet information.

This article with its confident opening statement was the result. There was a great outcry over the suspected leak but there was no Enquiry. Fisher got his Dreadnoughts.

2 February 1908

We are in a position to-day to give clear and authoritative answers to some questions touching the greatest of all national interests which have begun of late to disturb the public mind. The information following reaches us from a correspondent whose anticipations even when questioned at the outset have always proved remarkably exact.

For many months the present Board of Admiralty, and especially its professional head, have been assailed by every resource of attack. As to the present First Sea Lord, not only is his professional imbecility proclaimed, his patriotism is scouted. The Navy League has accordingly split as an example to the Germans. A new League has been formed. It is a very small organisation with a very long name [The Imperial Maritime League]; its simple thesis is that the Board of Admiralty is betraying the country. But above all an 'Enquiry' – always a plausible word – is demanded.

It was stated in a morning paper during the week that an 'Enquiry' is practically certain to be granted. In that confident prediction there is not a word of truth. There will be no Enquiry. There can be none. If it were instituted, it is notorious that the strongest board of Admiralty we have ever had would instantly resign in a body to the infinite joy of the German nation. As for Lord Charles Beresford, whose name unfortunately is always in the mouth of the panic-mongers, the issue is exceedingly simple. If any officer in high but subordinate position finds himself in disagreement with the policy for which his chiefs are responsible he must either acquiesce in the ordinary course of discipline or attest the seriousness of the position by resigning his command.

◆

Lord Charles Beresford, in his dispute with Fisher, had the support of some Unionist MPs. More important were economy-minded Liberal Cabinet members.

Suffragists on the march. 'A false move on their part might have caused a storm of ridicule. There was no false move.'

SAYINGS OF THE WEEK

'Sayings', the paper's shortest regular feature, has proved to be the longest-lasting.

11 July 1909

If we all made shorter speeches we should all have shorter hours.
The Attorney General

Providence is a very bad thing to trust to for the house-rent.
Judge Bacon

Every man over fifty is a Cassandra, talking of the brave days of old, and of the bad times in which we live. *Lord Curzon*

I am to get £500 a night – which, after all, is a very reasonable sum.
Signor Caruso

It is of little good for people to live the stereotyped life they were born into. *Mrs Garrett Anderson*

There is less cruelty in the slaughter-houses than there is in any one day on Blackfriars Bridge, where we constantly see horses struggling with heavy loads. *Mr J. Lindsay*

The principle of the Budget is to take a man's shirt when he is alive, his skin when he is dead, and if he does not die quickly they skin him alive. *Mr Pretyman*

Of all the peoples of Europe only the French and English possessed the power, the energy, the adventurous courage, the opportunity and the occasion for expansion across the Atlantic. *Mr Root*

The Divorce Court is a fount of corruption, perjury and collusion.
Lord Halifax

I apologise to Inspector Jarvis, and regret Inspector Jarvis had to receive what I should have liked to administer to H.M. Government. *Mrs Pankhurst*

SUFFRAGE DAY

14 June 1908

'Fine lot o' sportswomen; I wish 'em luck!' exclaimed a major of an exclusive line regiment as the tail of the great suffrage procession passed one of the Service Clubs in Piccadilly yesterday afternoon and became merged in the crowd. He spoke for London. His views were those of the vast majority of those who thronged the streets. They had gone out, so far as one could judge, with vague ideas of the attitude they intended to adopt. It was touch and go. A false move on the part of the women might have caused a storm of boos and a hurricane of ridicule. There was no false move. Miss Emily Davies, LL.D., frail but determined, set the pace bravely along the streets. She was one of the women who presented the first women suffrage petition to John Stuart Mill many years ago.

The grizzled Major's opinion permeated the crowd. They made jokes, but they were jokes spiced with good-humoured appreciation, and the smallest attempt at derision was instantly drowned by indignant cheers. So the procession went its spirited way, up Piccadilly to the Albert Hall; and there it assembled in imposing array, a mixture of brilliant gowns and hoods amongst the summer frocks. The hall was white with the waving of thousands of handkerchiefs, and the vast dome rang with a deafening chorus of cheers . . . Lady Frances Balfour gave a final word of advice to the audience, urging them never to turn their backs upon the march they had begun today.

FORCIBLE FEEDING

3 October 1909

Writs have been issued in connection with the action for assault to be brought by Suffragette prisoners against the Home Secretary and the Governor and the Medical Officer of Winson Green Gaol. The Home Secretary has refused the request made by relatives of some of the prisoners that their family doctor should enter the prison to report on their state of health. Mr Gladstone states, in reply to Mr. Keir Hardie, that six of the seven imprisoned Suffragettes who refuse to feed themselves, now accept food when it is administered to them from a feeding-cup. Only one requires to be fed by tube. When a tube had to be used the ordinary soft rubber feeding tube used in hospitals was employed. No screw gag was used, and the prisoners were not strapped down.

Dr. Forbes Ross, of Harley-street, protests strongly against the forcible feeding of Suffragettes in prison. 'I am not advocating the cause of the Suffragettes. I am protesting against the brutality of Englishmen who can treat women in this way. To me it seems typical of the brutality that in the last century could hang a man for stealing a sheep, or transport him for life for shooting the squire's partridges. No other nation in the world does such a thing.'

ONE CAKE FOR TWO WEDDINGS

3 October 1909

A young woman obtained from the Kingston magistrates yesterday a summons against her husband for desertion. She stated that she had been married only seven weeks, and that three weeks ago her husband left her and married another woman. He took with him her marriage certificate and half of her wedding cake, which was used at the second wedding breakfast.

A PLEA FOR A TRUCE OF GOD

Even more intractable than the dispute over the Navy were those over Ireland, with the Liberal Government committed to some sort of home rule, and economic reform. In late 1909 the Lords threw out Lloyd George's Budget, with its graduated direct taxation and taxation on land values. In January 1910 a General Election gave the Liberals a majority of some hundred and twenty but left them dependent on their Labour and Irish Nationalist allies. On the night of Friday 6 May Edward VII died. Sunday's Observer *carried Garvin's historic call for a political version of the medieval Truce of God, the Church's device to prevent anarchy after the breakup of the Charlemagne empire.*

The politicans took notice and meetings of leading members of both parties behind closed doors began in June. The Garvin Truce lasted four months. Another election in November produced a result similar to January's. The Parliament Act, definitively destroying the possibility of Lords resistance to money Bills, was passed in 1911 (with George V agreeing to create more peers if necessary, so playing a role similar to William IV's in 1832). The Irish problem was not solved until after the Great War, and then only after a fashion, by partitioning the island, which has produced its own problems; the Troubles are still with us today. But the Truce was a singular achievement for a mere journalist.

8 May 1910

We have passed from the old reign to the new. No tribute to King Edward can compare in sincerity and worth with service to King George. His task is to safeguard and develop that just influence of the Crown which was restored by his two predecessors, and to leave upon the monarchy, more than ever indispensable to the Empire, a right impress of his own.

But King George's task is in some ways more difficult than has yet confronted any of our modern Sovereigns. If he is to discharge it well to the enduring fame of this reign and with lasting benefit to the State, he must be supported with decisive resolution on the part of the average mass of reasonable men throughout the country and assisted by strong self-control on the side of every party in the State. In other words the nation must see fair play for the King.

Let conference take place before conflict is irrevocably joined on terms of war to the knife. If King George invites his leading statesmen of both parties to consult each other before any prerogative of the Crown is made a direct issue in an almost un-quenchable conflagration of party passions, we are certain that the overwhelming mass of the nation will expect all who may be concerned to meet the wishes of their Sovereign. We repeat that if ever in the whole record of domestic politics there was a moment for a truce of God that moment is now, when King George ascends in a critical hour his father's Throne while King Edward lies upon his deathbed.

The immediate meaning of a truce of God is delay. The House of Commons, which invariably meets at once upon the death of a Sovereign, has already begun to assemble. Let there not be this year – what we hope there will never be – a General Election with the Sovereign's name involved. Let reason have 'time and space to work and spread.' Whether there is conference sooner or conflict later, let there at least be the suspension of arms – a truce of God proclaimed on behalf of the King as the first great public event of his reign after the burial of the father. So much is due to the living and to the dead. So beyond the grave the reconciling influence of 'Edward the Peacemaker' may endure to serve his son.

VICTIM OF 'X' RAYS

10 July 1910

The death took place, yesterday morning, of Mr. Harry W. Cox, at his residence at Lower Clapton. Mr. Cox, who was only forty-six years of age, died a victim to the science of 'X' Rays, of which he was a pioneer. About twelve years ago he placed, by accident, the tube of the apparatus near his face with the result that through the rays he contracted 'X' Ray dermatitis. Although afflicted with this dread disease, Mr. Cox threw himself into the work of perfecting the apparatus. He took out some eighty patents, one of them being a valuable invention which locates not only the position of a bullet but also its depth. This apparatus was used with success during the South African War.

Mr. Cox's efforts in this field of science were recognised by the medical profession, and King Edward himself took a deep interest in his work. On the death of King Edward, Mrs Cox wrote to the Queen-Mother offering her respectful sympathy on behalf of her husband and herself. In reply, Mrs Cox received the following gracious message on 22 May:

Dear Mrs Cox,

Owing to the thousands of letters and telegrams which have been pouring in during the last sad fortnight, very many of them have remained unopened and unanswered.

I regret to say yours was among the number. But now I am commanded by the Queen to assure you that she values your kind sympathy most highly. Her Majesty prays that your husband may still be spared to you, but hers, alas! has gone for ever.

Yours very truly,

Charlotte Knollys

THE LAMP

21 August 1910

Florence Nightingale died on 13 August

Had Florence Nightingale lived in the Middle Ages she would probably have been canonised as the patron saint of nurses, but they by themselves are a minority, though one of the best of all the good minorities. Her wider influence was that of her character upon modern men and women, who cannot imitate her special activities, but can adapt her example to their own tasks. In the Crimea she had fairly won immortal honour. When she came back nothing could turn her head or induce her to pose or mar the noble unity of her nature. In her ninetieth year and up to her last rejection of the thought of burial in Westminster Abbey, she continued the tradition of what was strongest and best in an earlier England. Florence Nightingale was the Lady of the Lamp – not of the limelight. When she moved through the night at Skutari, that little shielded flame she carried was a better symbol even than she knew. Duty in its most earnest sense was to her the lamp of life. We hope that means will be found to connect that symbol and that idea with her name, so that the children of England may never forget either the memory of the lady who was buried yesterday or the greater meaning of the Lamp.

True to an earlier tradition.

DR RICHARD STRAUSS

5 February 1911

Dr. Strauss was at Munich on Monday evening to witness the first production of *Der Rosenkavalier* at the Bavarian Royal Opera. It was coldly received, and the plaudits bore unmistakable evidence of being a mere personal compliment to the composer. The impression gains ground that Dr. Strauss's newest creation is not destined to be an enduring masterpiece.

Richard Strauss. Not an enduring masterpiece?

*I*n 1911, after a series of disagreements between Garvin and Lord Northcliffe, primarily on tariff reform and imperial preference, Northcliffe bowed out – but gave Garvin three weeks to find a new owner.

William Waldorf Astor, American by birth, became that new proprietor. In 1915 he gave **The Observer** to his son Waldorf who remained proprietor until 1945.

'ABOVE PARTY'

Lloyd George's National Insurance Act was his greatest achievement in social legislation.

7 May 1911

There is not the slightest doubt as to the attitude that ought to be and will be adopted by the Unionist Party towards the greatest scheme of social reconstruction ever yet attempted by a single effort of legislation. In spirit it transcends all partisanship. It adapts and extends the memorable principles of State Insurance founded just thirty years ago by Bismarck. It develops the constructive example set by Mr. Chamberlain and fulfils the ideal of progress foreshadowed by Lord Beaconsfield and advocated by Mr. Balfour.

In Mr. Lloyd George's proposals there is not a main purpose that has not been advocated in these columns, though to the Chancellor himself belongs the high and imperishable credit for the personal energy, determination, and resource – and, above all, for the final touch of conciliatory genius – which have at last enabled the nation to pass from dreaming to doing.

The Chancellor has had an infinitely difficult and intricate task. He has brought to bear upon it exhaustive labour, practical aptitude of the highest kind, thorough moral courage, and with these a certain inimitable reasonableness and skill which are all his own. His exposition on Thursday was a great speech and a quiet speech. Everyone who heard it saw in him a far bigger man when he sat down than he was thought to be, when he rose.

In all this business we have to pay a higher national premium for the results of an unexampled social neglect. Our machine-age began earlier. Our slums are older, wider, fouler. We have allowed squalor, dirt, disease and destitution to breed degeneracy and multiply the unfit. As Mr. John Burns says, 30 per cent of pauperism is unquestionably due to sickness among the working classes. The rest is largely due to unemployment, which hitherto they have been no more able to prevent or influence than to control the tides of the sea.

Maternity benefit is to be paid at the rate of thirty shillings on condition that the mother does not return to work for four weeks. We think the figure might even be somewhat increased. Neglect of mother and infant following child-birth is perhaps the very worst of all the initiating causes leading to physical infirmity, degeneracy, unfitness and pauperism. We regard this as the very best thing in the Bill.

RE-ENTER THE 'ROSENKAVALIER'

25 June 1911

Der Rosenkavalier, after a conquest of practically every other important city or provincial town of Germany, is at last about to make its triumphant entry into Berlin. When the opera was first produced last January, some of its Rabelaisian humours were deemed unfitted for the select atmosphere of the Berlin opera, and all hope of its production there seemed to have been abandoned, but apparently it has been found inexpedient to keep so widely advertised a work longer out of the repertory. At a performance in Cologne a few days ago Dr. Strauss himself conducted the opera for the first time, and, according to report, had a brilliant personal success.

Scene from Act I of Der Rosenkavalier, *photographed at the 1911 production. A 'brilliant personal success' for Richard Strauss.*

THE FALL OF THE COMMONS

In the same parliamentary session MPs, until then unpaid, voted themselves a salary of £400 a year

20 August 1911

Having put the House of Lords in chains, the Government have wound up the session in a blaze of glory by degrading the House of Commons.

What will the feelings of the old age pensioner be when he discovers that the altruists who voted him five shillings a week from the national purse as a reward for a life of toil have now voted to themselves out of the same receptacle just thirty times that sum for the labour of reposing on cushioned benches?

The saving touch of humour in the sordid business is supplied by the fact that income-tax at the rate payable by unearned income is to be deducted. We hardly expected this unwonted candour. But when we come to think of it, how just is the distinction! Men so conspicuous for their desire to do as they would be done by must necessarily feel that the *douceur* voted to them by their grateful selves for lounging in the smoking room of 'the best club in London' could hardly be placed on the same footing as the generally more modest remuneration which barristers, doctors, and, let us add, journalists, earn by the sweat of their brain. The more so that membership of the House is not necessarily a bar to the acquisition of a competency by other means. On the contrary, it is often sought as an aid thereto, as witness the case of the gentlemen who indite weekly London letters from the comfort of the smoking room, and, not improbably, on the nation's stationery. Four hundred pounds a year, a good dinner at a shilling a time and four to five months' holiday in the year: it is enough to make the mouth of the work-shy water.

Scott writing his diary before setting off. 'A nobler immortality than better fortune would have won.'

THE GREATER VICTORY

Captain Robert Falcon Scott RN reached the South Pole on 17 January 1912, four weeks after Amundsen. Months later Scott and two companions were found eleven miles from safety. Oates, the 'very gallant gentleman', and Evans had died earlier. Scott was given a posthumous knighthood. His statue by his wife Kathleen, who was granted the title she would have received had he returned, stands in Waterloo Place, London.

16 February 1912

For nearly eight months Scott and his lost companions – surviving for a few weeks two others whose bodies may never be found – lay unburied where breath had left them within a few miles of safety. One day's good march would have delivered them. Within eleven miles of the depôt with the final supplies, they had to part with hope of life and home. Without food or fuel, starved, numbed, doomed by frightful calamity, broken to the uttermost in all but soul, they died orderly and quiet in a mood that sets the greatest stamp on all we mean by heroism. Their names, with that of Captain Oates, are secured by a nobler immortality than better fortune could have won. Their story becomes part of the moral being of all the Britains to bear harvest from the seed of their souls while generations endure.

Artist's impression of the sinking Titanic. 'The saddest tragedy wrought amidst the peaceful nations of the world in the whole history of the seas.'

THE TRAGEDY OF THE TITANIC

21 April 1912

A great wrong has been committed in the world. Safety can never be absolute. But we are not dealing with the inevitable in this case. We are dealing with a preventable disaster, for which no man upon the Titanic was mainly to blame. By error and inadequacy on shore, by unimaginative routine and official inertia, by the decay of national interest in mercantile seamanship sixteen hundred souls have been sacrificed. She had been warned that ice was thicker in the path than usual. Well, vigilance at look-out and on the bridge would perceive it. At evening the Titanic – following, remember, the route of possible death deliberately chosen by the shipping companies in concert as against the slightly longer path of assured safety to the south – was in the region which can only be called the great ship-trap of the seas. The companies have ordered in the last few days that the route shall be changed. Why did they not change it before? Why was the Titanic sent into the ship-trap when it is certain that by making the course only a few hours longer the sixteen hundred lives now sacrificed would never have been lost?

There are other issues not less urgent. It would surpass the sombre power of a Dantesque imagination to enforce the horror of this commonplace of ocean traffic: that the modern ocean liner with two or three thousand souls on board only provides enough boat accommodation for about a third of her passengers and crew. There is no technical reason why the proportion should not be largely increased or why other devices should not be employed, giving every man a chance for life.

Behind the grief for the Titanic is a sense of bitter waste. There will be a cloud upon the conscience of England and America until the lessons of the saddest tragedy wrought amidst the peaceful nations in the whole history of the seas, shall be so applied that the lives of those who did well upon the Titanic shall not have been offered in vain.

THE WOMAN'S WEEK

19 January 1913

Towards the end of this week, Sir Edward Grey will move to strike the word 'male' out of Clause I of the Franchise Bill. Should he be successful, every adult woman, as well as every adult man, will become eligible to vote at a Parliamentary election. We are opposed to the innovation. We do not base our objections to it on the desire to maintain masculine ascendancy.

Force of circumstances is bringing women ever more and

more into the arena of economic life, and they suffer, we admit, even more than men from its harsh conditions. It is an appalling thought, but we fear it is true that they are sweated and underpaid because they have a last direful resource for keeping body and soul together.

In every department of social life we need the aid of valiant women who will fight the battle of their wronged sisters. But the actual casting of the ballot is the least of the ways in which they can do so with effect. The State is primarily organised for defence: for the preservation, that is to say, of internal and external peace. We cannot, therefore, consent to place the power to choose its executive government in the hands of those on whom the responsibility for defence does not rest.

On 26 October 1913 The Observer *carried the advertisement below.*

The caption proudly announced: 'The advertisement below is of unusual interest. It was specially drawn and written by Lt.-General Sir Robert Baden-Powell, K.C.B. for Boots Pure Drug Co. Ltd., who have pleasure in presenting it to the public as a striking demonstration of the fact that the Hero of Mafeking is no less proficient in the arts of peace than in the sterner art of warfare.'

As for the product itself, 'invalids may take it without any misgiving. It will not nauseate their fastidious palates, but will nourish and build up their frames.'

BURIAL OF THE LATE ARCHDUKE

The Archduke Franz Ferdinand, heir to the Austrian throne, and his wife were assassinated on 28 June by the young Bosnian fanatic Gavrilo Princip at Sarajevo: the spark that set off World War I.

5 July 1914

Pochlarn (Lower Austria), Saturday. The train carrying the bodies of the late Archduke Francis Ferdinand and his consort, the Duchess of Hohenberg, arrived here at half-past twelve this morning. The coffins were removed in heavy rain and placed on biers in the waiting room, where twelve officers of the Uhlan Regiment, which bears the name of the Archduke, kept watch over the bodies.

WILL THE WAR LAST LONG?

9 August 1914

Reasons for thinking that six months and perhaps a shorter period should see the end of it are chiefly economic. The cost is stupendous now, and for Germany we believe will soon be found to be insupportable. A couple of million men at the least have got to be fed and supplied in every war. In Germany, more than in any other country, the working of the railways is diverted to military traffic. The bulk of the export trade is stopped altogether. Imports of raw materials and food have ceased or are severely reduced. All ocean shipping is suspended. The sufferings of the whole working population will be worse than in any other country, Austria not excepted – far worse than in agricultural Russia, or in France for whom the British Navy keeps the seas open. It is almost certain, if the early stages of the war do not pursue a course very favourable to German arms, that this situation will not be endured by the German people.

FRENCH AND BRITISH AT BAY

30 August 1914

An age seems to have elapsed since we last wrote in these columns, and, by comparison with the tremendous events which are shaking the world, all the beginnings of the war, seem far and dim. We have come swiftly to the sternest trial in all the centuries of our country and to an hour big with fate for the whole Empire.

At sea we know that our old naval spirit still shines undimmed. While the ruins of Louvain are still smouldering and Belgium lies trampled by the modern Huns, the British Fleet still stands between us and destruction by an enemy whose patrols already behold our cliffs from near Calais and Boulogne.

Ten days ago the opportunity seemed still open of shattering the whole German plan staking all upon the invasion of France through Belgium. Now the cause of France rocks in the balance, and with the hazard of our gallant allies is inseparably connected the fortunes and even the existence of our own glorious little army.

We now know that the German numbers were larger and the French less than anyone had ventured to apprehend. It looks as though the Allies had never succeeded in getting into Belgium anything like even numbers to pit against the invaders. By Saturday the enemy were swarming from all sides upon the French at Charleroi. For two days the battle for the town raged on until the narrow streets were jammed with dead.

The following Sunday the struggle was renewed amongst the slag heaps and the houses of the suburbs. The French, charging once more, swept the Germans back across the Sambre. The bridge was captured and recaptured again and again. The Germans, in pursuit of their infernal policy fired the town. But by Sunday night the French, magnificently as they had fought, knew it was time to retreat. They must already have heard that the whole Allied line along the Sambre had been jeopardised. Our own men had held their own from dawn till after dark last Sunday in the hardest battle a British army had ever sustained.

They were now occupying the hill round Mons. On Saturday morning the attack began. Between that time and Sunday night the British force, solid as a rock, withstood six attacks by German troops coming on mass after mass. Altogether over a hundred thousand of the Kaiser's best soldiers assailed our men, but could not break them. When Sunday night fell the British Army had proved itself man for man and gun for gun to be as good as the best in any army in the world. There was no doubt of German bravery. Again and again their ranks were withered by the incomparably cool, sure rifle fire of our men. Again and again the resolute enemy came on against the batteries and the lined trenches.

Even in this first battle we wrought more damage among the enemy than we suffered. We lost over 2,000 of our best. It was the least we could expect to escape with after the fiercest day's work that a British Army ever went through up to then. Mons had been well held, but Charleroi and Namur had fallen. There was nothing for it but to leave Belgium and fall back on France.

SCANDALOUS LEAFLET

6 December 1914

The following is a copy of the scandalous leaflet which is being largeley circulated in the South of Ireland:

Irishmen! It is absurd to talk against British tyranny in Ireland when you join, or let your sons, brothers, or friends join the British Navy and the British Army.

If there were a weak British Navy and British Army, the British Government would not be able to maintain the infamous Union under which your Industries have been ruined, your soil given over to the bullocks, your population cut down one-half, and your taxation increased fivefold.

The Irish are the real fighting element in England's armed forces. Without the Irish England would have been beaten by Napoleon a hundred years ago and by the Boers yesterday.

MEN of the 1st SPORTSMAN'S BATTALION
at Hornchurch Essex. All are Sportsmen.

A Chance for British Sportsmen

Hunting-men, Golfers, Cricketers—in fact every line
of Sport is represented in the first Corps of the

Sportsman's Battalion

Royal Fusiliers

Colonel-in-Chief - THE KING.

The War Office has now called for a 2nd Battalion.
As the 1st attained its full strength in three weeks—
all Varsity men, Old Public School Boys—men who
are hardened to the soldier's life by strenuous pursuit
of sport should enlist at once in this splendid corps.

Sportsmen from 19 to 45 Years of Age—Join To-Day.

Candidates should in the first instance apply in
person or in writing to the Chief Recruiting Officer,
Indian Room, Hotel Cecil, London, for Enrolment Form,
which, when duly approved at Headquarters, can
be presented at the nearest Recruiting Office, when
candidate will be immediately examined and attested.

Pay at Army Rates.   Financial obligation optional.

Show the King's enemies what British Sportsmen are.

*This battalion fought in East Africa. One of its officers, Frederick Selous, founded the Selous Scouts,
which became notorious in modern Rhodesia. He was killed in action in 1917, aged 66.*

The Fighting at Neuve Chapelle

14 March 1915

The following descriptive account has been communicated by an eye-witness present with General Headquarters. At 7.30 a.m. on the 10th the battle began with a bombardment by a large number of guns and howitzers. Our men in the trenches describe this fire as being the most tremendous both in point of noise and in actual effect they have ever seen or heard. The shrieking of the shells in the air their explosions and the continuous thunder of the batteries all merged into one great volume of sound. The discharges of the guns were so rapid tht they sounded like the fire of a gigantic machine gun. During the thirty-five minutes it continued our men could walk about in perfect safety. Then the signal for the attack was given, and in less than half an hour almost the whole of the elaborate series of German trenches in and about Neuve Chapelle were in our hands. Except at one point there was hardly any resistance for the trenches, which in places were literally blotted out, were filled with dead and dying partially buried in earth and debris, and the majority of the survivors were in no mood for further fighting. The enemy for the time being was beaten and on the run. It was the consciousness of this which filled the hospitals and the ambulances with the cheeriest crowd of wounded ever seen there.

The War of Exhaustion

2 May 1915

We can now give a fuller account of the battle round Ypres than the scanty and inconclusive news of a week ago enabled us to furnish. We have ourselves no doubt whatever that the enemy hoped to break through the Allies' lines to Dunkirk and the sea. But for the magnificent heroism of the British troops, with the Canadians foremost, the plan might have succeeded, and the whole front of the Allies in Flanders might have been pierced and smashed. Between the Canadians, on the British extreme left, and the canal the line was held by French troops. Some way beyond these again were the Belgians.

The storm burst on the evening of the 22nd, and in a manner that might well test the nerve of any troops. The wind was blowing from the north-east against our Allies and the Canadian division. The poison-fumes were let loose and rolled forward in a heavy greenish-yellow cloud, hanging low on the ground, at first about four or five feet high, like a moving wall but gradually becoming taller as it advanced. Those whom it first enveloped it either killed or choked and blinded. It was an ordeal like nothing ever before known in war. The noxious gases were of various kinds; a poison mixture patented by German frightfulness. Some think that wood-fires were lighted in front of the German trenches and fed with sulphur.

The Germans came on equipped with respirators and, in some cases, with rubber helmets like divers. Delirious with rejoicing, they may well have imagined that all they had hoped for would be won. The French, and no blame to them, broke to the north of Ypres. The enemy for two miles swept without resistance over line after line of abandoned trenches. On the left the canal was laid open to attack. On the right the British flank was uncovered. The Canadians were left in air. When night fell the Allies' line was very deeply driven in towards Ypres, and a catastrophe was threatened. The next three or four days were a continuous fight for life.

Foremost in saving the situation were the Canadians. Their deeds were even more heroic than we knew last week as their losses were more grievous. Enormously outnumbered, they fought through two days and two nights and were never broken. They only retired under imperative orders when it would have been madness to stay, and as they fell sullenly back they sold dearly every yard of ground. Some units were reduced to a quarter of their original strength, but the Canadians had saved a battle. When they were finally relieved last Wednesday their lion-hearted courage and tenacity had won a name second to none.

We cannot say less for the battalions of the Mother Country, than that they were equal to their comrades of the Dominion. A British brigade paused to cheer the Canadians to the echo before itself sweeping on into the face of death.

By Monday the force of the German blow was spent. The enemy was thwarted of his chief aim, in spite of the poison campaign. The five days' fighting on a five miles front was possibly the most intense and murderous struggle in which British troops have yet been engaged. The Germans in all likelihood lost far more heavily than the Allies, but they were nevertheless much encouraged.

In the circumstances we have described they can still claim to have gained more ground than we won at Neuve Chapelle, and their gains are, on the whole, somewhat more annoying to us than ours to them.

The moral to be drawn is that, while the Germans have lost their former general ascendancy, months of tremendous combat must be fought through before the Allies establish anything like an unquestionable mastery. We feel certain that beyond this year's campaign the war will still require from us the utmost doggedness of our traditional staying power.

The crisis of the fighting in Flanders was no sooner over than even the situation round Ypres was overshadowed by the interest of events on the Dardanelles. The landing has been effected in a way that will always rank among the historic feats of amphibious power.

The expedition had concentrated in Egypt – a strange assemblage of fighting men drawn from four continents, and including the Australian and New Zealand contingents. While we at home heard nothing, the wide fleet of transports covered by the warships had already reappeared in the Ægean. The disembarkment was expected to be at the outset the most difficult part of the operations. It is ticklish work to land large numbers of men from open boats under shellfire. The arrangements in the event worked to perfection. The disembarkment

began about sunrise on Sunday last and was carried out almost simultaneously at half-a-dozen different points.

On five of the beaches the operations were at once successful. North of Gaba Tepe the Australians and New Zealanders made good their hold on the lower slopes of Sari Bair, one of the highest hills in the rugged peninsula. They have the post of honour, and we may depend upon it that they will not be behind the Canadians in Flanders for resolute soldiership.

We warned our readers in these columns as long ago as February 28 that the shores of the Dardanelles would be 'a tough nut for the military crackers of the Allies.' Sir Ian Hamilton, who went through the Manchurian war as well as the Boer war, may be expected to frame his further plans with spirit and care.

THE CRIME OF THE LUSITANIA

9 May 1915

The sinking of the Lusitania has evoked a chorus of execration from the civilised world. The Press of New York sees nothing in the act but assassination – 'murder by savages drunk with blood.' The Dutch papers utter their horror and detestation of the perpetrators of the crime. America is awaiting evidence before taking steps. Whatever course the President may take in bringing the Germans to book he will have the support of the American people. The total loss of life is now estimated at 1,502. Of the 703 persons rescued 45 have since died as the result of exposure and shock. The great loss among the first-class passengers is accounted for by most of them being at lunch at the time.

W. G. Grace, who died yesterday, aged 67. 'No Englishman was better known' – Encyclopaedia Britannica.

EXIT AT GALLIPOLI

26 December 1915

The Dardanelles enterprise has now come to a strange and sudden close in circumstances still shrouded in mystery. It was bitter to let go after eight months of effort, costing over a hundred thousand casualties and nearly another hundred thousand sick. These things were the Dead Sea fruit of deficient imagination, resolution and capacity at home, the results of discordant counsels and a wavering policy behind an enterprise which either should never have been attempted or should have been put through at any price in the temper of thorough war, not of political compromises.

For the men of our flag afloat and ashore there was nothing at the end but immortal honour and glory exceeding praise. At Anzac and Suvla we were on a narrow front, partly rocky shelves, partly swamp-logged flats, almost literally between the devil in Turk-shape and the deep sea. The trenches in the hills were rain-swept and storm-lashed. Those below at Suvla were almost drowned out. Even those who had believed in further efforts to get through at any cost while there was still a fighting chance either on the peninsula or in its neighbourhood knew that it was now time to go.

But how to go? The Turks were everywhere in heavy force and close contact. Some who were against evacuation thought we must lose anything up to half our forces or more. The dénouement took away the breath. From Anzac and Suvla a British army with its array of guns, were spirited away as by magic. The Turks on higher positions within ear-shot of all were nonplussed and supine. Our casualties were – three wounded. We are not allowed yet to know by what means and devices this miracle, or conjury was wrought, when a whole army, with artillery and baggage, did a vanishing feat or disappearing trick like the neatest trap-door effect in melodrama.

That ground abandoned was consecrated by blood as good as was ever shed in war, nor shall Britain and Australia ever cease to hold it hallowed. We have left many thousands of graves behind us, and the foot of the Turk is upon them. We think of the un-matchable men of the Connaught Rangers, the Lancashires, the Ghurkas. The '29th Division' will remain a classic name in the records of the Army. The first landing, the storming of the beaches under artillery fire and against barbed wire was a deed that achieved what the Germans had thought impossible. Even that was beaten in August, when a contingent from Anzac forced its way upward by sheer dint of bayonet and butt-end until they won the very top of Sari Basir, and for a few minutes saw the Narrows beyond.

We say, God bless the men of Anzac, living and dead, for their part in the deathless epic of the Dardanelles. We cannot express the debt this country owes to our race 'down under.' In this struggle they have been of one bone and one flesh with us. Australia and New Zealand are in distance the furthest away from us of all peoples but in spirit they are with us shoulder to shoulder to fight it to the end. Their deeds at Galli-poli, like the morning light of fresh forces of freedom in the world, have been as much the battle-baptism of Australian and New Zealand liberty as Marathon was of Greek.

THE BATTLE FOR VERDUN

27 February 1916

The battle before Verdun still rages with unheard of violence; the Germans describe their own onslaughts as being made in a 'sea of fire.'

Before the weight of the attack the French have given ground rather than put forward men to resist in places where sacrifice of life would serve no serious military purpose.

Nevertheless, the advance has been opposed with unflinching tenacity, the enemy paying in losses which are characterised as 'fabulous.'

The Kaiser is present, and is, of course, urging his troops forward, as he has done before at Verdun and at Ypres, at the price of tremendous losses.

France is calm and confident. There are ample reserves to step in when the hour arrives, when the fury of the Germans shall have expended itself against the un-shakable valour of the defenders.

THE BATTLE IN THE NORTH SEA

Battle of Jutland: 31 May–4 June

4 June 1916

Although many details are yet lacking to fill in the picture of the naval battle in the North Sea, the general outline is clear. Sir David Beatty had practically the whole fighting force of the German Navy on his hands, and must have been outnumbered two to one in Dreadnought ships at least.

The losses are grievous. The Queen Mary was the newest and most powerful battle-cruiser in the Fleet with the exception of the Tiger. The Invincible was a historic ship. She carried Admiral Sturdee's flag in the battle of the Falkland Islands, and, moreover, she has carried down with her one of the most gallant and able of our younger Admirals, the Hon. H. L. A. Hood. The complements of the ships lost total somewhere between four and five thousand officers and men, of whom, it is to be feared, only a small proportion are saved, while many more must have been killed and wounded in the action. Most of these were the very pick and cream of the Royal Navy, and, whatever may be said about the ships, their loss is irreplaceable. The British Navy has suffered a heavier loss in men than in any previous battle in its history, and, with it all, has not obtained that complete and crushing victory for which our naval history and tradition has taught us to look. At present one cannot help feeling that the list of our losses has been unduly swollen by the inclusion of the armoured cruisers, Defence, Black Prince and Warrior, in the Fleet, and that the lives of those who went down in the two first-named were unnecessarily sacrificed. The loss of the Tipperary and seven destroyers is a serious matter, for the Fleet is notoriously short of this class of vessel.

The Admiralty's estimate of enemy losses is reserved. They claim positively that a German battleship of the Kaiser class, said to be the König Albert, was blown up as the result of a destroyer attack, and they make a similarly definite claim that a battle-cruiser – probably the Lutzow – was similarly destroyed. They believe that another battleship of the Kaiser class was sunk by gun-fire, while another battle-cruiser was "seen to be disabled and stopping." In addition, one light cruiser, six torpedo-boats and a submarine were sunk.

The result of the action is profoundly disappointing, through no fault of the gallant men engaged, and very much remains to be cleared up before we can dismiss from our minds the thought that someone had blundered. It is more fitting, however, to defer a critical examination of the facts to a future occasion.

THE LATE R.G. GARVIN

The Battle of the Somme (1 July-15 November) cost the British over 400,000 casualties. One was Garvin's son Gerard ('Ged'). He was born on 12 October 1895. In 1914 he was due to go up to Christ Church, Oxford, with a Westminster history scholarship. Instead he was one of Kitchener's 'First Hundred Thousand' volunteers, and was commissioned into the South Lancashire Regiment. A few days before his battalion went back into the line his commanding officer recommended him for promotion to captain and gave him a company. On 22 July, thirty-five yards from the German line, he was killed leading it into action. Waldorf Astor was told privately and broke the news to Garvin.

30 July 1916
News was received from private sources on Tuesday of the death of Lieut. Gerard Garvin, the only son of Mrs. J.L. Garvin and of the Editor of The Observer . . .

From the age of ten he seemed to know that when he grew up it would be to fight for Britain in a war of wars, and there was sometimes that about him which suggested that, with all the grave, happy serenity and forethoughtful kindness which made him in-finitely loveable, he had a steady intuition of his end. His last letter left to be sent in case he did not come back was like him: 'Dearest Ones, – Try not to grieve too much for me. I hope my death will have been worthy of your trust; and I couldn't die for a better cause.' Though his course is run at twenty, his strong young character left an impression which few who came much in contact with it are likely ever to forget.

BRITISH TANKS IN ACTION

17 September 1916
Paris, Saturday. The *Matin* says yesterday morning at dawn the Germans had quite a new surprise, when, from the midst of the assaulting British troops, enormous steel monsters emerged, the new armoured motor-guns which have been constructed by the British with so much secrecy and which now made their début with their ram-like fronts.

The cars advanced across the demolished defences and calmly passed over all kinds of obstacles, while the British airmen passed over the heads of the enemy and poured shot into them.

Troops in a trench near Thiepval, the tiny village that saw some of the heaviest fighting in the Battle of the Somme. British War Memorial site.

A GIANT UNBOUND

▼ *Crowd being harrangued in a square in Petrograd (now Leningrad) during the chaotic, turbulent days that followed the abdication of Tsar Nicholas II and the proclamation of the Provisional Government, which was itself overthrown by the Bolsheviks in November.*

18 March 1917

The Provisional Government came into being in Russia on 12 March. Petrograd, Friday night. Since last Sunday there has been accomplished the greatest revolution of the past hundred years, perhaps in the history of Europe. The revolt now embraces practically all the great centres in Russia. The news has been received with joy at the front.

The revolt began on Sunday. Order was partially re-estab-

lished on Wednesday, and to-day success is clean and complete.

The first troops that passed over to the side of the people occupied the streets round the Duma. In the workmen's quarters the troops also passed over. Troops sent to quell disorders similarly joined the people. Even the fortress signified its submission and hung out a red flag. I was in the Duma [Parliament] yesterday. The main hall was piled with sacks of munitions, machine-guns, etc., and soldiers and sailors were everywhere. If the Government is undisturbed by internal disagreement, I believe that the revolution will enormously help the cause of the Allies.

▲ *The militarily useless village of Passchendaele was captured in November 1917, ending the Third Battle of Ypres. It cost 300,000 casualties. When Haig's Chief of Staff visited the battlefield (pictured above) for the first time, he burst into tears, and cried, 'Good God, did we really send men to fight in that?'*

EASTER DAWN

8 April 1917
The United States entered the war on 6 April.

New York, Saturday. America has been formally at war with Germany since Good Friday afternoon, following the signing by the President of the Joint Resolution of Congress.

That President Wilson would abandon his long struggle for peace with a heavy heart was known to all men; that having taken the momentous decision he would support his new stand with such unstinted vigour was a hope rather than an expectation. The realisation exceeded even the hopes. Now, with one magnificent gesture, he has swept away the hesitation which have perplexed and divided the country for two years and supplied what it most wanted – leadership. The country as a whole has rallied behind him, though the pacifists rage and imagine vain things.

If the final entry of the United States into war was probable from the first and inevitable after the German decree of indiscriminate assassination by sea, it was undoubtedly hastened by event in Russia. Indeed, it is impossible to exaggerate the effect of the Russian Revolution both on Government policy and on public opinion. It enabled the President to say forthrightly that the United States was entering the struggle 'for democracy, for the right of those who submit to authority to have a voice in their governments'; and no part of his address met with more instant response than the eloquent passage in which he paid tribute to Russia, 'fit partner for a League of Honour.'

For the future of Anglo-American relations the prospect is bright as it was never before. The partnership in war, should cement a bond between the two Anglo-Saxon nations which will be the surest guarantee for the peace of the world. America as a whole is going to war rightly for its own honour first. Secondary and sentimental motives are democratic ideals, the defence of civilisation, sympathy for France and Belgium, and now for Russia.

One thing is needed to include England unreservedly in that sympathy, to rouse in this country such another storm of enthusiasm as greeted the Russian revolution, and that, of course, is a settlement of the Irish question. The American Press during the past few weeks has shown an unaccustomed moderation in discussing Ireland, an unusual insight into the difficulties of the problem, but inevitably the Russian revolution has called forth comparisons, unjust but plausible, and there are thousands of Americans, not only those of Irish affiliations, who will fight Germany less gladly because Ireland remains a thorn in the side of the British Empire. It is an opportunity for a great stroke of statesmanship, and the time for it is now.

THE BOLSHEVIK COUP

11 November 1917

Petrograd, 8 November. This long-expected rising has taken place and so far has been carried out very quietly. All the railway stations, telegraph, and telephone offices have been occupied, the State Bank captured, the Winter Palace surrounded, and the shock battalions dispersed. The armoured motor service came over to the side of the Bolsheviks, and the Cossacks have refused to obey the Provisional Government, which has been overthrown, and all power has passed to the hands of the Petrograd Soviet.

It is impossible to predict the outcome.

PEACE UNDER ARMS

17 November 1918

Germany signed the Armistice on Monday 11 November.

On Monday morning it was known that the war would end at eleven o'clock. At Westminster some watched the finger of Big Ben, as in the last minute it moved solemnly to the fateful point of the dial. The hour was reached. We knew that there was then a stange silence elsewhere in the world – that there was surcease of slaughter – that the guns were hushed at last. For over four years there had been no silence but that to which death received the dead. Now came a silence like no quietness that was ever before.

Then London, like other capitals, burst as by magic into the crowds and flags and joyriding and cheerful noises of the most wonderful scenes of human exultation it ever knew. The tumult of relief was human and harmless. Merriment rioted with decency. We owe this, as everyone knows, to the liquor control, and its continuance was ensured by that object-lesson. A sane and rising democracy cannot co-exist with unlimited facilities for alcohol. The old license and temptation never can be restored. Through all the rejoicing ran the deeper notes. The churches have been full. Round the Mansion House the City sang the Doxology while men's eyes filled with tears. Before Buckingham Palace, multitudes demanded the King and Queen.

Throughout London since, their Majesties have been repaid for their faithful service to the State by the boundless enthusiasm of a faithful people with whom they shared all the trial and the glory.

------◆------

Pilots of No.1 Squadron RAF in 1918, the year in which the force came into being.

JEWISH NATIONAL CHARTER

The Balfour Declaration, proclaiming a Jewish National Home in Palestine, was communicated to Lord Rothschild, a Zionist leader, on 2 November.

11 November 1917

Feelings of deep gratitude have been expressed by Jews all over the world at the British Government's declaration favouring the establishment in Palestine of a national home for the Jewish people. 'It is looked upon,' a high authority said yesterday, in an interview with a representative of *The Observer*, 'as the Jewish nation's charter. For more than eighteen centuries the Jews as a nation have been without a home, and the longing to recover their ancient home in Palestine has been the deepest and most abiding of their passions . . .

'With ordinary conditions of legal security there can be no doubt that the Jews in Palestine will increase, and within a generation or so should constitute the majority of the inhabitants.'

BORN AMID THE THUNDERS OF BATTLE

31 March 1918

History will appreciate the fact that the Royal Air Force came into being while the greatest battle ever fought was being waged, and that the aerial arm played a geater part than in any previous battle. Tomorrow is the date when the members of our Flying Services become Royal Air Force, and drop the designations Royal Naval Air Services and Royal Flying Corps.

May one repeat the suggestion made in *The Observer* a few weeks ago that the Royal Air Force should adopt the old motto of the Royal Flying Corps, 'Per Ardua ad Astra,' unless anyone can suggest a better?

PEACE AND DRAGON'S TEETH

The terms of the Versailles Treaty, with their punitive measures against Germany – surrender of all colonies; cession of Alsace-Lorraine, parts of East Prussia, Danzig and other territories; ridiculously vast reparations – were revealed on 7 May 1919. John Maynard Keynes, the Treasury's chief representative, resigned in protest against the economic terms. The Treaty, Garvin wrote in a powerful leading article, left the Germans 'no real hope except in revenge'.

11 May 1919

Our forecast a week ago of the paper-peace was right to the letter. A distinguished neutral calls it Peace with a Vengeance. Yet at the same time it is peace with folly. These terms give no fundamental solution to any European problem. They raise more dangers than they lay. They try to do what Louis the Fourteenth, Frederick the Great, the two Napoleons and Bismarck, attempted.

All the Treaty – apart from the incorporated and saving Covenant of the League – scatters Dragon's teeth across the soil of Europe. They will spring up as armed men unless the mischief is eradicated by other and better labours. They will prove as artificial, untenable and futile, as the morals are absent or execrable.

After the first £1,000,000,000 required from Germany, nothing in connection with the future of the indemnities will be sure. But vaguely the vanquished race is expected to keep working for others decade after decade. Tribute running for years to more thousands of millions will be a permanent incitement to unrest, protest, conspiracy, to international agitation and intrigue. The generation responsible for the war will pass away gradually, leaving much of the burthen on Germans now so young as to be practically as innocent of the original crime as babes unborn. How can the financial enslavement of the German race be maintained for thirty years except by a combined militarism with that of France in the forefront? How can all Germany left of the Rhine – a region amongst the dearest to the whole race – be held down under French domination for fifteen years, except by sheer militarism? How can the semi-annexed German population taken over, with the coal in the Saar Valley, be managed and mastered in these circumstances except by force?

The root-vice of the whole Treaty is that it leaves the German race no real hope except in revenge – no matter how long the revenge may have to be deferred. It offers the hundred millions of the beaten races in Central Europe, including Magyars and Bulgars, no good inducement whatever to become willing members of a new peace-system; in the whole Treaty there is no glimmering perception of the constructive necessities of Europe as a whole. This Treaty tends to Balkanise three-fourths of Europe . . .

Preserving the peace will mean the discarding of a large part of this Treaty, the reversal of some of it, and the decisive modification of the whole. The time has come for upholding in peace the principles and ideals by which the Associated Nations one and all professed to be inspired during the struggle. The best amongst us did not fight and work only to end by the adoption of German principles now repudiated by millions of the Germans themselves. We fought and worked for the redemption even of the enemy and for the reconciliation of mankind. That alone is worthy of the pure hearts of our young dead who fought without hate.

GERMAN FLEET SUNK

22 June 1919

The Secretary of the Admiralty announces that yesterday afternoon certain of the interned German ships at Scapa were sunk and abandoned by their crews. The crews will be detained in safe custody.

A later statement issued by the Secretary of the Admiralty said: According to the latest reports received from Scapa Flow all the intended German battleships and battle cruisers have sunk except the battleship Baden, which was still afloat. Five light cruisers have sunk, but the other three have been beached. Eighteen destroyers have also been beached by the local tugs and four destroyers were still afloat.

The German rear-admiral and most of the Germans from the ships are in custody on board H.M. ships. Some boats from the ships refused to stop when ordered and were fired on, and a small number of Germans were killed and wounded. In accordance with the terms of the armistice the German ships were interned with skeleton German crews as caretakers and without British guards on board.

ART AND ARTISTS

4 January 1920

Mr Stanley Spencer's *The Sacrifice of Zacharias* is not a picture to be dismissed with an impatient shrug, for it has a depth of feeling, a sense of awe, that makes unquestionably a very direct and powerful appeal, quite apart from the charm of a landscape background painted with a pre-Raphaelite's love of elaborate detail. But the picture gains nothing from the grotesque treatment of the figures in their semi-modern costume, Zacharias himself being disguised as a chef, with a white apron over his trousers. If the buildings and ruins of the Giotto-esques lacked architectronic stability, the primitive painters, nevertheless, did their best to make their walls look like walls.

In Mr. Spencer's picture, the thin, curved, round-edged, screen-like erection behind the central group looks more like a portion of an enamelled bath than like a wall. More satisfactory is the same artist's *Swan-upping at Cookham*. He has adopted a pleasing convention for the lapping water of the river under the iron bridge; the action of the figures is expressive of physical effort. The design is linked together with great skill, so as to make an agreeable pattern.
P.G. Konody

CHAPLIN

27 February 1921

I have a most vivid recollection of the first occasion on which I saw a Chaplin film. It was in France. A party of very tired and utterly depressed men were moving down from the 'line' to 'rest billets' after an arduous spell in outposts. The weather had been very hard and bitter, so that the ground was frozen like steel, and many of the men had sore feet and walked with difficulty. I remember the party losing its way in a road where misery had settled down so deeply that no one swore. And I remember one of them, a very cheery lad from Dublin, suddenly losing heart, and turning to me and saying, 'God Almighty's very hard on us, sir!'

In that state of dejection the lost party staggered into the rest billets at three o'clock in the morning and were told that at the end of the week, instead of the promised Divisional rest, they would receive orders to return to the line! Next evening, after tea, with some recovery of cheerfulness, the men went off to the big barn, in which the Divisional Concert Party gave its entertainments. There they sat, massed at the back of the barn, looking strangely childlike in the foggy interior, and listening without much demonstration to some songs. Their irresponsiveness was not due to inappreciation, but to an overwhelming collective fatigue, and to the dreadful loathing of one's kind that comes from continuous association in congested quarters. Then the singing ended and the lights were diminished and the 'pictures' began. On the screen came the shuffling figure of Charlie Chaplin and a great welcoming roar of laughter broke from them. That small, appealing, wistful, shuffling, nervous figure, smiling to disarm punishment, had only to show himself, and instantly a crowd of driven men remembered only to laugh. That is an achievement which is very great.

St. John Ervine

Gustav Holst: 'delicacy, rapidity, with a latent humour, essential but not gross.'

THE PLANETS

21 November 1920

It is, of course, gratifying to one's journalistic vanity to be proved a prophet, and the 'scene of excitement' I hinted at last Sunday morning duly took place on the Monday evening. Mr. Holst's 'Planets' Suite was not half concluded before there occurred applause of so violent and insistent a character that the conductor, Mr. Coates, was compelled to turn round, search for the composer in the audience and then compel him at the point of the baton to make his modest way to the platform and acknowledge the public's congratulations. The movement which thus carried the audience off its feet was exactly the one that might be expected to have that effect – 'Mercury,' whose delicacy and rapidity, with a latent humour (essential but not gross) make a most effective combination. 'Mercury' would in itself make a splendid little concert piece for occasions when the whole suite cannot be given, and if the composer is willing for it to be separately performed I should not be surprised if this 'Winged Messenger' carried his name wide and far.

Percy A. Scholes

GRIM TRAGEDY OF
FAMINE-STRICKEN RUSSIA

Millions Of Babes Slowly And Painfully Dying From Starvation

Masses of Humanity Leaving Their Homes and Wandering Aimlessly from Place to Place IN SEARCH OF FOOD

EVERYONE MUST HELP, THOUGH EVEN THEN MILLIONS MUST DIE !

THE greatest scourge of disease and famine in History is sweeping through Russia, and 20,000,000 people are doomed to die unless immediate help is forthcoming.

Remote corners of this once great Empire are in the throes of famine, just as much as the great towns. Through immense areas famine and pestilence sweep remorselessly—bringing death and untold agonies to myriads of unfortunate people.

Added to the horrors of pestilence and famine has been the great drought.

The torturing heat beating down remorselessly is driving people mad in thousands. They plunge into the river to meet death—they collapse by the wayside and die of Typhus or Cholera. The festering bodies are a menace to the hordes of men, women, and innocent children who stagger along every road in a vain endeavour to escape pestilence and find food.

An idea of the awful conditions can be gathered from the fact that in two great districts, Samara and Saratoff, not a single pound of Winter Corn came to maturity. This utter failure of crops can only accentuate the awful misery of the starving millions in Russia. Cholera snatches life as a reaper reaps Corn. Tens of thousands have died and millions more must die unless help is sent AT ONCE.

133,428 DEAD FROM DISEASE
52,000 CHILD VICTIMS OF DYSENTERY.

Fifty-two thousand children have already succumbed to the unspeakable agonies of Dysentery. Forty thousand other folk have died from Typhus. Pestilence stalking on every highway and byway has already claimed over 133,000 victims, and is laying the hand of death on thousands every hour. While you read these words some poor starving child is dropping by the wayside—foodless—almost—a mere bag of bones ! These poor, helpless, starving, and disease-stricken children cry aloud for food and succour. They see grim death all around them — they face famine and pestilence –they succumb to untold horrors while we go about our daily duties, enjoying life, seeking pleasure, and living just as we wish. Every hour—every MINUTE, a weakened, broken human being gives up its grip on life and goes to face its Maker. Every minute some poor mortal succumbs to agony and drops by the wayside never to rise again !

THANK GOD RELIEF IS AT HAND!
BUT YOUR HELP IS NEEDED!

The "Save the Children" Fund is fully organised to give immediate relief. It is the recognised Agency for Child relief, and its only interest is that the largest possible number of children shall be saved from starvation, disease, and misery.

It already has relief work in operation amongst Russian children. Its Representative is at the moment in Moscow, and details of relief measures on an extended scale are being completed.

Scattered all the way from Reval to Constantinople are starving children or refugee exiles—thousands of poor, helpless forms suffering from the effects of famine and pestilence. The ever-ready helping hand of the "Save the Children" Fund is extended to these children just as willingly as relief is given to the starving hordes in Russia.

Men and women are dying also—they drop with their children and expire. Their need is urgent, but WE MUST SAVE THE CHILDREN FIRST. This Fund exists solely for the relief of the little ones, and to them we call every man and woman of the Empire.

FORGET POLITICS AND PREJUDICES.

Whatever opinion you may have had of Russia's Government or its past atrocities, you surely cannot sentence a race where millions of children are starving. Give your help freely and generously. Forget politics and prejudices. Remember these starving babies are children of the great God in Heaven—the Creator of Mankind—and He looks to

YOU to help AT ONCE. Do not give from any interested motive or any desire to exploit Russia or to show adherence to any form of Government. Give out of the fullness of your heart—give because you cannot allow little children to suffer the most cruel death of all. Can you talk politics to a starving child ?

THEY STRUGGLE ON AND ON IN AGONY UNTIL THEIR SUFFERINGS BECOME UNBEARABLE AND THEY FALL BY THE WAY, VICTIMS OF THE GREATEST CATASTROPHE THE WORLD HAS EVER SEEN.

" 20,000,000 in Russia Famine Zone having eaten cats, rats and dogs, are now fleeing from their homes in a desperate search for some place where there is some Food."—DAILY EXPRESS, July 23.
" Bark is being stripped off the Trees for Food."—DAILY CHRONICLE, July 23.

The awfulness of the situation is inconceivable ! The full details are too terrible to print ! It is the children, though, that suffer most, despite the heroic sacrifices made for them by their parents. Think of it ! So barren has the country become that even the bark is being stripped from the Trees for Food. Can you read of this terrible catastrophe unmoved ? Do you not feel impelled by the spirit of Common Charity to do something to save as many of the children as possible from the terrible agonies of the lingering and most frightful death it is possible to conceive ? What will YOU do ? Whatever it may be, do it for Civilisation's sake—to-day—NOW !

The "Save the Children" Fund has in the past received consistent support from the great-hearted British Public in their widespread efforts to save children, and Lord Weardale, the Chairman, again specially appeals for generous Donations, for the present mission of Rescue surpasses all that they have attempted before. Add your quota of help.

Not a second must be lost—not a second WILL be lost. The great organisation is perfected, and the moment your gift is received it will go to relieve the sufferings of poor broken mortals who cry aloud in their agony.

It is all important that food should go at once. The ships are waiting. THEY ARE WAITING

BRITISH RELIEF UNDER BRITISH CONTROL.

Remember the administrator of this Fund in Russia is a Briton, and he will see that adequate steps are taken to ensure that every thing sent to Russia will be solely applied for the benefit of the children !

THE WORST DISASTER IN HISTORY'

Millions of starving, disease-infected people have left all that remains of their homes and are sweeping along the roads—suffering untold anguish and pain.

Drought, Famine, Cholera, Typhus, have combined to make ghastly death in Russia.

Crowds of tens of thousands swarm along the banks of the Volga seeking food and escape from death. They drop and expire upon the banks. The disease-infected bodies are flung to the water, and the flow carries them by district after district, spreading pestilence in their wake. And the people, thirsting and hungering, must drink of this water from the Volga—they must take into their systems the germs of certain DEATH. The living lie under a baking sun, suffering indescribable tortures. To think that innocent children should be called upon to face such horrors is unbearable. The very thought sears the brain of honest men and women—it is like a red-hot iron searing into the living flesh.

THE WHOLE WORLD IS THREATENED.

Disease and pestilence will spread—the winds will carry it over Continents, and the millions of deaths will mount steadily upwards.

Stop it in the name of Heaven ! Give in the name of Christianity ! Crush out the spectre of disease and famine as you would crush a venomous reptile under your heel.

Christians –Britons must give the help that is essential and urgent. Fail not—for you, too, are in peril if the Terror is allowed to spread.

10,000 DYING DAILY.

Every day that passes sees more than ten thousand souls cast from this world. Graves cannot be dug for them—they are left to rot by the wayside or cast to the waters. Every hunger-maddened being is striving for food—they swarm in millions—they die in thousands—they starve in tens of millions.

They tear the bark from trees and greedily devour it ! Grasses and tree bark take the place of bread—rats and vermin of every description take the place of meat. Oh, the horror of it ! To think that such suffering can exist in this enlightened world ! !

Whatever your creed—whatever your vocation in life—give to save the dying and the starving !

Can you allow it—must these infants call aloud to you in vain ? It is criminal to let these babies go beyond the border. It is brutal and cowardly.

IT MIGHT HAVE HAPPENED TO YOU.

Help the greatest cause the world has ever known. Give FREELY and QUICKLY. Do not delay one moment, lest a child be sacrificed and the account be laid to your charge in the book of doom.

AN APPEAL TO EVERYONE AND TO YOU IN PARTICULAR.

SEND A THOUSAND POUNDS if you can afford it. If you cannot do this, then send £500, £200, or £100. If you have the money it is your privilege, nay, your duty, is it not ? to send all you can to assist in this terrible crisis.

Should you not be in a position to make an offering of more than £25, £10, or £5, by all means send this. Thousands of readers will be unable to send more than £2, £1, or even 10s.

As all people of every class, from the rich, well-to-do, down to the humblest, are inspired to participate in this, the most wonderful appeal ever made in the cause of Suffering Humanity, even the Widow's Mite will be appreciated equally with the contribution from the rich.

SAVE THE CHILDREN FUND.
(Registered under the War Charities Act, 1916.)

PATRONS: H. Grace the Archbishop of Canterbury ; His Eminence the Cardinal Bourne, Archbishop of Westminster ; The Right Hon. The Speaker, Esq., J. L. Garvin, Esq.

To LORD WEARDALE,
Chairman of Committee of "Save the Children" Fund.
(Room 360 : 26, Golden Square, Regent Street, London, W.1.

NAME ....

ADDRESS ....

This advertisement in August 1921 launched a campaign to help the starving children who were victims of the Russian famine. Garvin was a patron of Save the Children, which had been founded two years earlier.

SAVAGERY IN BELFAST

19 March 1922

The weekend opened ominously in Belfast with murders and bomb outrages. Four lives have been taken, and several people have been injured. Yesterday evening when a tram, crowded with passengers, was returning from the Glasgow v. Irish League football match at Cliftonville, a man ran out of Churchill Street on Antrim-road and hurled a bomb through a window in the lower saloon. One passenger was blown to pieces and three others were injured. The tram was wrecked. The assailant was pursued by civilians into Lepper-street, where he escaped. He was quite a youth. The wounded were sent to hospital. The name of the dead man is not known.

MUSSOLINI IN OFFICE

5 November 1922

Some sixty years ago D'Azeglio said: 'We have made Italy; it now remains for us to make the Italian people.' It would seem as though Fascismo sought to finish the work of the Risorgimento. The spirit of the war, the sufferings of the people, love of their beautiful land, traditions of ancient Rome, youth struggling for recognition and glory, these were some of the themes which inspired D'Annunzio and Mussolini, and led the new generation along fresh paths. Mussolini, who personifies young Italy, has given the country a national Government after four years of suffering and shame. That is why Fascists all over Italy are being smothered in flowers; and as they return from 'the taking of Rome' with the words, 'Evviva Rome and the King!' scrawled upon their fezzes and helmets, they are treated like victors and heroes by deliriously happy crowds.

TUTANKHAMEN'S TOMB

17 December 1922

An alarmist statement appeared in yesterday's *Daily Mail*, whose Luxor correspondent suggested that in the event of rain, the tomb might be flooded in an hour and all its contents ruined. Even as the telegram was written panic was said to be spreading, 'the clouds were darkening; all eyes were

Howard Carter at Tutankhamen's tomb, which he and Lord Carnarvon discovered in the Valley of the Kings. 'No man is better able to deal with the situation,' said the professor.

turned on the last blue patch in the west, and fervent Mohammedans were beseeching Allah to turn back the clouds.'

Less disquieting views were taken by Egyptologists in this country whom *The Observer* approached. Professor Newberry, who is lecturing on the Valley of the Kings to the Egypt Explora-tion Society on Tuesday evening emphasised the fact that there is no man better able to deal with the situation than Mr Howard Carter. 'He has had great experience, and whilst it would probably not have occurred to anyone to protect the tomb of Tutankhamen from rain, seeing that rain only falls about once in twenty years, everything that can be done, if a storm should occur, you may be absolutely certain will be done. The entrance to the tomb is not large, and a little banking, for example, could be easily put around it and the water drained off in an hour or so. But I really do not think there is any danger.'

QUICKSANDS OF THE PEACE

2 September 1923

'My dear lady,' I said to the woman weeping on the sofa in the German Consulate in Silesia, 'do try to compose yourself, it is so painful to me' but at that moment the official entered. Mrs – had married a Czech miner, who had worked in German Poland for twenty years, now dead and never naturalised. Her three sons were miners. The Poles had informed her that she and her sons either had to become Poles or clear out. I inquired whether this was legal, whereat the clerks and even the poor woman smiled. 'Holy Mother!' she said, aghast at my ignorance, 'he must be a *Völker-bund* (League of Nations) man.'

She was a victim of self-deter-mination. After all, what was she? Husband a Czech, lived under Austria in Germany which is now Poland. Was he Austrian, Czech, Pole, or German? No, he was dead. What was his wife? The Czechs, now that the man was dead, were disinterested; the Poles wanted her three sons as soldiers; the Germans wanted them as Germans. The Consul ex-plained that this kind of thing was of daily occurrence. All over Europe tens of thousands of women had been de- and re-nationalised, willy-nilly, at Ver-sailles. The woman's only chance was to quit. I asked her what she would do? She said: 'Do? Why, die sooner than become a Pole.'

It is historically true to say that there is no true Germany, no true Poland, or true Russia; there are only true Germans, true Poles, true Russians, and they are to be found – war emigrants and colo-nisers – all over Europe. If the map-drawers had studied history from the angle of race, some prac-tical solution might have been found. But now Germans and Russians have joined the out-casts, without a unity; even the Poles are not really united, and now France has begun to colonise them. Lille to-day is a Polish city. This is a pretty big war position to leave in the air. Napoleon did better than that. He built roads. We have built quicksands.

I had a curious talk with a once-rich Russian, who fought against Russia because he hated Tsardom, then fought against Germany under Republican Russia, finally fought under Kol-chak against Bolshevism, and now had lost all his property and had become a Swiss. 'What about Russia?' I asked. 'Russia,' he said, 'never dies, though many Russians do. Our general is time. We have lost the Baltic; we have lost Constantinople. It is good. We now have a national aim when Marx has killed off suffi-cient Russians to understand, whereas before we had only a social or Socialist aim. We shall not bother about Poland. With-out us the map of Europe is a caprice.'

'And Latvia, Lithuania, Esto-nia,' I interjected. 'And Ireland,' he replied, 'and Catalonia, and don't forget Jerusalem, or the Arabs.'

Austin Harrison

LENIN IN HISTORY

27 January 1924

Lenin died on 21 January
Tsarism bred the Russian revo-lution, the war released it, and Lenin bridled and rode it. With-out Lenin war and the Tsardom would still have done their fated work. But without Lenin's fanat-ical strength, unscrupulous fidel-ity to his life's purpose, and power over men, the waters of the revo-lution would almost certainly have run their course into the sand. It was Lenin's achieve-ment, thus far, as it was also his original aim, to pull down one despotism and set another in its place. The years of his own reign are six or less. In that time the little refugee of the Swiss garrets became a household word through both hemispheres, a power to excite the enthusiasm and the execration of the Western World. The legend of Napoleon was a thing of slow growth beside it. Napoleon's conquests were less swift, less extensive, and, it would seem, less solid.

For some imaginations Lenin is the Genghiz Khan of our century, the enemy of the human and, in particular, of the Russian race. Others will argue more cynically that nothing is more to be re-marked in the revolutionary era than its continuity with the past. The new order has merely stood the old order on its head. Both are stained with crime and cruelty. In both there is the same conviction

that the masses exist for the State and for the satisfaction of the theory of government it represents. Both show organisation and elaboration on paper, squalor and disarray in fact. The one exploits education, as the other exploited religion, for the maintenance of the system. Thus through a score of parallels the argument might run to prove that under Tsar or under Soviet, in its internal as certainly as in its external aspect, the fundamental Russia persists.

Lenin – 'The Genghiz Khan of our century.'

TWO AMERICAN FILMS

28 September 1924

It must be the climate or the size of the country that gives these films their breadth, their paralysing gusto. And to say that one either liked or disliked them would be as irrelevant as blowing kisses to Vesuvius or reproving a typhoon. If you can imagine Sheherazade in delirium on Ellis Island, fighting her battles over again, you will get a dim idea of the marvels of *The Thief of Baghdad.* For two hours cloud-capped towers and gorgeous palaces, contending armies of human beings like flies or animated dust, beasts both normal and monstrous – elephants and gorillas, flying devils and giant octopuses, even Pegasus himself, cantering among the stars like a two-year-old at Newmarket – all these had passed before my eyes like phantasmagoria in a dream.

I had already seen Douglas Fairbanks as Robin Hood and as D'Artagnan, but his Thief as far transcends these ponderable heroes as he himself does you or me. He is less a man than a syndicate – Sindbad and Aladdin, Siegfried and the Flying Dutchman all rolled into one. His

valour, impudence, agility, and good-humoured resource are amazing. His normal way downstairs – even such stairs as link the floors of the prodigious palaces of Baghdad – is over the banisters. He does the rope trick in emergencies as coolly and successfully

as one might step into a lift. He vaults into the saddle with the ease of a thrush alighting on a twig. And if the languours of Oriental love weigh a little heavily on him, that is scarcely to be wondered at. Baghdad must be seen to be believed.

Douglas Fairbanks: 'Sindbad and Aladdin, Siegfried and the Flying Dutchman all rolled into one.'

Love and Sacrifice, the hitherto censored Griffith film, is almost human by comparison. It tells a romance of the War of Independence; and it struck me as an excellent kindergarten method of teaching history. We get glimpses of the court of George III; a set-piece or two with Pitt and Washington rather stiffly posed; a rousing night ride whose breakneck excitement is beaten into the brain by a tomtom obbligato. This film also goes for broad effects and knockdown climaxes. But Baghdad remains Baghdad, incomparable, delightful, and absurd.

'HAY FEVER'

14 June 1925

Mr. Noel Coward has brought off his first real theatrical coup.

Hay Fever is so good a comedy that description can say little about it. Its persons are an artistic family: the mother (Miss Marie Tempest) a retired actress; the father (Mr. Graham Browne) a pleasantly philandering novelist; and a couple of precocious children – a quarrelsome, greedy, Bohemian family, with much too much of the artistic temperament to be comfortable and agreeable to outsiders. Enter to them, at their house up the river, some ill-assorted week-end guests. The guests one by one almost perish of neglect and boredom, and finally all depart together on the Sunday morning.

That is all the play, but its small idea is worked out with happy adroitness. I shall not forget that curtain to the first act, where the family sits round so thoughtfully sipping its tea and enjoying its cakes, while the guests, neglected to the point of being utterly forgotten, hover miserably in the background; nor the last curtain of all, where, in the midst of a violent family quarrel, the flight of the guests is at last noticed, and the family, shocked into silence, turn to one another with the horrified cry of 'How rude!'

'THE GOLD RUSH'

13 September 1925

Tomorrow, at the Tivoli, a pathetically grotesque fellow wearing a smudge moustache, a crestfallen bowler hat, and 'bags' not distinctively Oxfordian will shuffle across a crowded dance floor with one foot tied up like a brown-paper parcel. He will sit down to a meal of old boots, pulling out a twisted nail for a wish-bone. He will rock in a hut on the edge of a precipice. He will sit waiting in a shack, all bedizened for a New Year's party, for a girl who does not turn up.

That will be Charlie Chaplin, the buffoon of the soul, in *The Gold Rush*, a film so long in the making – two years, actually – that it dropped Charlie's last income-tax return to that of a ten-cent-store clerk's. In this, which he regards as his finest work, Charlie joins the long, long trail of the early goldseekers to white Alaska. There are some 2,500 toughs on the job with him – Southern Pacific Railway 'bums' chartered specially for the film and taken up into the High Sierras in the Californian Rockies for a month's camera-shooting *in situ*. Equipment was hauled nine miles from

Charlie Chaplin: 'He joins the long, long trail of the early goldseekers to white Alaska.'

hours at a stretch, sometimes for a few minutes, at the end of which he would say, "It's no good. Come on. We'll go and have a coffee." He was always going off at new tangents, altering, reconstructing. In the middle of a walk he would strike an idea, get out pencil and paper, and say. "Yes, we must have it this way." The film is 8,200 feet. To get that we shot 400,000. He lived in the film, heart and soul.'

THE NEWSPAPER SOLILOQUISES

14 March 1926
Hardy was 86, The Observer 135.
Yes; yes; I am old. In me
  appears
The history of a hundred years;
Empires', kings', captives' births
  and deaths;
Strange faiths, and fleeting
  shibboleths:
Tragedy, comedy, throngs my
  page
Beyond all mummed on any
  stage:-
Cold hearts beat hot, hot hearts
  beat cold,
And I beat on. Yes; yes; I am
  old.   *Thomas Hardy, O.M.*

the railroad, and a pioneer's city of shacks built in order that Charlie might play the fool in it. About $1,000,000 was sunk in the whole enterprise, which included the erection of 200 tons of plaster Sierras at Hollywood, snowed under with 285 tons of salt, 100 barrels of flour, and four cartloads of blizzard confetti!

But enough of that. What of the magician himself during these two years of organised buffoonery? Mr. H. d'Abbadie d'Arrast, who has been Mr. Chaplin's assistant director for three years, can enlighten us on that. 'He worked fitfully, as the mood took him,' he told *The Observer* yesterday, 'sometimes for eighteen

'Sentries and policemen were swept aside by the huge crowds which had assembled and Lindburgh was carried shoulder-high to a pavilion where he was officially welcomed by the American Ambassador.'

CAPTAIN LINDBERGH'S TRIUMPH

22 May 1927

The first airman to venture the crossing of the North Atlantic alone has succeeded in his dangerous undertaking. Capt. Charles Lindbergh, who, in his Ryan monoplane, *Spirit of St. Louis*, left Long island at 7.50 a.m. on Friday for a non-stop flight to Paris, arrived at Le Bourget at 10.22 last evening.

The airman passed over Plymouth at 7.40 last evening, heading in a south-easterly direction, flying very high and very fast. The monoplane was sighted from Le Bourget about 10 p.m. As soon as the airman landed there were remarkable scenes of enthusiasm. Sentries and policemen were swept aside by the huge crowds which had assembled, and Capt. Lindbergh was carried shoulder high to a pavilion where he was officially welcomed by the American Ambassador.

WOMEN AND THE FUTURE

1 April 1928

On 29 March 1928 universal adult suffrage was at last achieved in this country.

Under ordinary forms in the British way one of the extraordinary revolutions in democratic history has been ensured. In effect, even accomplished. In spite of the romantic resistance of a corporal's guard in the No lobby, the supremacy of a male electorate in this country was virtually abolished last Thursday by an overwhelming majority of male votes. The result will be to enlarge the electorate to the total of 26,000,000 voters, amongst whom women-citizens to the extent of a couple of millions will outnumber the men.

Ultimately some woman pre-eminent as orator and leader will become Prime Minister. If women have been great as queens and empresses, why not some day as Prime Ministers? That experiment is bound to be proposed before the end of the twentieth century.

The introduction of universal suffrage is remarkable as terminating one of the longest and greatest processes in our own political history. The movement now completed has lasted for over a century and a half. The Duke of Richmond advocated manhood suffrage as far back as 1780. Looking back, the astonishing thing about the measure called the Great Reform Bill is that it made only the smallest and safest of changes. Even in 1867 Household Franchise only introduced a very limited democracy. That Act added about a million voters to the register. Still less than one-tenth of the people were citizens. There was a bigger change in 1884 when the vote was extended to the agricultural labourer. Then, in

1918, women's suffrage made the tremendous increase. The electorate at one sweep was enlarged from about eight millions to over twenty millions.

The critics of this historic measure protest against it on the ground that it gives a permanent majority to women. On any basis whatever of equal rights women would still be a majority in politics just as they are in national life – though a majority not combined as a sex, in the manner once feared by egregious pessimists, but distributed amongst the three parties and differing from each other like men.

BUILD THE TUNNEL!

13 January 1929

On the day when Bleriot flew the Channel England ceased to be an island. From that day onwards Englishmen have been slowly ridding themselves of their traditional attitude towards the neighbouring continent, exposing to their own minds the humbug inherent in comforting tags about the tight little island and the silver streak.

The tunnel should have been built forty years ago, when its construction would have secured to British engineers for another generation the supremacy which they won in the railway-building era. Lord Salisbury, with his contempt for sham thinking, was in favour of it. But an enterprise desirable then is essential now. Great as would be its benefits to us in peace or war, its value to Europe will be infinitely greater. Why then do we hesitate? Because hesitation is enthroned in high places. It is with the tunnel, as with the road programme and the penny post. Always an eye for the immediate risks, never the vision of the ultimate gain.

The country is in no mood for further temporising.

MENUHIN'S MUSIC

27 November 1932

Menuhin [then aged 16] combines skill, modesty, and youth, as one can hardly believe they have ever been combined before. They are great gifts, and with them he tells the simple truth of the music.

Everywhere there is buoyant youth with taut nerves and unclouded brain, busy and curious about ornamental detail, yet with a judgment beyond his years, which may develop into the grasp of an artist.

THE NEW B.M.A. BUILDING

22 September 1929

This is a cheerful sort of building with its arches in the base, its keystones, its heavy sash bars, its red brick columns, its broken pediments, and its stone Corinthian capitals. It belongs to the period of Wren and the full-bottomed wig. It has a porty flavour.

The general effect is so cheerful, so bluff, and so hale and hearty, that one wonders how this building came into the second quarter of the Twentieth Century, and certainly how it came to be the headquarters of so reticent a profession. The explanation is simple. It was designed by Sir Edwin Lutyens in those distant years before the war. Untroubled by the upheaval of Europe, this building has gone on in an imitation of the more spacious days of Wren.

Much has happened since 1914, and when some years hence this building stretches still further right and left, it will look down on a lean world of steel and glass that will not understand it.

THE HITLER PORTENT

1 May 1932

Last Sunday's Hitler vote was big enough to be an unmistakable portent. The Nazi poll was the biggest single party vote recorded since the revolution. In Prussia the Nazi seats are increased from nine to 162, in a Diet of 422 members. Herr Hitler now becomes an operative force in German politics. Fortunately, he is not a dictator, and will be forced to bend himself in harmonious national unity.

GERMAN 'MARXIST' CAMP

26 March 1933

Preparations are going on apace with the new concentration camp in the neighbourhood of Dachau, where 'all the Communists and Marxists who endanger the state' are shortly to be housed. After alterations have been made there are to be two thousand five hundred prisoners. The camp is strongly guarded, and is surrounded by a barbed wire fence. The rooms appear to be clean and airy, and the prisoners sleep on straw sacks. The eldest one in each gang is responsible for order. The food for the time being is being cooked in field kitchens.

The camp will probably be quite ready in about two months' time.

HITLER'S GERMANY

16 July 1933

Last week Herr Hitler made a pacific speech. His declared reason for thus suddenly applying the soft pedal, after doing nothing for weeks to stop a brutal and mean persecution, is that the revolution is now complete. Who can doubt it? Within a few weeks the face of Germany has been so violently assaulted that it is rarely recognisable. Communists, Socialists, Catholics, Pacifists, Jews have been herded into concentration camps. Even chess, with rabbit-breeding, has now joined the company of those pastimes that are closed to the non-Aryan. There is nothing here that will lift the oppressive intolerance that has driven an Einstein from Germany and is stifling German thought and culture.

It is now two months since the Chancellor made his famous speech in which he said that 'the German Government is convinced that today there can only be one great task, and that is to assure the peace of the world'. Yet nothing has been done to translate these excellent sentiments into something more tangible. The concentration camps are still swarming with pacifists. The German browbeating of Austria continues.

GERMANY OUT OF THE LEAGUE

15 October 1933

Germany announced yesterday that she will leave the League of Nations and the Disarmament Conference and that a new election would be held on November 12. The German people, Hitler said, had been 'deeply humiliated' by the negotiations at Geneva, and therefore felt that there was nothing else to do but to take no further part in them. Hitler also made the point that he was sure the election would show that the German people support him in this action 'like one man'.

BANNED IN BERLIN

15 October 1933

The Nazis ban *The Observer* because it attacks their philosophy at the base. Their creed of neo-barbarism is built out of a mass of naive and charlatan assumptions. If that creed prevailed, there could be no hope whatever for the future of mankind. Why? Because the advocacy of the spirit of peace is absolutely eradicated throughout that doped and duped nation; and because the organised glorification of war itself is substituted. It is a rubble of lies about race, history, life, and God.

Before the massacre: Hitler, right; Goering, left; in the middle the victim, Ernst Röhm, the organiser and commander of the whole army of Brown battalions.

Mr Christie's Glyndebourne

3 June 1934

Glynde, which lies at the east end of the South Downs, has become a name on the map of music, like Bayreuth and Salzburg. The one hope for those who love opera has always been that some day the head that holds the ideas and the hands that hold the wherewithal might belong to one and the same person. Committees, however enthusiastic, are naught: it must be a genial tyrant. Such is Mr. John Christie. On the subject of 'opera in idea' he believes in choosing the right man and trusting him. He chose Mr. Fritz Busch as conductor and he chose Mr. Carl Ebert as producer.

When Wagner came here to give concerts in 1877 his criticism of the Philharmonic was that they proposed to give a whole evening of the classics on one morning's rehearsal. For the two operas done at Glyndebourne Mr. Busch has had twenty-four rehearsals of orchestra alone, of course; the rehearsals were to secure balance.

It is within the truth to say that this is the first time in this generation, and probably much longer, that opera has been done *right*, under English management. Every singer and player there knows that it is so, and the public, a creature of habit, will gradually discover it to be so.

A.H. Fox Strangways

Hitler's Red Hand

8 July 1934

Hitler's Night of the Long Knives took place on 30 June

A great but unfortunate people are now more than ever outside the pale of normal civilisation. They cannot recover happiness and prosperity, nor true strength and dignity, until more freedom and sanity prevail. We have warned our readers for several weeks that something strange was brewing. It was supposed that nothing extraordinary would happen for some months. The Führer and his most formidable lieutenant decided not to wait. Better to make a thorough job while about it and slay on suspicion as well as on evidence. They resolved upon nothing less than a preventive massacre. Potential oppositions – left, right and centre must be beheaded. Amongst the Nazi leaders shot were three men who counted amongst the lions of the movement. Captain Röhm sent on leave by the Führer weeks before was the organiser and commander of the whole army of Brown battalions. He had rendered priceless services to Herr Hitler. With him perished Heines, the notorious tyrant of Silesia, and of this cruel sadist the earth is well rid. One of these men had lived in shameless luxury; the other was alleged to have been caught in infamous circumstances. Their deaths were elaborately described as a service to morals. Fudge! From the begining of the Revolution their immorality was known, flaunted, and tolerated. They were finished, not for their old vices, but for their new politics making for insubordination.

An imaginative spell is broken. The original Nazi dream is shattered. No new faith of that kind can replace it. The tyranny seems strengthened, concentrated, omnipotent. We dare to predict that its basis will prove to be fundamentally and irreparably weakened.

Herr Hitler's original foundations have collapsed. To stand at all he must stand more to the Right, which will never love him nor trust him.

'She adapts every technical resource of voice and body to the exact scope of the cinema medium, and adds warmth to each character from a kind of slumbering but undying inner flame.'

GRETA GARBO AS KARENINA

6 October 1935

I suppose more nonsense has been written and talked about Greta Garbo than about any other actress on the screen. She has become the archtype of the cinema woman, adulated, burlesqued, imitated, envied. And between her disciples and her traducers the real Garbo, I fear, has been badly let down. Great Garbo is, quite simply, a great screen actress. That is to say, she adapts every technical resource of voice and body to the exact scope of the cinema medium, and adds warmth to each individual character from a kind of slumbering but undying inner flame.

Her latest appearance is *Anna Karenina*. The film has not got the magnificent solidity of *Christina*, but it is a pretty good thing of its kind. The production has a certain opulence that fits its mood and period; it is handsome and dashing, with enough social sense to present divorce as a problem to an age which has come to regard it as a commonplace. I found it a little hard myself to believe in Frederic March's elegant Vronsky but the rest of the acting, I thought, was distinctly helpful. Basil Rathbone, in particular gave just the right sense of icy integrity to Karenin – from the crack of his knuckles in the taut interview with Anna, to the schooled pity in his night scene with the boy Sergei, this sketch was beautifully done.

There are, of course, bad moments. The picture frankly stems from Hollywood, not Moscow. The consoling scene after Anna's suicide is quite banal and vulgar. But, on the whole, *Anna Karenina* is a picture of merit and it certainly presents a Garbo in the high summer of her maturity, richer and more mellow than she has ever been before.

C.A. Lejeune

C.A. LEJEUNE (1897-1973) Always known as 'C.A.' around the office, never Caroline Alice. Film critic of The Observer *from 1925 to 1960, one of the first journalists to treat the new medium seriously as an art-form. Her career spanned the rise, great days and the beginning of the decline of the film industry. Perhaps because she was a pioneer, she exercised an influence which few other newspaper critics of any of the arts have achieved.*

KIPLING AND HIS WORKS

19 January 1936

Rudyard Kipling died on 18 January at the age of 71

At twenty-one he brought out *Plain Tales from the Hills*. Before he was thirty *Barrack-Room Ballads*, *Life's Handicap*, *Many Inventions*, *The Light that Failed*, and *The Jungle Book* had followed these. While the liberal West was worrying over the problems of democratic government, of the application of our institutions to other civilisations, and the relations between races, this youth broke in on it as the Man Who Knew, prepared, in brief and biting sentences, to tell the unpleasant truth about everything. He knew the facts and the conclusions: and he could squeeze an immense amount of controversy and affirmation into a phrase. 'One advantage of the Secret Service is that it has no worrying audit. The service is ludicrously starved, of course, but the funds are administered by a few men who do not call for vouchers or present itemised accounts.' The 'of course' was characteristic; anybody was a fool who disputed it; under a sentence like that, from the admirable book *Kim*, lay a whole world of assumption and preference, and deliberate provocation to all who thought in phrases like 'public control,' or had a distaste for the idea of 'Secret Service'.

One set of men denied his literacy greatness because they disliked his views; another set admired his inferior work because it embodied opinions which they shared. Both conspired to concentrate attention upon elements which, after all, do not dominate his writings, when one looks at them in bulk. It is typical of his fate that the one line from the superb *Ballad of East and West*, which is perpetually bandied about, is the merely incidental line 'Oh East is East and West is West, and never the twain shall meet.' The line has almost served to distract attention from the nobility and swing of the poem; certainly from the fact that it is the community between the finest things in East and West that is emphasised elsewhere.

Kipling: 'One of the greatest writers of his time.'

It has been said he lacked depth and mystery, that he too often achieved a merely surface brilliance; that many of his verses exhibited a sort of vulgar slickness. It remains obvious that he was one of the greatest writers of his time. A selection from his vast production would include enough masterly short stories and beautiful poems to make a dozen small literary reputations.

He summarised much of his thought in *If*. It has a bluntness of statement and cleanness of conviction rare in our day of fine shades and universal scepticism:

If you can bear to hear the truth you've spoken
Twisted by knaves to make a trap for fools.

The terms are unusual now. 'If you can bear to hear what you have said misinterpreted with the intention, or at least with the result, of giving a false impression to the simple and the innocent,' is more in our mode, and 'truth' is a word from which we tend to shrink.

MISS DIETRICH PASSES BY

13 September 1936

Marlene Dietrich gave me a non-stop two-minute interview this week in a Denham corridor.

As we talked, we were hurrying towards the stages. Doors opened miraculously in front of us. Heads peered out of dressing-rooms to stare at us. Executives stood back to let us pass. Miss Dietrich's eyes swept from side to side, very slowly, under dropped lashes. She smiled the secret smile that von Sternberg likes to shoot through gauzes. It was impossible, fantastic, like a scene in a dream.

Dietrich, I had learnt from the studio call-sheet earlier in the day, was to be on the set at 2 p.m. for a costume test. I got on to the set. Never mind how, but I got there. Twenty-six people were waiting to shoot the test, including one director, one producer, one production manager, one interpreter, one Paris dress designer, one hairdresser, one script clerk, six electricians, and me.

We waited two and a half hours, two and three-quarters. At 4.45 precisely Miss Dietrich came. She made her entrance on Alexander Korda's arm, rather a tall woman, draped in brown furs, hatless, looking unreal and lovely.

We rose to our feet like a congregation; stood to attention as she passed through. Afterwards I heard one man say to himself in a surprised whisper, 'Why the hell did I do that?'

Miss Dietrich passed straight through the set and disappeared. We sat down again to our waiting. Ten minutes later I sought out Korda.

'Alex,' I said, 'I must see Dietrich.'

He shrugged his shoulders.

'I, too,' he said, 'But I cannot find her again. Nobody can find her.'

'Let's hunt,' I said. We did.

'Do you know that these corridors are a third of a mile long?' asked Alex contemplatively at one point in the marathon, more to himself than me.

We ran for miles, following every rumour of Dietrich's passage. We looked in her dressing room – all pale wood and blue glass-topped tables, pink satin cushions, pink roses, a refrigerator, a bath. She was not there, only a new electric hair-dryer waiting solitary in her anteroom. We looked on the lot, here the old-fashioned barouche in which she was to ride for the film was being solemnly driven round and round, to accustom the horse to its jingling harness. When we got back to her dressing-room she was there. Korda tapped at the inner door, called 'Marlene' through the panels.

'I am dressing. In a moment I shall be ready,' said the slow Dietrich voice. A lovely hand and bare arm was thrust round the door, palpably for someone to kiss. Korda, doing the honours, kissed it gallantly.

She came out at last in an evening gown of black tulle, trimmed with mauve ruffles; a white flower on her shoulder, a mauve flower in her hair.

Her eyes slid round the room, rested on me questioningly. The beautiful, languid eyes considered, accepted me. She smiled just a little, offered me scarlet-tipped fingers.

'Come,' she said.

Then began that fantastic journey down the corridors to the stages. We were alone, the bodyguard half a pace behind us. I knew I had precisely two minutes to break the silence of which she was so completely mistress.

'This picture – *Knight Without Armour* – do you begin work on it soon?'

'On Monday.'

'With Donat?' – 'Yes.'

'Is he here?' – 'No.'

'He's ill, isn't he?' – 'Yes.'

'What's the matter?'

'Asthma,' she said, making the word seem somehow exotic. We rounded a corner. I tried again.

'The ending is sad, isn't it?' – 'Yes.'

'You die?' – 'Yes.'

'You like it that way?' 'Yes. I like to die.'

We passed through a crowd of extras. We were getting near the set. I made one last attempt at a conversational opening.

'Miss Dietrich,' I said boldly. 'Your part in the book was a very small one. Has it been rewritten for the picture?'

She didn't bat an eyelid, but I felt the atmosphere suddenly become electric.

'It is still a small part. I *like* to play small parts I prefer not to be on the screen the whole time.'

She swept through the sound-proof doors on to the set. The twenty-six faithful sprang to attention. 'Clear the stage!' someone yelled. 'Lock the doors! Draw the screens! Here's Miss Dietrich!'

The white screens were drawn round her, close, without a peep-hole.

Three hours and three quarters late, the costume test began.

C.A. Lejeune

'*A lovely hand and bare arm was thrust around the door, palpably for someone to kiss. Korda, doing the honours, kissed it gallantly.*'

'THE ROAD TO WIGAN PIER'

14 March 1937

Mr Orwell's book is a difficult one to place. The general reader may find it difficult to pick his way through the jungle of the author's impressions, prejudices, and social theories. But the book is certainly worth the effort. Mr. Orwell, although sometimes irritating, is a shrewd and original person, who has a great deal to say, and some of it is worth hearing.

He is very frank about his own position. He comes of a middle-class family, and in his youth seems to have been a thorough little snob, who found the working-class repulsive because they 'smelt'. His 'awakening' came when he was serving in the police force in Burma, and he returned to England with a 'hatred against Imperialism' and a sharpened social conscience. From that moment he was filled with a longing to free himself of all the ideas and conventions that he had learnt in his unrepentant middle-class life. He found the task by no means easy, for the 'stink' of the proletariat is prodigious and the nostrils of a bourgeois are apparently very sensitive. But no one would accuse him of not trying. Mr. Orwell first became a tramp, mixing with that floating army of the destitute that is drawn from every class, and later on attempted the far more difficult job of getting to know the real working class.

When he sticks to things seen he is very good indeed. His abstract reasoning is not so good partly because he is too emotional and partly because his statements are often supported by insufficient evidence. Far more pertinent and amusing are Mr. Orwell's reasons for the retreat of the Labour movement. First, there are the vegetarians the sentimentalists, the exhibitionists and 'the bearded fruit juice drinker,' who give the movement an air of crankiness that repels so

many sympathisers. Secondly, there is the way the Labour movement has identifed itself with 'Progress', and many people are by no means so bamboozled by the word as when Mr. Wells first began to lead us into a world of shining glass and brass. Thirdly, there is the fatal tendency on the part of many Socialists to underestimate their opponents and to assume that anybody who does not agree with them must be either a pimp, a liar, or a rogue. Incidentally, Mr. Orwell falls into the same error himself when he talks about 'Mosley and his pimpled followers'.

Hugh Massingham

George Orwell: 'Irritating, but shrewd and original and with a great deal to say.

A Punch view of what was seen as the pro-Italian policy of The Observer and Daily Mail, the only English papers allowed into Italy. The Pope (Mussolini) blesses Garvin and Rothermere.

LABOUR AND ARMS

25 July 1937

The Labour Party's unreason in instigating the country to warlike attitudes and at the same time refusing it the armaments to support them, has become too much for even its own members to swallow. At last week's meeting, when its leaders proposed to vote against the Service Estimates as usual, a majority of those present decided against anything of the kind. They had begun to realise at last that 'Defiance without Defence' was scarcely a policy to recommend them to a sane community. But their new course – that of abstaining from the divisions – is virtually an announcement that Defence is a matter they dare not touch for fear of burning their fingers.

JUDGMENT OF SOLOMON

25 July 1937

Palestine is a little land no bigger than Wales. At the time of the 1922 Census, when the Mandate was granted, there were 670,000 inhabitants, of whom about 83,000 were Jews. To-day there are nearly 1,300,000 of whom 375,000 are Jews. There are also 10,000 British graves. They were left there after the War, and were the initial purchase price paid for all that had been done in the country since – good or bad. The greater part of what has been accomplished since has been achieved by Jewish capital, labour, and enterprise.

Jewry throughout the world poured its treasure and, be it added, its highest aspirations, into this little country in order to afford to its least fortunate members the chance of a free and decent life. Palestine to-day supports twice the population that it did fifteen years ago. Not only does it support more Jews, but it supports more Arabs. The credit for this belongs to the Jewish immigrants, and to those who sent them there. Their right to a place in Palestine rests now not only on history and a British promise but on their own achievement.

To many in this country this great Zionist movement makes a very deep and natural appeal. To Israel the British people owe their religious faith; for centuries their imagination has been fired and ennobled by the records of Jewish prophecy, poetry, and history.

Even their literature has been profoundly affected by this influence. The grandest expression of patriotism in the English language was translated from the Hebrew, and was written of the love of Israel for the rough and stony land which provided for many centuries the only real home her people ever knew. 'Oh pray for the peace of Jerusalem; they shall prosper that love thee. Peace be within thy walls and plenteousness within thy palaces.' It is not only a Jewish patriot who feels a lump in his throat when he hears the Psalmist's words.

Yet though Palestine is the historic home of Israel, it is also the home of another race. For a thousand years Palestine has been the home of the Arabs. Even Jerusalem the Holy City of Israel, is also a Holy Place to the Muslims. Those who were responsible for the Balfour Declaration knew this. That was why what was promised to the Jews was a National Home *in* Palestine, and not Palestine itself, and why it was stated that nothing should be done that might 'prejudice the civil and religious rights of existing non-Jewish communities in Palestine.'

The strong patriotism, vitality, and racial consciousness of the Jew has aroused that of the Palestinian Arab, himself already deeply stirred by the widespread Arab national movement engendered by the war. And the Arabs, who had hitherto lived on not unfriendly terms with the comparatively small Jewish minority population, found themselves growing increasingly resentful of the new tide of Jewish immigration. For the first thirteen years after 1920 it did not average more than about 8,000 immigrants a year. But in the last three years, stimulated by world movements and terrible persecutions far beyond the ken of the Palestinian Arab, more than 130,000 Jews have entered the country. This, though a mere drop in the ocean of the necessities of persecuted Jewry, is a very remarkable figure. It is not surprising that it alarmed the Arab cultivator.

The Palestinian Royal Commission may not have achieved the ultimate solution of an apparently almost insoluble problem. But it certainly approached it in a realist frame of mind. It accepted the contention of the two parties that they could not agree over the beloved object of their contention. It therefore adopted the judgment of Solomon and proceeded to divide Palestine between them. Its members can have had small hope that the division would satisfy either side. It has not done so. But it has made them reflect. Both parties have now to reconsider their attitude. No mere pious declaration on the part of a third party, Britain, can bring them together.

Jew and Arab; each is the legatee of a noble civilisation. Both have suffered persecution and both are indestructible. A fraction of these two great races now meet in the historic land of Palestine. A continued clash between them does not only mean trouble for Palestine; it means trouble all over the earth. It threatens our imperial communications. It threatens our peaceful relations with those we live and trade with in every corner of the world. The problem of Palestine is not only a Jewish and an Arab problem but it is a British one as well. We live by trade and by orderly, reasonable, and just dealing between man and man. Without order we cannot live. *Arthur Bryant*

'Ultimately television sets will be in millions of homes as are wireless sets today.'

TELEVISION FOR ALL

5 December 1937

There were no television receivers in Greater London in September, 1936, but now there are nearly 9,000, and the rate of increase is rapidly accelerating – in the last four months the number has more than doubled. These figures confirm the opinion of those in intimate association with the development of the industry that ultimately television sets will be in millions of homes, as are wireless sets today. Developments now in hand will make it possible to televise all events of public interest wherever they take place, and to receive transmissions in practically any part of the country.

HITLER AND AUSTRIA

13 March 1938

With 400 warplanes circling overhead, tanks preceding him, and 250,000 people gathered to cheer him, Herr Hitler last night made a triumphal entry into Linz, capital of the Austrian province where he was born.

Leaving Berlin in the morning, he flew to Munich, whence he continued his journey by car.

Once over the border he broke his journey at Braunau to see the house where he was born, and at Leonding, where he placed flowers on his parents' graves.

At Linz he was met by Dr. von Seyss-Inquart, Austria's new Nazi Chancellor. In a short broadcast, Herr Hitler announced that a plebiscite would be held in Austria on the question of an immediate *Anschluss* (economic union) and the merging of the two countries into one State. Thousands of men and women wearing Nazi emblems marched in a torchlight procession through the streets of Vienna last night, watched by members of Dr. von Seyss-Inquart's Cabinet, who took the Nazi salute.

Hitler announced that a plebiscite would be held in Austria on the question of an Anschluss.

WHAT IT MEANS

2 October 1938

Up to last Wednesday the world, as we know it, seemed swaying to doom. Herr Hitler, holding his Godesberg ultimatum in an iron hand, giving only six days' respite, seemed deaf not only to the urgings of the Prime Minister but to the solemn appeals and entreaties of general civilisation led by President Roosevelt himself. As never before in any age the fate of the whole human race seemed to hang on the will of one man; and then the miracle of the deliverance won within twenty-four hours by the saving tenacity and resource of the Prime Minister above all men – a relief not only for to-day but containing in itself new promise for the peace of a generation.

It was then that the Prime Minister thought of his masterstroke. In the small hours of Wednesday morning he sent a personal message to Signor Mussolini, with whom fortunately his own relations had not ceased to be good:

88

'I have to-day addressed a last appeal to Herr Hitler to abstain from force . . . I have offered myself to go at once to Berlin to discuss arrangements with German and Czech representatives. I trust Your Excellency will inform German Chancellor that you are willing to be represented and urge him to agree to my proposal, which will keep all our peoples out of war.'

Prompt and good was the response from Rome. The Duce replied in effect that while in case of war he would stand by the Reich he would urge the Führer, without prejudice to his claims to give a further chance to negotiation.

That was the real turning point for the world. But that was not certainly known on Wednesday.

Next day, Thursday, Mr. Chamberlain flew to Munich. Everyone felt like the Prime Minister himself that in one sense the thing was done. Peace would be saved somehow. Yes; but on what terms? In this respect also the sequel happily was to represent the very best that could be achieved. Thanks, above all, once more to Mr. Chamberlain – and no less it must be said to the softened and more genial humour of the Führer himself – the tone and procedure of the Godesberg ultimatum were mitigated in favour of the Czechs to an extent that had seemed beyond reach . . . By the new arrangements at Munich the Czechs have at least a fair chance of creating in free association with the kindred Slovaks a new and more homogeneous State numbering about 10,000,000 . . .

When the Conference on Czecho-Slovakia was over the Prime Minister had a separate meeting with Herr Hitler on the larger issue. Personally, and it counts, these two men, after their tough encounters have become friends for good, like British and German soldiers in the war. The Führer and the Prime Minister agreed on a signed declaration which proclaims 'the desire of our two peoples never to go to war with one another again.'

At the head of 80,000,000 of reunited Germans and with an irresistible influence now over many

more millions of other races on the further side of Europe, Herr Hitler stands forth as the mightiest sovereign and ruler since Napoleon, and perhaps since Charlemagne. On the other hand the Prime Minister has been rewarded by a welcome of thanksgiving and appreciated never yet surpassed.

Whatever else may come it will be his abiding fame that for one magical moment in an age that threatened to become one wide anarchy of hate and death and woe, he restored the touch of nature which makes the whole world kin. That touch evoked

The still sad music of humanity;
Not harsh nor grating, though of ample power
To chasten and subdue.

J. L. Garvin

Chamberlain being greeted at Heston, bringing back 'Peace with Honour' from Germany. He was rewarded, wrote Garvin, with an 'unsurpassed welcome of thanksgiving and appreciation.'

SAVAGE WORK IN GERMANY

13 November 1938
On Monday Herr Vom Rath, Third Secretary of the German Embassy in Paris was shot by a seventeen-year-old Polish Jew born in Germany. It was an abominable crime, committed by a demented boy whose misguided motive was to register his protest against Nazi Germany's maltreatment of his fellow Jews, including his own parents. As a 'reprisal,' the entire Jewish population throughout Germany and Austria were subjected to an organised campaign of personal violence, robbery, and indignity. In Berlin synagogues were set ablaze and shops were looted and wrecked. In Vienna the synagogues were blown up by bombs and the Jews arrested in thousands. Many of them committed suicide.

NO GERMAN JEWS TO DRIVE CARS

4 December 1938
Berlin, Saturday. Two more rigorous decrees against German Jews and stateless Jews were published here to-day. The first, issued by Herr Himmler, chief of the Secret Police, forbids them to drive motor-vehicles of any description or to possess cars or motor-bicycles. They may, however, own lorries. The German Official News Agency writes:

'Germans have long considered it a provocation and a menace to public life that Jews should appear in German streets driving cars, and especially that they should profit by Adolf Hitler's roads built by the hands of German workers.' The second decree comes into force on Tuesday, The following places are forbidden to the Jews: all cinemas, theatres, cabarets, night clubs, fun fairs, amusement parks, concert halls, lecture rooms, museums, exhibitions, sporting events, public baths, and skating rinks.

The shilly-shallying was over. The British were at war again.

BRITAIN PREPARES FOR WAR

Chamberlain, speaking on the radio, announced the declaration of war at 11 a.m. on Sunday morning, 3 September. The Observer *had, of course, already gone to press the night before.*

3 September 1939

Parliament met yesterday to pass urgent measures necessary to face the eventuality of war. With only seven dissentients the House of Commons carried the second reading of the National Service (Armed Forces) Bill, which makes men of eighteen to forty-one liable for military service. Parliament is to meet again at noon to-day.

Hitler has not replied to Britain's last warning that German troops must get of Poland or we would fulfil our pledge to Warsaw. Warsaw sources stated that German air attacks on Polish towns were increasing.

LIGHTER SIDE OF WAR WORK

10 September 1939

It would be so dreadful a thing for anyone to be or to feel lonely at such a time. You see an older woman passing down the street where sandbags are being filled. She stops, parks her fox stole and her handbag on the spikes of some railings, and joins in the filling of the bags. The handbag trade, by the way, had best call back its models and re-equip them with shoulder straps, for the problem of looking after your money and working at the same time calls for the return of pockets.

'Got your box o' sweets with yer, lady?' the conductor on the

Housewives in Southend taking a short break to practise communicating in spite of gas masks.

bus says, thinking I have come without my mask. Owners of gas masks are divided into the haves and the have-nots, the ones who have secured cases for them and the others who are still on the waiting list. I am the proud owner of a black two-and-elevenpenny: in Bond-street the beauty special-ist sells cases of proofed velvet, with compact and purse added, for thirty-one-and-six; and a shop higher up has elegant Russian leather ones in the tubular shape which the waitresses carry. It is strange how much pleasanter faces have become since the beginning of hostilities. We look into each other's eyes as we pass along on our business, and every woman has a half-smile for another, stranger though she be.

Alison Settle

MR. CHURCHILL AS PREMIER

Germany occupied Denmark and attacked Norway on 9 April 1940. Early in May Chamberlain announced defeat in Norway. On 8 May tension in a fraught House of Commons was heightened by Leopold Amery's denunciation of Chamberlain in Cromwell's words to the Long Parliament in 1653: 'You have sat too long here for any good you have done. Depart, I say, and let us have done with you. In the name of God, go.' On 10 May Chamberlain resigned and Churchill became Prime Minister.

12 May 1940

Despite the conventional predic-tions that for all his genius he would never arrive, Mr. Churchill becomes Prime Mini-ster at sixty-five. He takes the helm in a hurricane.

He is the choice of both Houses and of all parties. His Premier-ship is welcomed with enthusiasm by the nation and the Empire. It will be supported with unlimited determination. It is a wonderful call. It is a tremendous task.

Churchill leaving the Admiralty – he had been First Lord – to meet the King at Buckingham Palace after becoming Prime Minister.

B.E.F. FIGHTING IN HOLLAND

12 May 1940

British and French troops, having raced across Belgium, are now fighting alongside the Dutch in repelling the German invasion of the Low Countries.

R.A.F. planes have heavily bombed the airport of Rotterdam, which had been seized by Ger-man air-borne troops. A great battle is taking place in Rotter-dam itself, where the Dutch are busy mopping up more German air-borne troops who have succeeded in reaching the centre of the city.

In the Maastricht region the Belgians admit that the enemy have gained a foothold in their defensive positions.

MORE THOUSANDS OF B.E.F. SAVED

On 10 May Hitler launched his blitzkrieg on the Western Front. Between 27 May and 4 June more than 200,000 British troops and 120,000 French were evacuated from Dunkirk, many of them in 'little ships' with evocative names such as Gentle Ladye and Resolute of Rye.

2 June 1940

Every type of ship brought the Allied soldiers in an almost unending stream. Four warships entered one port within a very short time, their decks crammed. On the other hand, one small ship had not more than thirty troops on board. It was revealed that the men's terrible ordeal had continued until the ships were well on their way home.

As they had waited on the beach at Dunkirk these men had endured not only attacks from low-flying planes and shelling, but fire from the German troops drawing ever closer.

With tired faces, in torn and muddy clothes, the Flanders heroes trooped ashore.

All of them, like all those who had preceded them, showed that their spirit was utterly unbroken by the hell through which they had passed. On the carriage doors of the trains which bore them away they scrawled, 'Back to Blighty – but not for long,' and 'Look out, Hitler. We haven't started on you yet.'

They were full of admiration of the Navy and the Air force. They said the French troops had fought magnificently.

Their only hint of bitterness

was when they spoke about the lack of planes at the Front.

'In seven days in Belgium,' said a R.A.F. man, 'I saw far too few British planes and far too many Germans.

'And the Germans are afraid of us in the air. If you see three Spitfires you won't see any German 'planes about for long.'

Boys of seventeen, who on Thursday night were working in factories on the South-East coast, reached home yesterday after having been to Dunkirk to help to evacuate the troops.

Many of them had never seen a shot fired in their lives, but a naval officer who was with them when they returned said he had never seen such coolness in his life.

Off the coast they were bombed and shelled for twenty-four hours. All the time they were helping soldiers into their small craft.

One of them said 'The trouble was the smoke. For twenty miles round Dunkirk there is a pall of smoke a mile high, and the sea seems to be full of smuts.

'We were wading up to our necks half the time and I'm black all over now.'

Soldiers being evacuated from Dunkirk. 'As they waited on the beach these men had endured not only attacks from low-flying planes and shelling but fire from German troops drawing ever closer.'

MUSSOLINI STRIKES

Mussolini declared war on Great Britain and France on 10 June.

16 June 1940

Mussolini has timed his stroke like a Machiavellian adept in modern *Machtpolitik*. We have to measure him justly to beat him.

The Italian dictator reckons on Nazi victory in a short war in Europe. He does not see that the war, outside Europe, cannot be short; and that his calculations will be destroyed when the war-production of the United States comes in with full weight.

LOST A BATTLE BUT NOT THE WAR

On 16 June Marshal Pétain announced in a broadcast, 'It is with a heavy heart I say we must cease the fight'.

4 August 1940

Thousands of posters bearing the tricolour of France are going up on hoardings in every large city and town of Great Britain this week-end.

Addressed to all Frenchmen, the poster is a 'Declaration of Faith' by General de Gaulle, who declares: 'France has lost a battle, but France has not lost the war.'

General de Gaulle asserts that while a makeshift Government may have capitulated, given way to panic, forgotten honour, and delivered their country into slavery, yet 'nothing' is lost, because immense forces not yet brought into action will one day crush the enemy. General de Gaulle's message concludes with a call to all Frenchmen, wherever they may be, to unite with him in action, in sacrifice, and in hope. His rallying cry is 'Our country is in danger of death. Let us fight to save it.'

Battle of Britain as seen by a German raider which took this photograph of a Heinkel 111 over London's docklands.

BIG AIR BATTLE OVER LONDON

8 September 1940

London's biggest daylight raid of the war raged for ninety-eight minutes last evening, when massed formation of German planes attacked the capital, seeking vengeance for the R.A.F.'s bombing of Berlin. Guns thundered almost immediately.

Over a London bathed in sunshine one picked out the shapes of bombers escorted by fighters, flying many thousands of feet above, and saw white puffs from our A.A. guns.

Then came the crash of bombs, the crackle of machine-gun fire, and, above all, the boom of anti-aircraft guns. Steeply diving R.A.F. fighters set the air quivering. But even the inferno above them did not disturb the amazing equanimity of Londoners. Dozens of people stood in the streets watching the battle.

London, 'grim and gay,' a day after Mr. Churchill had forecast harder air fighting, had felt and seen Goering's vicious assault, and still laughed, and went on watching football matches.

It was unofficially estimated that something like 500 raiders approached the Thames Estuary.

THE KING VISITS COVENTRY

17 November 1940

The King yesterday visited Coventry, the scene of Thursday night's concentrated raid by the Nazi bombers. He made a tour of the damaged areas, and expressed personally to many of the sufferers his sympathy and his admiration of the courage everyone had shown.

George VI at the devastated Coventry Cathedral. Rebuilt after the war, it was reviewed by R. Furneaux Jordan (see 20 May 1962).

VICTORY IN EGYPT

To set against the disasters in Europe was one brilliant but short-lived victory. In December General Wavell's Western Desert Forces (later Eighth Army) drove the Italians out of Egypt and nearly halfway across Libya. However, early in 1941 General Rommel landed in North Africa with two German divisions. In March he was substantially reinforced and Wavell seriously depleted – he had had to send a force to Greece, which Mussolini had invaded. In April Hitler struck against Greece and the British had to evacuate. German paratroops dropped on Crete on 20 May, and another evacuation followed. RN ships sunk included the destroyer Kelly, commanded by Lord Louis Mountbatten. There was worse to come.

15 December 1940

At dawn last Monday the British army struck. Its main forces, without alarming the enemy despite brilliant moonlight, were moved during Saturday and Sunday nights across nearly eighty miles of wilderness, before the signal for attack. Then, they stormed Sidi Barrani, broke up the whole quadrilateral of fortified camps, and separated Graziani's advanced positions from his main body. They drove clean through to the sea at Buq-Buq. Three Italian divisions have been shattered. Near 30,000 prisoners have been taken. Huge quantities of material have fallen into our hands – tanks, mechanised transport, artillery, machine-guns, rifles, and ammunition.

WAVELL SWEEPS ON

9 February 1941

The King has sent a message of congratulations to General Sir Archibald Wavell, G.O.C.-in-C., Middle East. It reads: 'The capture of Benghazi is a notable landmark in the campaign in North Africa. I warmly congratulate all ranks of the Army of the Nile, and of the sister Services on this further success, which will rank high in the military annals of the British Empire.'

Wavell: A message from the King.

THE CRUX OF THE WAR

20 April 1941

General Wavell seems most likely to make his stand at Mersa Matruh. There his defences and communications are the best. To a certainty General Rommel will try to circumvent him. This will be the greatest and most critical battle for Egypt that has been fought for centuries. The German objectives are Alexandria, Suez – and beyond. We need not dwell on the immense implications.

HITLER AND RUSSIA

29 June 1941

At dawn last Sunday Hitler plunged from subjugated Europe into Russia. As the tanks and bombs went into action on a 1,500-mile front, the German people were given a Hitler proclamation by wireless. Trained to swallow anything from their Führer, the German people were suddenly ordered to regard Russia as an enemy, to reverse what they had been told before, and to face gigantic war on two fronts.

Ribbentrop, who two years ago declared that Russia and Germany were natural friends, now declared that they were natural enemies.

Last Sunday night Mr. Churchill broadcast to the world the British decision, despite the difference between Russian and British principles, to fight side by side with Russia against the common enemy, Nazism.

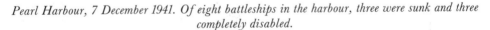

Pearl Harbour, 7 December 1941. Of eight battleships in the harbour, three were sunk and three completely disabled.

JAPAN'S BLITZKRIEG

14 December 1941

Japan's stroke was a masterpiece of treachery, admitted by Mr. Roosevelt to be 'brilliant.' At dawn last Sunday her whole forces by land, sea, and air launched what at once appeared to be a gigantic simultaneous attack upon American and British outposts in the Pacific.

The initial attack on Pearl Harbour inflicted what Mr. Roosevelt in his Address to Congress called 'severe damage to American naval and military forces.' Among them the battleship Oklahoma was sunk. On Wednesday it was announced that British losses off Malaya included the sinking of the Prince of Wales and the Repulse.

'In my whole experience,' said Mr. Churchill, 'I do not remember any naval blow so heavy or so painful.'

In 1941 tension had begun to build up between Garvin and Waldorf Astor, mainly because Garvin disagreed with Astor's view that Churchill should cease to be both Prime Minister and Defence Minister. Also in 1941, Astor persuaded Garvin to provider space for a new feature entitled 'Forum' organised by David Astor.

On 15 February 1942 The Observer published a Forum piece, entitled 'What's Wrong?', which called on Churchill to give up his role as Defence Minister. Astor claimed that Garvin had passed 'What's Wrong?' at proof stage. However, on 22 February Garvin published a leading article, entitled 'To Win the War', which denounced the idea. (It is printed overleaf.)

Garvin's contract expired on 28 February and Astor decided not to rernew it. The Observer of 1 March was produced without Garvin. The leader in that issue paid tribute to Garvin's achievements as editor and was almost certainly written by Astor.

WHAT'S WRONG?

15 February 1942

Norway; Dunkirk; Greece; Crete; Libya; Singapore. It is high time that we found the answer to the question as to what is wrong with our general conduct of this war. If we do not find the answer to that question before it is too late we shall lose the war.

There is so far as I am aware no divinely appointed ruling to the effect that the British shall never lose a war. Historical evidence exists to show that (fortunately for the world) we did lose a war 150 years ago. We were within five weeks of losing the 1914-18 war in April 1917. We are not winning this war because at the moment we do not deserve to win it. We do not deserve to win it because we are not fighting the war on the home front with whole-hearted determination and furious energy.

Our men at sea, our troops ashore, our aircrews are doing their duty, but they are inadequately equipped. The higher direction of the strategy of the war has been muddled. In our munition factories many thousands of men and women are working hard. Many managements are thinking solely of the war effort. But there is also a sense of a lack of urgency in many parts of our war effort. There is avoidable absenteeism, and there are managements who are thinking in terms of post-war advantages.

According to a telegram from Singapore, at a time when the Japanese were within a few miles of the city, there was an attitude of business as usual in Singapore, and cars were setting down guests as usual for the afternoon tea-dance at the Raffles Hotel. I have only mentioned that story not to criticise people who were on the edge of disaster but because it is the kind of attitude to the war which is not at all unusual amongst many people in Great Britain.

There is too much attempt to do business and have pleasure as usual. One cannot fight Total War except by making a total war effort; the Russians have proved that. In Great Britain to-day we like to deceive ourselves into believing that 'Party Politics' are dead for the duration. It is a non-sensical delusion. Party Politics are not dead but viciously alive inside and outside Parliament. Vested interests intrigue against each other. The Whitehall War rages day and night.

We shall begin to win this war when every day and every night the great mass of our people say to themselves with anxious inquiry: 'Have I this day done everything I could in every way open to me to slave and toil for the war effort? Have I produced as much as I could? Have I wasted anything? Have I *felt* I was fighting the war?' But in order that this spirit may rush like an electric current through the bodies and souls of our people there must be leadership.

In our democracy that leadership must come from the Prime Minister. At this critical moment in our history we have not got a Prime Minister. That office has been swallowed up and eclipsed by our energetic and pugnacious Minister of Defence.

We must recapture our lost Prime Minister, and Mr. Churchill must make the great personal sacrifice of abandoning the congenial task of Minister of Defence and devote his great talents to the job of being Prime Minister.

To Win the War

22 February 1942

At the sternest hour since Parliament was founded the impending debates in Parliament threatened a storm. Instead, Mr. Churchill has drawn the lightning. He has made his own indispensable and saving contribution to the national unity.

A fortnight ago we judged that Mr. Churchill's mind was not closed against Ministerial changes. Last week we said that his wisdom even more than his genius were now required for the management of a great people, and for the strongest conduct of the war.

What was Mr. Churchill asked to do? One group pressed him while remaining Prime Minister to resign his prime function. That is, his position as Minister of Defence. As addressed to him, of all men, this was an impossible proposition. As well might it have been suggested to Chatham [Prime Minister in the Seven Years War, 1756-63] that he should remain in some kind of office but cease to be Minister for War. Mr Churchill is adamant in refusing this demand. He bears a tremendous and fearful responsibility unparalleled in our annals. Never for one instant will he consent to bear that responsibility without power in proportion. But his load of late has become more than any mortal man could shoulder with impunity. A Napoleon could not attempt to carry that burthen with any rational expectation of continued success. The Prime Minister needs extensive relief. His method of reconstruction meets that imperative need by delegating to others the general run of domestic business. The number of members in the new Cabinet is reduced from nine to seven. The one astonishing thing is an omission. Though invited to remain a member of the War Cabinet Lord Beaverbrook declines. We judge that his present separation from the Government is unlikely to be permanent. Emergency will become compulsive.

Churchill at No. 10 giving one of his famous broadcasts, wearing his famous 'siren' suit.

A Great Journalist

1st March 1942

Mr. J.L. Garvin relinquished yesterday that editorial chair which he has held for thirty-four years. Throughout that period he has been not only a great editor but one of the most distinctive and distinguished figures in the journalism of the English-speaking world. We deeply regret the severance, and desire to put on record our abiding gratitude to one who for so many profoundly eventful years has been this journal's life and mind and soul.

When Mr. Garvin first came to *The Observer* it was no more than a shadow of its former self. Mr. Garvin not only recreated it and raised it rapidly to heights which it had never reached before but in the process set the pattern for a form of Sunday journalism which has since been widely followed elsewhere.

Wealth in all other things is nothing in a journalist without the power of clear and convincing expression, without eloquence when eloquence is needed, without an individual, arresting and at call a challenging style. We need not dilate to our readers on Mr. Garvin's style. We need not say that we shall deeply miss its balanced periods, its resource, its sparkle, its sonorous cogency, its incomparable turn of phrase. He has set a standard which his successors will do their utmost to emulate, and he may rest assured that the gratitude of proprietors and staff alike for his long and conspicuous service to *The Observer* is ardent and profound.

THE
MODERN
OBSERVER

1942-1991

David Astor

Donald Trelford

For thirty-four years The Observer *had been Garvin and Garvin* The Observer. *Now Garvin was gone. He left behind a news-cum-production editor; his assistant; a literary editor (Garvin's eldest daughter Viola); a sports editor. 'As far as there was an editor during those dreadful weeks,' David Astor said some forty years later, 'it was me in my lunch hour.' He was now a captain in the Royal Marines, working in Whitehall. Somehow he found the time and energy to keep in touch with the tiny staff. The paper continued to come out, not only with no noticeable falling-off in quality but with new, crisper, more pertinent features, as below. Another was the profile. This one was almost certainly by Sebastian Haffner, one of those brilliant Central Europeans that Astor was gathering around him. Haffner, a German emigré (real name Raimund Pretzel), usually wrote as 'A Student of Europe', but he also shared the pen-name 'Liberator', with a close friend of George Orwell's, Jon Kimche, a Swiss Jew, who wrote on military matters (Haffner wrote on world and European politics). There was the historian Isaac Deutscher, of the* Economist *(as were two more helpers, Barbara Ward and Geoffrey Crowther); Deutscher was later the author of classic biographies of Lenin, Trotsky and Stalin. There was Astor's Rhodes Scholar friend E. F. Schumacher, later the author of* Small is Beautiful. *With writers like these. The Observer's intellectual eminence was unique. However, it desperately needed an editor who could be in the office full-time. Ivor Brown, the paper's drama critic, was called in and admirably filled the role of acting editor until David took over in 1948.*

ROMMEL DRAWS NEARER TO MERSA MATRUH

Operations in the Western Desert had settled into stalemate. In May 1942 Rommel struck. In 1941 Tobruk, then garrisoned mainly by the battle-hardened 9th Australian Divison, had defied an eight-month siege. It now surrendered and the Afrika Korps advanced deep into Egypt.

29 June 1942

It was reported from Cairo yesterday that up to the afternoon the main forces in Western Egypt had not come in contact. The Eighth Army awaits Rommel's attack around Mersa Matruh. He was reported to be still a few miles from there.

MOOD OF THE MOMENT

19 April 1942

There is not much grumbling about the Budget. Common ale at tenpence a pint and cigarettes at ten for a shilling, now seem hardly worth bothering about. It is criticised mainly for what it has not done. This is not a budget which 'soaks the rich.' It benefits the lowest income groups, but imposes no fresh burdens on the higher groups. It is not much use demonstrating to the common man that, on paper, large incomes don't exist nowadays. It is still not true – and everyone below £500 a year knows it – that we 'are all in it together,' as we felt ourselves to be during the big air-raids. The British people are not envious as peoples go, but they would like to feel, now, with the enemy at several of the gates, that we *are* all in it together, sharing the petty hardships as well as the great ones.

Since 1940 public opinion has generally been a little ahead of the Government. It has demanded an invasion of Europe, more aid to Russia, and a tougher attitude towards hostile neutrals. The Budget swings attention back to home affairs. 'Cut us to the bone – but cut us *all* to the bone' would probably express what people are thinking. They want equality of sacrifice at home just as they want effective action abroad, and it is probably a sound instinct which tells them that the two things are interconnected.

George Orwell

GEORGE ORWELL (1903-1950) *Regular contributor to* The Observer's *leader-page Forum slot, which was started by David Astor during the Second World War to provide a leavening of liberal thinking and lively writing on pages that had been dominated for years by J.L. Garvin's majestic pronouncements.*

THE CITADEL

Stalingrad, on the lower Volga (it is now called Volograd) was the farthest point the Germans penetrated into Russia. On 5 September 1942 they were checked there. It was a turning point in the war.

27 September 1942

The defence of Stalingrad caught the wonder of the world and probably in the long run, it has caught Hitler by the throat. The fury with which the Russians have rallied again and again to the dust and ashes of their homes has been like a blazing torch in the eyes of mankind. The opposition of men to metal has been staggering in its courage; but it is a battle of wits as well as of will, and Russian ability to adapt war from steppe to street has been brilliant. Men have often stood by their city. Was ever such loyalty to its ruins?

Stalingrad, 1942. 'The fury with which the Russians have rallied again and again to the ashes of their homes has been like a blazing torch in the eyes of humanity.'

PROFILE: HIMMLER

The Profile, modelled on the New Yorker*'s but much shorter, is one of David Astor's many important contributions to British journalism – the first* Observer *profile was of his friend Stafford Cripps, just back from being ambassador to Moscow and about to go to India for talks on possible dominion status. Profiles were unsigned; they represented editorial judgment. they were not hatchet jobs: as Astor wrote in his last year as editor, 'men of positive, deliberate evil are exceedingly scarce'. Even today, nearly fifty years after appearing, it strikes a chill.*

18 October 1942

He has by now killed so many people as to make the activities of a Torquemada or a Robespierre appear petty in comparison. He has thought out and constantly refined the most nearly perfect system of scientifically calculated torture the world has ever known. He has fashioned the ubiquitous Gestapo and the armed SS, an army of 500,000 trained and completely dehumanised killers. He is, at this moment, the most powerful man in Europe, not excluding Hitler, who by now rules more or less on his sufferance and whom he could have put out of the way any day it suited him.

All this, however, in his own view, is scarcely more than a modest beginning. He is in the prime of his life – just forty-two. He intends to open up a new world-age. While Hitler modestly speaks of inaugurating a millenium, Himmler is reported to have said that he is laying the foundation of a world order to last twenty to thirty thousand years. He hopes, during his lifetime, to exterminate one of the major races

'Always polite with the ladies.'

of the old mankind, the Jews, and intends to plough under several of the old European nations: for a beginning the Poles and Czechs. And in one of his rare literary utterances he writes: 'We are going over the Germanic races, selecting and crossing the most perfect surviving specimens.' The SS to him, is not only an instrument of power and a ruling caste but the foundation of a new race, 'a new species of man': the stud-farm where the superman is bred.

Looking for the man behind these thoughts and deeds, one has a surprise. This man is the very embodiment of indifferent, non-descript mediocrity. A quiet, correct rather dull, good-tempered fellow. This is the horrible puzzle of Himmler. He is Mr Average-man turned demon.

His is the kind of face which is the despair of the cartoonist; just a mass of plump, clean-shaven flesh with a nipper hooked on it. His eyes are colourless, his gaze is sleepy, and he does not look people in the face. He cannot speak. For years now he has avoided any public performance as an orator. Nor can he write. His few articles are made up horrid cliches, strung together in an almost ungrammatical way. But, like many illiterate people, he is a good entertainer in a small homely circle. Ribbentrop's British nurse found him the most charming guest of the house. 'One wouldn't have dreamt that this was the chief of the dreaded Gestapo.' A teller of funny stories, modest, quiet-mannered, very middle-class, 'always polite with the ladies,' industrious, a reliable worker, somewhat pedantic but efficient, a pleasant and useful nobody – this is to what all accounts of Himler before his present eminence boil down. This is the man who has become the hangman of Europe.

He is the son of a Munich schoolmaster. He studied a few years without winning any academic honours. He was a minor clerk in some industrial concern. Later he took to poultry-farming in a small way. As a poultry-farmer and 'agricultural expert' he joined the Nazi party sometime in the late Twenties. Like Goebbels, he was a discovery of Gregor Strasser's, at that time Hitler's rival for the leadership of the party, who made young Himmler his private secretary. It was on Strasser's recommendation that Himmler was appointed leader of the SS in 1929 – at that time a troop of 280 men. Later, it was on Himmler's orders that SS-men arrested Strasser on 30 June 1934, while he was sitting down to lunch, took him out to a wood and there trampled him to death.

This thirtieth of June was Himmler's big day: with a stroke, the insignificant, little-known sub-leader, so far only police chief of Munich, burst into the limelight as the Reich's executioner-in-chief. Apart from this it is difficult to fix his career to definite dates. He slowly, steadily, methodically, wormed his way into power. His passion for record-keeping and lists-compiling served him well: so did his reputation for unambitious insignificance. When in 1936 the year-long struggle between him and Goering for the key-positon of German Police Chief was at last decided in Himmler's favour, was it perhaps because he seemed less dangerous than the ambitious, boastful, popular Marshal?

Today he rules supreme in all but in name. He flies from capital to capital, and wherever he takes off, he leaves a patch of blood behind. And Europe groans under the heel of the most hideous tyrant she has ever known: not a full-blooded monster, but a soulless, faceless, godless nonentity.

THE NEW OBSERVER

1 November 1942

Today *The Observer* appears in an altered form. The chief and most recent news will now be printed on the front page. The alteration is being made to suit the pressure of the time and to improve the service which a newspaper seeks to offer.

On such an occasion we think it well to put the policy of *The Observer* before the public. In its first number, in a period, like our own, of vast social upheaval, this journal explained its arrival in 'the present extraordinary era which opens upon an astonished world.' There is certainly no less cause for 'astonishment' today.

Amid this chaos the transient nature of existing Parties and alignments becomes obvious, while the permanence of principles is plainer and more precious than ever.

The Observer is not a party paper. It is tied to no group, no sect, no interest. Its independence is absolute. But merely to stand alone, challenging and bracing as that attitude may be, is not enough. One must also stand for a system of ideas and for a pattern of constructive reform.

The Observer's war-policy is to prosecute the war with loyalty to all our Allies until complete victory over the dictatorships has been won.

There must be no negotiated peace with the present regime of the Axis powers. Not only the dictators, but also their whole scheme of life, must be overthrown.

In the prosecution of the war there must be no uncritical respect of persons or reputations, but an un comprising search for the best possible machinery of war-direction and for the younger, fresher minds which are so much needed to cope with the rapid changes of technique in all forms of fighting and production.

It was the function of the nineteenth century to liberate. It has so far been the function of the twentieth century to control, a task wherein the failure has been calamitous in international affairs. In the control of our national life, in prevention of gross inequalities and cruelties, certain successes had already been won. (After all, the Britain of 1939, so violently criticised now, was far more humane and civilised than the Britain of 1839.)

But much remains to be done in creating a society which will get rid of injustice without losing freedom. To unify the past functions of the two centuries, liberation and control is *The Observer's* social policy. Those who work to this purpose will be supported without distinction between political parties.

The first task is to end the mad competition of nations by a world-wide control, a control not static but susceptible always to necessary changes. The second is to destroy the social injustices of an ill-balanced society without creating a sluggish conformity and dull inertia.

In our rebuilding we shall drive at the old Athenian ideal of seeking beauty without extravagance while pursuing new ways of efficiency and of mastering the machine which has so often been the oppressor rather than the liberator of mankind. That, in broad outline, must be the ideal of a dynamic democracy. It is also the policy of this paper.

EIGHTH ARMY STRIKES AGAIN

El Alamein is fifty miles west of Alexandria. Auchinleck's checking of Rommel in the first battle of that name (30 June-25 July), like Stalingrad, was a turning point in the war. In August Montgomery took over Eighth Army. The second battle began on 23 October.

1 November 1942

General Montgomery's Eighth Army resumed its attack on the El Alamein front in Egypt early yesterday morning, according to a German News Agency message last night. This report said that no news was yet available of the progress of the attack.

EIGHTH ARMY ON HEELS OF FLEEING ENEMY

8 November 1942

Cairo, Saturday. Britain's Eighth Army is steadily pushing ahead with the destruction of Rommel's German-Italian forces in North Africa. Besides the 20,000 prisoners so far officially stated to have been captured, five Italian divisions – which would normally total some 75,000 men – are trapped, with little or no hope of escape.

Rommel is now very short of armour, but he still commands a fighting force capable of giving a good account of itself.

WHERE CAN WE SURRENDER?

8 November 1942

With the Eighth Army. Saturday. Driving along the coast from El Daba to Fuka to-day, writes Reuter's Special Correspondent, I had the unusual job of directing parties of 100 or more Italians who were disconsolately asking where they could surrender. So rapidly did the Eighth Army advance that large pockets, mainly of Italian troops, were found waiting to be rounded up. All the tracks and roads going east were crammed with Italians driving their own lorries and asking the way to the nearest prisoners' camps.

I was stopped by a little Cockney rifleman with a perplexed look on his face, who asked me to take over about 100 Italians from him as he wanted to get on with another job. 'I don't know what to do with 'em,' he complained. 'They keep following me about – demanding to be allowed to surrender to me.'

Member of a German tank crew surrendering to a British infantryman. In the first few days of November hundreds of enemy tanks, guns and motor vehicles abandoned in the haste of retreat, had been taken. As for the prisoners, most of them seemed to be pleased to be out of the war after the pounding from the air of the last few days. Even the Germans were smiling.

PRODUCTION FOR VICTORY

Daimler Armoured Cars with their famous

Fluid Flywheel Transmission served in North

Africa, Sicily, and Italy with distinction. Such is

the testing of the peacetime Daimler to come.

Daimler goes to war

THE DAIMLER COMPANY LIMITED · LONDON AND COVENTRY

NAZI BARBARISM IN POLAND

13 December 1942

The Polish Government has recently received from Poland one of the grimmest documents of the war – a report on the brutal measures taken by the Germans to exterminate the population of the Warsaw Ghetto. This was created in October 1940. All Jews in the city were ordered to move by November 1 to the Jewish quarter assigned to them. After November 25, 1940, the ghetto was completely closed. Anyone leaving the ghetto without a pass became liable to the death sentence. Month after month the mortality rate within the walls rose steadily. Epidemics and want caused many deaths, and the Germans killed dozens of victims daily.

After the outbreak of the war between Germany and Russia news began to arrive of the mass machine-gunning of Jews in the more easterly parts of Poland. The terror moved west. In the spring of 1942 news came that a fresh extermination camp had been opened at Sobibor. On July 24 10,000 people were assembled for deportation, and 7,000 on every subsequent day. The quota was made up of people taken from their homes or rounded up in the streets. The process was carried out more and more brutally by the Germans with the aid of the *junaks* the Polish security battalions. The Germans separated and old and infirm who had escaped so far, carried them straight to the Jewish cemetery, and killed them there. The others were packed into goods trucks, 120 being crushed into trucks, with room for forty, which were then sealed up. The floors were covered with quicklime and chlorine. By September 1 some 250,000 people had gone. For the month of September 120,000 ration cards were printed, for October only 40,000. Only 40,000 skilled workers are to be left in the ghetto, held in barracks as suitable for German war production.

For a German to shoot someone on the spot is regarded as an act of humanity. Suicides are numberless. Every day someone takes poison; several people, even up to a score, will commit suicide in an hour, and all the chemists' shops in the ghetto have been closed as a precaution. Some of the victims implore the *junaks* to kill them, but the *junaks* demand fees of 100 zlotys for shooting. Here, surely, is the crowning horror.

DIS-APPEARANCE OF 1,600,000 JEWS

17 January 1943

Stockholm, Saturday. It was accidentally admitted to-day in the official journal of the German Governor-General in German-occupied Polish territories that 1,600,000 Jews have disappeared in Poland since the war started. The revelation came in a statement on the concentration of Jewish populations into fifty-five reservations, including thirteen ghettos inside big towns and forty-two all-Jewish towns. Quite casually it is said that there are two million Jews in the area controlled by the Governor-General and none outside. But the 1931 censure recorded 3,133,900 orthodox Jews in Poland. By 1939 there were undoubtedly at least 3,500,000 Jews of all kinds in Poland and since the war at least 100,000 European Jews have also been sent there.

A Russian divisional command post in one of the devastated buildings in Stalingrad, waiting for the imminent collapse of the trapped and exhausted German Army commanded by General Paulus.

NAZIS TOLD 'YOU ARE DOOMED'

A Russian relief force under General Zhukov cut off communications from the Germans at Stalingrad in November 1942, and the besiegers became the besieged. On 31 January Paulus and his army were captured. Twenty-one German divisions fought there. The Russians took ninety thousand prisoners.

17 January 1943

The ultimatum to the trapped German Army at Stalingrad to surrender was made 'to avoid useless bloodshed,' the special Russian communiqué stated last night. It was addressed to 'The Commander of the Sixth Germany Army, Colonel-General Paulus, or to his deputy, and to all the officers and men of the forces completely surrounded since 23 November.

'In the event of your non-acceptance of our offer of capitulation, we give you warning that the Red Army troops and air force will be compelled to engage in the annihilation of the encircled German forces, and the responsibility for their annihilation will rest on your shoulders.'

GETTING READY

7 February 1943

In spite of the last peace, of its long disillusionment and of the defeat of most of the hopes with which it began, shall we now be unready for the next peace?

Sir William Beveridge's Report on Social Services and Allied Services is a plan for abolishing want. But the Report itself names four other giant evils calling for attack – Disease, Ignorance, Squalor, and Idleness. The treatment given hitherto to one of these five Giants – Squalor – to the problem of Town and Country Planning and of ensuring sufficient and healthy housing for all, is far from reassuring. The Barlow Report on the distribution of Industry was made two and a half years ago, and the Scott and Uthwatt Reports nearly six months ago. The only overt action up to the present has been first a step in one direction – of uniting Works and Planning in a single Ministry by Act of Parliament – and then a step back – of disuniting them and setting up a new Ministry of Planning with undefined powers and no suggestion of a policy.

Behind the five Giants there are hosts of other problems – of international justice, of security from war, of constitutional change in relation to the Colonies, of relations to the other countries now allied to us or neutral, or enemy. Shall we be able to deal with the cataclysm of peace when it comes? Since we cannot have one Government for war and another for peace, those who lead the country to victory must take the responsibility of framing now the policies required when the fighting ends and establishing now the machinery for their realisation.

Beveridge at a Liberal Party meeting. His Report attacked the five Giants of Want, Disease, Ignorance, Squalor and Idleness.

The D-Day Landings, 6 June ▶ 1944: troops wade ashore from a British landing craft on one of the Normandy beaches during the invasion of France.

LIGHT DIET

7 February 1943

While patriotism would pile the potato on every plate, doctors frequently have to warn their patients to avoid starchy foods. Whither, in a rationed world, do the poor wretches turn for the makings of a light diet? It is one of the ironies of the time that a heavy, starchy meal is easier to come by than a light one.

A good mixed diet is particularly necessary at this time of the year. February habitually fills sick-beds as well as dykes; its very name sounds feverish and it behaves as such: its 'influence,' in the old sense of a magic power descending upon us, is the influenza. This year influenza carries jaundice for its ugly sequel. Here is more need for the lightest and least fatty of diets.

Fish is an obvious solution, but fish is extremely scarce. It has been 'zoned' into thin air. The fishmonger's slab is a marble desert, a gravestone of the housewife's hopes. None blames the fishermen. Many have gone to other labours and angle for mines instead of food. They have suffered terrible things, attacked by bomb and machine-gun from above as well as by destruction under water. We are immensely their debtors for having fish at all.

Whether or not the supply can be better organised, the distribution should certainly be based on medical merits. A light diet, with hardly any fish, eggs, or fruit, means almost no diet at all. Hospitals, nursing homes, and sanitoria should come first and home-keeping invalids should be guaranteed their share of the fish if a doctor's certificate be shown on their behalf. Thus, with a little use of reason, might the slender flow of sole be best employed.

SICILY: INVASION GOING TO PLAN ON 100-MILE FRONT

In November 1942 the enemy retreat in the Western Desert became a rout. On 23 January 1943 the British flag was hoisted in Tripoli, a thousand miles west of Alexandria, much further by road. Libya had been cleared, though Rommel had by now been strongly reinforced and it took heavy fighting to break the Mareth Line and enter Tunisia. The Eighth Army now made contact with the Americans and British First Army, who had landed in Algeria in November. On 10 July 1943 the Allies landed in Sicily.

10 July 1943

A communiqué from Allied Force Headquarters broadcast by Algiers Radio last night said: 'In spite of unfavourable weather and a swell off the Sicilian Channel, the Allied landing in Sicily started before dawn. Many beaches and landing places used for these first assaults extended over about one hundred miles.'

THE LANDING – SEEN FROM A 'GRAND-STAND'

11 June 1944
(Five days after the D-Day landings in Normandy)

I sat perched on the upper bridge of the American cruiser *Quincy* during the beach-head landing last Tuesday. We were at the extreme right flank nearest Cherbourg, and we had a sort of grand-stand seat for the whole thing. With binoculars I could see about 20 or 30 miles of cliff and beach. I shall never forget the aerial bombardment that preceded our attack. We were under heavy cumulus clouds, through which the moon occasionally peeked. During a four hour wait our nerves were frayed almost beyond endurance.

All that time, out-of-sight overhead bombers rumbled past like an endless freight train going over a viaduct. Streams of incendiaries went up like fountains from France, and clusters of flares were dropped twisting long smoke trails behind them. I saw two airplanes go down like falling stars and flare up suddenly when they hit.

Then I remember crouching behind the splinter rail of the open bridge, wating for our 8-in. guns to return the first German fire. We flinched at the first salvo – at least I did – but after a while got used to it. We were splashed but not hit.

Watching a little American destroyer slowly demolished by shore batteries that had it bracketed was a hard experience. They caught it again and again. The ship up-ended in narrow water and soon formed a landmark for binocular observation. Another destroyer bravely went in under fire and took off survivors.

From our distance the busy, animated scene of disembarkation looked like a couple of ant-lines to and from a crumb of bread, small boats going in with supplies; empties coming back again.

I watched an amphibious craft slowly moving along with a white ruffle of foam; turned away my glasses to give it a chance to cover the last mile; then watched it waddle up the beach.

Most spectacular sight and I think one of the most soul-stirring things I have ever witnessed, was the arrival of the first glider-borne troops. This was something right out of H.G. Wells. I wish he could have seen it.

FUTURE OF A RUINED GERMANY

Typically George Orwell used his space for hard, deep, imaginative thinking far beyond the scope of the run-of-the-mill 'war correspondent'.

8 April 1945

As the advance into Germany continues and more and more of the devastation wrought by the Allied bombing planes is laid bare, there are three comments that almost every observer finds himself making.

The first is, 'The people at home have no conception of this.' The second is 'It's a miracle that they've gone on fighting.' And the third is, 'Just think of the work of building this all up again . . .'

Bombing is not especially inhumane. War itself is inhumane and the bombing plane, which is used to paralyse industry and transport rather than to kill human beings, is a relatively civilised weapon. 'Normal' or 'legitimate' warfare is just as destructive of inanimate objects and enormously more so of human lives. Moreover, a bomb kills a casual cross-section of the property. Whereas the men killed in battle are exactly the ones that the community can least afford to lose. The people of Britain have never felt easy about the bombing of civilians, and no doubt they will be ready enough to pity the Germans as soon as they have definitely defeated them. But what they have still not grasped – thanks to their own comparative immunity – is the frightful destructiveness of modern war and the long period of impoverishment that now lies ahead of the world as a whole. To walk through the ruined cities of Germany is to feel an actual doubt about the continuity of civilisation as a whole. It is not only Germany that has been blitzed. The desolation extends all the way from Brussels to Stalingrad.

Where there has been ground fighting the destruction is even more thorough than where there has merely been bombing. Even in England we are aware that we need three million houses and that the chances of getting them within measurable time seem rather slender. But how many houses will Germany need, or the U.S.S.R. or Italy? If millions are to be deported to the victorious countries for reconstruction work, the recovery of Germany itself will be all the slower. The impoverishment of any one country reacts unfavourably on the world as a whole. It would be no advantage to turn Germany into a kind or rural slum. *George Orwell*

THE DAY

The murderers' plan for Europe
has to cease.
The millions of young men are
free to live.
You, who have power of beauty
in you, give . . .
Nothing but sunlight in us will
bring peace.

John Masefield

Devastated Dresden – the frightful destruction of modern war. As George Orwell reported, 'To walk through the ruined cities of Germany is to feel doubt about the continuity of civilization as a whole.'

109

LOOK BACK

6 May 1945

Looking back from the close of the war in Europe, what do we see? First, the last summer of peace. It is another world: roads crowded with cars, lashings of food, cricket and tennis and bathing in the sun. Then the black-out and the darkened streets, the queues of evacuees at the stations, the Prime Minister's broadcast on Sunday morning, the gas-masks and the first sirens, and we were in it – the war we had often been told would destroy civilisation and reduce large cities to rubble in a few hours. And we were in it obviously unprepared. But soon we found that we were not in *that* war, yet. That first winter was a winter of illusions; they lasted until they were torn away during the agonising weeks that led up to Dunkirk and the fall of France.

Four things saved us. The English Channel; the combined prowess of the Navy and the R.A.F; Mr Churchill's leadership; the fourth was something in the national character which refused to take in the staring prospect of defeat. In high and humble quarters there was no weakening through that summer; nor was there as the nights lengthened and the sirens sounded and the winter of the blitz drew on.

It is right that we should now remember and take pride in these things. But there should be no illusions in our pride. We can never again afford to bask in a dream of island security. That will call for a much greater effort of continuous national preparedness than we have been used to in the past. But it would be equally an illusion to suppose that we can protect ourselves by standing self-reliantly alone. War prevention depends on lasting international collaboration. But on what does international collaboration depend? There can never be much prospect of it if in periods without overt war the nations are engaged in economic warfare; if they are struggling to ease their social problems by capturing markets and exporting unemployment wherever they succeed. Here, too, as we look back over the years of struggle, we may feel that we have accomplished a great deal. Not only have we mobilised our resources to an outstanding pitch; we have shared in a great pooling of Allied resources by methods previously unknown.

In Europe a nightmare has lifted. What the world has been saved from, Belsen and Buchenwald show. Of the victors the British Commonwealth alone has fought continuously from the first. That is our achievement; history will rank it high. But it is not a war to end war that we have won. That war begins when peace is declared: we lost it in the twenty years after 1918. Now our second chance is coming; let us learn from looking back how to seize and hold it firm.

THE NEW WORLD : TRUE FREEDOM OR A 'PEACE OF TERROR'

Mussolini was killed by Partisans on 28 April. Hitler committed suicide on 30 April. The Germans officially surrendered on 8 May. The first atom bomb was dropped on Hiroshima on 6 August, the second on Nagasaki on 9 August. The Japanese surrendered on 14 August.

12 August 1945

New York, Saturday. The second world war is ending. It has lasted six years for Britain, four for Russia, and three and a half for the United States. It has lasted fourteen years for China. Mankind threw into this war all that it possessed and drew upon its descendants as well. Its dead are as yet incalculable. Certainly, civilians contributed as many and probably far more casualties than armies, and this is not over. Those who perished in the cities of Hiroshima and Nagasaki died, we are told, 'a death no one ever died before.'

At the outbreak there were the following 'Great Powers' on earth – the British Empire, the United States, Germany, Japan, Italy, France, and the Soviet Union. Britain was the strongest naval Power; Germany the strongest land and air Power; Japan the leading Power of Asia; France was rated high; the Soviet Union was rated low. The United States was rated strongest economically and technologically, dubious militarily, inactive politically.

Today the United States is the strongest Power on the sea and in the air, and, with economic and technical factors added, overwhelmingly strongest from any point of view. Great Britain has lost the mastery of the seas, and the Soviet Union, which has no challenger on the European continent, is checked only by American technology.

Until the invention of the atomic bomb, there was some chance of stabilisation on that basis. But with the perspective that rival continents can blow up each other and the planet, this hope is no longer tenable. The two great complexes of power left from this war, Anglo-American and Soviet, cannot go to war against each other. And no one else can even dream of going to war against them.

The message of the Unknown Soldier comes in the very words of Christ, 'Ye must be born again – or we have died in vain.' He needs no wreath and wants no tomb, he, who carried into this war so vast a burden of doubt, so great a light of hope, the doubts and the hopes of the whole of suffering mankind.

On 12 August, after Hiroshima and Nagasaki, The Observer
*reported: 'Across Britain's rain-swept holiday flashed first of all
the news of destruction's masterpiece, then the blazon of its
triumph, the downfall under catastrophic pressure of Japan'.
Above, the signing of the surrender aboard USS Missouri; right, a
grief-stricken Japanese woman hears the names of the dead.*

The struggle is not over. It enters another realm in the hearts and the minds of individual men and collective men, persons and nations. We have wrestled with the enemy and conquered. Now we must wrestle with ourselves.
Dorothy Thompson

THE SOUND OF THE HAMMERS

19 August 1945

My own first impression – it is only as an outsider just arrived in the British Zone after a few weeks' absence from Germany – is that things here are in some respects visibly improving. In the little and medium-sized towns of Westphalia I find many more signs of revival of normal life than I saw in Southern Germany two months ago. A surprisingly large number of shops are reopening. Here in Herford, for instance, local railways have just resumed civilian passenger traffic. German newspapers published by the Military Government carry columns of small advertisements which reflect some revival of business. As one walks in the town one is constantly accompanied by the pleasant sound of hammers knocking at the walls of damaged buildings. People are busy repairing flats for the winter. (It is perhaps also natural that one comes across more signs of black market now than immediately after the 'cease fire.')

The characteristic air of stunned apathy which hung over all German towns in spring and early summer seems to be vanishing and giving place to a new spirit of enterprise. This is so at least in smaller towns which have not been utterly ruined. In large industrial centres human enterprise continues to be baffled by the prodigiousness of destruction.

Isaac Deutscher

REVIVED GERMAN HOPES OF A WAR BETWEEN THE VICTORS

10 March 1946

Berlin. The impact of Mr. Churchill's Fulton speech – *'An iron curtain has descended across the continent'* – has been instantaneous and powerful. Every conversation with a German begins now with questions about the meaning of that speech. The German newspapers published in the Russian sector have summarised the whole speech in not more than two or three sentences, and given 20 times as much space to every bit of British and American comment suggesting that Mr. Churchill's views are not representative of British and American policy.

Most of the people here take it for granted that Mr. Churchill's speech was a clarion call to war against Russia. If one tries to tell them that he called for a firm policy, *vis-á-vis* Russia, in order to prevent war and not to provoke it, they reply with sceptical head-shaking and incredulous smiles. So many Germans, especially from the middle classes and intelligentsia, live in the constant expectation of war between the victors! So many of them believe that Germany's power would rise from the ashes through new armageddon! Obsessed with this hope, they cling to every symptom, real or illusory, that seems to confirm it.

Isaac Deutscher

SECRETS OF THE JULY PLOT

21 July 1946

Prevailing British opinion about the events which took place in Germany two years ago, on 20 July 1944, when the attempt was made to assassinate Hitler with a bomb, can be summed up under three heads. Most people believe that the affair was a 'Generals' revolt.' They assume that it had no deeper cause than the hopeless military situation of Germany, and no larger aim than to get out of the lost war cheaply. And that, since the revolt failed anyhow, it has only modest historical interest and no importance at all for the present and future.

All these three theses are false. The conspiracy had matured for several years, quite regardless of the military situation, and its aims were not short-term and opportunist but long-term and in the broadest sense political and moral.

It is true that in the actual events of the day itself, the military were most in evidence. It was, after all, they who had to be the instruments of the intended *coup d'état*. But, most of them were really instruments only, and bewildered instruments at that. A very few, such as Generals Beck and Olbricht, and especially Colonel Count Stauffenberg – who actually placed the bomb and by all accounts must have been a very extraordinary human being – formed the 'military wing' of the actual conspiracy and knew exactly what they wanted. Most of the others, half convinced and often trying to the end to run with the hare and hunt with the hounds, fumbled. It was their fumbling, even more than Hitler's lucky escape, that lost the day.

Behind them, however, stood a very different group of men, who for years had tried to drive the reluctant army forward to action, and who had prepared the plans for the political liquidation of Hitlerism which was to follow the physical liquidation of Hitler. All that was left them after the failure of the *Putsch* was to die for their cause – and die they did, hundreds of them, nearly all after prolonged torture, and nearly all with great courage and dignity.

The executions went on from the early days of August, 1944, right up to the end of April, 1945. Almost the entire political élite of anti-Nazi Germany was liquidated – leading elder statesmen and diplomatists such as Goerdeler, Count Schulenburg, Count Bernstoff, as well as those younger man on whom some of the greatest hopes for a post-Nazi Germany had rested – men like von Trott, von Moltke, Pastor Bonnhoeffer and Mgr. Delp, to name a very few only.

The history of their movement will show the gradual clear-cut, fully-worked-out political programmes that were finally laid down in August 1943 in the so-called 'Kreisauer Papers.' (Kreisau, the Silesian estate of the Moltke family, was a frequent meeting place for the conspirators). The papers, still unpublished, make saddening and fascinating reading. Saddening, because so much of their vision seems to have been lost in the chaotic, hand-to-mouth politics of quadripartite Germany. Fascinating, because their content is a peculiarly German version of European ideas which grew up simultaneously in certain groups of the French Resistance and in war-time Britain. The most striking of these ideas is that of a simultaneous development – 'inwards and outwards' – towards smaller and more intimate and at the same time towards wider and more comprehensive political units.

Would it all have worked in practice? Probably not. We have seen similar intellectual efforts of creative political thought (especially inside the French Resistance) peter out in the drab day-to-day politics of the aftermath of war. How much more disillusioning must have been the aftermath in Germany if the men of 20 July had survived, either through a successful *Putsch* or through attempting no *Putsch* at all. It was their noble purpose – born of the fantastic strain of perpetual subterfuge and constant hideous danger – to produce, immediately and almost without transition, good out of evil: a German renaissance out of the deepest German debasement; a Christian society out of a Nazi society; a united Europe out of a Europe wounded, split, and humiliated as never before; lasting reconciliation out of un-dried blood and fresh hatreds.

But their vision remains; and, fortified by their martyr's deaths, it gains a curious persistent power.   *Sebastian Haffner*

OPERATION SQUATTERS

15 September 1946

There is an ironical flavour now about the promise, subscribed to by all parties, that after the war housing would be treated as a military operation. The Government having failed to act with anything like the drive and urgency suggested by the phrase, the Communists stepped in. Their Operation Squatter, like most successful military coups, was swift and opportunist; it apparently took the enemy – the Labour Government – completely by surprise. Moreover, unlike most invasions, it will rank as a tactical success for its commanders even though it ends in retreat.

It must end in retreat: to ensure that is the Government's first task. There is no difference in principle between seizing empty houses and seizing any other kind of property, anyone who justifies it might as well justify raiding the shops. The enforcement of property laws is not a device for keeping the rich comfortable and the poor in their place; it is an essential protection against anarchy in which the weak would be at the mercy of the strong.

All this is obvious; it must be obvious to the government. The root of the trouble is that Whitehall officials and Whitehall Ministers simply cannot visualise the dreadful plight of families in blitzed towns and other places where housing is more than usually scarce. This complacent remoteness is a vice to which all Civil Services and all Governments are prone. But it is a vice peculiarly dangerous to the credit of a Labour Government which claims to be a people's Government in a special sense. The squatters' invasion should make the Government realise how badly, over housing, it has failed to live up to this claim.

THE PASSING OF THE BRITISH RAJ

10 August 1947

At midnight next Thursday British rule in India, extending back for nearly two centuries, will end: India will become two independent Dominions. There is no parallel in history for this act of statesmanship, nor for the moral and material benefits the British Raj has brought India. What the great change will mean for India herself is beyond prediction. One hope there is, however, and it is bright. In the very act of separation, Hindu and Muslim seem, by the speeches of their leaders, to have the means of agreements. The renewed threats of famine in some areas should forcibly remind Indian politicians that independence will not profit their country unless its menacing economic problems are taken promptly and firmly in hand.

HANGING AND MURDERS

30 November 1947

The study of factual evidence shows, broadly, that countries which have abolished capital punishment have not experienced a rise in the murder rate. In Holland, Denmark, Norway, Sweden and Switzerland the murder rate has fallen since the death penalty was renounced. In America, six States have abolished the penalty; in all of them the homicide rate is below the average for the United States as a whole. Of course, this evidence is not conclusive. It may be argued that the countries and States to which it applies are unusually orderly and peaceable, or that other causes have brought the murder rate down. But at least the evidence disproves the idea that there are sure to be more murders if hanging is abolished.

In the last resort a person's verdict on capital punishment must be influenced, perhaps decisively, by moral and religious considerations – by his views on the purpose of life and the meaning of death. But in voting against hanging he has no need to ignore the evidence; a substantial weight of it is on his side.

GANDHI: A LAST LOOK

1 February 1948

*Gandhi was assassinated on
30 January.*

It is the violence of Gandhi's death, this complete and contemptuous negation of everything he lived for, which is the shocking thing. Yet paradoxically, this is the aesthetic end to a life of non-violence, the end which, one imagines, the old man would have chosen for himself. I remember, in the very middle of the war, I went as a war correspondent to interview him in Delhi. It was an excessively hot afternoon and I sat cross-legged on the floor sweating through my Army uniform. Gandhi leaned back on a white bolster, wearing nothing but a loincloth, and he said amiably: 'What is the good of our talking? You and the people you represent are committed to violence. I am interested only in non-violence. We have nothing to say to one another.' I asked him if he was prepared to see the Japanese invade India (they were then very close in Burma) 'Why not?' he said. 'They can't kill us all.' He went on to propound his famous doctrine: Never oppose

'Jawaharlal Nehru and other political leaders didn't expect practical politics from Gandhi: but they were inspired by him just the same. They loved him passionately.'

violence with violence. 'Non-violence,' he said 'requires an even higher kind of courage than violence. You must be just as prepared to lay down your life – even more so.'

I remember how cheerful he was that afternoon, how healthy with his great brown barrel of a chest, and how wittily (unfortunately I have no shorthand note – there was no time to take notes) he talked.

Nor was he much changed when I went to one or two of his prayer meetings in Delhi this winter. He was still getting up at four o'clock in the morning to exercise, he was still the nimblest (and I think the gayest) good brain in India, and he was still talking in parables on precisely the same theme.

Of course he becomes a martyr now; more than that – a mystical legend and a god. It is probably a waste of time trying to assess him in Western terms. Inevitably the mysticism and the fatalism intervene, blocking out all logic. I do not think Jawaharlal Nehru and the others ever expected practical politics from Gandhi; but they were inspired by him just the same. They loved him passionately. I never met anyone in India who came away from a meeting with the old man without being captivated and in a slightly elevated condition of mind for some little time afterwards. He had an overpowering charm under that humility. He talked hard common sense as a rule and the mysticism ran between the lines. And all the furniture of his life – the robes, the fastings, and the evening prayers – was not just ballyhoo but something that came straight out of peasant India.

What happens now? It seems almost impossible to be optimistic. The country has lost its figurehead, its living public conscience. Who is to speak against racial hatred now with that authority? The British kept the peace with police and prestige, and Gandhi did it with love. Now, within six short months, both police and love have vanished together. Perhaps enough of his followers will obey his creed of non-violence. It depends on how much one believes in the sanity of human beings. Whatever the immediate effect may be, at least his influence in the long run can only be for the good. *Alan Moorehead*

THE BRITISH LEAVE PALESTINE

The State of Israel was proclaimed on 14 May 1948 and was promptly invaded by the armies of five Arab countries. The Israelis, fanatically determined and brilliantly led, had somehow managed to get arms, mainly from Czechoslovakia. By the end of the year they had won. Half a million Palestinians were beginning to drag out a miserable existence in refugee camps in surrounding Arab countries.

25 June 1948

Haifa. When General MacMillan stepped aboard his launch in Haifa harbour he was the last British soldier to quit Palestine. The launch sped across the crowded harbour, breaking across 31 years of British administration in Palestine.

It was a quick and neat operation. At first light this morning there were nearly 3000 men on the shore. The Grenadiers and Coldstreamers marched in section formation straight on to the quay and on to their troopships. They carried their bayonets fixed and their rifles loaded. Cromwell tanks stood at the cross-roads with their engines ticking over and their guns moving to and fro, feeling for danger. As the troops passed their platoon billets on the slopes of Mount Carmel, the little faded Union Jacks were whipped down and the sentries left their posts and joined in. The port was surrounded with a rim of machine-gun posts manned by men of 40 Marine Commando in full battle kit. This unit fought in Dieppe, Sicily, and Anzio and was the last to leave.

By nine o'clock the town was empty of British soldiers. The huge troopships Eastern Prince and Ocean Vigour put out to sea. Three L.C.T.s swallowed up the last of the tanks and trucks. They closed the big doors in their square bows and away they went abroad, singing and laughing like children released from a difficult term at school. As the troops closed into the port 140 specially picked Jewish policemen took over the empty camps and harbour installations. They watched the final ceremony with expressionless faces. Formally the Jews took over the harbour. The British handed over a working port. There were no demolitions. One of the Jewish port administrators said: 'Everything is in excellent condition. There has been practically no damage at all.' And an American officer supervising the withdrawal for the United Nations said 'Everything is in perfect condition – I am most impressed.' On the cookhouse wall yesterday's menu was still chalked up. A few orders still flapped on the notice-boards. A sign still pointed the way to St. Andrew's Church of Scotland. A dozen disconsolate dogs mooned around the quays, left behind by the soldiers. They alone showed any signs of regret.

Patrick O'Donovan

PATRICK O'DONOVAN (1918–1981) Joined The Observer *after the Second World War, made his name as a foreign correspondent in the late 1940s covering China, where he was one of the first journalists to recognise that Chiang Kai-shek would be defeated by Mao's revolutionary forces. Later covered Africa, the Korean War and Washington in the Kennedy years. Descriptive writer of outstanding talent, with an unerring instinct for the meaning of events.*

THE GREAT NEW UMBRELLA

4 July 1948

The vast umbrella of National Insurance opens out tomorrow simultaneously with two sister reforms, the National Health Service and National Assistance, which jointly aim at economic security for all in perpetuity.

There will be nearly 26,000,000 of us under the Insurance umbrella, an increase over the present scheme of about 4,000,000. The explanatory booklet of the National Insurance Ministry pleasantly depicts us as owls wisely roosting out of adversity's rain. We are being wise as much by compulsion as by choice. There is no opting out of millennium for anybody except the self-employed or 'non-employed' person with less than £2 a week who, after the necessary form-filling, will be excused paying his statutory 6s. 2d. a week (5s. 1d. in the case of women). Hundreds of thousands of workers in jobs hitherto excepted, and nearly as many who were barred from the old scheme because they get more than £8 a week now become weekly contributors and beneficiaries not only to the grave but (bearing in mind the £20 death

grant) beyond it also.

The parson, the G.P., the taxi driver who is hire-purchasing his taxi, the independent barrow boy, the company director with £5,000 a year, the commercial agent with commission from a dozen firms and special allegiance to none – these and all others in class 2 (self-employed) are required to go regularly to the post office, buy their stamps, stick them and date them weekly, and send their cards when they are full to the local N.I. office.

Umbrellas have spokes: also it is possible to trip over them. There are bound to be grumbles. Among the humbler ranks of the self-employed grumbling seems in certain cases to be justified. The Ministry has been invited to consider, for example, the case of the crofter weavers of the Hebrides, who, classified as sub-contractors, have to pay the higher contribution rate, namely, 6s. 2d. a week, yet, when they fall on bad times, are not entitled to a penny of unemployment benefit. There appears to be a pleasant fiction that a self-employed person, whatever his status, can never be out of work.

*D*avid Astor's wartime job in London had been liaising between Combined Ops. H.Q. and the Press. Shortly after D-Day, he had taken part in a mismanaged, disastrous airdrop in France, was wounded and spent some months in hospital. In 1946 he joined The Observer *full-time as Foreign Editor under the Acting Editor Ivor Brown. (Lord Astor had always made it clear that David would take over eventually, though 'acting' was never used publicly.)*

Astor wanted many good foreign correspondents, but six-page papers did not offer much scope for such ambitious ideas. Instead, he created the Observer *Foreign News Service, which syndicated articles to newspapers world-wide, including to the* Washington Post, Los Angeles Times *and* Melbourne Age.

This made economic sense, and provided an outlet for good stories that had been crowded out of the paper. Two such were Patrick O'Donovan's piece from Haifa in 1948, and from Hong Kong in 1949. Both first appeared in the Liverpool Post.

In 1948 Astor formally took over as editor.

OURSELVES

1 May 1949

With this issue we open a new chapter. There are some new features; we have changed the arrangement of pages so as to group kindred subjects together and give each page a distinctive character. It is perhaps an occasion for restating our policy and aims.

The Observer is an independent newspaper, bound to no party, the servant of no hidden interests, the spokesman of no special group. Some readers, not unnaturally, find this puzzling. Are we lapsed Conservatives, disguised Liberals, or subterranean Socialists? Where do our loyalties lie?

The answer is that in politics our loyalty is to the community and its free institutions. We believe profoundly in democracy because it is only through the practice of self-government that men and women can grow into responsible citizens, able, through a freely elected Parliament, to check the perils and abuses of political power.

We respect all political parties that accept these values and institutions.

Towards parties or persons with dictatorial aims, whether of the Left or Right, we are frankly hostile. Nevertheless, we inquire closely into their ideas, and on occasion we give space to reporting those of their activities which they had rather were not publicised.

In economic matters we are not dogmatic. This country, in our view, is going through a period of arduous experiment; the whole answer to our problems will not be found either in indiscriminate State control or in a reversion of *laissez faire*. We have to seek an economic system which will combine the immense productivity and elasticity of free enterprise with the social justice and stability which national planning can provide.

In foreign policy we believe that Britain must be resolutely prepared to break with many habits and traditions of the past. The nations which enjoy political freedom, are not in a majority on this earth; if they are to survive, they must progressively combine. This will require a radical change in their ways of thought and conceptions of sovereignty. They must never forget that freedom is not preserved by words, or even by treaties, but by the efforts of those who value liberty so highly that they are prepared to live and die for it. Against the ambitions of dictators the free nations must be constantly on guard, ready and equipped to act in concert before they are overwhelmed.

In one respect we differ from many newspapers. We are not devotees of doom. At a time when it is a common feeling that the world is running down from bad to worse, with some ultimate catastrophe not far ahead, we affirm our conviction that this century, though most certainly perilous, is rich in challenge, fertile with opportunities. We believe that mankind is not wretchedly living out an old epoch but breaking into a new one; the times are arduous and hazardous, but they hold a promise for those who can see it.

A TALE OF TWO ENGLISHWOMEN

Fighting between Chiang Kai-shek's Kuomintang Government and Mao Tse-tung's Communists broke out almost as soon as World War II ended. By 1947 it had developed into full-scale civil war. The People's Government was set up in Peking on 1 October 1949.

29 May 1949

I have seen two incidents in this war, incidents so small, so local, and so unimportant that neither history nor the local papers will record them. A little while ago, an Englishwoman on the edge of Shanghai had a garden and a half-timbered house with an iron lantern over the door.

One day four Nationalist soldiers strolled into the house telling the Englishwoman they had come to cut down the trees to improve their defensive position. She protested and they went. Later a captain came and, after accepting a reasonable present, he also left. The next day a colonel came and said they would at least

Street scene in Shanghai, 1949. A policeman who has just killed a Communist prisoner is photographed as he is about to shoot another.

have to remove the bamboo fence, but nothing happened for a week. Then one night a general telephoned – the Englishwoman was of some influence – and said that of course no one would touch the house or garden. The next morning the garden was filled with several hundred soldiers not only hacking down the tall trees and the little flowering ones, but scything and carefully stamping in the flowers and jumping in dozens on the little bridge until it broke, laughing like naughty children in a play pit. Others were in the house trying the breakfast. One of the house servants was bleeding about the head and all the household were too frightened to move. Two soldiers were throwing clods at the windows in a reflective way while a captain had an armchair taken to the lawn with a tin of bisuits he had

found. The Englishwoman was told she must leave at once, taking no more than a suitcase. Later she took a lorry load of goods into the city and no one stopped her for long. By threats and bribery she almost cleared the house and took the stuff into Shanghai. The captain and his men moved into the house to help defend Shanghai and the cut trees lay where they had fallen, providing even more admirable cover for an enemy. It was all perfectly traditional.

In Tientsin, a similar thing happened when the Communists arrived. But it was a new pattern for China. The Englishwoman here had a house with an orchard and a company of infantry were billeted on her. There was no refusing. They marched in and the captain took an inventory of the house. Four days later they prepared to leave and the captain

and the woman together checked the house. 'Is anything missing?' he asked. 'Nothing', she said, 'and I know of no other troops who could have behaved so correctly. Really, the only thing I can't find is a small face towel from upstairs. I am most grateful'. The captain interrupted her, paraded his men and searched their kits. One lad of nineteen had the towel, and he explained that he had packed it in error for his own. His comrades took him down to the orchard and shot him.

Apologising formally, the captain, as he left, gave the woman money for a new towel and for the burial of the young corpse at the bottom of her garden. They padded away and left the woman with a fistful of silver, and cold with horror at what had happened.

Patrick O'Donovan

*M*echtild Nawiasky, right, was hired by David Astor as The Observer's *first permanent Picture Editor, (1948-57). As Picture Editor of* Lilliput, *the pocket-sized monthly magazine, she had introduced the double-page spread of contrasting yet look-alike photographs, which brought her to Astor's attention. She was born in Austria, of Russian, French and Scottish descent.*

The first two photographers she hired were Michael Peto and Jane Bown – who learnt that she was definitely working for the paper only on receiving a telegram instructing her to report at nine a.m. next morning to photograph Bertrand Russell.

Mechtild was also involved in producing a film, Brief City, *for the 1951 Festival of Britain; and mounted* The Observer's *acclaimed Diaghilev Exhibition in 1954. She was the founder of* The Observer's *continuing reputation for brilliant photography.*

A Rebel's Progress

29 January 1950
George Orwell died on
21 January aged 46.

An English critic recently called George Orwell the most honest writer alive; his uncompromising intellectual honesty was such that it made him appear almost inhuman at times. He was merciless towards himself, severe upon his friends, unresponsive to admirers, full of understanding sympathy for those on the remote periphery, the 'crowds in the big towns with their knobby faces, their bad teeth and gentle manners; the queues outside the Labour Exchanges, the old maids biking to Holy Communion through the mists of the autumn mornings . . . '

Thus, the greater the distance from intimacy and the wider the radius of the circle, the more warming became the radiations of this lonely man's great power of love.

His life was one consistent series of rebellions both against the condition of society in general and his own particular predicament; against humanity's drift towards 1984 and his own drift towards the final breakdown. Intermittent haemorrhages marked like milestones the rebel's progress as a sergeant in the Burma police, a dishwasher in Paris, a tramp in England, a soldier in Spain. Each should have acted as a warning, and each served as a challenge, answered by works of increasing weight and stature. Shortly after *Nineteen Eighty-Four* was completed he became bed-ridden and never recovered. Now that he is dead, the time has come to recognise that he was the only writer of genius among the littérateurs of social revolt between the two wars. Cyril Connolly's remark, referring to their common pre-school days: 'I was a stage rebel, Orwell a true one,' is valid for his whole generation.

His seven books of the period 1933-9, from *Down and Out* to *Coming up for Air* all remain fresh and bursting with life, and will remain so for decades to come, whereas most of the books produced by the 'emotionally shallow Leftism' of that time, which Orwell so despised, are dead and dated to-day. As for all the pamphlets, tracts and exhortations which the war produced, hardly anything bears re-reading today – except, perhaps, E.M. Forster's *What I Believe*, a few passages from Churchill's speeches, and above all, Orwell's *The Lion and the Unicorn*. Its opening section, 'England Your England', is one of the most moving and yet incisive portraits of the English character, and a minor classic in itself.

Animal Farm and *Nineteen Eighty-Four* are Orwell's last works. No parable was written since *Gulliver's Travels* equal in profundity and mordant satire to *Animal Farm*, no fantasy since Kafka's *In the Penal Settlement* equal in logical horror to *Nineteen Eighty-Four*.

The resonance of Orwell's solitude and the quality of his despair can only be compared to Kafka's – but with this difference: that Orwell's despair had a concrete, organised structure, as it were, and was projected from individual to the social plane. And if 'four legs good, two legs bad,' is pure Swift, there is again this difference: that Orwell never completely lost faith in the knobby-faced yahoos with their bad teeth. Had he proposed an epitaph for himself, my guess is that he would have chosen these lines from Old Major's revolutionary anthem, to be sung to a stirring tune, something between *Clementine* and *La Cucuracha*:

Rings shall vanish from our noses.
And the harness from our back . . .
For that day we all must labour.
Though we die before it break;
Cows and horses, geese and turkeys,
All must toil for freedom's sake.

Somehow Orwell really believed in this. It was this quaint belief which guided the rebel's progress, and made him so very lovable, without his knowing it.

Arthur Koestler

Arthur Koestler (1905-1983) Leading proponent of The Observer's *successful campaign to end capital punishment in the late 1950s and early 1960s. Born in Budapest, educated in Vienna, travelled widely as a newspaper correspondent. Captured by the Fascists while covering the Spanish Civil War in 1937 for* The News Chronicle, *condemned to death as a spy, spent 100 days in prison waiting to be shot before being exchanged with another prisoner. Wrote in German, his first language, until he was 35, then became one of the most distinguished writers in English of this century.*

Nijinsky

9 April 1950
Vaslav Nijinsky died on
8 April, aged 60

Vaslav Nijinsky, the greatest dancer of this century, died in London yesterday. Born in 1890 in St. Petersburg, he came of a family of dancers and acrobats, and entered the ballet school of the Imperial Maryinsky theatre at the age of nine.

When Diaghilev brought Russian ballet to Paris and London in 1909 the quality of the male dancers was one of the several surprises he held in store for the western world; among these Nijinsky was pre-eminent. All agreed that his physical prowess was no less astonishing than his sublime classical style and intuitive genius for interpretation; perhaps his most fabulous feat was the seeming ability to stop still in mid-air. 'It is quite easy,' he said. 'You jump, you stay still, and then you come down.' As choreographer he created

L'Après-midi d'un Faune, Jeux and *Le Sacre du Printemps.*

History is changed by great men and women. Nijinsky made his mark on our century and retired long ago into the twilight. His death can only be regarded as a release. The Spectre of the Rose has flown out of the window and is dancing again.

Richard Buckle

McCarthy's Shadow

21 May 1950

In the past few months a sort of poison-pen campaign has rocked Washington to its foundations. The political and international implications of Senator McCarthy's campaign are very great, but the personal disruption it has caused is even more striking. This young mid-western Senator has challenged the very basis of communal life in Washington, or any small town: trust in a man's word. He has done this by accusing several hundreds of unnamed people in the Government of being Communists, or Communist sympathisers, citing many by name. Among them is no less a figure than Dean Acheson, Secretary of State.

Of course, the charges are denied, but McCarthy simply repeats them with a knowing wink, hinting that to deny that you are a Communist is such a well-known Communist trick that it almost clinches his case. At the same time he supports his charges by the evidence of ex-Communists who are prepared to swear that certain public figures were well known to them as fellow-members of the party. This 'evidence,' which is broadcast and filmed, fills columns in every newspaper. The luckless victim can only say: 'It is not true' which is undramatic, brief and, to the suspicious, quite unconvincing.

Since Alger Hiss was convicted, denial has, as McCarthy well knows, lost all validity. Hiss was a well-established, highly re-

Nijinsky as Petrouchka, one of his most celebrated roles for Diaghilev's Ballets Russes.

spected senior State Department official, who was accused of passing secret documents to the Communists. He denied the charge as absurd, and the great majority of decent, intelligent people, led by Acheson, Franfurter and Jessup, believed his denial and spoke up for him. After two trials he was convicted, and few could question the verdict. If Hiss was guilty, how can one be sure who is innocent?

To-day the capital of the United States lives under the shadow of Hiss and McCarthy. President Truman is deeply concerned about it, and it has done more than any other factor to slow up the State Department in the formulation of foreign policy.
William Clark

CITY UNDER SIEGE

Dr Daniel Malan, the creator of apartheid, had become Prime Minister of South Africa in 1948. The 1950 Group Areas Act required the establishment of separate residential areas in cities, towns and villages for Whites, Blacks, Indians and Coloureds.

17 September 1950

Johannesburg. It is as if a ragged and despairing army had laid siege to the city. In the centre, Johannesburg sits on its gold reef as massive as a mountain. On three sides there are suburbs, scarcely more permanent than army camps. They creep over the low hills, squalid and lawless. The citizens within seem hardly aware of the camps outside their walls. In fact they think they are winning the siege; the White army is on their side, and already they have out-flanked some of the Black camps, have built suburbs beyond and around them, and by the terms of the Group Areas Act, a big, undiscriminating gun, will one day force them to move on.

Of these sad dwelling places you may have heard of Sophiatown. The houses are little tattered bungalows. Women shout like sergeants down its streets, young men over-dress and go rotten. Too many people stand in the shade and do nothing. Most houses consist of a single room dominated by a bed, with perhaps a few pious pictures on the wall and a photograph of royalty.

Some 80,000 people live here, sleeping more than one family to a room. There are no drinking shops, but women brew beer in basins under their beds. Smart young men without jobs and in cheap American suits, with wide-brimmed hats turned up all the

way round, stand on corners to assault strangers or rob workers of their pay packets. Priests in this town are not called to the dying at night. They wait until morning. Among these houses there are even meaner houses. I went to one built of squashed oil drums. Its tenant leant against his door filing a piece of his bicycle. He came from Basutoland. He earned £8 a month in a dairy – fine wages for

an African. Each month he paid £1 5s. for the hutch in which he could not stand upright. He would not look up nor smile, nor in any way declare his heart. His woman was cooking in a bucket on wood, and his children were scratching naked at a game in the hard earth.

I went into one hut. A woman from Bechuanaland dressed in a blanket and suckling a child opened the door. There were holes in the roof. She had a narrow bed and a pile of blankets for three other children that slept on the floor. There was a pile of tins in the corner in which she cooked. Her husband works for the municipality; it takes him an hour and a half to get to and from his work. Such huts, adequate for chickens, filled the valley; around them the bush veld stretched away as limitless and uneventful as the sea; and above, the blue emptiness of the South African sky.

This army of rootless men has no part in the wealth or pride of South Africa. If such an Army were camped outside my city I should fear for the future of my people.
Patrick O'Donovan

Dr Daniel Malan borne shoulder-high by supporters shouting, 'Een volk, een land, een taal *[language]!*'

ASTONISHING SPLENDOUR OF THE SOUTH BANK

6 May 1951

The South Bank exhibition presides on the banks of the Thames, as English as a pudding and yet as splendid as a crown. London has seen nothing like this. It is What Might Have Been. For, in a way, it is the evocation in glass and steel of the sort of Britain the old reformers planned and that soldiers in France thought they were fighting for, where white cities stand beside clean rivers. But this is, alas, only one bombed site, and County Hall and Waterloo Station peer heavily over its coloured screens, and the mean streets of South London, the grim churches built to a budget, the pubs built for beer drinkers and the narrow houses left standing too long crowd against its gates to mock it.

The place is an enormous joke. It is light hearted and a little wry. If it had a message, it is that Britain is old but not decrepit, that its real wealth is still in its preposterous people. And every now and again the exhibition steps back from this statement and laughs at it, with a humour that is as privately made as Edward Lear or country clergymen in books.

A disembodied female hand in a court glove of purple velvet claps the White Knight's shoulder and tells him he can ride better than anyone. There is a mandoline made of matchsticks and a tiny tea-set made of salmon bones. There is a screen of illuminated drawings which light in turn to produce the British clichés. 'Oh, he was a gentleman, danced with me all night and never held me close.' (Not working yesterday morning.)

Some things give special pleasure. Inside the Land of Britain building there is a dell built round an oak tree. It has a stream, and its banks are alive with lilies of the valley and bluebells. And they are growing out of a carpet of *real dead leaves*. Above is a wall of pictures of British birds, and each in turn lights up and a recording plays its song – missel-thrush, blackbird, cuckoo and curlew. there are never fewer than 40 people standing in front of it, listening and smiling.

And there is a line of pampered farm animals, sleek Guernseys and flesh-pink pigs. There is a corner devoted to the Modern Hen, which to me looks much like the old hen. The hens live in wire cages and their eggs roll out on to a tray, and nobody tries to steal them. For this is Britain and other people are watching. Finally, there is eleven-year-old Grey Lad, a vast pneumatic shire horse. He is grey and placid and perhaps the most charmingly out of place thing on the whole South Bank. He goes back to Kent in seven days.   *Patrick O'Donovan*

Henry Moore photographed by Jane Bown. 'Sculptor, craftsman, English romantic, poet of the female principle.'

HENRY
MOORE

13 May 1951

Of the many claimants to be the 'Cinderella of the Arts' sculpture has the best case and it is remarkable to find a sculptor as the principal artistic figure of the Festival.

Henry Moore has expressed his own aims more clearly (and stylishly) than most of his commentators. In 1930 he wrote: 'The sculpture which moves me most is full-blooded and self-supporting ... It is static and strong and vital, giving out something of the energy and power of great mountains.' A fine description of the best of his own work.

It is the work of a craftsman – limited, finished, and rich in subtle variation: the work of an English romantic – instinctive and passionately attuned to nature: the work, above all, of a poet, one who sings of the female principle – the curve, the hollow and the heavy enveloping form, of the moon and the cave – a poet of rest and brooding mystery.

In some of his most recent sculpture – notably in the 'Standing Figure,' to be seen at Battersea – there is a harder, tenser feeling. Moore has by no means worked out the rich vein of his invention.   *Nigel Gosling*

The Observer's *gardening correspondent, Vita Sackville-West. Her husband, Harold Nicholson, was another Observer writer.*

IN YOUR GARDEN

13 May 1951

There is a race of little irises, flowering in April and May, too seldom grown. They do not aspire to make a great splash; their colours are frail; they grow only six to twelve inches high; they must be regarded as intimate flowers, to be peered into and protected from the vulgar slug. I am referring to miniature versions of the Bearded Iris. If you can buy what nurserymen usually call *Iris pumila* you will get a reward. They cost about 1s. 6d. each. Having paid this price, where is it best to plant them? I have grown a patch of them in a stone sink for some ten years and they have never flowered better than this year. The behaviour of plants is indeed inexplicable. It breaks all the rules; and that is what makes gardening so endlessly various and interesting.

I have come to the conclusion, after many years of sometimes sad experience, that you cannot come to any conclusion at all. But one simple thing I have discovered in gardening: It is many plants do better if they can get their roots under stones. May I suggest that you might plant your little early irises into the cracks between paving or along the edges of a paved path, where they will not be walked on? They are so unobtrusive and take up so little room that their few weeks of flowering-life entitle them to a place where they can subsequently grow forgotten.
                                  V. Sackville-West

Victoria (Vita) Sackville-West (1892-1962)
Novelist, poet and travel-writer. Creator of the famous garden at Sissinghurst in Kent. Contributed a distinguished series of gardening articles to The Observer.

Katherine Hepburn, Humphrey Bogart (and director John Huston)
'rarely let the spectator's interest falter.'

'THE DAY OF THE TRIFFIDS'

26 August 1951

The Day of the Triffids is such a very jolly and exciting piece of – I suppose one should call it science-fiction, that it recalls the great days of H. G. Wells. Mr Wyndham pictures an England in which nearly everyone has been blinded by a single act and giant vegetables of infinite malevolence stalk the land. The hero's private

story is quite as good and thrilling as the broader ingenuity, and a good time can be had by any reader who likes this kind of phantasmagorical catastrophe, including those who may care to speculate on the reason for the recent appearance of so many novels based on the end of our civilisation.

Marghanita Laski

LOVE AND LEECHES

6 January 1952

The New Year has got off to a spanking start with *The African Queen*, which delighted its first audience and will certainly go on to delight more.

The story is based on an early novel by C. S. Forester, and has the beauty of direct simplicity. An English missionary (Robert Morley) and his prim, missish sister are working among the natives of East Africa at the outbreak of the 1914-1918 war, when the village is fired by the Germans. The missionary dies. The sister makes her escape down-river with the only other white man in those parts, the skipper of a wheezing, Emett steamboat called The African Queen.

Little by little, under the influence of their enforced companionship, and in the excitement of combating rapids, crocodiles, Germans, mosquitoes, mudflats, engine trouble, torrential rains and leeches, the lady loses her missishness and becomes a tough campaigner. She discards her cotton gloves, her picture hat, her buttoned boots, her whaleboned blouse, and gets down to work in her frilly underwear. Nor does her enterprise stop there, for it is she, and not the skipper, who conceives the idea of attaching makeshift torpedoes to The African Queen, and blowing up the German gunboat that guards the lake between the river and the estuary.

Except that the pair fall in love during their long and adventurous voyage, that is really all there is to the story; but of this little, Mr Huston, Mr Bogart, and particularly Miss Hepburn, manage to make a great deal, and rarely let the spectator's interest falter. We always knew that Miss Hepburn was a dab hand with the timing of a comic line, but it is a long while since she gave us so much heart and tenderness in a role. To sustain such a long and complex part without a fault, and keep the character constantly developing, is something of a *tour de force*. My only regret is that the *The African Queen* should be crowned by a gimcrack climax aboard the German gunboat. But for that, and an early comedy scene about stomach-rumblings that keeps the joke going twice too long, *The African Queen* seems to me a splendid picture.

C. A. Lejeune

THE KING I KNEW

10 February 1952

The death of King George the Sixth last week came as a great shock to all his people. I had had the privilege of serving him as a Minister for eleven years, during the last six years of which I was Prime Minister. During this latter period there was seldom a week in which I did not see him to discuss affairs of State. The longer I served him the greater was my admiration, respect and affection. No Prime Minister had a kinder or more considerate master.

The functions of Kingship have changed during the centuries from the times when Kings not only reigned but ruled, but it would be a mistake to think that constitutional monarchy does not demand high qualities from the occupant of the Throne. On the contrary, the constitutional head of a democracy has an exacting task. He needs to have a broad and sympathetic appreciation of the feelings of the people, for he is in a special sense their representative. King George was, I think, fortunate in not being born to succeed to the Throne. He was able to live a life more like that of his future subjects. He served as an officer in the Navy during the First World War. Subsequently he was interested in industrial welfare and in boys' camps, and he acquired a wider knowledge of industrial conditions and social and economic questions than is usual in a member of a Royal House. He was happily married and could enjoy family life without the heavy responsibilities that fall upon a King. He was called to the throne in circumstances that must have caused him distress. It is a tribute to him and to Her Gracious Majesty the Queen Mother that they so soon established themselves firmly in the hearts of the people.

King George had in a high degree the qualities which are required in a constitutional Monarch. I think that I would put first his great sense of duty. Few people perhaps realised how hard he worked; they did not know the close attention which he gave to every side of public affairs. Masses of telegrams, reports and other State papers came before him and he never treated them perfunctorily. I was always careful to be up to date in my reading whenever I went to see him, for I knew that he would be well informed on everything, whether foreign or domestic. He often told me how surprised visiting statesmen were at the extent of his knowledge. 'They don't seem to realise I have to work,' he would say. I knew, too, that I would always get from him a well-balanced judgement.

I think I would put next his courage. Physical courage, of course, he had to the full, as he showed in two wars, and most notably when he was stricken with illness. He faced the danger of an operation with complete calm. But he also had moral courage. He was not afraid to take difficult decisions. Throughout his life he was sustained by his strong religious faith.

King George had great personal charm. He had a ready

Three queens – Mary, Elizabeth the Queen Mother, and Elizabeth II – waiting at Westminster Hall for George VI's lying-in-state.

sense of humour and was a delightful host. He never in any way derogated from dignity, but at the same time he freed one from any feeling of awkwardness or constraint. He was broadminded and tolerant. It cannot have been easy for him to have had a government pledged to make sweeping changes, but he accepted the position. I never knew him to depart from strict constitutional propriety. Whether or not he agreed with the policy of the Labour Government, he understood very well the reasons for it.

The earlier part of his reign was overshadowed by the growing menace of Hitlerism. Then came the long strain of the war and, later, the tensions of the period in which we live. I think that this continual anxiety weighed upon him. Looking round the world situation he saw all too few bright spots and far too many clouds on the horizon. He had, on the other hand, a happy family life, and he knew how great was the affection in which he was held by his peoples throughout the Commonwealth and Empire.

C. R. Attlee

THE NEXT EIGHTY YEARS

18 May 1952

My last ten years, according to the Scriptures, ought to have consisted of labour and sorrow, but in fact I have had less of both than in most previous decades. The world takes a lot of getting used to, and I have only lately begun to feel more or less at home in it.

My early youth was passed at the very summit of the Victorian epoch. I saw Disraeli driving to the opening of Parliament in 1879. In Paris I went to tea with Whistler and there met the poet Mallarmé.

England in those days was still aristocratic. Country houses and town houses retained all their pomp. Democracy had begun to exist as a theory, but not as something that coloured people's everyday thoughts. There was an old Duchess of Cleveland whom I knew who was outraged by the institution of Bank Holidays and exclaimed acidly, 'What do the poor want with holidays? They ought to work.' This was thought a little extreme even in those days.

I well remember the first crack in the imposing aristocratic façade. It was when Keir Hardie, came to the House of Commons in a cloth cap instead of a top hat. When it was found that no thunderbolt struck him down for this impiety, strange new doubts began to germinate in men's minds. The flood of revolution was let loose. The landed aristocracy was reduced to a ruin which began with Lloyd George's Budget. Those who had thought that the poor ought to work became themselves poor.

The revolution which has taken place in the social life of England has been accomplished without the use of the guillotine or the concentration camp, though it has been more profound than anything that the guillotine achieved in France. And as the great have lost status in England, so England has lost status in the world. For old people like myself the mental adjustments involved have not been easy. I have two entirely different visions of the future,

Bertrand Russell, philosopher, mathematician, writer, pacifist, photographed by Jane Bown in 1949. He died in 1970, aged 98.

according as I happen to feel cheerful or the reverse.

On gloomy days I foresee a third world war in the near future, lasting for years and ending indecisively after unparalleled destruction. In the course of these struggles I see Western Europe with its cities reduced to rubble and its countryside transformed into a radio-active desert. I see the total expulsion of all white men from Africa, and Asia rendered even poorer than at present by internal strife. I see Latin America throwing off the yoke of the United States and reverting to barbarism. I see the United States shorn of power, surviving like the Byzantine Empire as the last fading glimmer of a more civilised age, endeavouring to survive behind defensive walls and living on old ideas which the rest of the world will regard as archaic. This is what I see on a gloomy day.

On cheerful days I see a quite different vision. I see Russia and America gradually growing less suspicious of each other, and arriving at last at the point where a genuine accord is possible. I see an international authority more capable than the United Nations of enforcing its will upon recalcitrant members, and therefore able to make world peace secure. I see Communism losing its fierceness and white men learning to acquiesce in equality for those of different pigmentation. I see science at last allowed to bring to mankind the happiness it is capable of bringing, instead of the universal death and destruction which is now threatened.

I do not know which of these two visions has the greater likelihood of being realised. What does seem to me nearly certain is that things must get either much better or much worse. Man has survived hitherto because his ignorance and incompetence have made his folly ineffective. Now that science has shown us how to make folly effective we must abandon folly or perish.

Bertrand Russell

A Disintegrating Society

23 November 1952

An hour after sunset you can drive out of the bustling brightly lit centre of Nairobi for fifty miles into the Kikuyu country without seeing a single African or a flicker of light anywhere. The curfew imposed under the colony's state of emergency draws a heavy curtain over the silent countryside. A special police pass is required to get past guards. Even the African member of the Legislative Council, one of eight Kikuyu business and professional men at a party, arrived late: his official pass had not prevented the guard from taking him to the police station for questioning.

The attitude of these eight men was that the campaign against Mau Mau was necessary. 'But,' they asked, 'is it necessary to treat all Kikuyu like criminals, including those of us who have publicly offered to help fight Mau Mau?' Since the emergency was declared five weeks ago every Kikuyu has been treated as guilty unless he could prove himself innocent of Mau Mau connections. This policy has made the Kikuyu feel that the whites have branded them indiscriminately.

The 'Kukes' as they are called half in contempt and half in affection, comprise one quarter of Kenya's population of 5,500,000 Africans and occupy an area of roughly 2,000 square miles. They have acquired the reputation of being trouble-makers, but they are also recognised to be among the most intelligent and skilful tribesmen in East Africa. A cold war has been going on between the Kikuyu and the whites for thirty years. The primary cause is the Highlands, reserved exclusively for white occupation, that border on Kikuyuland.

And many of the whites have too glib an explanation for the resentment. 'The Kukes,' they say, 'aren't really bad chaps, you know; the trouble is the people behind them.' And, of course, everybody knows who they are. They are the Communists, or they are the Asians, 'who want to turn Kenya into a colony of India,' or they are Fenner Brockway and his Fabian comrades in London.

There is agreement among many settlers and civil servants that the present trouble is caused not by any domestic difficulties inside Kenya's plural society but by external factors. This avoids the need to answer awkward questions. The settlers who adopt this attitude do not have to decide why so many Kikuyu peasants have been prepared to take an anti-White oath; why there is a vendetta against the Government-appointed 'chiefs', or why the Administration knows so little about what has been happening inside Kikuyuland.

One has the impression that these questions spring from the fact that the Kikuyu peasant society is in a painful process of disintegration. Its old values and loyalties are being destroyed and nothing worth while has been put in their place. Among the peasants on the overcrowded lands has grown up a curious Kikuyu patriotism, and among the landless peasants in the white areas, a vigorous sense of nationalism which feeds on racial discrimination. The impact of this new spirit of African nationalism on tribal patriotism has produced Mau Mau.

Until the arrival of the whites the Kikuyu peasant society was based on deeply-knit family and clan loyalties. Each family jointly owned a block of land, and because the *Githaka*, the unit of land tenure, consisted partly of cultivated and partly of undeveloped land, there was room for expansion. The stability of this system depended on the availability of land to support a slowly increasing population. White settlement on the border areas closed the natural frontiers to Kikuyu expansion, and at the same time the good results of settled Government increased the rate of their population growth.

Soon there was not enough to support the people. Communal ownership began to give place to individual ownership. Fathers had to divide their land among as many sons as possible, and the 'surplus' sons went to work for the whites. The son who inherits a shamba is in a superior position to the sons who are driven into the Highlands or towns, with their uncertain employment, low wages, and racial discrimination.

The Kikuyu traditional society was democratic, and there were no chiefs. But the traditional tribal organisation was destroyed by the introduction of 'chiefs' who are, in effect, under-paid Government agents without real power, and often with little influence. The only surprising feature about Kenya is that anybody should be surprised that Mau Mau has developed. It provides an outlet for both the conscious and unconscious feelings of resentment of the Kikuyu as they see their traditional way of life being broken up and destroyed.   *Colin Legum*

COLIN LEGUM (b. 1919, S.A.)
Writes with unparalleled authority on Third World affairs, especially African. Consulted by most African leaders, many of whom he has known in office and/or exile.
Joined The Observer *1951.*

Mau Mau suspects waiting to be screened. 'The only surprising thing about Kenya is that anyone should be surprised that Mau Mau has developed.'

31 May 1953
*'If we look for an explanation of our political good fortune, our eyes are drawn, voluntarily or
involuntarily, towards the serene and majestic steadying power and continuity of our central
institutions; and towards the exemplary reigns of those two dedicated Kings, George V and George VI,
whose heritage is now assumed by our beloved and gracious young Queen . . . In celebrating our
Monarchy, we celebrate a triumph of the unifying, civilising and healing powers of human nature.'
from 'Monarchy revived', an unsigned leading article by Sebastian Haffner*

129

KOREA: UNFORGETTABLE FRAGMENTS

27 December 1953

Panmunjom. It is customary at the new year for broadcasters and journalists publicly to display a little optimism and a great deal of good will. Somehow this year it does not seem to settle so easily, particularly in the Far East: almost all the things I shall remember of this year were terrible. True, the Coronation made a distant rumble of splendour; but it were better that the things that stuck in the memory here should never have happened.

There was that single file of United States Marines struggling upwards to take the crown of a minor hill. They moved very slowly in a majestic uproar of explosions. They often lay pressed against the ground. They went up and lay for a little close to the dreadful summit. They came down and tried once more and then withdrew, slowly. The file was smaller when it got back.

There were three American soldiers, just back from prison, their hair still powdered with insecticide. A journalist asked the sergeant if he personally knew of anyone who had 'betrayed his buddies.' The sergeant said, 'Do you really want to know?' and the reporter said, 'Yes.' The sergeant said, 'There's one sitting right next to me,' and the wretched boy went white and scrambled off the bench and hurried through the silence out of the tent.

There were the children. The place was Seoul, and the icy wind was like a continuing physical pain. The building had been a Japanese temple and was little more than a shell. It housed some of the hungry and frequently delinquent little orphans who ran wild through the broken city. It was the most terrible place for children I have ever seen. In one room they sat in rows on the floor, huddled in blankets, and they refused to uncover their faces. The place stank of drains and boiled barley. The director was unpaid and you could not blame him because he sometimes sold things that soldiers gave for the children. When I revisited this place, a few days ago, the director had gone and the place was run by a relief organisation. Windows were mended and rice replaced the barley. The children no longer ran away. When we walked into the yard, someone blew a bugle out of a window and all the children came running out laughing, dressed approximately as Boy Scouts, to salute the flags of South Korea and America. They do it several times a day for visitors.

And then there was the hatred. Curiously, this was never so apparent during the fighting. Here at Panmunjom for fourteen months, and almost ritually, was celebrated that new and very articulate hatred that a large part of the East now feels for the West. The Communist delegates would sweep past with set expressions. Their journalists would wait with us on the same road and, with the exception of the two English-speaking ones who had their mission to perform, they would speak to no one. Each man stood alone, took no notes, almost as if wrapped in some private sorrow. The conference concerned peace, but there was no trace of the behaviour that visitors to youth festivals report.

At Panmunjom the delegates merely registered and administered the calculated moves that had been made elsewhere. But if anyone still believes that things are not terribly changed in the Far East, a few visits to this village that no longer exists would be enough to convince him. Of course, one could certainly find something more appropriate to the season in the quiet beauty of Japan, in the activities of soldiers at Christmas time, or in the shining good intentions of the Indians who came to help. But these things happened in Korea, and Korea was the outward and visible sign of the world's deep sickness. And to write of anything else from this part of the world would seem a little insincere and silly.

Patrick O'Donovan

Prisoners-of-war crouching on the ground in Korea – 'the outward and visible sign of the world's deep sickness.'

'LUCKY JIM'

24 January 1954

Lucky Jim, by Kingsley Amis, is one of the brightest books that has been published in Britain since *Decline and Fall*. This is one of the rarest of novels in that it is both comic and true. Mr. Amis's achievement is to have made the gayest of bricks with the most common straw, some of it very crumby and dusty indeed.

His hero, or anti-hero, is a history lecturer in a provincial English university, insecure in his job, which he is quite unfitted to hold, and thereby fated to suffer every possible sort of deserved and undeserved discomfiture. It may suggest to the reader the sort of young man he is to say that he is a grown-up version of *The Catcher in the Rye*, that unique piece of adolescent comedy by J. D. Salinger. It is typical modern satire in that its butt is not wickedness but kindness, idealism, goodheartedness, and even (in a mild sense) heroism – i.e., all those noble impulses which, when misguided or unguided, turn men into sentimental mugs: the sort of people whom, for example, Marcel Aymé is always torturing on the grounds that it is such people that the toughs of the world exploit to destroy good, honest bourgeois like (I trust) you and me. The fact is, heroism has gone over from fiction into auto-biography where (the quip is Carton de Wiart's) heroes nowadays sell their 'Lives' as dearly as possible – to the public.

Only one major criticism do I wish to utter about *Lucky Jim*. Could so utterly incompetent and Chaplinesque a figure as Jim Dixon rise to as much as the post of bottle-washer, even in a provincial English university?

Sean O'Faolain

End of the Dien Bien Phu siege and of French involvement in Indo-China. Reinforcements are parachuted in to 'this awful basin whose green walls offer no hope of escape.'

A BATTERED MIRACLE

The conflict in Indo-China, with the French colonial power resisting takeover by Communist Vietminh forces from the north, came to a head with the siege of Dien Bien Phu, which lasted for 55 days and seized the attention of the world. It ended on 8 May. French involvement in Indo-China came to an end on 21 July with the Sino-French pact which divided Vietnam into north and south along the 17th Parallel.

25 April 1954

You cannot help seeing the place even under its constant artillery barrage as a comfortable little rice valley set fortuitiously among the wild green of mountainous jungle.

It takes more than shells to destroy rice fields that have served for generations, and even now defenders of Dien Bien Phu, in their bitter, persevering counter-attacks, shelter temporarily behind foot-high bunds that separate the little fields.

Dien Bien Phu is at once a military miracle and a military outrage. It defends nothing. The roads which cross in the valley are dust and will soon be mud. No town is protected by the defence of this small oasis 200 jungle miles from Hanoi.

A small Franco-Vietnamese force seizes a point that has the essential asset of an airstrip. The Vietminh, marching inexhaustible troops over jungle ridges, tries to bring up overwhelming numbers against the defenders. The French High Command reinforces: so does Vietminh. In a few weeks two armies are poised for battle.

At Hoabinh and Nasan, with bluff and courage, French managed to disengage themselves before Vietminh dared mass to attack, but General Navarre cannot evacuate Dien Bien Phu without raising the siege with a relieving force.

The surrounding mountains run up to 5,000 feet. Every move of the Franco-Vietmanese is observed by the enemy, and though the 'several thousand' parachutists stated by the French to have been dropped in since the start of the battle have done so in darkness there is little doubt the Vietminh by now know almost everything about them.

But Dien Bien Phu is a miracle of organisation even if it is a battered miracle. Before the fighting started staff officers would display with pride the cavernous excavations and wine cellars; the dugout stores that held weeks of supplies for troops with such varying diets as Moroccan, Algerian, Vietnamese and European. In the sandbagged mess the beer was icy cold, the meals far from rough, and the wine circulated rapidly. But none can help being anxious about this accident of military geography which has seized the attention of the whole world.

In the main position the Vietminh are slowly infiltrating, slowly making it harder for the Franco-Vietnamese to supply or relieve their forward posts. While casualties mount the seriously wounded, who at present have no hope of evacuation, lie underground without even sufficient light by which to read. At any one time about one third of the less injured must be in the firing line.

There is immense courage in this awful basin whose green walls offer no hope of escape and which swarm with enemy that any relief force must dislodge. Though the American-supplied fleet of Flying Boxcars can now drop in tons of supplies, the tantalising parachute so often swaying into the Vietminh lines is the only physical link for Dien Bien Phu with the outside world.

Men are dying in thousands in a battle which can never settle the dispute between Ho Chi-minh and Bao Dai but which is a classic of the Indo-China war.

Rawle Knox

Groucho, the wisecracking, cigar-chewing, writing Marx Brother – his books include an autobiography and a serious study of American income tax – photographed by Jane Bown.

MEETING GROUCHO MARX

27 June 1954

Smart women, and men in dark suits for business lunches, strolled past the mirrors and pink sofas in the hotel lounge. Mr. Marx, with lady secretary following, came across travelling fast like a shark through the shoals of porters and pageboys – a small athletic figure with pale blue suit, blue shirt, white tie, cigar between teeth and on his head a large white cap of the sort Gene Sarazen used to wear for golf. We greeted him, and together made for the door. As we approached it, he put a hand out to slow us down for a moment: 'Cricket, eh?' he said flatly and headed towards a taxi.

Our attempts at ordinary conversation seemed unnecessary as Mr. Marx sat there, looking wary and sardonic, smoking away at his cigar. We said we hoped he wouldn't be bored coming to Lord's with us, that it wasn't a very important game, just the M.C.C. playing Cambridge University – like Yale and the Dodgers – and that Cambridge would be fielding.

'Fielding?' said Mr. Marx abstractedly. 'Didn't he write *Tom Brown's Schooldays*?' Well, no, he wrote 'Tom Jones.' 'Tom Jones' Schooldays?' said Mr Marx, looking out at the Edgware road.

The taxi drew up at the Grace gates. Mr. Marx was first out. He offered to pay for the taxi, holding out a neat brown hand with two florins in it: with this gesture, somehow, everyone relaxed. We bought his and Miss Hartford's tickets.

'Come on, let's go,' he commanded. We stepped forward into the ground as he wheeled round, cigar held in front of him, travelling through the gates.

He accompanied us round the back of the silent stands, looking marvellously incongruous in his white cap. Could there really be a game on, he asked: a baseball game in New York could be heard blocks away. He glanced sideways as we passed at the notice on 'Q' stand which says Members and Friends, remarking: 'That's the most ambiguous thing I've *ever* heard.'

We rounded the back of the Pavilion and there it was. The ground was practically empty: a hundred people outside the Tavern, a few in the stands, twenty or thirty Members in front of the

Pavilion. The players, one of them an Indian in a pink turban, stood in two motionless groups waiting for a new batsman. The scoreboard said 74 for 5. The place was quite silent. It looked like rain.

We sat down in the front seat of 'A' stand: we were alone there. Mr. Marx's eyes went round. 'Is it always as crowded as this? Does it get enough money to pay for the ball?' he continued, observing the scene. 'What a wonderful cure for insomnia. If you can't sleep here you really need an analyst. Does Oxford do this too? Doesn't that Maharajah with the whiskers get tired pitching? Even the men in the tradesmen's coats are trying not to watch it. Umpires, eh?'

He noticed the small crowd in front of the Tavern, asked if that was where they put the dead bodies. We explained there was a bar there open all day. How long did the game go on? Eleven-thirty to six-thirty. 'Boy, by six-thoity they must be really loaded,' he reflected.

Would Mr. Marx like to visit the Pavilion? On the way, a spectator leaned over with his score-card. 'It is Mr. Groucho Marx, isn't it?' Groucho signed with a sudden accusation: 'Were you the guy making all the noise back there?'

As we approached the door of the Pavilion, we explained that this really was the altar of English cricket, a venerable place. 'Don't worry,' he said, 'I've met stuffed shoits before.' In the Long Room, with its air of linoleum and dignity, Groucho sniffed and looked around.

'Where's Haabs?' he asked. 'That's the only name I know in this business.' We showed him the large painting of W. G. and other portraits. Suddenly he leaned forward: 'I never knew girls played cricket.' We asked what he meant. He gestured with his cigar at an eighteenth-century painting of a boy with fair hair standing among trees and leaning on one of those curved bats.

Groucho inspected it closer. Under the painting was written: 'Youth with Cricket Bat, c. 1790.'

'Youth, huh? 1790, eh? I guess this business started earlier than we thoight.'

From time to time Mr. Marx glanced out through the closed windows at the game. 'How long can they be without running?' We said it could be a matter of days, theoretically. 'Is that so? And at night they play with phosphorescent balls?' He shook his head in wonder.

Mr. Marx was then introduced to a high official of the M.C.C., accustomed to dealing with visiting celebrities. 'You're over here on holiday, are you, Mr. Marx?' Groucho stroked his chin: 'I was until I saw this game.'

As we left, the doorman suggested that we show Mr. Marx the Museum. Groucho's eyebrows went up. The doorman reminisced enigmatically: 'We had Mr. Rockefeller here too – he used

a lot of baseball terms.' 'Ah-ha,' said Groucho, 'but he was richer than I am.'

Out in the street he bent down to make a funny noise to a child in a pushchair. He looked happy, but he had never actually smiled the whole afternoon.

The next day we called to say goodbye. There he was with Miss Hartford, standing outside the hotel waiting for a car to take him to the airport. He had on a neat brown trilby and no one recognised him.

He and Miss Hartford climbed into a large car. They had not much time to get to London Airport. As they were leaving, Groucho flung open the door. 'Can I drop you any place?' We said no, we were going in the other direction. 'Cable me the result of that game,' he called.

Michael Davie and John Gale

MARTYRDOM

31 July 1955

Have you ever dreamt that you were exposed in your shirt-tails on a brilliantly lit stage? If you have the smallest claim to be a celebrity, you may find that this nightmare has become fact in front of the television cameras. *This Is Your Life*, the B.B.C.'s latest import from America, is specially designed to transform one man's embarrassment into sentimental entertainment for the millions.

On some pretext, a famous person is decoyed to the studio. There, before cameras and audience, his past is unexpectedly retold through the testimony of people who have known him at different stages of his life.

On Friday night the programme was introduced by the American inventor, Mr. Ralph Edwards, a chubby man with the nervously jovial voice of one who used to chant forty-three commercials a week. Now he looked as though butter was positively evaporating in his mouth. His victim was Eamonn Andrews, a young Irishman who has

achieved enormous fame as a panel game chairman and sports commentator. Normally a brash, glib talker, he fell into a dishevelled silence when he was marched on to the stage. With all the dignity of a man who has just slipped on a banana skin but is determined not to show his pain, he had to listen to his mother talking about his childhood fear of bogymen, his first employer describing his promotion to assistant surveyor after four years as a junior clerk, and his wife recalling the beginning of their honeymoon. After such a half-hour of suffering Eamonn Andrews deserves to be famous – as television's first home-grown martyr.

Whether the programme deserves its reputation is less certain. Hardly one of the witnesses had anything very novel to tell us. We learned that our hero has a mother and sisters, that he used to box, that he has written a play. Only the most severe famine can excuse this willingness of the Corporation to devour its own young in a public place.

Alan Brien

New Writing

7 August 1955

Mr Samuel Beckett's *Waiting for Godot* is a dramatic vacuum: pity the critic who seeks a chink in its armour, for it is all chink. It has no plot, no climax, no *dénouement*; it has a situation, and it might be accused of having suspense, since it deals with the impatience of two tramps, waiting beneath a tree for a cryptic Mr. Godot to keep his appointment with them; but Mr Godot is not going to arrive. *Waiting for Godot* frankly jettisons everything by which we recognise theatre. It arrives at the customs house, as it were, with no luggage, no passport; yet it gets through as might a pilgrim from Mars. A play, it asserts and proves, is basically a means of spending two hours in the dark without being bored.

Its author is an Irishman living in France. Passing the time in the dark, he suggests, is not only what drama is about but also what life is about. His two tramps pass the time of day just as we, the audience, are passing the time of night. Were we not in the theatre, we should, like them, be clowning and quarrelling, aimlessly bickering and aimlessly making up – all, as one of them says, 'to give us the impression that we exist.'

Mr Beckett's tramps for the most part converse in the double-talk of vaudeville: one of them has the ragged aplomb of Mr. Buster Keaton, the other is Mr. Chaplin at his airiest and fairiest. Their exchanges are like those conversations at the next table which one almost but not quite deciphers: human speech half-heard and reproduced with all its *non sequiturs* absurdly intact. From time to time other characters intrude. Fat Pozzo, Humpty Dumpty with a whip in his fist, puffs into sight with Lucky, his dumb slave. They are clearly going somewhere in a hurry: perhaps they know where Godot is? But the interview subsides into Lewis Carrollian inanity. Lucky stammers out a ghostly, ghastly, interminable tirade, compounded of cliché and gibberish.

The play sees the human condition in terms of baggy pants and red noses. Hastily labelling their disquiet disgust, many of the first-night audience found it pretentious. What vexed the play's enemies was, I suspect, the opposite: it was not pretentious enough to enable them to deride it. I care little for its enormous success in Europe over the past three years, but much for the way in which it pricked and stimulated my own nervous system. It forced me to re-examine the rules which have hitherto governed the drama; and, having done so, to pronounce them not elastic enough. It is validly new: and hence I declare myself, as the Spanish would say, *godotista*.

Kenneth Tynan

Beckett's play 'forced me to re-examine the rules which have hitherto governed the drama.'

KENNETH TYNAN (1927-1980) *One of the most influential theatre critics of the post-Second World War period. Joined* The Observer *in 1954 after stints on* The Spectator, Evening Standard *and* Daily Sketch. *His years as a critic coincided with the early triumphs of the supposedly 'angry' new school of dramatists led by John Osborne, and he became identified with the drama of social protest. He was one of the first British critics to popularise the ideas of Brecht. His greatest gift, however, was the ability to record with extraordinary liveliness the texture of a theatrical performance. Became literary manager of the National Theatre, returning to* The Observer *in 1964 for a couple of years as a film critic.*

THE QUIET AMERICAN

4 December 1955

We are off again on one of those brief and captivating trips which are periodically conducted for us by the most deftly courteous of all modern novelists. How adroit he is, with his introduction of local colour, his subtle preliminary arrangement of atmosphere and situation! There is no English writer who knows better how to lead his reader irresistibly onward. He engages us to such an extent that criticism is unthinkable until many hours after the book has been closed and the marvellous spell has been removed.

And yet . . . And yet I *will* rub my eyes and write that every single one of Graham Greene's recent novels has suffered from a fatal moral flaw, a fault of both feeling and argument which only his astonishing literary skill could for an instant disguise from us.

His latest novel, *The Quiet American*, is riven by a fault in the psychological argument which is serious and destructive. The scene is Indo-China during the early stages of the French war against the Vietminh. The narrator is an English journalist, one of those world-weary, sardonic figures with whom we have become so familiar from the private-eyes of Californian fiction. In the strongest possible contrast to this tired and sophisticated cynic is the figure of Pyle, the Quiet American.

Pyle, with his crew-cut and his innocence and his ignorant good intentions, is a believer in Third Forces everywhere – forces of honest democrats who will oppose with equal vigour both the Imperialists and the Communists. Against the weary wisdom of the narrator Pyle supplies plastic bombs to an absurd terrorist called General Thé, in the belief that this self-interested bandit will use them in the cause of Third-Force democracy. The result is a disgusting and useless massacre of civilians – instead of the massacre of French and Vietnamese soldiers which Pyle had hoped for. Fowler, the narrator, moving at last into dubious acton, organises the murder of the unrepentant Pyle.

The main moral thesis of the book is concerned with Pyle. Mr Greene wishes to demonstrate the dreadful results of opinionated innocence, the hells which lie fatally ahead of ignorant good intentions. But Pyle is all wrong. Pyle is a monstrous and impossible combination of two opposing forms of moral error. As an innocent, and above all as an American innocent, he would never have indulged in terrorism. His blunders would have taken a different and far more high-minded shape – with results perhaps no less calamitous.

Mr. Greene has mixed up his quiet American with the distorted monsters of *The Possessed* and the brutalised commissars of Koestler. He has mixed up the error of *naïveté* with the error of too much experience, the error of ignorance with the error of heartlessness. This emerges with particular sharpness at the moment when Pyle contemplates the bodies mutilated by his bomb and resolves to make more efficient use of his next one. It is not in character. It is not consistent with the moral thesis of the book.

On every level except the most important one this is a magnificent novel. But Graham Greene is a novelist who must be judged on the most important level.

Philip Toynbee

PHILIP TOYNBEE (1916-1981) Joined The Observer *in 1950, serving first as foreign correspondent, then as one of the most respected literary reviewers of his day. His contributions helped to create the special quality of the paper's book pages. Author of* Friends Apart, *a classic memoir of the 1930s (non-treasonable) Left.*

Graham Greene 'engages us to such an extent that criticism is unthinkable until many hours after the book has been closed.'

RICHARD III

18 December 1955
Laurence Olivier's Richard III is the deep-dyed villain of the Tudor chroniclers; a hunch-backed monster with a withered arm; a long-distance planner who waded to the throne through seas of blood, and died at Bosworth fighting like a demon and shouting for a horse. Olivier plays him like a demon king in pantomime; thin-lipped, skulking, gamesome, fascinating, intoxicated with evil, and always ready to share the fun with others. He inducts the cinema audience in new ways of utter wickedness, with a whisper behind the hand, an ingratiating smile and wink.

It shows great courage in Oliver that he has yielded not an inch to modern sentiment, and has tried to film a play of Shakespeare's in such a way as to re-

Laurence Olivier, unforgettable in the title role of Richard III, a milestone in British cinema. As director and producer he 'inducts the audience in new ways of utter wickedness'.

create the impact made on a popular audience of 400 years ago.

Olivier may have savaged the play's text, but he has cut deep and true to the play's spirit. As a director he grows in stature film by film. 'Richard III' is full of moments one will remember. The deliberate use of shadowplay; bleak country rides through the snow; the long look exchanged between Hastings and Jane Shore across King Edward's deathbed; the terrifying partnership between Richard and Buckingham, and its chill ending; Mary Kerridge's face as she gazes through the window towards her children in the Tower; the wicked jollity of two kind uncles leading a boy to murder hand-in-hand; the superb shot in which the sweep of a sword in the dust brings up dragon's seed; the hostile circle closing on a single man; the galvanic throes which will never let anyone who watched them forget that King Richard III died horribly at Bosworth.

The more I consider it, the more highly I regard this film.

C. A. Lejeune

REFLECTIONS ON HANGING

5 February 1956

Great Britain is that peculiar country in Europe where people drive on the left side of the road, measure in inches and yards, and hang people by the neck until dead.

On 2 November 1950, Mr. Albert Pierrepoint was called to testify as a witness before the Royal Commission on Capital Punishment. He was asked how many people he had hanged in his career as an executioner, and answered: 'Some hundreds.'

Q. Have you had any awkward moments? *A.* No, I have only seen one in all my career.

Q. What happened? *A.* He was rough. It was unfortunate; he was not an Englishman . . . and he kicked up rough. In short, hanging is all right for Englishmen.

At the beginning of the nineteenth century British criminal law, known as the Bloody Code, was a unique curiosity. It listed between 220 and 230 offences to be punished by death, from murdering the king to stealing a turnip, from the sex-slaying of a child to damaging a fishpond, associating with gipsies, writing threatening letters, impersonating out-pensioners at Greenwich Hospital.

There were about one hundred public executions a year in London and Middlesex alone; and London craftsmen were wont to apologise to their customers with a shrug: 'That will be a hanging day and the men will not be at work.' The crowds assembled at the 'Tyburn Tree' (Now Marble Arch) sometimes amounted to 100,000 and more.

Children were publicly hanged from the age of seven upward if there was 'strong evidence of malice,' because malice was considered by the Law 'to supply age', without strong evidence of malice, the age limit was fourteen. Greville describes the trial of several young boys who were sentenced to death 'to their excessive amazement' and broke into tears. He laconically remarks: 'never did I see boys cry so.' The last cases on record are: Andrew Brenning, aged thirteen, publicly hanged in 1801 for stealing a spoon; a girl of *seven*, hanged in 1808 at Lynn for an unknown offence; a boy of nine, hanged in 1831 at Chelmsford for arson, and another aged thirteen, hanged for an unknown crime in the same year at Maidstone. The philosophy behind all this may be gathered from the following:

In 1748, William York, a boy of ten, was sentenced to death for murder. Chief Justice Willis postponed the execution to find out whether it was proper to hang the child. All the judges concurred that it was, for it would be a very dangerous consequence to have it thought that children may commit such atrocious crimes with impunity . . . 'Though the taking away the life of a boy of ten years old may savour of cruelty, yet as the example of this boy's punishment may be *a means of deterring other children from the like offences* . . .' [italics mine].

That was a century-and-a-half ago: but compare the arguments with Lord Goddard's summing-up to the jury in the case of Craig, sixteen, and Bentley, nineteen. It will be remembered that Craig, at sixteen, could not read and that Bentley was a Grade Four mental deficient.
'Now let us put out of our minds in this case any question of films, or comics, or literature of that kind. These things are prayed in aid nowadays when young prisoners are in the dock, and they have very little to do with the case. These two young men – boys or whatever you like to call them – are both of an age which makes them responsible to the law . . . '

At the beginning of the eighteenth century there were no more than fifty capital offences. At the beginning of the nineteenth, there were five times as many. This was one of the by-products of the Industrial Revolution. The new urban proletariat of wage earners, uprooted from their rural existance, were transformed into a race of shiftless slum-dwellers. The spreading of extreme poverty with its concomitants of prostitution, child labour, drunkenness and lawlessness, coincided with an unprecedented accumulation of wealth as an additional incentive to crime. To counter public insecurity, Parliament resorted to emergency legislation, with hanging as the all-cure for every new type of offence. This development continued, with gathering momentum, until a new remedy was found: the modern police force, which Sir Robert Peel created in 1829.

Had this been done a century earlier, the whole shame and terror could have been avoided. The reason why it was not done was the fear that a regular police force, once established, would be used to curtail his individual and political freedom.

In the fifteenth and sixteenth centuries, most European countries adopted written codes based on the Roman Law, in replacement of their old customary 'common law' or 'folk-law'. A second wave of codification swept over Europe in the wake of the *Code Napoleon*. England alone has adhered to this day to Common Law. The benefits of the Common Law were enormous. Continental law was *inquisitorial*, English law *accusatory*; it admitted of no pressure being exercised on the accused. Hence the superiority of English judicial procedure in giving the accused a fair trial.

But these benefits were heavily paid for. Dislike of regimentation by the police was a major cause of the prevalence of the hangman; dislike of law by code and statute left English legislation at the mercy of the wigged oracles who, since precedent must be their only guidance, by the very nature of their calling had their minds riveted on the past. They not only administered the law; they made it. Elsewhere no such monopoly existed: the law was codified, the judges doled it out for better or worse, but they had no power to make it. Penal legislation on the Continent reflected the social currents of the time; England alone let herself be guided by an ex-

clusive class of alleged experts who, like the medieval alchemists, lived in a mysterious world of secret formulae, impervious to changing conditions.

In 1810, Samuel Romilly brought in a Bill to abolish the death penalty for shoplifting to the value of five shillings and over. The Bill was passed by the Commons and defeated by the House of Lords on no fewer than six occasions, in 1810, 1811, 1813, 1816, 1818, and 1820. In the first Lords debate on the Bill, in 1810. In 1822, Chief Justice Lord Tenterden, defended the death penalty for horse- and sheep-stealing with that traditional bray of the learned asses: 'We have at present in this country no substitute for the punishment of death.' In 1883 Sir James Stephen

demanded the reintroduction of the death penalty for forgery and the receiving of stolen goods, and added:

'These views, it is said, are opposed to the doctrine that human life is sacred. I have never been able to understand what the doctrine means, or how its truth is alleged to be proved.'

That last sober phrase sums up the attitude of the oracles from the sixteenth century to this day. The terror of the French Revolution preserves in retrospect the grandeur of a tragic but essential chapter of history. The terror of the Bloody Code was wanton and purposeless, alien to the character of the nation, imposed on it, not by fanatical Jacobins, but by a conspiracy of wigged fossils.

Arthur Koestler

*1*956 was a climactic year. In February, at a secret session of the Twentieth Soviet Congress, Khrushchev denounced Stalin in astonishing detail. The Observer got a copy, the scoop of scoops and ran all 26,000 words of it in one issue (10 June). Also in June the Poles rose against their Communist masters and gained a measure of freedom. In November the Hungarians also rose and were brutally put down. The Observer's Lajos Lederer was there to give an eye-witness account. In November too the paper strongly attacked the Prime Minister, Sir Anthony Eden over Suez, for which it suffered a severe drop in readership and income.

The year had started with five page-long pieces by Arthur Koestler on capital punishment – the first of which starts on page 138 – the climax of the paper's long campaign. Louis Blom-Cooper, QC, writes: 'The campaign had a marked effect on MPs of all parties. The fact that about two-thirds of all murders are committed by individuals within the domestic circle brought home the absurdity, not to say gross injustice of applying the ultimate sanction.'

THE VOICE OF THE YOUNG

13 May 1956

'They are scum,' was Mr. Maugham's famous verdict on the class of State-aided university students to which Kingsley Amis's *Lucky Jim* belongs; and since Mr. Maugham seldom says anything controversial or uncertain of wide acceptance, his opinion must clearly be that of many. Those who share it had

better stay well away from John Osborne's *Look Back in Anger*, which is all scum, and a mile wide.

Its hero is a provincial graduate who runs a sweet-stall. With his flair for introspection, his gift for ribald parody, his contempt for 'phoneyness,' his weakness for soliloquy and his desperate conviction that the time is out of joint,

Jimmy Porter is the completest young pup in our literature since Hamlet, Prince of Denmark. His wife, whose Anglo-Indian parents resent him, is persuaded by an actress friend to leave him: Jimmy's prompt response is to go to bed with the actress. Mr. Osborne's picture of a certain kind of modern marriage is hilariously accurate: he shows us two attractive young animals engaged in competitive martyrdom, each with its teeth sunk deep in the other's neck, and each reluctant to break the clinch for fear of bleeding to death.

The fact that he writes with charity has led many critics into the trap of supposing that Mr. Osborne's sympathies are wholly with Jimmy. Nothing could be more false. Jimmy is simply and abundantly alive; that rarest of dramatic phenomena, the act of original creation, has taken place; and those who carp were better silent. Is Jimmy's anger justified? Why doesn't he *do* something? These questions might be relevant if the character had failed to come to life; in the presence of such evident and blazing vitality, I marvel at the pedantry that could ask them. Why don't Checkhov's people *do* something? Is the sun justified in scorching us? There will be time enough to debate Mr. Osborne's moral position when he has written a few more plays. In the present one he certainly goes off the deep end, but I cannot regard this as a vice in a theatre that seldom ventures more than a toe into the water.

Look Back in Anger presents post-war youth as it really is, with special emphasis on the non-U intelligentsia who live in bed-sitters and divide the Sunday papers into two groups, 'posh' and 'wet'. To have done this at all would be a signal achievement; to have done it in a first play is a minor miracle. All the qualities are there, qualities one had despaired of ever seeing on the stage – the drift towards anarchy, the instinctive leftishness, the automatic rejection of 'official' attitudes, the surrealist sense of humour (Jimmy describes a pansy friend as 'a female Emily Brontë'). The casual promiscuity, the sense of lacking a crusade worth fighting for and, underlying all these, the determination that no one who dies shall go unmourned.

One cannot imagine Jimmy Porter listening with a straight face to speeches about our inalienable right to flog Cypriot

John Osborne, author of Look Back in Anger, *which exploded into the public's consciousness after Kenneth Tynan's review.*

schoolboys. You could never mobilise him and his kind into a lynching mob, since the art he lives for, jazz, was invented by Negroes; and if you gave him a razor, he would do nothing with it but shave. The Porters of our time deplore the tyranny of 'good taste' and refuse to accept 'emotional' as a term of abuse; they are classless, and they are also leaderless. Mr. Osborne is their first spokesman in the London theatre. He has been lucky in his sponsors (the English Stage Company), his director (Tony Richardson), and his interpreters: Mary Ure, Helena Hughes and Alan Bates give fresh and unforced performances, and in the taxing central role Kenneth Haigh never puts a foot wrong.

That the play needs changes I do not deny: I agree that *Look Back in Anger* is likely to remain a minority taste. What matters is the size of the minority. I estimate it at roughly 6,733,000, the number of people in this country between the ages of twenty and thirty. And this figure will doubtless be swelled by refugees from other age-groups who are curious to know precisely what the contemporary young pup is thinking and feeling. I doubt if I could love anyone who did not wish to see *Look Back in Anger*. It is the best young play of its decade.

Kenneth Tynan

THE KHRUSHCHEV EXPOSURE OF STALIN

*T*he production of The Observer's *issue of 10 June 1956 is one of the strangest, most stirring stories in journalism. The credit belongs to three men: Our Man On Russia, Edward Crankshaw, who got his hands on the crucial document; David Astor, who bore the ultimate responsibility; most of all, the Managing Editor, Kenneth Obank, who had the idea and the seemingly impossible task of putting it into effect.*

It began on Thursday, 7 June, typically for The Observer *of that time, in the Waldorf Hotel, where a small editorial lunch was held every week. Crankshaw, according to an eyewitness, 'modestly mentioned that he had obtained complete transcripts of Khrushchev's speech'. For all the modesty this was obviously a scoop among scoops and, the eyewitness goes on, 'it was agreed to run the lot, 26,000 words, in next Sunday's paper, despite the appalling obstacles'.*

The eyewitness was Obank; no one knew more about the technical, physical difficulties. This was decades before computer setting. Stories had to be set in hot metal on Linotype machines and transferred to galleys and thence into formes, to be made up into pages.

By now, Thursday, in Ken Obank's words, 'half the paper had been set, corrected and was being made up. Worse, we found that we would have to hold out almost all the regular features – book reviews, arts, fashion, bridge, chess, leader-page articles, the lot.

'The Khrushchev copy, page by page, began flowing. As we began making up pages it became clear that still more space would be needed, so we gulped and turned to the sacred cows – the advertisements. The printer Bill Aylott, kept count with, literally, a piece of string, measuring galley after galley of Khrushchev in Fleet Street metal.

'At the first count the General Manager patiently surrendered two precious columns of adverts. At a second count, some hours later, we squeezed two more columns out of him, pained but ungrudgingly. I had to ring him at home after the third and final count. It was nearly midnight. I desperately needed three more columns. The response was better than I feared. "What are you doing to us?" he said, wearily. I felt I was squeezing the revenue out his own bones. "Don't call me again, will you?"

'In the meantime Ronald Harker [head of The Observer Foreign News Service *and Night Editor on Saturdays] and I had been writing a seemingly endless number of page headlines, sub-headings, cross-heads, and captions, planned to match the copy as it wound its way through the paper.*

That issue won the paper the first of its three awards organised by Printing World *under the patronage of the Linotype Corporation for Best-designed Newspaper of the Year'. After two more awards, in 1957 and 1962,* The Observer *was asked to withdraw from the contest.*

Letters from readers in response were highly favourable. They included:

Sir, I am just a chargehand in a factory, hardly a place where you might expect The Observer *to have a large circulation. But my copy of the Khrushchev edition has been going from hand to hand and from shop to shop in the administration offices, transport etc.*

Those of use who have followed events in the Soviet Union for the last thirty years, Communist Party members and non-Communists, as well as the youngsters who come to work in drainpipe pants, have all read most of the speech. I was quite amazed at the serious interest shown as a result of the very minute examination of the speech.

Sir, I was profoundly shocked that you had the impertinence to publish Mr. Khrushchev's speech in English. It was a grave mistake to underestimate your readers and not publish it in the original Russian. I hope you will not do it again.

When Obank retired, in 1979, David Astor wrote: 'For over thirty years Kenneth Obank has played the central role in the journalistic life of The Observer. He *has contributed more towards building up the character and competence of the paper than anyone else. Apart from his technical contribution he has infused an energy, liveliness and a downright honesty into the paper that has been invaluable. He has managed to remain lovable and human throughout this marathon of journalistic achievement.'*

ANTHONY EDEN AND SUEZ

In July 1956 the Americans and British cancelled their shares in the World Bank loan raised by Nasser to pay for building the Assuan High Dam. The deal fell through and Nasser announced that he would nationalise the Suez Canel and use the revenues to build the dam. Months of international wrangling followed. On 29 October the Israelis invaded Sinai. Britain and France issued an ultimatum to stop fighting – despite Government denials there was certainly collusion; probably no one will ever know how much. Israel accepted the ultimatum, Egypt refused, and HMG sent in the bombers. The leading article that follows appeared on 4 November. Next Sunday the paper said that of the 1,227 letters in response, eight hundred and sixty-six were hostile; more than half of these said the writers were giving up the paper. Marshal of the Royal Air Force Lord Portal resigned from The Observer Trust; Sir Keith Murray announced that he was retiring from it at the end of the year; Arthur Mann, former Editor of the Yorkshire Post *(and David Astor's first employer), resigned his honorary trusteeship.*

The leader was drafted by Dingle Foot but drastically revised by David Astor, especially the first paragraph (which caused most of the offence): 'If ever one was going to be outspoken,' he said years later, 'then this was the time.'

Sir Anthony Eden, prime minister at the time of Suez, bitterly criticised by The Observer *for his handling of the crisis.*

4 November 1956

We wish to make an apology. Five weeks ago we remarked that, although *we* knew our Government would not make a military attack in defiance of its solemn international obligations, people abroad might think otherwise. The events of last week have proved us completely wrong: if we misled anyone, at home or abroad, we apologise unreservedly. We had not realised that our Government was capable of such folly and such crookedness.

Whatever the Government now does, it cannot undo its air attacks on Egypt, made after Egypt had been invaded by Israel. It can never live down the dishonest nature of its ultimatum, so framed that it was certain to be rejected by Egypt. Never since 1783 has Great Britain made herself so universally disliked. That was the year in which the Government of Lord North, faced with the antagonism of almost the whole civilised world, was compelled to recognise the independence of the American Colonies. Sir Anthony Eden's eighteenth-century predecessors succeeded in losing us an empire. Sir Anthony and his colleagues have already succeeded in losing us incalculable political assets. So long as his Government represents this country, we cannot expect to have a good standing in the councils of the nations. It has attempted to provide those councils futile by rendering them futile. This it has done by, first, frustrating the Security Council of the United Nations through the use of the veto, and then by defying an overwhelming vote in the General Assembly. The Eden Government has become internationally discredited.

Ever since 1945, there have been two cardinal features of British external policy. The first has been to uphold the rule of law with special reference to the United Nations. The second has been the steady progress away from imperialism, exemplified in the full emancipation of Burma, India, Pakistan, Ceylon, West Africa and the West Indies. Neither of these cardinal features of our national policy was sincerely endorsed by the leaders of the Conservative Party, as we now see. In the eyes of the whole world, the British and French Governments have acted, not as policemen, but as gangsters. It will never be possible for the present Government to convince the peoples of the Middle East and of all Asia and Africa that it has not been actively associated with France in an endeavour to reimpose nineteenth-century imperialism of the crudest kind.

Is there any way of retrieving, in some degree, the errors of the last six days? There is one essential. Sir Anthony Eden must go. His removal from the Premiership is scarcely less vital to the prospects of this country than was that of Mr. Neville Chamberlain in May, 1940.

The Eden Administration has shown that it does not understand the sort of world we live in. It is no longer possible to bomb countries because you fear that your trading interests will be harmed. Nowadays, a drowning man on a raft is the occasion for all shipping to be diverted to try to save him; this new feeling for the sanctity of human life is the best element in the modern world. It is the true distinction of the West. Our other distinction is our right of personal independence and responsibility in politics – a right that must be exercised.

Nations are said to have the governments they deserve. Let us show that we deserve better.

EYEWITNESS IN BUDAPEST

In the summer of 1956 Poland obtained a measure of independence from Moscow. In the autumn the Hungarians rose. On 4 November the Russians sent in their bombers and tanks.

18 November 1956

On Sunday, 4 November I got back to my hotel, shaken and exhausted, at 2 a.m., only a few hours before the avalanche began. I had a last look at my young friends – some thirty wounded boys – who were quartered in an improvised field-hospital in the hotel. They knew the Russians were coming back. They did not wish to be consoled. They only regretted that they were not fit to fight. I shall never forget those young faces, some in their very early teens. After that I had joined a handful of Hungarian intellectuals, who had lost their homes and found refuge in the hotel, to listen to the B.B.C. news. They were the *élite* of Hungarian cultural life. The news was chiefly about the Anglo-French action in the Middle East, which seemed very far away and irrelevant. From their bitter but restrained comments it was clear that they felt that Hungary had been 'let down.'

At 2.30 a.m. I had a telephone call from London – a friend asking who was in charge of Hungarian relief – where and to whom to send medical supplies. This was the last call from London. Though I had hardly slept for a fortnight, I could not sleep now.

Instead, I sat on the balcony of my room, looking out over the city. It was a grey dawn. With flickering candles in the windows, the city was deathly quiet – except for the agonising cries of wounded who had had to be left unaided. Then, suddenly, there was the rattle and rumble of tracked vehicles. Soon the skies were flickering with the flash of gunfire, and the roar of guns shook the air. The Battle of Budapest had begun.

My journalistic colleagues and I decided to migrate to the British Legation. We felt very ashamed as we deserted that hotel, leaving so many helpless ones behind. I had no more strength to bid a last farewell to my wounded young friends. I was in tears.

We were all to be underground by 11 o'clock that morning because the Soviet Commander-in-Chief had issued an ultimatum: unless the city surrendered by noon it would be bombed from the air.

But there was no aerial bombing, after all. And after a time we were allowed to go up on to the roof. We were also given permission to telephone our friends in various parts of the city. We heard of the blind shelling of all houses along the boulevards where resistance continued, of the bombing of strategic points. But it soon became clear that the Russians had not been able to dislodge the Hungarians from any of their strongpoints. And by nightfall we were satisfied that Budapest was not going to surrender.

Just before midnight we heard the rumbling of heavy Soviet tanks, some of them passing our building in the direction of nearby Andrassy Street. There they were concentrating and making a *laager* for the night. Thousands of freedom fighters moved into an extemporised attack before dawn. This attack on the tanks led to one of the heaviest battles. I watched it from my window. More than thirty tanks were destroyed. And after that the Soviet tanks never stayed in the centre of the city at night. Every night, before midnight, they moved out, to come back at dawn.

The new day broke to the deadly roar of tanks. They were coming in in much greater force than on the day before. The Soviet tanks shelled every house in this boulevard with total savagery. This was the order of the day. And reports came in all that morning saying that the same sort of thing was going on in many other places. By evening there was scarcely a building in the main boulevards of Budapest which had not been torn open by Soviet shells. People swarmed to the Legation all day, hundreds more telephoned, imploring the Great Powers to intervene. 'Tell the world what they are doing to us!' they cried. And we could do nothing. The outside world was busy elsewhere, in Suez. We were ashamed. We could offer nothing but a promise that we would do our best to tell the world about these horrors. In spite of the restrictions understandably imposed on us by the British Minister, we managed on the third day to get out into the streets. I saw small children standing by the tanks and cursing the crews for what they had done. 'Do you really believe,' one little girl was asking in Russian (which was compulsory in schools) 'that you have come to liberate us from a handful of Fascists?'

'You unspeakable swine,' another shouted. 'You won't get away with this!' The tank crews themselves looked tired. They were dirty and bewildered. At first they would try to argue back: but in the end they gave up. They themselves were hardly more than boys, some of them obviously of Mongol blood. They were shabby in the extreme – shabbier than those I met in Budapest and Vienna at the end of the war. Dumbly, they put up with being spat at and cursed. Their expressions seemed to say that they knew they deserved nothing better. They sat motionless by their machine-guns in their turrets, but they did not shoot. This day marked the end of the really heavy fighting in Budapest.

As the fighting died down we moved out of the Legation build-

ing, and this gave us greater freedom of movement. Now there was time to look round and see the worst-hit parts of the city. It was a heart-breaking tour.

It was not only the damage looked at – damage blessedly confined for the most part to the main avenues (because Soviet tanks will not venture into narrow streets, where they cannot turn). I was also looking at the spirit of the Hungarian people, symbolised in a multitude of ways. There has been a great deal of loose talk about rapine and looting. I should like to testify that the Budapest rising must have been the cleanest revolution in history.

Before the Russians came back there stood in the main thoroughfare large boxes bearing notices: 'Give to those who remain alive!' These were full of 100-forint notes. They were unguarded. They were emptied periodically by small boys sent to collect the contributions. Nobody else touched them. After the battle they were still there.

In the main streets there were nothing but broken shop windows. After the battle the goods were still in the windows, untouched, among the broken glass. Valuable jewels and watches lay there for the taking. Nobody took them (and here the Russians, too, exercised restraint).

The only thing the Freedom Fighters took was food. They had no food. They entered the food shops at night and took what they needed. But they made lists of what they had taken, and left these lists in the shops, together

with the money which they thought was due.

One other thing. In all the streets were poems. The most celebrated Hungarian writers had pinned up their tributes on broken walls, in their own handwriting. They did this while the fighting was going on: short, declamatory verses:

You are heroes
But not the heroes of our songs of the
  past
We have no word for you
We shall not rest until we have found
  the word.
Or:
Every minute a hero dies
But every minute a new hero is born.
These verses flutter above the graves of the unknown.

Lajos Lederer

LAJOS LEDERER *(1904–1985)*
Born in what is now
Czechoslovakia, son of a
Hungarian newspaper editor and
politician. He came to London in
1926 and met, among others, the
royal family: Princess Elizabeth,
when a child, sat for his sculptor
friend Strobl. Early in World War
II he was interned but soon
released, thanks to his friend
Randolf Churchill.

In 1945 he began writing for
The Observer. *(In that year too*
he made a successful undercover
trip to war-torn Central Europe to
find priceless paintings lent by
another friend, Lord Rothermere,
to the Budapest Gallery of Fine
Art and seized by the Russians.)
Lederer's greatest scoop was
forecasting Tito's break with
Stalin in 1948.

THE ORDEAL OF GILBERT PINFOLD

21 July 1957

Mr. Waugh has never written a book in the least like this one before. Fictionalised autobiography? Nightmare? An essay in the macabre?

The book opens with a brilliant and only very slightly romanticised self-portrait. It proceeds to tell the story of 'Gilbert Pinfold's' appalling voyage to Malta and

the aural hallucinations which he suffered on it.

As a result of heavy drinking, an ill-chosen combination of drugs and some sort of change of life the hero suffers from a frightful near-psychosis. Lying sleepless in his cabin he hears a multitude of voices talking either to him or about him and planning various forms of persecution.

Meanwhile the normal life of the ship proceeds in the bar, in the dining-room and on deck.

The book is extremely deft. It was a *tour de force* to tell the story entirely from the hero's point of view and yet keep the reader constantly aware of the line which divides reality from hallucination.

I was tempted to write the word

reality in inverted commas, for the hallucinations are described with a dreadful vividness which wholly persuades us that they are no less real than the normal events of the voyage.

I confess that I have never been a great admirer of Mr. Waugh as a stylist, although it is clear that he takes very great pains to write as he intends to write. This book was marred for me by the mannered precision of its writing. Indeed I find it very hard to say whether it is a good book or not. But it is certainly an interesting and a moving one. And one reason why it is so moving is that Mr. Waugh has not a trace of self-pity in his character. Pinfold's ordeal is a truly shocking one, and it would be an odd reader who did not find himself deeply involved in it.

However, the hero and his creator retain their courage throughout, and retain as well an ironical detachment which is very rare in books of this kind.

What interests me most about the book is that the hero's imaginary persecutors are not, as one might have expected, parlour pinks, pacifists, non-believers, men with the wrong accent or any of the other stage villains of Mr. Waugh's mythology. They are colonels, public school men, upper-class thugs, anti-Semites, Fascists and bullies – just the kind of people, in fact, to whom Mr. Waugh has sometimes seemed to be a little over-indulgent in the past.

It is deeply interesting that the ultimate horror in the recesses of

Evelyn Waugh, his wife Laura and their children, taken by Jane Bown, some years before this article was written. 'Self-revelations of a remarkably honest and brave man.'

Mr. Waugh's mind is the same horror which has obsessed so many of us who experienced the normal torments of public school life. For the bully, of course, is an enemy not only of weakness, not only of sensitivity, not only of loving kindness, but also of intelligence.

It is the appalling, nagging, shrewd *stupidity* of the imaginary persecutors which is best brought out and which will haunt my own imagination for many days.

These are the self-revelations of a remarkably honest and brave man who has also allowed us to see that he is a likeable one. It is a book which seems to suggest that Mr. Waugh has shifted gear and has begun to explore depths of experience which were previously beyond his reach – or at least beyond his desire. Whatever will he do next?

Philip Toynbee

SEX AND SENSE

15 September 1957

An issue which involves attitudes to sexual behaviour arouses strong emotions, and what is needed at such a time is the calmest possible consideration of the Wolfenden recommendations. The heavier penalties recommended for solicitation by prostitutes have been, on the whole, welcomed both editorially and in public opinion polls, though some misgivings have been expressed about the wisdom of sending prostitutes to jail.

Because prostitution is a more mentionable topic than homosexuality, public feelings have been less violent than on the committee's other main proposal – which is that homosexual behaviour in private between consenting males over the age of twenty-one should no longer be a criminal offence. Even on this issue, despite the ferocious obscurantism of certain papers the public reaction seems to have been more understanding and constructive than might well have been expected. It was foreseeable that the habitually indignant Mr. John Gordon of the *Sunday Express* would describe the report as 'the Pansies' Charter'.

It is expected that the Government will soon introduce legislation along the lines suggested in that part of the report which deals with prostitution. The Government should not shirk from implementing at the same time the proposed change of law on private homesexual behaviour. This would remove the special discrimination against male inverts over twenty-one, and leave such behaviour, together with lesbianism, adultery and fornication, as a matter of private morality outside the criminal law.

The Government will need courage if it is to reform the law on homosexuality as the Report recommends. There appears to be a small but definite public majority against the implementation of this proposal and, as on all such issues, those who are opposed to reforms are likely to be much more clamorous than those who support it. This was true both on the issue of flogging and on that of capital punishment.

The fears expressed by some

that the toleration of homosexual acts between men will lead to an increase in offences against boys have been carefully examined and specifically discounted by the Committee. Adult homosexuals who turn towards other men are, with very few exceptions, in quite a different category from paedophiliacs who seek boys as partners – as different as is the normal heterosexual male from the man who is attracted exclusively to little girls.

JOGGING ALONG

5 January 1958
Tomorrow, Monday, Mrs. Dale and her performing family – they talk! they move! they crack jokes like old nuts! – will have been at it for ten years, a record for radio serials. By this time it must almost count as public-service radio, and any demagogue could

make out a good case for treating it like *To-day in Parliament* and putting the B.B.C. under a statutory obligation to broadcast it. The plot is phoney, but at least it chronicles genuine events like births and quarrels (the emphasis and selection are the trouble). The dialogue is the wholly inex-

cusable thing. All the back-breaking inanity of people without thought, wit or conscience is packed into the daily quarter-hour. If the Dale audience was quietly withering, going about its other business, all this wouldn't matter. But it isn't: it's getting bigger. This is the most preposterous and significant fact about radio in the New Year.

Paul Ferris

DUMB KAFFIR NOTEBOOK

26 January 1958
Johannesburg, Saturday. In a village of the Baphurutse tribe, among the hills and thorn bush of the north-western Transvaal, an African sat alone by a fire. It was very hot. To men who paused in surprise to ask him why he sat beside a fire on such a day he said simply that he was cold. But to inquiring women he said: 'This is a good fire and I thought that if you had any pieces of paper, any *rubbish* you wished to burn, then this fire would burn it up quickly.' Whereupon the women laughed and went away to fetch the Passes (identification certificates that Africans must at all times carry) the Government had just issued to them and threw them into the man's fire. News of this reached the White Baas, the Native Commission. He told the Police Sergeant of this wickedness and the Sergeant went off to end it.

The Sergeant was an Afrikaner, ready to be reasonable towards Natives who were good

but hating all *dom Kaffers*, the stupid ones, who listened to agitators and opposed authority. These he would chastise and the Sergeant was proud of the reputation he had for his mastery over them. So the Sergeant went forty miles to the village and the Chief – who knew that the Government paid his wages – found for the Sergeant the names of the women who had burnt their Passes. There were twenty-five names on the list.

'Have them,' said the Sergeant, 'at the place of the tribal assembly in the morning and I will come with the *kwela-kwela* [the pick-up van that Africans call the rock 'n' roll] to take them to prison.' The next day the Sergeant came again, but at the assembly place there were not twenty-five women. There were 233. So the Sergeant asked which were the twenty-five whom he was taking to prison. 'They are among us,' said one of the women, placidly. 'Take all of us to the prison and you will take them.'

Thinking to confound them, the Sergeant sent for two of the big buses that belong to the Railway and into these he loaded all the women and took them to the Native Commissioner's court in the town. Meanwhile, someone had telephoned to Mrs. Muller, the woman lawyer in Johannesburg who looks after the Baphurutse people when they are in trouble. 'We belong to Mrs. Muller,' they say. And Mrs. Muller telephoned to the Native Commissioner, reminding him of the law and of the need to charge the women who had broken it by burning their Passes, and to proceed against them without delay. But the Commissioner was at a loss to sort the wrongdoers from the guiltless and things dragged, and the women sat on the ground, and once every hour Mrs. Muller telephoned.

At sundown the Commissioner sent the Sergeant to tell the women they could go home, but that they should come again to the court in three weeks' time. But where, said the women, are the buses that belong to the Railway, and the Sergeant said brusquely it was not the business of the Government to provide free transport. 'Never mind,' said the women, 'we will sit here until you want us again in three weeks from now.' The Sergeant rebuked them bitterly, but they would not move. And once every hour Mrs. Muller telephoned, quoting the relevant Section. So the Sergeant sent for the buses and the women went home.

Three weeks later, the court assembled to hear the cases. But no women came. Angry messages went out to the village and back came the answer that the women were there and so were the buses, but the women could not move because the Sergeant had not come to fetch them.

'You are not our Baas to tell us what to do,' said the women to the bus men. 'Only the Sergeant is our Baas.' And in his way the Sergeant was flattered by this. He gathered his fleet of vans together and drive off to the village.

The women greeted him cheerfully and said *now* they were ready to go. But this time there were not 233. There were nearer 400 and beyond counting. And when they had risen to leave, the suddenly sat down again and told the Sergeant there was another woman in that hut on the hill a mile, who had also burnt her Pass and should go with them, to make it fair. The Sergeant, recognising the co-operation only a personality as strong as his could win from Kaffirs, went off to fetch the stray lamb. And when he got back, the women said they had remembered, in his absence, another woman, somewhat further away, who was likewise guilty. . . They kept this up until late into the hot afternoon, until even the Sergeant began to feel the uneasiness of self-doubt. And then at last the women agreed that it was time to go and marched off towards the town in a great column, with the Sergeant among them.

When it was almost dark, the women suddenly turned off the road together and sat down, leav-ing the Sergeant in the roadway, dusty, sweating and alone. We are tired, they said, and must rest, for it is a long way to town. It was late. The Native Commissioner would have gone home anyway. So, conquered and worn down at last by the dumb Kaffirs, the Sergeant strode angrily away, up the long straight road to the crest of the ridge. And as he dwindled the women sang again, in time to the fall of his feet: '*Onward, Christian soldiers* . . .' And the twenty-five women never did go to court.

This is a story they tell now in the villages of the Baphurutse, who have never heard of passive resistance.   *Cyril Dunn*

Cyril Dunn (1908–88)
Wrote with wry humour and, like Orwell, fierce integrity – his obituary was headlined, 'Last of the puritan reporters.' His own word would have been 'Irresponsible': 'Whenever some official accused me of being "irresponsible",' he once said, 'I knew I'd hit some hidden nail firmly on the head.' One of the finest writers the paper has had.

The burning of the hated identification passes became a symbol of passive resistance in South Africa.
This bonfire of passes and copies of the Natal Daily News *was stoked by ANC members.*

FROM DREYFUS TO DJAMILA

16 February 1958

The men governing France today, who have hushed up so many violations of human rights, would be unwise to count too much on the continuing apathy of the French people. This is the same France which was roused to furious protest during the 'Affair Dreyfus' for the good reason that one man had been unjustly condemned.

It is just sixty years ago this week that Zola was sentenced to imprisonment for his famous pamphlet *J'accuse*, in which he had castigated, in what the court judged to be slanderous terms, the men responsible for convicting the innocent Dreyfus, and shielding the real criminal, Esterhazy. It was the Zola trial which really marked the turning-point of the Dreyfus affair.

Once again a patent miscarriage of justice is being smothered by official untruths and public apathy.

Ostensibly the Dreyfus case has very little in common with the case of the twenty-two-year-old Algerian girl, Djamila Bouhired, sentenced to death last July for alleged complicity in a terrorist bomb outrage. Captain Dreyfus was loyal to France: Djamila has publicly proclaimed her loyalty to an independent Algeria. Dreyfus was tried when France was at peace: Djamila is a victim of the Algerian war.

Acts of bestial cruelty by the terrorists of the 'National Liberation Federation' (to which she admits belonging) explain, though they do not excuse, the cruelty with which F.L.N. members are treated when they fall into French hands. Djamila spent two weeks in the hands of the parachutists before being handed over to the judicial authorities. The indignities suffered by Captain Dreyfus were trivial compared with what she has suffered physically at their hands.

Nevertheless, there are many revealing points of comparison between the two trials. To begin with, both accused were tried by a military tribunal, which was determined to convict them. Both were the victims of racial prejudice. The public benches at Djamila's trial were occupied exclusively by Europeans – Muslims were not admitted – who howled 'Death to the assassins' before the trial began. In both cases there were 'reasons of State' for finding the culprit guilty – and a stigma of treachery on those who challenged the verdict. In both cases weak coalition Governments needed a verdict to satisfy a wobbly Parliamentary majority. In both cases the prosecution produced only the flimsiest evidence – in the first Dreyfus trial, only a single document, secreted from the German Embassy and wrongfully alleged to be in Dreyfus's

handwriting: in Djamila's case, only the self-contradictory evidence of a hysterical co-detainee, Djamila Bouazza, whom the court refused to have examined by a psychiatrist. In both cases the counsel for the defence was not allowed to see the principal document for the prosecution. Both victims were wrongly declared to have confessed.

Again both cases, the French Army was desperately trying to preserve its reputation after suffering serious defeats. After the verdict against Zola, a German newspaper unkindly commented that this was the first victory of the French Army since its defeat in 1870-71. This time not only 1940, but also the retreats from Indo-China, Morocco and Tunisia, have made the Army sensitive of its 'honour'.

There is, however, one important difference. During the Dreyfus affair, the case for putting order above justice 'in the interests of the State' was widely accepted by the Roman Catholic Church.

Today, on the contrary, *La Croix*, the principal Catholic daily, which was violently anti-Dreyfusard in the 1890s, has helped to awaken the Catholic conscience to the moral responsibilities of acquiescence in the more criminal aspects of the 'pacification' policy.

Nora Beloff

TORTURE IN ALGERIA: THE FORBIDDEN SARTRE ARTICLE

The Observer*'s Sartre article, banned in France, was reprinted in English, microscopically small, by the satirical pamphlet* Le Canard Enchaîné.

9 March 1958

The Paris police yesterday raided a publisher's printing works to seize and destroy a tract by Jean-Paul Sartre against torture in

Algeria.

The tract, called 'La Victoire,' from which we publish an extract below, was written after the publication of Henri Alleg's book *La Question*, in which he describes his victory over French parachutists who tried to extract information from him by the use of torture and drugs.

In 1943, in the Rue Lauriston

(the Gestapo headquarters in Paris), Frenchmen were screaming in agony and pain; all France could hear them. In those days the outcome of the war was uncertain and the future unthinkable, but one thing seemed impossible in any circumstances: that one day men should be made to scream by those acting in our name.

There is no such word as impossible: in 1958, in Algiers, people are tortured regularly and systematically. Everyone knows this is so, but almost no one talks of it. France is almost as mute as in the Occupation, but then she had the excuse of being gagged.

During the war we watched the German soldiers walking inoffensively down the street, and would say to ourselves: 'They look like us. How can they act as they do?' And we were proud of ourselves for not understanding. To-day, we know there was nothing to understand. The decline has been gradual and imperceptible. But now when we look into the mirror we see an unfamiliar and hideous reflection: ourselves.

Appalled, the French are discovering this terrible truth: that if nothing can protect a nation against itself, neither its traditions nor its loyalties nor its laws, and if 15 years are enough to transform victims into executioners, then its behaviour is no more than a matter of opportunity. Anybody, at any time, may equally find himself victim or executioner.

Jean-Paul Sartre

THE LEBANON

Philby was taken on by The Observer *in early 1956. Although Robert Stephens complained his pieces were boring ('He's always toeing the Foreign Office line!'), his reports from Beirut were competent and knowledgeable.*

22 June 1958

Beirut, 21 June. The name Lebanon usually stands for the Westernised society of Beirut, for the summer resorts perched on the surrounding hills, for the ski lifts at 'The Cedars' and perhaps for a visit to the Baalbek Festival. The last six weeks have exposed a harsher reality. Yet its harshness has been overdone. Hate is there, but not a lust to kill.

What, then is the reality? The Lebanese crisis is scarcely a rebellion, since rebel leaders have been wandering freely in and out of Government controlled territory. It is not a civil war, since there has been precious little warfare. Yet is is clearly more than a strike or riot. Perhaps it is best described as a calculated defiance of authority by at least one-half of the population, which is determined by a show of strength occasionally backed by actual violence to impose its will.

The origins of the struggle are diverse in the extreme. Antagonisms at work are religious, social, political, regional, tribal and personal. Each of these interact on the others so that it is impossible to point to any one as being a decisive influence.

There is a difference between Christian and Muslim. Since Lebanon became independent in 1945 the Christians have tended to dominate the country's political life: They look to the West, whence they derive their religion, their culture and the trading links that enriched them. The Muslims, on the other hand, look to the rest of the Arab world, with which they share Islam and the common experience of foreign domination at the hands of the Turks, French and British.

Leaders on both sides, however, strenuously disclaim any intention of launching a religious war. The danger is that the longer

149

the conflict continues, the likelier it becomes that those antagonisms which everyone wants to stifle will rise to the surface.

The present trouble came to a head with the murder of an Opposition journalist. The leaders of the Opposition issued a call for a general strike. This call was widely observed in the Muslim cities of Tripoli, Sidon and Tyre; and in Tripoli attempts to enforce the strike on reluctant business men led to serious riots.

It was three days before Beirut joined in, and then only because forced to do so by a series of bomb outrages. The Christian areas of Mount Lebanon remained quiet while the rest of the countryside became a sort of no-man's-land with the Army and gendarmerie playing hide-and-seek with armed bands of Muslims, Druzes and dissident Christians.

It may seem astonishing that in the seven weeks of the struggle the military situation has remained virtually unchanged. The Opposition still hold large areas of Tripoli, Sidon and Tyre and a smaller area in Beirut itself. There has been no attempt even at a blockade, and the adherents of the Opposition can leave and enter their strongholds at will.

From the first it was evident that the Opposition had formidable armaments only part of which could have been acquired within the country. Indeed, it was so obvious that arms had come in from Syria that the Opposition never bothered to deny it. They merely insisted that the arms had been purchased and smuggled into the Lebanon without the connivance of the Syrian authorities. Such assurances must be taken with a pinch of salt.

The real argument is about the degree of intervention. Was it 'massive interference' as the Government insists? Or was it just spontaneous encouragement from sympathisers across the border, as the Opposition claim?

The truth probably lies somewhere in between the two extreme views. Syrian aid certainly made the Opposition a redoubtable force. Yet it seems more than probable that the present struggle would have broken out even without foreign interference.

What will happen to this beautiful countryside with its narrow coastal strip of orange groves and banana plantations crowded into the sea by meticulously terraced ridges of limestone, and with its miraculous Bekaa Valley like a green lake set deep among high mountains?

It is possible that a serious attempt will be made to seek a military solution. If it were tried, the future would be dark indeed, with strong secessionist movements developing in Muslim areas which, if successful, would leave of the Lebanon nothing but a Christian rump of high mountains and Beirut.

The strong tendency among supporters of the Government to canvas the chances of Anglo-American intervention is a measure of their apparent helplessness to impose an internal solution. It is also a measure of their desperation. The arrival of British parachutists and American marines would deepen and perpetuate the present bitterness and lead to another outbreak of anti-Western fanaticism far beyond Lebanon.

The Lebanese must help themselves. With their borders sealed off from Syrian interference by United Nations observers and with Western Powers observing a wise discretion, the Lebanese will at least have a chance of putting their own house in order undisturbed.

H.A.R. Philby

TRIVIALITIES THAT LEAD TO DEATH

Terrorism in Cyprus in support of Greek Cypriot demands for enosis, *union with Greece, broke out in 1955 and went on, sporadically, until the island became independent in 1960. During the state of emergency Rawle Knox, then the paper's Chief Middle East Correspondent usually based in Cairo, was stationed there for some time – too long, in his opinion. He cabled:* OBSERVER LONDON AUTHORISED LUKE TWENTYTWO SIXTY EIGHT KNOX. *('And if I shall also ask you, ye will not let me go.') The reply read:* KNOX NICOSIA AUTHORISED DANIEL TWELVE TWELVE GENESIS FORTYSEVEN SIX OBANK. *('Blessed is he that waiteth . . . The land of Egypt is before thee'.)*

13 July 1958

Nicosia, Saturday. 'Of course, we should really take over all the newspapers and see that they publish only good things.' The Gunner major who spoke was standing in the rock-strewn village square of Avgorou where only a few hours before an attack by the villagers on a Royal Horse Guards patrol had resulted in many casualties, including two Greek Cypriots dead.

'What good things?' asked a newspaperman tentatively.

'Oh, So-and-so married Such-and-such – that sort of thing.'

'Don't you think,' ventured another newspaper man, 'that people might soon stop believing what was in their newspapers?'

'Nonsense! If you go on printing things long enough everyone believes them.' This was the same major who insisted later that we return to brigade headquarters under escort – rather than anywhere else we might want to go – so that we might get 'the proper story.'

We had been forbidden to speak to villagers in Avgorou. In Cyprus 'the proper story' is assuming an ever-increasing importance in the Army mind. If the major were an isolated bigot it would not be necessary to quote him. But he is not. The Army has a rotten job in Cyprus, a job the keenest professional in it would never have chosen for himself. Soldiers, dirty and often hungry (the temporary quarters in which they live never have enough showers and the food, they almost all say, is insufficient), tread the dusty, baking streets on patrol, cradling their guns with bayonets fixed in their arms. What are they looking for? Few of them can tell you because no one has told them; no one has had time to tell them. But if anyone shows signs of giving trouble they will 'sort him out.'

The two Greek Cypriot dead in Avgorou were avenged this week when a cornet and a trooper of the Royal Horse Guards were shot in the back in a shop in Famagusta, a tragic and squalid waste of young lives. In the ensuring search of the area the Army discovered bombs in a Greek club opposite the shop and exploded them and the club in a thunder of retribution. Three reliable eye-witnesses say that before the demolition took place they saw soldiers taking more explosives into the club to make sure that the bang would be a good bang.

Let us get this straight. I believe that the troops in Avgorou had every right to open fire – they were in very serious trouble. But the trouble would never have started if the troops had not been obliged by their orders to demand that the Avgorou villagers remove a poster which was signed 'Eoka.' That triviality led to the death of two Avgorou villagers and two young soldiers.

You must understand it all to appreciate the mind of the Army in Cyprus and to understand why soldiers dipped into their beer mugs in appreciation when they heard the Greek club go up in smoke and rubble. Someone had hit the Army; the Army was going to hit someone back. You cannot quarrel with that as a military attitude.

It is not, however, the attitude that will lead Cyprus gently into the 'experiment in partnership' and co-operation which the

Governor, Sir Hugh Foot, insists, in my opinion rightly, is the only immediate answer to the island's race-ridden problems. It is this Army attitude that has caused critics to make the observation that Sir Hugh is not kept fully informed by his officers and advisers. Sir Hugh has now forcefully denied that charge.

Recently late at night in the ugly village of Omorphita, not far from Nicosia, I was stopped and nearly shot by a patrol of Britons, some half-uniformed, others not at all, who seemed unhappy that I and my colleagues were not good shooting material.

'We'd better wait for the sergeant-major,' said the one who stopped us, waving his automatic unevenly into the side window of the car. 'He's drunk as usual.' This, I learned, was a Viking patrol – a volunteer organisation permitted by the Army in dangerous areas where Service families are living. There are 40 to 50 Service families in Omorphita, which is a constant battleground between Turks and Greeks. One of my inquisitors had stopped a Cypriot car earlier. 'I asked him about a tin on the floor,' he said, 'He said it was a can of car polish, but as it had a fuse attached I took the liberty of doubting him. I drove him to the police station with the bloody bomb under my knees.'

Another night while I was talking to the same Norsemen in Omorphita a pathetic group of British women came round the corner of the street. They were the Vikings' wives. 'Come home,' they cried, or words to that effect.

'It's all very well for you to go out and have a few beers and show your muscles,' said the senior and very Lancashire of the wives, 'but it's us you're supposed to be protecting, you know.' 'Never see him at nights at all,' said a young wife who had been in Cyprus only five days. 'I was dying to come here and now all I want is to get home.' The Vikings laughed: they were enjoying themselves: and they warned us to drive more slowly next time or they'd put a shot through the window. When I mentioned the Vikings to Sir Hugh Foot he had never heard of them.

There is no question that both Sir Hugh and the Army want violence to end in Cyprus. But Sir Hugh has to contemplate the ensuing peace and the Army does not – hence the inevitable different approach. An army – any army – can contemplate the final victorious battleground, strewn with human and material wreckage, with the knowledge that it has done a job well and without having to ask, let alone answer, the question 'Where do we go from here?'
Rawle Knox

THE ANGRY YOUNG CUBAN TAKES OVER

4 January 1959
Fidel Castro's victory in Cuba has been welcomed with remarkable unanimity in all the free countries of Latin America. It is seen as a kind of New Year present to democracy. Part of this feeling is undoubtedly emotional: the appeal of an honest young David routing a corrupt, cynical and powerful Goliath.

The deposed Batista was among the most unpleasant of the dictators. He could not claim even to have bettered the lot of

workers, like Perón, or to have brought peace to his country, like his present host, Trujillo of the Dominican republic.

But there is more to it than that. The overthrow of other Latin dictators has had popular support, but in almost every case it has been made possible by the assistance or at least the benevolent neutrality of the professional armed forces, who have remained intact with all their implicit power of intervention in politics. In Cuba it has been a straight fight, and the civilian 26 de Julio movement is now on its own, free to shape the country's future according to its own ideas.

It is precisely this which has caused disquiet in some quarters – particularly in the United States. Castro formerly advocated the nationalisation of sugar estates, compulsory profit-sharing in industry, and other 'dangerous' ideas. Some of his supporters are known to be Communist sympathisers.

Most of the members of the movement, including Castro himself, are young. Will they be able to govern effectively? The pessimists can point to the looting and violence in Havana as evidence that they cannot. But an outbreak of public disorder after a protracted civil war was only to be expected, and Batista's rule had been so arbitrary and so corrupt that it had brought the law into contempt. As in an occupied country, patriotism had become identified with law-breaking, an attitude which may take time to eradicate.

The political misgivings have more justification. The line that the Castro movement is Communist was, of course, taken by Batista to impress United States opinion, and for a long time it was pretty successful. But it was never true in the sense that Castro himself was a Communist or that the movement as a whole was Communist-dominated – it had, in fact, the sympathy of the Roman Catholic Church.

It is true, however, that the willingness of foreign firms to do business with the dictator encouraged a leftward trend of thinking in the 26 de Julio movement. It is also true that Castro himself is a Socialist (though he denies being a Marxist) and has in the past proposed far-reaching economic measures.

He is representative of a generation of purposefully angry young men in Latin America, part of whose make-up is a serious idealism. They are about as different from wayward tyrants like Batista as it is possible to be.

J. Halcro Ferguson

J. HALCRO FERGUSON (1920-1968) The Observer's Man on Latin America: 'He invented it for the ignorant British,' John Gale wrote in an obituary. 'He was almost certainly the first British journalist to write regularly about it.'

The piece ended: 'I once entered Jock's office to find him doodling, watched by a small, dark man. When Jock had finished his doodle he looked up and said: "Oh, by the way, I want you to meet the Prime Minister of Malta. I think it's time we took him for a drink."'

Ferguson welcomed Batista's fall but he soon saw that Castro's Cuba was not El Dorado.

THE DEVLIN JUDGMENT: GUILT IN AFRICA

In 1953 it was decided to group Northern Rhodesia, Nyasaland and Southern Rhodesia into a Central African Federation. This, so The Observer wrote later, was 'without the consent and against the manifest will of the overwhelming majority' of the first two countries, who feared 'that they would be subordinated for ever to the 300,000 white settlers of Southern Rhodesia' (now Zimbabwe). Unrest grew and, in March 1959, led to a state of emergency in Nyasaland (now Malawi). A commission of inquiry was set up under Mr Justice (now Lord) Devlin.

26 July 1959

The judgment of the Devlin Commission on Nyasaland is fair but devastating. Its judicial tone bears the unmistakable quality of its chairman, Mr. Justice Devlin. But it is not important only as a judicial statement; it ranks as perhaps the best study in modern colonial politics ever written. The four authors of the report were carefully chosen for their special attributes. Mr. Justice Devlin is one of the greatest lawyers of his day. Sir P. Wyn-Harris spent his whole working life in colonial administration, ending as Governor of the Gambia. Brigadier E. T. Williams was Director of Intelligence on Field-Marshal Montgomery's Staff. Sir J. Ure Primrose is the Lord Provost of Perth. All are conservatives, a point worth remembering in view of the wrath with which their report has been received by a nettled Government.

The Commission reports that the troubles in the Protectorate started long before the disturbances that led to a state of emergency earlier this year. Its roots lay in the British Parliament's 1953 decision to force Nyasaland into the political strait-jacket of the Central African Federation. The Government sought by oppressive restrictions to overcome the opposition of the African National Congress, and Congress, in its turn, resorted to intimidation, though the 'extent and effect' of this, says the Commission,'was exaggerated.'

Thus, long before the President of Congress, Dr. Hastings K. Banda, returned home in July, 1958, 'the prospect of collision sooner or later was almost certain.' For six years the critics of Federation had tried to convey the sense of this growing crisis, while the Government and the apologists for Federation tried either to deny these dangers or to minimise them. The Commission leaves no room for doubt as to who was right. It is wrong to suggest, as the Government now does, that its critics were opposed to the declaration of the emergency or that they denied the existence of violence and lawlessness in Nyasaland. The gravamen of the charges made against the Government at the time was that it had failed to substantiate its allegation that Dr. Hastings Banda and other Congress leaders had planned to massacre Europeans and Africans through a carefully prepared 'murder plot.' This plot is supposed to have been hatched in a secret forest hide-out. The existence of such a plot and of Dr. Banda's complicity in it were seriously questioned. The Mau-Mau like bush meeting turns out to have been a very different thing from the picture of it presented by the Governor and widely published at the time in British newspapers. Although it was held in secret, there was 'nothing sinister' about it. Robbed of its primeval colour, it was nothing more than an emergency conference of Congress held in the open air.

Although Dr. Banda does not emerge from the report as a lily-white saint, the Commission describes him as a charming and frank person – if not a modest one – and by no means as inflexible as the Government would have one believe. Although he freely admitted that he chose to work with the militant young men rather than with the moderate, older and discredited Congress leaders, he always sought to oppose anti-European feelings. His policy was against violence, but he was not prepared to rule it out under all circumstances. Most importantly, the Commission thinks 'that Dr. Banda would never approve a policy of murder and that he would have intervened decisively if he had thought it was so much as being discussed.'

To sum up. The British and Nyasaland Governments are found to have been justified in declaring a state of emergency, although not on the ground of the sensational 'massacre plot'; they were right to believe that Congress was turning towards violence.

But the Government is guilty of the major charges levelled against it in that there was no 'murder plot'; Dr. Banda was falsely

Devlin: 'One of the greatest lawyers of his day.'

accused; the situation after the imposition of Federation had been allowed to deteriorate to the point where a conflict had become inevitable.

Dr. Hastings Banda is acquitted on all the serious charges levelled against him. He emerges with an almost blameless character, except that he might have been expected publicly to condemn violence (which he had all along done privately), and that he had not exercised sufficient control over some of his lieutenants, who appear to have succeeded in pushing Congress towards violence after long resistance to such a policy.

The Commission's job was not to apportion guilt or to propose remedies. But its judicial verdict is unmistakable. Nyasaland today, says the Commission, is a police State. All the effective African leaders are in prison; constitutional reforms are in abeyance; and tension remains high.

It can be brought back into the ways of peaceful and democratic government only if the findings of the Commission are understood and acted upon. All policy must flow from a recognition of the strength of the African Congress and of the Africans' 'almost universal' opposition to Federation.

Hastings Banda: 'Not a lily-white saint, but a charming and frank person – if not a modest one.'

Mr Harold Macmillan affirms unequivocally Britain's stance against apartheid in his 'Wind of Change' speech to the Assembly and Senate in Cape Town on 3 February 1960.

THIS IS A MILESTONE

'The wind of change is blowing through this Continent, and whether we like it or not, this growth of national consciousness is a political fact' – Harold Macmillan, Cape Town, 5 February 1960.

7 February 1960

Mr. Macmillan's astonishing speech last Wednesday has changed in retrospect the whole strategy of his African tour. As he cruises between Cape Town and the Canaries, he can safely surmise that the African continent will never be 'quite the same again.'

It is already being insisted that the Cape Town speech contained no change in Britain's policy, and no doubt every statement has at some time been made before. But the important new feature of the speech – apart from the fact that it

was made in Cape Town – was that it was free from ambiguities: in particular it contained no suggestion that, 'when the chips are down' Britain will be on the side of South Africa.

The speech had no hint and no possible interpretation that Britain would be prepared to forfeit black allies for white under any circumstances: and the point has been taken in South Africa. The *Cape Times* said: 'Our isolation is practically total.' *Die Burger*, the leading Government paper, said: 'South Africa has been given formal notice of a state of emergency in her relations with the West.' No other speech has penetrated so deeply into South Africa since the Nationalist Party came to power twelve years ago. What, in practical terms, will be its repercussions?

It will be some time before the

eventual response of the South African Government becomes clear: but on the British side some effects are certain. In the first place, it is now known that Mr. Macmillan told Dr. Verwoerd that Britain would no longer be able to vote for South Africa at the United Nations. This decision, that *apartheid* was no longer a domestic concern, was clearly in his mind when he said in his speech: 'Mind your own business, of course, but mind how it affects my business, too.'

Secondly, having once made her views known within South Africa, Britain cannot easily go back. There can be no question of explaining away this unambiguous speech. Now that the Afrikaners may appear to many Englishmen to be in a situation of profound and genuine difficulty, it would obviously do no good to

154

offer false assurances of support.

But the most important result of the speech may well turn out to be its effect on the concept of the Commonwealth. Until Wednesday, it had seemed as if the Commonwealth connection had restrained, rather than encouraged, Britain's frank criticism of South Africa. If Mr. Macmillan *had* met the President of the African National Congress, Chief Luthuli, he would have been told that Africans would prefer South Africa *not* to be in the Commonwealth, so that Britain could be more outspoken.

But now that Britain has withdrawn her U.N. support and made a thorough criticism which has been all the more effective for being invited and broadcast throughout South Africa, the Commonwealth connection has become more, not less, real. It is by no means certain that, with the hardening temper of his Government, Dr. Verwoerd will wish to remain in this club, where members have begun to speak to one another without restraint, there is already doubt whether he will join his Commonwealth colleagues in London in May.

But the practical reasons for South Africa wanting to remain a member are still good ones. All the other countries are members of several other clubs, usually more important ones for them – the NATO club, the SEATO (South East Asia Treaty Organisation) club, the uncommitted club. But South Africa belongs to only one – the Commonwealth: and if she left that, she would find herself in a state of total isolation which is becoming a growing nightmare for thinking South Africans.

Anthony Sampson

EYE-WITNESS AT SHARPEVILLE

27 March 1960

Johannesburg, Saturday. We went back into Sharpeville the back way, around lunch-time last Monday, driving along behind a big grey police car and three Saracen armoured cars. As we went through the fringes of the township many people were shouting the Pan-Africanist slogan 'Izwe Lethu' (Our land). They were grinning and cheerful. Some kids waved to the policemen sitting on the Saracens and

two of the policemen waved back. It was like a Sunday outing – except that Major A. T. T. Spengler, head of the Witwatersrand Security Branch, was in the front car and there were bullets in the Saracens' guns.

At the main gates of the fenced-off location, policemen were stopping all cars coming in from the outside. Spengler and the Saracens headed for the police station which is deep inside the settlement, and we followed. The

policemen were by now all inside the Saracens, with the hatches battened down, looking at Sharpeville through the chinks of the armour plating. Yet the Africans did not appear to be alarmed by the cars. Some looked interested. Some just grinned.

A constable shoved the butt of his rifle against my windshield. Another pointed his rifle at my chest. Another leaned into the car, shouting: 'Have you got a permit to be in this location?' I

After the shooting of more than 200 unarmed blacks, South African police casually eye the dead and injured. Photograph by Drum *photographer Ian Berry, whose editor wrote the above report.*

said no, whereupon he bellowed: 'Then get out, get out, get out! or I will arrest you on the spot. Understand?' He had a police gun in his holster and a black pistol tucked into his belt. We decided to go around the other side of the police station, where we parked in a big field.

We could see a couple of the Saracens, their tops poking starkly above the heads of the crowd, just over 100 yards away from us. This was about seven minutes before the police opened fire. The crowd seemed to be loosely gathered around them and on the fringes people were walking in and out. The kids were playing. In all there were about 3,000 people. They seemed amiable and relaxed.

I said to Ian Berry, *Drum's* chief photographer, 'This is going to go on all day.' He replied: 'Let's hang on for a bit.' Suddenly there was a sharp report from the direction of the police station. 'That's a shot,' Berry said. There were shrill cries of 'Izwe Lethu' – women's voices, I thought. The cries came from the police station and I could see a small section of the crowd swirl around the Saracens. Hands went up in the Africanist salute.

Then the shooting started. We heard the chatter of a machine-gun, then another, then another. 'Here it comes,' said Berry. He leaped out of the car with two cameras and crouched in the grass, shooting pictures. The first rush was on us, then past. There were hundreds of women, some of them laughing. They must have though the police were firing blanks. One woman was hit about ten yards from our car. Her companion, a young man, went back when she fell. He thought she had stumbled. Then he turned her over and saw that her chest had been shot away. He looked at the blood on his hand and said: 'My God, she's gone!' Hundreds of kids were running, too. One little boy had on an old black coat, which he held up behind his head, thinking, perhaps, that it might save him from the bullets. Some of the children, hardly as tall as the

grass, were leaping like rabbits. Some of them were shot, too.

Still the shooting went on. One of the policemen was standing on top of a Saracen, and it looked as though he was firing his sten gun into the crowd. He was swinging it around in a wide arc from his hip as though he were panning a movie camera. Two other police officers were on the truck with him, and it looked as if they were firing pistols. Most of the bodies were strewn in the road running through the field in which we were. One man who had been lying still, dazedly got to his feet, staggered a few yards then fell in a heap. A woman sat with her head cupped in her hands.

One by one the guns stopped. Nobody was moving in our field except Berry. The rest were wounded – or dead. There was no longer a crowd and it was very quiet. Berry ran back to the car, saying: 'Let's go before they get my film.' We drove out through the main gate, looking straight ahead.

Before the shooting, I heard no warning to the crowd to disperse. There was no warning volley. When the shooting started it did not stop until there was no living thing on the huge compound in front of the police station. The police have claimed they were in desperate danger because the crowd was stoning them. Yet only three policemen were reported to have been hit by stones - and more than 200 Africans were shot down. The police also have said that the crowd was armed with 'ferocious weapons' which littered the compound after they fled. I saw no weapons, although I looked carefully, and afterwards studied the photographs of the death scene. While I was there I saw only shoes, hats and a few bicycles left among the bodies.

It seems to me that tough stuff was behind the killings at Sharpeville. The crowd gave me no reason to feel scared, though I moved among them without any distinguishing mark to protect me, quite obvious with my white skin. I think the police were scared, though, and I think the crowd knew it. That final shrill cry from the women before the shooting started certainly sounded much more like a jeer than a battle-cry. And the first Africans who fled past me after the shooting started were still laughing. *Humphrey Taylor*

HEARTHRUG WEDDING

Princess Margaret married Mr Anthony Armstrong-Jones on 6 May. He was later created Earl of Snowdon.

8 May 1960
The wedding, televised, was a triumphant mass communication. The effect of being there, in spite of no colour, was almost supernaturally strong. Many millions must have had the sensation that Princess Margaret was being married on their hearthrugs. It took you some time to re-integrate yourself from the Abbey. As usual, some of the off-beat moments were the best. The curtsey on the way out. The Queen in profile singing a hymn, but not joining in the National Anthem. The Duke of Edinburgh

rallying the bride, who needed no rallying, for the march-in, was a gift for trained lip-readers.

The gravity of the bride-groom's father emerging from signing the register was almost alarming coinciding with the pause that followed. But only for a moment. *Angst* was steadily routed throughout the entire ceremony, and the absence of Mendelssohn much lightened the end. Some of the old Abbey hands, like Lady Churchill, were delightfully at their ease during the settling in. The Commonwealth Ministers looked near enough to touch. There must have been some sharply contrasted prayers from their row.

Dimbleby was superb, fluent, friendly, full of colour adjectives (sign of a healthy psyche) and not too pompous. He remembered everything from names of carriage horses to what Princess Alice did with the myrtle sprigs from her bouquet. His infectious elation seduced me clean away from I.T.V., though the Rev.

Simon Phipps put up a firm display, pausing between his theological commentaries to use his social expertise and score with some lesser-known Royal relations. Outside the Abbey, Cocteau, with his frizzy blue rinse, and Betjeman, with his chummy

dome, stole some of the show from the hats. Anne Edwards, who was doing the 'Jennifer' act, suddenly remarked on a 'fellow journalist not looking as smart as the rest of us.' Was this a case of lady dog eating lady dog? I couldn't see.

Maurice Richardson

SOUTH BANK WASTELAND

23 October 1960

Architects are not noted for self-loathing and most of us like occasionally to revisit our old battle-fields – buildings to you – and to finger in retrospect the scars and medals of triumph or disaster. Yet few, I suspect, of those architects and engineers who were so busy on the South Bank site ten years ago will be found to-day mooning and brooding over the windswept tarmac of its promenades.

The truth is that for all its clean seaside light, its gay flowers, its magnificent panoramic range of architectural pictures the South Bank is a sad place to visit.

The Festival Hall looks as if it has the hump. The Shot Tower, decapitated and bolted up, clearly knows it is under sentence of death. The Riverside Café hangs only by its grimy and ragged fingernails to what must be one of the finest sites in London. The pools are cracked and empty, the fountains dismantled, the sculpture removed.

Yet it was here, ten years ago, that day after day we strolled among the courtyards and gardens of the brief light-hearted

city, and night after un-British night that we dined and danced under the stars with London's riverside lit up for our enjoyment. Was it all just an extravagant jamboree?

What did it achieve? A new stretch of embankment, four and a half acres of new land reclaimed from Thames mud, a fine new Concert Hall, a new pier. But more important were the lessons to be learned from it and later to be developed by those now engaged upon the replanning of our towns and cities.

First, the value to city life of traffic-free pedestrian promenades. Parks and gardens are nice, but they are no substitute for the pleasures of walking safely about and between buildings.

Secondly, the importance in re-development of taking advantage of the existing features on or around the site – a railway bridge, or an old wall, a tree, a change of level, an unexpected viewpoint.

Thirdly, the awareness that the spaces between buildings are as important as the buildings themselves – even more so perhaps as our buildings become increas-

ingly uniform, anonymous and non-committal in character.

Fourthly, the importance of detail. Whether it be a lamp-post or the profile of a kerbstone, the shape of a litter-bin or the selection of a manhole-cover, everything is worth taking trouble with.

Anything else? Yes. Public good will – just as important to the beginning of a new development as fine buildings and an imaginative layout. For nearly 300 years the South Bank was a disgrace to Central London. For a year at least it was a place of pleasure and interest.

The South Bank is still the most splendid building-site in London. It has restored to the city what it has always lacked – a true riverside to be publicly enjoyed. There is still a spark left of the warmth that glowed and glittered there ten years ago. Cherish it, and the South Bank could become once again a place with its own character and life. Neglect it, and the South Bank will become just another built-up area, tidy, well-meant, lifeless and unloved.

Sir Hugh Casson

LADY CHATTERLEY'S TRIAL

6 November 1960

Now that the case is over, and Lady Chatterley's adventures are speeding two-hundred-thousand-fold to every outpost of literacy in the country, it seems suddenly unthinkable that the jury could have brought in any other verdict. But it was desperately thinkable right up to three o'clock on Thursday afternoon, as anyone

knows who sat through the six days of the trial, and sweated out the dragging hours of the jury's retirement; more than most people, Gerald Gardiner, counsel for the defense knew it, and looked the reverse of optimistic as he prowled up and down like a wounded lion, waiting for those twelve inscrutable citizens to come to their conclusion.

How we had all stared at them, seizing on each smile, each sniffle, each sign of inattentiveness as evidence of sympathy or hostility to Lawrence's cause! The lean, middle-aged man at the right-hand end of the back row seemed prematurely grey: did this betoken sensitivity or hyper-sensitivity? And the quietly eccentric behaviour of the woman, upstage

157

right, left many of us baffled; she was given to strange, secret smiles, and would take notes at inexplicable moments.

In front of her sat a younger woman, sedate and pretty, perhaps a teacher; some of us pictured her as the Henry Fonda character whose gentle persistence would finally win over her colleagues, as in *Twelve Angry Men*.

In all our ears there still rang the voice of Mervyn Griffith-Jones, counsel for the prosecution, high-cheek-boned and poker-backed, a veteran of Eton, Trinity Hall (Cambridge), the Coldstream Guards and many previous obscenity cases; a voice passionate only in disdain, but barbed with a rabid belief in convention and discipline; a slow, scaly voice, listening to which one almost felt that if Penguin Books were acquitted, the prostitutes would dance in the streets, as they did after Oscar Wilde's conviction.

On Lawrence as a literary artist, the voice (for so I think of Mr. Griffith-Jones, since from where I sat only his head was visible) – the voice had done some dedicated homework. 'Is that expert, artistic writing?' it would ask, having cited a passage in which a phrase was several times repeated. The mind's eye saw a man holding up one brick after another and demanding: 'Is that expert, artistic architecture?' The voice marked Lawrence as if he were an examination paper, and its interrogations had much in common with *vivas*.

It exhaled class-consciousness as effortlessly as air. Would the jury wish their servants to read Lawrence's novel? And was it natural for the lady of a great house to 'run off and copulate with his husband's game-keeper?' The voice took on a positively vengeful rasp when cross-examining people who distinguished between sex as Lawrence saw it and sex as a trivial diversion. Wasn't it true that by 'tenderness' the book actually meant tenderness towards the genital organs? (One wondered how else the voice

would want them treated.) And could anyone deny that in the 'bouts' of love-making the emphasis was on the 'pleasure and satisfaction' involved? Leisurely and deadly, the voice hounded Connie Chatterley, a traitress to her class in that she not only enjoyed sex, but enjoyed it with a quasi-peasant. *A propos* of a passage in which she removes her night-dress before making love, the voice enquired why this 'strip-tease' was necessary; one assumed, charitably, that the question had been carelessly phrased. Throughout the trial, one longed for a witness who might challenge Mr. Griffith-Jones in Lionel Trilling's words:

'I see no reason in morality (or in aesthetic theory) why literature should not have as one of its intentions the arousing of thoughts of lust. It is one of the effects, perhaps one of the functions, of literature to arouse desire, and I can discover no ground for saying that sexual pleasure should not be among the objects of desire which literature present to us, along with heroism, virtue, peace, death, food, wisdom, God, etc.'

But nobody made that answer; and we, anxious in the corridors, had all but persuaded ourselves that no jury could withstand the impact of Mr. Griffith-Jones when the verdict was returned and Lawrence exonerated.

Looking back, I think I can isolate the crucial incident, the exchange wherein the case was psychologically won. It occurred on the third morning during the testimony of Richard Hoggart, who had called Lawrence's novel 'puritanical.' Mr. Hoggart is a short, dark young Midland teacher of immense scholarship and fierce integrity. From the witness box he uttered a word that we had formerly heard only on the lips of Mr. Griffith-Jones: he pointed out how Lawrence had striven to cleanse it from its furtive, contemptuous and expletive connotations, and to use it in the most simple, neutral way: one fucks. There was no reaction of shock anywhere in the court, so

calmly was the word pronounced and so literally employed.

'Does it gain anything,' asked Mr. Gardiner, counsel for the defence, 'by being printed "f———"?' 'Yes,' said Mr. Hoggart, 'it gains a dirty suggestiveness.'

Rising in cross-examination, Mr. Griffith-Jones wanted to know what Mr. Hoggart meant by 'puritanical,' receiving an answer to the effect that a puritan was a man who felt a profound sense of responsibility to his own conscience. Counsel then read out a series of excerpts from the novel. It must have been by chance that he chose the most impressive passages, the most solemnly ecstatic, the ones about 'the primeval roots of true beauty' and 'the sons of men and the daughters of women' but slowly, as he recited them, one realised that he genuinely thought them impure and revolting.

With every defiling inflection he alienated some part of his audience, seemingly unaware that what he had intended for our scorn was moving us in a way he had never foreseen; yet still he continued, bland and derisive, utterly unconscious of his increasing loneliness. Having finished, he triumphantly asked the witness whether a puritan would feel such 'reverence for a man's balls.' 'Indeed, yes,' said Mr. Hoggart, almost with compassion.

I remembered his earlier reply to the suggestion that Lady Chatterley's affair with Mellors was due solely to her husband's impotence. '*It is not*', he said: and in those words we heard, for the first time in the trial, the stubborn, uncompromising voice of the radical English moralist.

Its volume and assurance grew as the cross-examination proceeded; and before long both jury and audience knew that the real battle had at last been joined – between all that Hoggart stood for, and all that Griffith-Jones stood for; between Lawrence's England and Sir Clifford Chatterley's England; between contact and separation; between freedom and control; between love and death.

Kenneth Tynan

EVAN EDWARDS, SHEPHERD

Christmas in the countryside is supposed to be more traditional than Christmas anywhere else. Evan Edwards is a Welsh shepherd. His life is hardly romantic; his Christmas will be commonplace; but because we are all susceptible to the season, this is the kind of man who comes to mind.

25 December 1960

Shepherds keep dogs, blow whistles, carry crooks, wear oil-skins in storms, and know one sheep from another. On the Scottish border and in the north of England they may have a couple of thousand acres to look after; in South Wales one farm has 15,000 acres and nine shepherds, and a sheep-stealer with a van can make a dozen disappear in a night.

Mr. Edwards has a 500-acre sheep-walk on a mountain, with 400 sheep, employers who never bother him, and no thieves. He comes from the mountains, and, like most people, does what he does for the simple reason that anything else would be worse. He has a hard, quiet face, with dark hair; he is in his mid-forties. Welsh is his first language. The small stone house where he lives with his wife and two children is 1,000 ft. up, in central Wales, facing east into the Cambrian Mountains, which are among the oldest rocks in the world. Above the thin, perpetual wind a jet can almost always be heard, very high. A lot of rain falls, and at times of bomb-testing has given this part of Britain more radio-activity than most: Cwmystwyth, five miles away, was renamed Cwmstrontium by the wags.

Shepherds usually turn out to have had shepherds for fathers. The father of Mr. Edwards lived deeper and higher in the mountains, but the Army took over the land for an artillery range in the Second World War, and the family moved down to the present house. Now the son has it, rent-free from the three brothers who employ him. All he has to do for long stretches of the year is to get up at 7.30, hear the weather forecast on the new red battery radio with antennae, have breakfast – with his wife's salty butter, and cocoa, which he drinks instead of tea – then go out to see the sheep are all right at the top of the mountain, 1,500 ft. up, where they will have spent the night. After that he can get on with mending a fence or chopping wood or digging a ditch; he goes home for mid-day dinner, and may doze with one of his newspapers, the *Cymro* or the *Cambrian News*.

But the fixed points of his year turn Mr. Edwards into a furious man of action. His voice is harsh when he calls to his dogs. At lambing time he will kneel with the sheep; 'Sometimes you've got to take hold of the lambs and bring them out.' A month or two later comes the ear-marking – 'We always keep the day, the last Thursday in May.' With a sharp knife the ears are nicked in a pattern, distinctive to this flock, a slit in the left ear and a piece off the top of the right. Above the dresser, in the kitchen with mats and linoleum on the floor, is a tattered notebook containing 355 earmarks from the surrounding hills. Mr. Edwards lifts it down carefully and turns the pages slowly with thick fingers. He knows the marks as far as Rhayader, fifteen miles away. Some go back for centuries.

Shearing is in July, when twenty men and boys, with wives and other interested parties outnumbering them, come up the track from the next valley. Mrs. Edwards cooks a sheep and eighteen pounds of beef, and the noise is tremendous.

In the summer Mr. Edwards rides a pony. There are campers in the valley, and for twenty years now they have had a regular summer visitor, a retired soldier from the Midlands who comes for the fishing, or, as Mrs. Edwards says approvingly, just to go off for the day with sandwiches and lie on the grass. There are hikers. Extra sheep have come up for the summer pasture, at ten bob a head from May to October.

There is the marking and dipping, and sheep to be driven down to the lorries for market. The hills are busy. Then, in the autumn, the rams are let out among the ewes. Then winter settles down, black and wet.

The school taxi squelches through the field to the bottom of the track, a quarter of a mile away. It's too cold to ride a pony. Mr. Edwards squelches over the hills in wellingtons, stuffing pills of carbon tetrachloride down unwilling throats to prevent the fluke. In the evenings the parents play whist with Lewis, aged fourteen, and Sara Eleanor, aged ten, while the paraffin lamp hisses and Luxemburg comes through powerfully on the radio.

Lewis is mad about sheep and football, but it's not clear whether he'll be a footballer or even a shepherd. His father says: "If it goes on like now there'll be no need for shepherds here. The other side from us, it's all bought for forests. No one wants to come and live up the mountain now. When a sheep farm is going for sale the Forestry Commission give good money. They say they've got trees to grow anywhere, right up the mountain."

This doesn't depress Mr. Edwards unduly. It's a fact of life, like snow in February. He is reasonably content: goes to chapel occasionally, visits Aberystwyth for the pictures; has never been to London, of course, has a bank account at Tregaron, thinks "the electric is very handy" but doesn't pine for it, never tires of eating mutton; has five good dogs, a few cows, a hazel crook made by his cousin with "E.E." cut into the curly part, and a pair of geese for Christmas.

On Boxing Night there will be a whist drive in Bont, the nearest village, while the children stay with grandparents there. Soon it will be next year, and Mr. Edwards will be busy again.

Paul Ferris

THE FORGOTTEN PRISONERS

On 26 August 1990 Emily Bell reported in The Observer *how Amnesty International was founded 'following an overwhelming response' to an article in the paper in 1961. Here is that article. The introduction read: 'On both sides of the Iron Curtain, thousands of men and women are being held in jail without trial because their political or religious views differ from those of their Governments. Peter Benenson, a London lawyer, conceived the idea of a world campaign, Appeal for Amnesty, 1961, to urge Governments to release these people or at least give them a fair trial. The campaign opens today, and* The Observer *is glad to offer it a platform.'*

28 May 1961

Open your newspaper any day of the week and you will find a report from somewhere in the world of someone being imprisoned, tortured or executed because his opinions or religion are unacceptable to his government. The newspaper reader feels a sickening sense of impotence. Yet if these feelings of disgust all over the world could be united into common action, something effective could be done.

The important thing is to mobilise public opinion quickly, and widely, before a government is caught up in the vicious spiral caused by its own repression, and is faced with impending civil war. By then the situation will have become too desperate for the government to make concessions. In October a Penguin Special called *Persecution 1961* will be published as part of our Amnesty campaign. In it are stories of nine men and women from different parts of the world. One story is of

the revolting brutality with which Angola's leading poet, Agostino Neto, was treated. Dr. Neto was one of the five African doctors in Angola. His efforts to improve the health services for his fellow Africans were unacceptable to the Portuguese. In June last year the Political Police had him flogged in front of his family and then dragged away. He has since been in prison in the Cape Verde Isles without charge of trial.

From Romania, we shall print the story of Constantin Noica, the philosopher, who was sentenced to twenty-five years' imprisonment because, while 'rusticated' his friends and pupils continued to visit him, to listen to his talk on philosophy and literature. The book will also tell of the Spanish lawyer, Antonio Amat, who tried to build a coalition of democratic groups, and has been in prison without trial since November, 1958; and of two white men persecuted by their own race for preaching that the coloured races

should have equal rights: Ashton Jones, the sixty-five-year-old minister, who last year was repeatedly beaten-up and three times imprisoned in Louisiana and Texas for doing what the Freedom Riders are now doing in Alabama: and Patrick Duncan, the son of the former South African Governor-General, who, after three stays in prison, has just been served an order forbidding him from attending or addressing any meeting for five years.

The success of the 1961 Amnesty Campaign depends on how sharply and powerfully it is possible to rally public opinion. It depends, too, upon the campaign being all-embracing in its composition, international in character and politically impartial in direction. How much can be achieved when men and women of good will unite was shown during World Refugee Year. Inevitably most of the action called for by Appeal for Amnesty, 1961, can only be taken by governments. But experience shows that in matters such as these governments are prepared to follow only where public opinion leads. Pressure of opinion a hundred years ago brought about the emancipation of the slaves. It is now for man to insist upon the same freedom for his mind as he was won for his body.   *Peter Benenson*

NOT SIMPLY BLACK OR WHITE

5 November 1961

Instinctive liberal reaction to the Commonwealth Immigrants' Bill is to reject it out of hand. Whatever its intentions, it will weigh more heavily on coloured peoples than on others for the simple reason that (the Irish apart) most immigrants happen to be coloured. Even if one accepts (as we unhesitatingly do) that the Government has not brought forward its Bill under pressure of the anti-colour claque inside the Conservative Party, the Bill cannot

easily be dissociated from the campaigns led by some Tory M.P.s who ask: 'Do you want to see Britain go black?'

Nor can the strong feelings aroused by this Bill in some parts of the Commonwealth be ignored by those who genuinely care about preserving our multi-racial concepts even though no other member-nation maintains an 'open door.' (Most of them, in fact, control immigration very strictly.) There will also be causes of genuine hardship. Closing

Britain's door, however slightly, condemns many of the Commonwealth's underprivileged citizens to a blighted future in their impoverished societies. Even if 'we're all right, Jack,' they are not. Finally, an inescapable corollary of the limitation on immigration is that the colour problem is proving as hard for us to face as it has proved for others. It is a confession of social failure.

All these reasons make it easy to understand why liberals in all parties should wish to cry out 'racialism, intolerance, selfishness,' and consign the Bill to the devil. But the case is not quite so simple. To accept all the arguments against the Bill does not demolish the case for some control of immigration. We have not, in fact, maintained an 'open door' policy for many years past. If India and Pakistan had not *voluntarily* agreed to control emigration to Britain at their end, restrictions would inevitably have been imposed much earlier. All the signs now point to an accelerating rate of immigration. Britain has neither the resources nor the space to go on indefinitely adding to its population, white or coloured. Britain can progress only by planning *all* her resources, and this must include control over the rate of inflow of new labour from whatever source – Commonwealth or Common Market.

If the door were kept wide open, a time would inevitably come – in three or perhaps five years – when we should be faced with a glut of largely unskilled, mainly coloured immigrants. And by then we should have a social situation in which any proposal to limit further immigration would have to be fought through in an atmosphere of bitter racial antagonisms. The seeds of such a crisis are already present – not only in the repugnant emotional attitudes of certain politicians but also among the workers who are directly involved in the social strains of competing with immigrants for houses, hospital beds and social services. Certainly, we want more of all of these; but, again, there is a limit to what is possible. And although race and colour *should* not complicate these problems, it is hypocrisy to pretend that they do not.

Britain cannot afford, either for her own sake or for the Commonwealth's, to allow the impression to gain ground that we are running away from the implications of a large and growing number of coloured people as an integral part of our society. The immigrants who come to Britain are benefactors as well as beneficiaries. Without them, industrial development would long since have slowed down. But once they are here, we are responsible for their welfare, and must see that they can enjoy all the benefits of our society.

THURBER: MAN AGAINST MONSTER

5 November 1961

James Thurber died on Thursday 2 November, aged 66

Thurber had no more passionate admirers than his English ones, possibly because that specifically American wryness did not produce in America the same shock of delighted surprise as it did here in the thirties and forties. We had read writers like Mark Twain; but Thurber somehow gave us a sense of revelation, a new kind of wit in a perfected literary form.

Many people, if they thought of the man in those early days, must have envisaged someone vaguely unathletic, permanently middle-aged, endomorphic, something between Walter Mitty and the strange boneless men, apprehensively staring, mouths glumly turned down, of his drawings. (Thurber relates in his book on Ross how E. B. White, catching him in an attempt to make his drawings look more three-dimensional, said: 'Don't do that. If you ever got good you'd be mediocre.')

But when, later, we *saw* Thurber on his frequent post-war visits to England, we found someone very different: neat but restless, slim, upright, elderly, an ectomorph. Above all, Thurber was a precisian. He was always restlessly building neat walls against Old Chaos. His humour was the first that could be regarded as a genuine literary product of an age in which the ordinary man, heir to centuries of peasant and family life, suddenly (for art telescopes these processes) is up against the menace of industrial civilisation.

He was Committed, in a very much deeper sense than that commonly denoted by the word. He was committed to Man, and his enemy was a kind of shifting monster of Inaccuracy – whether the moral inaccuracy of scientific lunacy, the inaccuracy of people's knowledge about each other, or the inaccuracy of the misremembered quotation (he had total recall and never forgot anything. The last time I met him, at the Stafford Hotel in London, he was wondering whether Whitehead, the philosopher, could have been any good at all because of a misquotation he had made). Another frequent form of the enemy was inaccuracy in English construction, about which there are some splendid explosions in *Lanterns and Lances*, his last book ('a woman came chattering into my dreams saying, "We can sleep 20 people in this house in a pinch, but we can only eat 12".') It is not surprising that his great literary hero was Henry James.

Words were *things* to Thurber, and this became more and more evident as blindness descended on him during the last quarter of his life. He could see the whole thing hanging up there in his mind, he just went on restlessly choosing the words. Perfectly-fashioned pieces came out, showing an innocent dreamland, where there was no confusion or inaccuracy, only joy.

It is hard to think he is gone, even though the climate of his work grows larger and more inviting all the time. He created a *genre* and was a giant in it. In a century's time, critics may acknowledge Walter Mitty as a basic twentieth-century figure. If Faust is pure intellect and Don Juan is pure sense, Mitty is pure fantasy. It is fitting that the native city of the man who gave form to the Mitty-idea – this wonderfully new, big, true discovery – should be Columbus.   *Paul Jennings*

161

THE WALL

26 November 1961

Fortification of the wall through Berlin is still going on. The two parts of the city are now almost completely severed. The elevated and underground railways no longer connect the two parts of the town. There is no direct telephone communication. Only the mails are left.

The wall starts in a bird sanctuary on the banks of a stream called the Tegeler Fliess. It flows through a marshy valley 200 yards from the village of Lübars, which has four big farms, a policeman, a duck pond – now frozen – and an inn called The Merry Finch. The village is reputed to be the coldest place in Berlin. It might have been moved here from Wiltshire.

It belongs to the French sector of the city and the high road leading out of it leads only to the Russian sector. The barrier is seven minutes from The Merry Finch, but the East German People's Police can see you sooner. Here, as everywhere along the wall, they operate in pairs, one man with field-glasses, the other with a gun.

The barrier consists of three barbed-wire fences supported on concrete posts seven feet high and six inches thick.

The ground between the second and third fences has been cleared and can be lit at night. A line of poles thirty feet high, carries a power line, with a cluster of electric lights. There is a line of watchtowers twenty feet high spaced 600 yards apart.

Farther south, where the suburbs become denser, the border is marked by a railway embankment. In Berlin, as in Surrey, railway lines in leafy suburbs tend to be flanked by gardens. By this week the People's Police had managed to get rid of most of the gardens that were in their way on the east side of the tracks. On Wednesday they were burning the rubbish, the tool sheds along with the cherry-trees.

A mile south of the Hertha foot-

ball stadium the sector boundary runs east and west and coincides with the building line on the south side of the street. Here, the People's Police have made their wall out of houses. At first they bricked up the front doors and the ground-floor windows. Later they blocked up all the windows: people who lived on the south side of the street were talking to people who lived on the north side.

In Neukölln, the wall twists between blocks of flats, shops, houses, gardens. In two streets the boundary follows the building line, but here the houses belong to the West, the pavement to the East.

Where this happens the People's Police have built their wall in the gutter. A notice at the end of one such street reads: Citizens of the Sebastianstrasse! We draw your attention to the fact that the pavement you use belongs to the territory of the German Democratic Republic and that the building line is the State frontier. We expect you to refrain from any provocation on the territory because otherwise we will take the security measures that are necessary.

The wall ends four miles on in Rudow, a distant, pleasant southern suburb on State Highway 179, the road that leads to the East Berlin Airport and to the site of Hitler's most powerful broadcasting station. The road now ends in two rows of barbed wire and a slit-trench.

The last house in West Berlin is No. 197: small, neat and loved. What must have been No. 199 has been bulldozed away. It was, by all accounts, as neat and modest as 197. In the place where it used to stand the earth has been cleared and flattened. The cherry trees have been flung aside to make way for the wire.

Mark Arnold-Forster

163

THE SEVEN YEARS WAR

25 March 1962

The desperate resistance and lunatic atrocities of the O.A.S. (*Organisation de l'Armée Secrète*) in Oran and Algiers should not be allowed to conceal the immense importance of the Algerian peace treaty. The long, cruel war is ended. An independent Algeria has been born. France has been freed at last from a burden which was crippling her morally, politically and economically. For this achievement General de Gaulle deserves the highest praise. In 1958, when he returned to power, *The Observer* wrote that all the dubious tricks and dishonesties of the *coup d'état* would be forgiven if he could bring peace to Algeria. Now he has done it, and done it far sooner than most experts believed possible. (English critics should remember that in the case of Ireland, the closest parallel in our own history, Gladstone became convinced of the need to grant Home Rule in 1885, yet it was not until 1921 – thirty-six years later – that Ireland won her independence.) The difficulties are enormous, for the Europeans in Algeria are not a handful of settlers who could be compensated and brought back to France, but a nation in miniature who regard Algeria as their home and had been promised repeatedly that France would never abandon them. Partition – our own solution in Ireland – was geographically impossible.

But if General de Gaulle deserves praise, the Algerian leaders deserve equal praise. These men, who for seven years have been hunted, tricked and imprisoned, who have seen their comrades killed and tortured and their families uprooted, have shown an astonishing far-sightedness and generosity in making peace on terms which should make possible a more fruitful collaboration between France and Algeria. They have emerged from their long ordeal as the most mature and disciplined of all the Arab leaders, and should have great influence in the Arab world. If France too can forget the past and act as mediator and interpreter in this part of the world – a task for which she is well fitted – these two nations may be able to repair some of the damage done to relations between the West and the Arabs since 1945.

But the cost has also been terrible. A war of extreme cruelty has undermined the moral sense of both sides. Frenchmen have come to take torture for granted and to tolerate atrocities by their own armed forces which they fiercely resented when employed by the Nazis. France herself has been infected by the contagion of civil war. Although by an almost miraculous chance Algeria never became a theatre of the cold war, the West suffered infinite harm by association, and many moderate neutrals wondered how it was that Britain and America could accept so calmly what was happening in Algeria, when they protested so bitterly at events in Hungary and Tibet and East Germany.

Fortunately the determination of General de Gaulle and the courage and wisdom of the Algerian leaders have given the world a chance to make good the damage. France should recover quickly, and the removal of the Algerian problem, the last big colonial issue in French politics, should enable the non-Communist Left and Centre to emerge again as a vital influence in France.

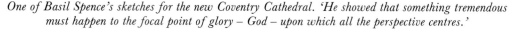

One of Basil Spence's sketches for the new Coventry Cathedral. 'He showed that something tremendous must happen to the focal point of glory – God – upon which all the perspective centres.'

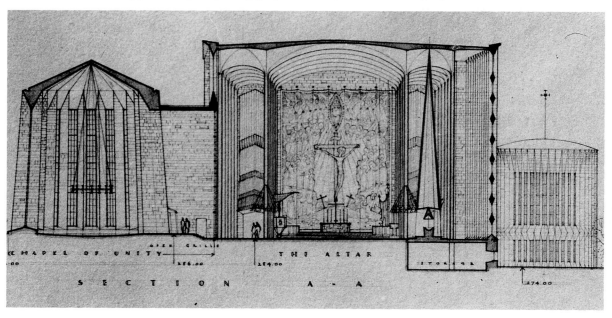

ARCHITECTURE:
VERDICT ON COVENTRY

The new cathedral at Coventry, built beside the old one destroyed in the war, was consecrated in May, 1962.

20 May 1962

There was nothing particularly 'Gothic', traditional or 'unmodern' about Sir Basil Spence's choice of a plan for Coventry Cathedral. It was both architecturally and liturgically desirable and correct.

Cathedrals are built not to exercise architects, or even for the delectation of tourists, but for oblation. Cathedrals must not only have complete architectural unity – that is true of any building – but something further, something born out of that unity: an absolute tranquillity, an absolute absence of the irrelevant, an absolute reservoir of calm silence within which the mind can both rest and concentrate – not the negative silence of the grave, but the silence of aspiration, which, I suppose, is prayer.

In some tiny village church in the Balkans, in some deserted cloister in the valleys of central France, one may find this miracle. In the great cathedral, with all its subsidiaries and distractions, it can never, even in the golden ages of faith, have been very possible. The faint ghost of it all may still be there at Chartres, at St. Apollinare, in the marshes outside Ravenna, or at Sant' Ambrogio in Milan, but it is, of necessity, no more than a ghost.

To suppose, against all this, that Basil Spence could actually 'succeed' in creating a cathedral would be absurd. One cannot overnight divert the dynamic of an age. Painters and poets, self-evidently, are children of their own time. How much more so, then, are architects.

The most that Spence could ever hope to do was to create a lovely shell, an aura, within which there could be some music and pageantry, within which the thoughtful could think and pray,

the less thoughtful find comfort or confirmation of simple beliefs. All this is – historically – hardly a definition of a cathedral, but within that definition, such as it is, Spence has – subject to reservations – done something altogether brilliant.

It is brilliant because if Spence has, inevitably, got some of the small things wrong, he has got almost all the big things right. Many of our cathedrals, having duly 'Anglicanised' the chancel more and more through three centuries, have destroyed the *raison d'être* of the basilican plan, destroyed the focal point of glory – God – upon which all the perspective centred. Spence showed in his very first sketch that, somehow, something tremendous must happen to that focal point. That something was a seventy-foot high Majestas dominating all.

That Sutherland, a painter in oils, was almost bound to fail when designing in wool, might have been foreseen. Titian failed when designing mosaic; Joshua Reynolds failed when designing stained glass. All that one can say in extenuation is that the architect's *idea* was architecturally right, the painter's execution a failure.

Again, the whole structure, vault, columns and tall windows, is a complete acceptance of all the rhythms, all the spatial qualities, all the romantic half-tones of the 'medieval' plan. Yet the vault is an airy canopy, the columns are matchsticks, the windows are grilles. In other words, they are all the very opposite of their Gothic counterparts. They are light and tense and thin – all directly derived from the wonderful nature of reinforced concrete. Spence almost certainly found inspiration of a sort in the 'jewelled casket' churches of the fourteenth century; his interpretation is his own, and it is one which would not have been possible in any other age.

Also – if Spence used a painter to design a tapestry, he at least used real craftsmen for his windows. Whether or not this age has much use for stained-glass is a moot point; Coventry Cathedral may well go into history primarily as the starting-point of a renaissance of English glass.

There are failures at Coventry – the west wall, the choir stalls, the tapestry. There are also many glories – great and small. The windows are the greatest by far.

R. Furneaux Jordan

TAKING PAINS WITH PINTER

10 June 1962

Harold Pinter was last week rehearsing his play, *The Collection*, directing with Peter Hall. Pinter, strong black hair, gleaming spectacles, dark suit, well-polished black shoes, was, superficially, more solid than one might have expected from his work. At first glance you might have taken him for a person who enjoyed discussing fast cars in pubs. He directed with confidence, his actor's voice authoritative. It was when he

took off his glasses and twirled them that you noticed the dark eyes and sensitive face that looked as though it had its worries.

Nuance and timing meant a great deal to Pinter: 'I'm probably complicating things,' he said to John Ronane, a young actor, 'but it's worth complicating. We haven't really ever quite examined this speech, have we? Until we find out what it means to you, there can't be any real.... You know?' Pinter coughed and took off his glasses. 'We have to find. . . . Don't be worried.'

'I'm not worried.' said Ronane. 'I'm just completely – lost.'

'I'm not really getting the way you were committed to yourself,' said Pinter, 'and to what you were committed. I feel you must be committed to a possibility, d'you know what I mean?'

In a break, while the cast of four drank tea and coffee out of Y.M.C.A. cups, Pinter sat down and took pains to discuss exactly what he wanted from an actor.

'The thing is, Harold's plays take such bloody concentration.' Kenneth Haigh said to Barbara Murray. She was playing with a small white kitten that had quite a large part. A man in a white coat brought in a tray of red sawdust for the kitten's W.C. Miss Murray liked the kitten, but it was troublesome. 'Bloody cats,' she said to it kindly. 'It'll have to be sedated.'

While the rehearsals went on. Pinter walked round, smoking, threw his lighter in the air and caught it. At times he lay back in a chair, feet up, hand to mouth, frowning. There was a Y.M.C.A. flag pinned to his dark vest-like jersey.

'John, I think this. . . . Since it's quite clear, I think, that the thunder. . . . And when you say, *"not again."* For Christ's sake! And the more you go on with this. . . . If you want to know what you feel about women and all that. . . .' Pinter snapped his fingers. 'Make it a clean start, as it were.' Fingers clicked. 'Switch in.'

'I should think that *olives* is *the* word. Whereas, as the change of concentration is very clear. Your, slight, thing. . . . It's a change at the silence, the change is there.' Several times people, presumably lost, opened the door of the rehearsal room in the Y.M.C.A., hesitated, apologised, went out. Pinter looked cross.

Oh, by the way, I've seen your wife [said one of the characters]. *What a beautiful kitten she has! You should see it. Bill, it's all white.*

If I were you, I'd go home and knock her over the head with a saucepan and tell her not to make up such stories.

'Okay, Michael, let's go from *"What about another drink".*'

In the shadows of the Aldwych, Pinter leapt on to the stage, stood there with his hands in pockets, spectacles gleaming. He walked with his arm round Barbara Murray.

She: 'What's *his* attitude?'

Pinter: 'What's *your* attitude?'

'I think we've done, I think it's essential to get this scene, er. . . .' Pinter's hands spun like a mouse's exercise wheel. 'Right. When you're ready, let's get on.' He lit a cigarette 'Okay, John. We're off.' Pointed and snapped fingers. 'Well, let's go, let's go, please, John.' Stands on stage, lies on stage, crouches on stage, sits on stage, flicking ash into a huge shining cylindrical tin that he carries about with him. Makes a gesture of easing collar, as though it were tight. Does this several times. 'Right, right.'

Oh, what a beautiful kitten! What a really beautiful kitten.

'In a sense it's too, rather . . . what's the word?' Fingers click, 'It was a bit too fishwifery.'

Oh what a beautiful lamp!

'Michael, you see, it's not good taste at all. The whole thing's horrible.'

'No, let's try. We've got that bloody Scarlatti. What the hell happened to it?'

Hungry? I've got some olives. Like one? Don't like olives? What on earth have you got against olives?

'Right. Good. Yes. You're there. Okay. Yeah, Let's just go back to the beginning. The whole speech, John. I find it a little elaborate. You're not swinging it.'

What on earth have you got against olives? 'I think this a qualification. You are, at the moment, shoving away, while. . . .'

I've come to a decision. I'm going to see him.

Who? What for?

John Gale

JOHN GALE (1926-1974)
'Sharp and clean as a bleached bone on a beach' – that is how Cyril Dunn described John Gale's prose. In 1956 he was in Cairo when it was bombed by the British. Algeria followed. His writing was always distinguished, but he particularly excelled in The Observer's *informal Notebook reporting* – he once said, 'I want to capture the sunlight on a butterfly's wing.' When his autobiography Clean Young Englishman *appeared, in 1965, the poet and novelist John Wain wrote in* The Observer: 'His account of forty years as an Englishman in our time is not likely to be surpased for truthfulness and accuracy.'

Playwright and director (Peter Hall) in rehearsal: 'Pinter was, superficially, more solid than one might have expected.'

NELSON MANDELA: THE BLACK PIMPERNEL

At the trial mentioned here Mandela was jailed for five years. In 1964, still in prison, he, with other black leaders who was arrested in a police raid on a farm at Rivonia, near Johannesburg, was sentenced to life imprisonment. He was only released in February 1990.

19 August 1962

Whoever betrayed Nelson Mandela to the South African police has given them an impressive victim. As an underground commander he had become a figure of unusual importance on the African scene. He directed a stay-at-home strike which disrupted and discoloured the Africkaner Nationalists' celebrations to mark the achievement last year of their new Republic. He compelled them to expose the armed strength with which they intended to subdue non-white resistance. For fifteen months since then he skilfully – even impudently – evaded arrest, so that people now call him the Black Pimpernel. A few days ago he was captured at last and was brought before a court in Johannesburg.

Mandela himself would probably reject his popular title as too romantic. He is a responsible, intelligent and resourceful man, a lawyer who in any free society would surely have won the utmost distinction. He is in fact the closest equivalent yet produced by the liberation movement to a true leader of the Resistance in Occupied France. He is a huge and strikingly handsome man of forty-four, with a broad, formidable face. His natural elegance and nonchalantly royal bearing are enhanced by a passion for good clothes. He talks in a booming, carrying voice which he rarely tried to modify, sometimes exciting apprehension in those who had secret meetings with him in Johannesburg.

Nelson Rolihlahla Mandela was born to be Chief of the

Nelson Mandela. An exile said of him, 'I have never worked with anyone who did more to banish my fear.'

Tembu, the biggest single tribe in the Transkei. His father died when Nelson was twelve. He was trained thereafter for the chieftainship, under rigid discipline, by his uncle and under the austere rules of Methodism by his mother. It seems that Nelson was by nature rebellious, unhappy even as a boy about the settled pattern of his life. He wanted to 'do something out of the way'. His vague discontent hardened into firm purpose when he went to Fort Hare, the college for Africans, and got friendly with Oliver Tambo, later President of the African National Congress.

After two years of political discussion in the college dormitories, Nelson determined 'never to rule as chief over an oppressed people.' He finished his degree

course by correspondence and went on to the University of the Witwatersrand to study law. He found the place in a political ferment, with the young Africans planning their Youth League, designed to inject new militancy into the ANC. Nelson is remembered as having been 'rather aloof' and already by far the best-dressed rebel. He did not neglect his studies quite so much as others did and in due course was launched on a legal career. He married a girl who was herself 'political' but was not eager to see Nelson ruin his practice for the cause.

Mandela and Tambo set up in partnership as attorneys, in offices on the shabby side of Johannesburg. But this was 1952 - the year of the Defiance Campaign' Against Unjust Laws. Chosen as Volunteer-in-Chief, Mandela left the office, allowed his marriage to break up and went off to travel the country. Africans now speak with awe of Mandela's achievement. He prepared and disciplined many of the 8,500 who ended up in jail. And as he was helping to train the army of volunteers, Mandela was also evolving a scheme of more enduring value, one which now reduces a little the damage to the liberation movement by his arrest. This was the M Plan, dividing the whole black part of the country into cells under the care of Congress activists. Its aim was to allow all Africans to feel themselves involved in the freedom struggle. When the iron will of the Afrikaner Nationalists forced Congress to go underground, there was at least the nucleus of an organisation that could carry on.

Mandela is self-effacing by nature. Perhaps, too, like the original Pimpernel, he has found it useful to exploit his elegance as a disguise, sometimes embellishing it with an air of indolent detachment. But he also genuinely believes in active leadership and does not wish to stand out as a hero. His real faith rests on organisation – coldly planned, tough tempered, ready for rough action in the 'war' he is sure has already been declared by the Nationalists.

Mandela had been underground since April 1961. Everyone knows about the debonair role he played in organising the stay-at-home. Everyone knows how he ran his Press relations from call-boxes, how he made appointments in the heart of Afrikanerdom and kept them all, on the dot. Several times he has slipped out of South Africa, visited many countries, and slipped back again. He popped up in Addis Ababa last February at a Pan-African conference, and made a sensationally moving speech. In this he began to ask whether a Government bent on using the utmost force to crush the freedom struggle could for ever be countered by peaceful and non-violent means.

In 1958 he married again. His second wife, Winnie, is a child-welfare worker in Johannesburg and keeps going, in Orlando township, the little brick house where the books, the record-player and the pictures still reflect her absent husband's tastes. Nobody knows how often Nelson contrived to see his wife and their two youngsters – or the three children of the first marriage now at school in Swaziland. But we may be sure that the courage with which he has faced these denials will be seen again when the Nationalists bring him once more into court. For Mandela is a brave man who can induce bravery in others. As one of the self-exiled Congress leaders says: 'I have never worked with anyone who did more to banish my fear'.

DAYLIGHT ON CUBA

In October, 1962, the two nuclear Great Powers had a showdown when President Kennedy took direct action to enforce the withdrawal of Russian missiles from Cuba.

28 October 1962

At nine o'clock on the morning of Tuesday, 16 October, Robert McNamara, Secretary of Defence, paid an early call on the President at the White House.

What he had to show Kennedy was powerful photographic evidence of Russian nuclear missile sites in Cuba, taken from American reconnaissance planes over the island.

The news confirmed the President's worst suspicions, but he reacted cautiously. He had already been given intelligence reports of missile bases in Cuba, but remembering the failings of the Central Intelligence Agency which had led to the 'Bay of Pigs' fiasco of 1961, he had ordered a stepping up of reconnaissance to provide more conclusive evidence.

This time he had to be doubly sure. For it was no longer Castro but Khrushchev with whom he had to deal. If the evidence were true, it meant Cuba was no longer a local 'irritant' but, like Berlin, the spearhead of a new military and diplomatic challenge from Russia on a world scale.

On Saturday morning Kennedy decided the evidence was irrefutable. Not only were some missiles already there, but the sites for others, with Washington in their range, were being installed with extraordinary speed.

Kennedy considered four possible courses. First, he could do nothing. Second, he could invade Cuba. Third, he could institute a blockade to prevent further shipments of missiles and combine it with a high-explosive aerial strike to eliminate existing missile sites.

Fourth, he could institute a blockade alone – and at the same time make a diplomatic demarche at the United Nations. It was not a decision that the President was to make without profound agony.

He called for the views of the Presidential inner circle, but the decision was his own and he took it before he went to bed on Saturday night.

Mr. Khrushchev had to be faced down, but he also had to be left some way of more or less honourable retreat. The partial blockade seemed the answer.

Having decided to enforce the blockade, Kennedy and his advisers clearly felt it necessary to play up the crisis, and to generate an atmosphere of 'maximum peril'. The speech that was prepared for delivery on Monday made no attempt to calm world fears. The accusation twice repeated, of Russian duplicity, the concentration on Cuba to the exclusion of everywhere else, and the brisk, jerky language, all emphasised that Kennedy was reacting to an immediate challenge with a bold, dramatic response.

An hour before President Kennedy was due to broadcast in Washington, Adlai Stevenson walked into the offices of the Acting Secretary-General U Thant, and told him that the Russians had missile bases in Cuba and that the United States intended to call an emergency meeting of the Security Council.

On Tuesday the crisis gathered speed. From Washington, Kennedy completed his opening moves: the U.S. fleet deployed off Cuba, the Western allies expressed their support. (Publicly the British Government gave its loyal support. Privately it expressed some dismay: 'We are not sure,' said one Cabinet Minister, 'what this young man is up to.') Stevenson tabled a resolution in the Security Council, demanding immediate dismantling and withdrawal from Cuba of all offensive weapons.

As the world prepared reluctantly to face war, all sides looked hopefully towards the U.N. But, from U Thant's vantage point, the outlook was grim.

On Thursday, at the UN, the atmosphere was still strained, but more hopeful and Moscow reported that Khrushchev, too, had agreed to talks.

The next day Khrushchev told U Thant that he had ordered Russian ships to stay out of the interception area. Kennedy said that everything possible would be done to avoid confronting Russian ships outside that area. The dreaded clash at sea had been averted, and the first part of the crisis was over – with the U.N. as the undisputed peacemaker.

But a second and more serious crisis was only just beginning. Although Khrushchev had indirectly given Kennedy a mild public answer, he had not committed himself to removing the missile bases from Cuba. On the contrary, American air surveys showed the Russians were working feverishly to complete them.

The blockade might stop more missiles coming in, but it could not stop the Russians from finishing the bases already started. The speed with which this second crisis developed was dictated by the speed of the continued Russian build-up.

Kennedy had warned in his broadcasts that if the offensive preparations in Cuba continued, 'further action would be justified'. Now, inspired leaks to the Washington Press corps ominously began to speak of possible American bombing attacks on the missile bases.

If this was part of the war of nerves, the Russians had already shown – more gently – they could play the same game. In Moscow on Thursday, Marshal Malinovsky declared in the closing speech at an army conference on ideological questions that Soviet forces were in a high state of readiness.

With the new crisis in mind U Thant sent another message to the two leaders urging restraint.

But the public mediation of the U.N. was taking second place to secret diplomacy between Washington and Moscow.

At the U.N. the American delegation was astounded to be called up by Washington at 11.30 on Friday night – after dawn in Moscow – and told that Kennedy had just received a secret message from Khrushchev going far beyond the compromise that U Thant had been trying to negotiate.

The text is still secret. It is said not to have been published by the Americans because of its violent and vituperative language. But, behind this smokescreen, Khrushchev made the key move of the week. The Soviet leader admitted in it for the first time the presence of bases in Cuba, reassured the Americans they were in Soviet not Cuban hands, and agreed to take them out in return for no more than the assurance that the Americans would not invade Cuba.

It was clear later that this was the turning-point of the crisis. At the time the world, ignorant of the message, could see only a rapid slide towards war. Evidently Khrushchev had at last been convinced that if he did not withdraw his missiles the Americans might really attack them.

In Washington that night it must have looked as though the game was won. But on Saturday morning more disturbing news began to come from Moscow. Moscow Radio announced that it would be broadcasting an important statement.

It was an offer to America to swap the Soviet bases in Cuba for the American missile bases in Turkey, which was received in Washington with bewilderment and alarm.

It coincided with the news that Russians round the Cuban missile sites were firing at American reconnaissance planes and had shot one down.

Had Khrushchev suddenly changed his mind? Or had he lost control in the Kremlin and been forced to take a tougher line? Whose finger was now on the trigger on the other side?

On Saturday evening, President Kennedy replied to both Khrushchev's messages. He rejected a deal over Turkey. He was ready, he said, to talk about disarmament generally, provided the Russian missiles in Cuba were 'rendered inoperable'. But he offered Khrushchev another way out. He gave him the promise the Soviet Premier had asked for in his secret Friday message – that America would not attack Cuba if the Soviet missiles were withdrawn. American officials at the U.N. spread the word that unless an agreement were reached within the next few hours the U.S. would take direct military action to wipe out the bases.

This was the brink. For no one knew what Khrushchev would reply. For the next 15 hours the tension reached its peak.

In London on Saturday night, it was realised that the situation was heading for disaster. Macmillan had seen Khrushchev's unpublished letter to Kennedy of the day before and believed that the risk of war was greater than at any time in the crisis.

But by 2.15 on Sunday afternoon the teleprinters everywhere tapped out the text of Khrushchev's message agreeing to the President's terms.

169

A Bellyful of the Warm South

23 December 1962

I suppose I did get to bed after dragging myself away from Fabulous Fanny's strip-tease act at some dawn-like hour. But never, as I sat with my milk shake in the sun-scorched courtyard of Brennan's waiting for my breakfast, had a morning after seemed such an unbroken continuation of a night before.

Milk shake may give the wrong impression, for it was Absinthe Suissesse, but it wasn't (unfortunately) absinthe either. Even in New Orleans there are a few things that one is not allowed to do and drinking absinthe is one of them.

Breakfast also isn't quite the word, not as we know it in Kent. At Brennan's it is an occasion as well as an all-purpose meal that you can ask for at any time from nine in the morning until midnight. We ate pineapple stuffed with banana, Oeufs Gran Vefour and crêpes suzettes, and we drank and drank Château la Dame Blanche and coffee, and we talked. After two hours we had to break off to catch a plane, with euphoric confidence in the pilot's skill as we took off towards Phoenix, Las Vegas and Los Angeles (all of which I expect to see again on my way to hell).

Our progress down the east coast had not prepared us for New Orleans, and if they had not still been fighting the American Civil War there we could have been in another country. The brochure on the city put out by the United States Information Service starts, 'Fun loving, easy going old New Orleans, since World War II, has become a striving, forward-surging metropolis. It still has its gaiety and gusto, its sun-splashed patios, and its Greek Revival mansions, shaded by palms and moss-draped live oaks. But everywhere there is a new thrusting vitality.'

The forward-surging bit is also roughly what the mayor said when showing us a model of a rocket and handing us our scrolls of honorary citizenship. We then went out and enjoyed ourselves with food, drink and jazz among the Tennessee Williams backcloth of balconies, patios and palms. The striving element must have been at it somewhere else; we found the relaxed, gently-decadent lot. Not the hot South – chambré, rather, if you like your rooms fairly warm.

We lunched at Antoine's (est. 1840) in one of those determinedly bare rooms that only the French would dare to serve food in. Each setting on the empty expanse of white linen gave you as much space as a double bed (the night before in Miami Beach I had been breathing down bosoms *across* the table).

Kennedy did his best to spoil the day with the crisis-starting broadcast on Cuba, but an argument over State and Federal rights during dinner at the Commander's Palace got us safely out of the present again.

A few confused hours ahead, filled with Dixieland jazz, gin and nudes, lay breakfast at Brennan's – which is where we went out. I long to go back, but not for too long. New Orleans is no resting-place for even long-lapsed puritans.

But San Francisco could be for ever. Falling in love with it is so common as to be tedious, since, as with a man or woman you adore, you cannot rationally explain why, but merely drool on.

It is beautiful, built on hills that the inevitable grid-iron street plan does its best to ignore. It is friendly, not just talkative – and you feel the same warmth in the most luxurious bars on Nob Hill as in the most doubtful ones in the Latin Quarter. It will feed you excellently and clothe you well. It is young, yet mature and slightly old-fashioned. It is tolerant and gay – but without the sweat-under-the-arm odour of New Orleans. It is utterly endearing, and I am enslaved.

In the doom-heavy days of our stay I could think of no better place to die. But the warm, kindly San Franciscans were determined that I should not. By my bed the local Disaster Council had fixed a notice advising me that the attack might come suddenly. Possibly the first warning would be a brilliant white light, probably the most brilliant I had ever seen. I was instructed to take refuge under a heavy piece of furniture. I felt cared-for and safe.

George Seddon

A Great Week for British Cinema

10 February 1963

Lindsay Anderson's *This Sporting Life* is a stupendous film. It has a blow like a fist. I've never seen an English picture that gives such expression to the violence and the capacity for pain that there is in the English character. It is there in Shakespeare, in Marlowe, in Lawrence and Orwell and Hogarth, but not in our cinema like this before.

Perhaps it is best to begin, like the film, with the physical facts. Frank Machin, the hero, magnificently played by Richard Harris, must weigh fourteen stone. On the football field he has the power of a tank. His instinct in any situation is to get his head down and push; you see him first in a Rugby League scrum and then working in the mines in the same fierce stance, chewing gum as though his mouth were a treadmill. He looks as proud as a legendary animal; when his front teeth are smashed in a scrum the stumps are like the broken horns of a bull.

Lindsay Anderson's films before this have been documentaries, but his first feature certainly isn't a documentary about Rugby League. Nor is it a sociological study of a kind of contemporary man. Frank Machin could have lived at any time, and he is not anyone's representative; the film is about a unique man who suffers an absolutely personal kind of pain.

The first time you see him with his landlady, Rachel Roberts, you wonder what on earth the pressure is between them. This is the way it happens in life (and in Ibsen's plays), but hardly ever in cinema; their lines carry a terrific charge of the past. There is something about her put-upon Englishwoman's silences that makes him behave like a pig, and he could boot her for the way she droops over the memory of her dead husband; but at the same time there is a kind of purity about her withdrawal that somehow consoles him, although he

does everything to wreck it. When he has sold himself for £1,000 to the North Country businessmen who run the team, he puts the cheque in front of her like a dog laying a putrid bone on a pillow.

Part of the quality of David Storey's script, from his own novel, is that the characters never offer explanations. Often what they say is not what they mean at all, which is one of the things that give the film its agonising tension between a rich instinctive life and a poverty-stricken expressive life. There is a very good scene when Frank unwraps a fur coat for her before taking her out on a spree. The cramped kitchen suddenly freezes over with the classic English repressiveness, and the neighbour who has come in to baby-sit behaves as though the place had turned into a brothel.

But when Mrs. Hammond pitches into a row after his best

friend's wedding, her grievances about what the neighbours are saying are not really the root of her misery: they are simply the easiest reason to find for it.

The difficulty isn't that they aren't married, it is that he disturbs her. In their last fight, which brings on a brain haemorrhage, all she can do is yell that she wants peace.

The football game after her death is like the awful scene in a bullring when a Spanish audience whistles scorn at a matador because they suspect him of cowardice. His supporters are suddenly booing, and they are booing his pain. Something primitive and tragic is happening.

The black subjective spirit of the film is overpowering. It floods the sound-track, which often has a peculiar resonance as though it were happening inside one's own head; Roberto Gerhard's score is

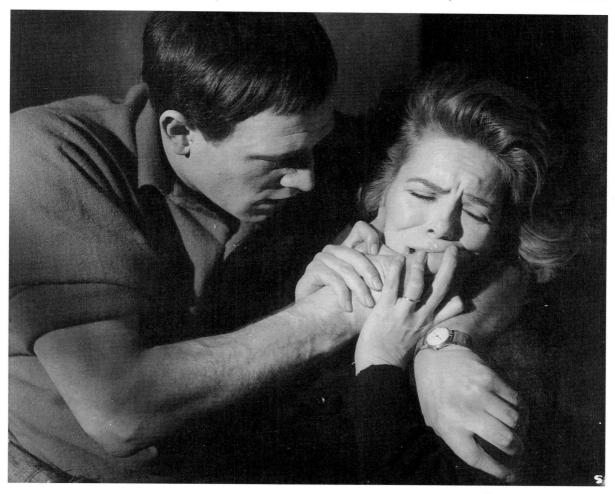

Richard Harris and Rachel Roberts give expression to 'the violence and capacity for pain there is in the English character. This Sporting Life has a blow like a fist.'

one of the best I have ever heard. Technically *This Sporting Life* is like a rock.

For one thing, it has obviously been made with a clear idea of how it was to be edited, which is rarer than it sounds. For another, the actors rehearsed for ten days first, and the scenes between Richard Harris and Rachel Roberts were done roughly in continuity; how else can serious actors work and how often does the cinema bother about it?

The tension between the two of them is suffocating. There is also a remarkable performance by Colin Blakely as Frank's friend, who is his ear at the end for his one helpless attempt to understand himself. Like the classical tragic hero, Frank has no power to change his life because he has no insight into it; all he has is a final stab of knowledge about how he looks to other people. 'She called me a great ape on a football field,' he says about his mistress. And about the football crowds: 'They want someone to act big for them.' This is what heroic art is about.

Penelope Gilliatt

THE ROOTS OF VIOLENCE

5 May 1963

There is no mistaking the change in temper in South Africa in the three 'quiet' years since the Sharpville shootings. On all sides now there is a fatalistic acceptance of the inevitability of violence.

The juggernaut of *apartheid* is now highly geared and has begun to roll heavily over the lives of the people. An order goes out from BAD (the Bantu Affairs Department) that 200,000 of Natal's 550,000 Zulus are to be moved from their traditional reserves to make one solid 'black area' for a Zulu Bantustan. Orders go out for the removal of 9,000 Indians. 700 Chinese, 7,500 Coloureds (people of mixed blood) from Johannesburg; for 6,000 Indians from East Rand towns: for two-thirds of Pretoria's 7,000 Indians; for 83,000 Indians, 81,000 Africans and 1,000 whites from Durban.

Alexandra is one of the most crime-ridden African towns around Johannesburg. Already 43,000 people have been removed, another 20,000 are being moved at present; soon only 30,000 will be left. But the sole test of who must go and who can stay is whether a person works in a particular peri-urban area outside Johannesburg or, in the case of women only, whether they provide domestic service in the city. The rest must go, or be moved. Daily, police come to search out the 20,000 permitless people. In one week Alexandra welfare workers found four small children left alone after both their parents had been arrested, another two little girls whose mother had been

An all too familiar scene in South Africa. 'There is no mistaking the change of temper. On all sides now there is the fatalistic acceptance of the inevitability of violence.'

taken away at 5.30 in the morning, and two hungry boys whose parents had been removed three weeks before.

The process of removal is known as being 'endorsed out'. It is an endorsement in the pass which forbids the holder to go on living or working in a particular urban area. An 'endorsed out' African loses his home and his right to look for work in an area of his choice. If it happens to be a woman she must leave her husband. Sometimes the man is 'endorsed out' but not his wife. His choice then is whether to split up his family or take them all into the reserves with him.

This whole system is controlled by the Pass Laws. One thousand Africans a day are prosecuted under the Pass Laws. In one week in Port Elizabeth last January, fifty Africans were fined a total of £770, or 1,610 days in prison, for pass offences.

The urban African townships have the highest crime rate in the world. Sixty-eight people are hanged every year – fives times as many as in Britain with a population three times as large. In 1961 there were 2,610 murders – 20 times higher than in Britain. As for the police, the last available figures, for 1959, show that 566 police were charged with assaults on prisoners; 311 were convicted, but only 29 were discharged from the force. Recently the courts stayed the execution of three men on the grounds that confessions had been extorted from them by the application of electric currents to their heads which were swathed in wet blankets.

Now violence has begun to wear a new face – becoming political as well as ordinarily criminal. The Government has struck back hard through the Sabotage Act. It has also introduced a variety of methods for dealing with political opponents. They are banned, banished and confined. More than 140 people have been banned. They lose all civil rights. If they are journalists they are not allowed to write. Nineteen people mostly whites, have been confined to house arrest for a period of five years. Many of those banned are chiefs or headmen who have opposed the introduction of Bantustans.

Despite bannings and banishments and the Sabotage Act, the tempo of political crime continues to rise sharply. In less than a year 585 people have been charged with serious crimes of political violence, many of them for sabotage. Four have already been sentenced to death. Scores of people have been sent to prison for terms of between twelve and twenty-three years.

Poqo is a Xhosa word meaning 'pure' or 'stand alone'. It is avowedly anti-white and has streaks of tribal atavism. It works through an elaborate cell system. Its members, significantly, are Xhosas: the people chiefly affected by the Western Cape removal scheme and by the Transkei Bantustan. A number of Poqo leaders have been 'endorsed out'. It first achieved prominence last October through its attack on the police station at Paarl, near Cape Town where several white people were killed. Subsequently it blazed a trail of violence through the Transkei – attacking police stations and killing five whites.

What was supposed to be an inquiry into Poqo became equally an inquiry into the practices of petty bureaucrats holding the power of decision over who should be 'endorsed out' to lives of insecurity and misery and who should be allowed to stay. It exposed, too, the disregard shown by the all-white Paarl town council to the grievances of the voteless people in Mbekweni township where Poqo's leaders were more feared than the police.

The authorities claim that Poqo has been destroyed: that may be so. But the root causes that bred Poqo still remain.

Colin Legum

PHILBY: AS WE KNEW HIM

7 July 1963

At first, for the initial hour or so there was nothing abnormal about his absence. As a journalist with a difficult, largely unpredictable, Middle East beat to follow he had schooled his wife, Eleanor, to accept unexplained leave-taking and appointments as routine. For the initial hour or so, any foreign correspondent's wife would have been impatient but at ease.

That evening, 23 January, Philby had left his flat in Beirut at about 6 p.m., saying he would join his wife later. They were due at a small dinner party at the house of Hugh Balfour-Paul, First Secretary of the British Embassy, a close friend of theirs, by 8.30 p.m. About 7 p.m. he telephoned to say he would be late and that Eleanor should go along without him. One of the Philby children took the call and later said he sounded 'in a hurry' but otherwise not abnormal.

When Philby failed to show up next day his wife alerted the British Embassy and they the Lebanese police. It is significant that the first reaction of his wife and close friends should be that he had had an accident.

Next day Eleanor organised a thorough search of all the hospitals in the district. Two days later, she called off the search – or, rather, attempted to – by telling the authorities that she had had a reassuring letter from her husband. He had left this in the flat. It had apparently been placed so that Eleanor would discover it the morning after his disappearance. But by mischance, or because of the first distractions of the search, it had been overlooked till now.

Looking around later, Eleanor also found that her husband's small attaché-case had gone, the one he normally managed with on even the longest reporting assignments. His typewriter had been left behind. But she was soon to receive letters from Cairo that had been unmistakably typed on it before departure. It all pointed one way. However briefly, in whatever rush, his departure was premeditated. It now looks as though when he said a very casual cheerio to a wife and children he was devotedly attached to that evening, he somehow knew he was burning his boats, that he was radically changing his life and theirs. He was leaving for a reason and a destination that, it seems, he could not discuss or disclose to his wife, a tolerant and understanding woman.

It is significant of the impression that Harold 'Kim' Philby had made on close friends and newspaper colleagues in London and Beirut, particularly in his last six and a quarter years as correspondent in the Middle East of *The Observer* and the *Economist*, that there should have been such bewilderment. Every newspaper office hauled out its bulky files of the Burgess and Maclean case, noted Philby's acquaintance with Burgess at Cambridge and the Washington Embassy, his apparently ready admission of early Communist associations.

Reporters arriving in Beirut (as I did in March) to look for clues or knit their surmises could only look closer at the man, his past, his present life, his habits, his known inclinations, then attempt to fit it into a Middle East context, and see which way the shadow fell. The mystery began and ended somewhere inside Philby.

He was 51. He was born in India and spent much of his boyhood there – hence the Kipling-esque nickname – apparently happily. He went to Westminster School and was a scholar at Trinity, Cambridge. He joined the University Socialist Society, but unlike Guy Burgess and Donald Maclean there was no sign that he was a Communist. When he came down in 1933 he spent a year or so travelling in Europe and studying German in Vienna. He then worked in London, on the *Review of Reviews*. In 1937, when he was 25, he went to look at the Spanish Civil War and *The Times* took him

'He was leaving for a reason he could not disclose to his wife, a tolerant and understanding woman.'

on as their correspondent with the Franco side. He was wounded by a shell that killed a fellow-journalist near by. He was decorated by Franco.

In World War Two Philby was recruited by the Foreign Office for counter-intelligence work. He stayed in this until the end of the war, part of the time in the same outfit as Guy Burgess and got the O.B.E. for his work. He became successively First Secretary in Istanbul and, in 1949, temporary First Secretary at the Washington Embassy where Burgess arrived also, in late 1950.

By all accounts Philby's work was highly regarded, but in July 1951 he was asked to resign from the Foreign Office because although cleared by British and

American investigations of complicity as the Third Man who had tipped off Burgess about the suspicion falling on Maclean, it became known that he had had 'Communist associations' in the past.

For Philby, with a promising career abruptly cut off, there now began a lean period of three or four years. His means of livelihood are obscure, but with a wife and children to keep, he may have been having a difficult time.

About the spring of 1956 a member of the Foreign Office staff known to the paper, who made it clear that his approach was official, asked the Editor of *The Observer* if he had a place for Philby. He said the Foreign Office felt it was unfair that, in spite of the full clearance of Philby's name in 1955, he was finding it impossible to practise his profession of journalism. In the autumn of 1955 Mr. Marcus Lipton named Philby in the Commons and suggested that he was being shielded as the Third Man who had tipped off Burgess about the suspicion falling on Maclean, both of whom had defected in 1951. Mr. Macmillan, then Foreign Secretary, then cleared Philby in these terms: 'No evidence has been found to show that he was responsible for warning Burgess and Maclean . . . I have no reason to conclude that Mr. Philby has at any time betrayed the interests of this country, or to identify him with the so-called Third Man, if, indeed, there was one.' Now, in 1955, a cast-iron promise was given that he had no further connection with British intelligence and that he would not be involved in Government work of any kind while in *The Observer* employment.

When Philby vanished, the paper shared the bewilderment of his closest Beirut friends. Any answer had to be reconcilable to one firm factor: Philby was strongly attached to his wife and family. When away on assignments he made a point of writing home daily. Only some desperate move could have persuaded him to cause them so great a sorrow.

He was in good health and an apparently rational state of mind when he left that evening. Some, however, had noticed signs of increasing depression and heavier drinking over the last year or so.

Speculation was ended when Mr. Edward Heath announced in the Commons last week that the security services were 'now aware that Mr Philby worked for the Soviet authorities before 1946 and that in 1951 he in fact warned Maclean through Burgess that the security services were about to take action against him.'

Mr. Heath conceded that this also meant that Philby was now known to have been the Third Man. Mrs. Philby had received letters from her husband purporting to come from behind the Iron Curtain.   *Roy Perrott*

THE COMMUNICATIONS INDUSTRY

14th July 1963

Journalism, advertising, public relations, satire – we're all one big happy family in the communications industry. More and more we're setting our minor differences to one side, and pulling together as a team.

That's why I find it heartwarming news that one of my colleagues in the satirists' lodge has now made a film sponsored by the Advertising Association in which, according to the *Financial Times*, he 'helps to demonstrate how modern advertising has imposed on itself rigid codes of conduct.'

There is no less encouraging news about another of our Brother Communicators. He has appeared in a film about an industry, sponsored by a manufacturers' association, and, again according to the *Financial Times*, the aim of the film is to hit back at the critics who are – to quote the film brochure – 'ill-informed and prejudiced' in regarding the manufacturers as 'wicked profiteers'.

The *Financial Times* also reports another very friendly piece of co-operation in the same field – the use of television newsreaders in industrial films. 'To hear the familiar voice of a TV announcer,' says the *Financial Times*, 'speaking the commentary of a sponsored film immediately adds authority to its message.'

I have to report, more in sorrow than in anger, that I have heard ill-informed and prejudiced members of the public criticising these warm-hearted and brotherly arrangements of ours for mutual assistance. It is difficult to believe that anyone could be so cynical as to sneer at the humble efforts of human beings to help one another on their way through this vale of tears.

Let us set prejudice to one side and think about this matter calmly and logically. Aren't the aims of all of us in the communications industry pretty much the same? Where would this or any other paper be if it was not supported by advertisers? Some rather boorish journalists, I know, take a perverse pleasure in biting the hand that feeds them, but isn't it more logical to grasp it, full of food as it is, and shake it warmly?

Take my case, I can see nothing to be ashamed of in both working for *The Observer* and writing humorous advertisements for Fub. After all, when you come down to it, are they such very different activities?

Aren't I, in writing articles for *The Observer*, trying to help sell the paper? Is it so ignoble to condescend to turn aside and help the more humble packet of Fub on its way?

Anyway, I don't actually advertise the Fub, I just write entertaining little pieces about quite irrelevant subjects, and if people happen to notice it says Fub at the bottom, that's their business.

I mean, I'm allowed to make *jokes* about Fub if I want to. So if you buy Fub and it doesn't turn out to be any good, don't come and blame me. I never said it was, did I?

Or take the booklet I wrote putting the case for the Advertisers of Advertising, or the script I wrote for the film sponsored by the Committee of Public Relations for Public Relations. I was able to be of real assistance there because obviously you're much more likely to believe them when you see they're written by honest Mike Frayn. You know I wouldn't tell you anything but the fearless outspoken truth. The fact that I sometimes criticise advertising and public relations here makes it that much more striking when I praise them somewhere else.

There's no contradiction in that. After all, I just criticise them for the laughs. For heaven's sake, I don't mean every word I say to be taken *literally*.

Anyway, how do you know I'm not telling the simple truth when I say I'm convinced of the utter sincerity of the advertising profession? For all you know, I may actually believe it (you wait till I whack a writ in on you, and you have to prove in court that I'm not the credulous moron my counsel will make me out to be). And if I believe it, what possible harm can there be in accepting a fee to state that belief? I take it nobody objects if I accept a fee from *The Observer* to state my honest beliefs in articles. To start quibbling if the cheque happens to be signed by the Advertisers of Advertising instead of *The Observer* is more Jesuitical hair-splitting.

Let's not get all solemn and upright about it. After all, nobody believes what they read in the papers these days. Anyway, I need the money. And what right has anyone got to come pointing the finger at me when people like Profumo carry on the way they do?

I think we ought all to band ourselves together and set up a Committee for Mutual Assistance in the Communications Industry to deal with this cynical criticism. We'll hire some impartial commentator like myself and pay him a large fee to make an utterly independent inquiry showing how absolutely right we are.

Michael Frayn

MICHAEL FRAYN *(b. 1933) Joined* The Observer *from* The Guardian *as humorous columnist from 1962 to 1968 before becoming comic novelist and playwright. Satirist of 1960s middle-class trendies, creator of the imperishable Rollo Swavely, Horace and Doris Morris and the Don't Know Party. Later contributed occasional series of travel pieces, incomparably invoking the spirit of Berlin, Vienna and other great cities. His witty novel* Towards the End of the Morning *was based on his years at* The Guardian *and* The Observer.

THE ROOTS OF BEATLEMANIA

10 November 1963

It doesn't do to knock the Beatles. Our own jazz critic, Benny Green, did so, almost by accident, on Granada TV the other night.

Without any deep feeling one way or the other, Green said he thought there wasn't much musical value in what the Beatles do. Now he gets letters with menacing beetles drawn on the envelope and enclosures which say, for instance:

'Listen Mate, I jus won to say dat your gob on telly 2 night was last. The Beatles, mate, make a better and original sound than any other group. If you think you can make an original sound from your trumpitt and sacks then record it and see if people will buy it and mob you and Q up for you for days. If there were more groups as good as the Beatles this land we call Eng would be gear. So go buy yourself a surgical boot and go criticise yourself sum jazz.'

Actually, dissenting voices are few and nervous. People may be found along London's Tin Pan Alley who say 'Don't quote me, but . . .'

What they go on to say is never very harsh, they simply deny that the Beatles are creating an entirely new sound.

But Mr. George Martin thinks differently. He is chief record producer at E.M.I., now making the booming Beatle discs. Elegant and relaxed, with Prince Philip good looks, Mr. Martin is everything not usually associated with pop records.

'I didn't make the Beatles,' he says. 'They would have been great anyway.' And he is quite sure they have made a new sound, that the sound-before-the-Beatles was an amalgam of Cliff Richard and the Shadows, and that the Beatles sound will be the pattern until the next pop-mutation happens.

But people are evidently drawn to the Beatles by factors other than the extraordinary noise they make. The main body of truly obsessed fans – the compulsive screamers – seem to be extremely young, taking in the 10-12 age-group as well as the teenagers. But even the grown-ups who reacted with sharp distaste to the Elvis Presley cult a few years back now speak about the Beatles with real affection.

Even the Queen Mother seems to have been impressed. She talked to the Beatles after the Royal Command Performance the other night. She asked them where they would be appearing next, and they said Slough. 'Ah,' said the Queen Mother, with obvious approval, 'that's quite near us.'

Musicians may find nothing unique in the Mersey Sound, but the Beatles are broadcasting the true and unique voice of Liverpool's working class and this is what most people admire. The Beatles were all born during the blitz on Merseyside. They have grown up in a tough, violent city and have developed an immense self-confidence.

The working-class accent is exaggerated, not refined away but made to sound as crude as it can be. But the tone is triumphant, not resentful.

The Beatles are intelligent, too. They talk in a Goonish witty way and it all comes straight from under their own mops. They have no gag-writers. And there's something beat and Kerouac-like in what they say.

We have been investigating Merseyside this week. It is a wild place. Our car was broken into outside a club called The Sink and a portable radio stolen.

One group called The Undertakers wear top-hats and black crêpe and have loudspeakers shaped like coffins. They once turned up at the Locarno carrying a dead cat and have been photographed in graveyards. Another amplified group call themselves

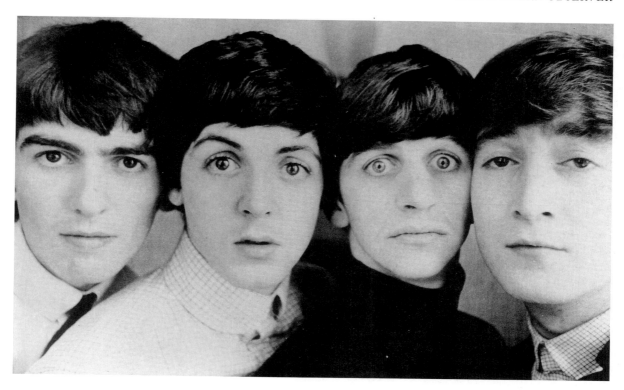

From left to right: George Harrison, Paul McCartney, Ringo Starr and John Lennon 'talk in a Goonish witty way straight from under their own mops.'

the Ghost Squad. They wear white hoods and skull masks and look like white citizens on a night out in the Deep South.

But Liverpool's also a seaport, edged up against a wide estuary, a kind of dead end with a tremendous sense of community. And it's also in touch with America. New 'sounds' reach Liverpool before anywhere else in the island because young seamen bring home with them American pop records not yet released in Britain.

Liverpool seems to breed self-assured, vital young people who are nowadays learning the guitar as soon as they are big enough to hold one. They have a ganging-up tradition – street gangs at one extreme, boys' clubs at the other.

The gangs, clubs and groups rate loyalty very high. And the unforgivable sin is big-headedness. The Beatles are still enormously popular in their home town because they have avoided this breach of ethics. In fact, the Beatles are strong on ethics altogether; at early record-making sessions they regarded over-dub-

bing with suspicion until Mr. Martin convinced them it was no more unethical than an electric guitar. If anyone shows off in a Liverpool group-performance, he's liable to have someone pull out the plug of his electric guitar in mid-phrase.

The Beatles' promoter is Mr. Brian Epstein. He is a handsome, poised, urbane young man, rather amused by the 'highbrow' interest now being taken in the group he helped to make famous.

He is a director of a family firm owning three record shops in Liverpool. His interest in the Beatles dawned when youngsters started demanding the records of a group he didn't know.

Our correspondent does not get from Mr. Epstein the impression of a brilliant manipulator, but of a shrewd young man who has caught the lightning. And the overwhelming emotional reaction of the fans to the Beatles is, Mr. Epstein says, as much a mystery to him as to anyone else.

Psychologists, however, seem less inclined to reckon this phenomenon mysterious. Beatlemania,

they say, has a long pedigree. Apart from compulsive dancing to drum-beats among Africans, they mention the young girls known to have swooned when 'the blades' swaggered through medieval Florence and squealed in eighteenth-century England as the redcoats marched by.

What seems to have emerged is an age-group solidarity of a new intensity. The old play-group of the city streets used to be deliberately exclusive; shutting someone out – usually someone diffident and unglamorous – was part of the fun. But when the Beatles start hammering the Mersey Beat into the floorboards and swaying behind those guitars, anyone can join in and scream with her fellows.

We got this final piece of wisdom from a teenager who felt old enough to throw a tender light on the Beatle fans whom she saw as being younger than herself. Asked why she thought these young ones so readily joined the Beatles frenzy, she said: 'Because they're lonely, of course.'

Cyril and Peter Dunn

John Fitzgerald Kennedy shortly before his assassination.
'The dead President was not universally loved in this city.'

THE
DISGRACE
OF BIG D

1 December 1963

President Kennedy was assassinated on 22 November in Dallas

Dallas, Texas. 30 November. People who live this city call it 'Big D'. They've always used the top of their corporate voice to boast about anything thought likely to spread their fame – the tallest office building west of the Mississippi, the biggest and richest Baptist Church, the only bank with a lobby ceiling of pure gold.

Now, suddenly, Dallas finds itself on everyone's lips everywhere in the world, but in a terrible context. The appalling prospect confronts it that in the end Dallas will be remembered only as a place where somebody important was assassinated, like Sarajevo.

Some confused citizens are still inclined to boast, perhaps from force of habit, perhaps from a longing to feel normal again. The cab driver who brings you in from Love Field, one of the city's airports, invites you to agree that 'this has sure been an historical week for Dallas', makes a sightseeing detour round by 'where it happened' and brags about knowing Jack Ruby, the night club operator who shot Oswald, the supposed assassin.

Most people you talk to seem hurt and ashamed. They feel that Big D has been disgraced. But they also insist that fate has hit them unfairly; they vehemently reject the idea that they ought now to be tormented by feelings of guilt. 'This could have happened anywhere else' is what they go round saying, repeatedly.

Even so, Dallas is being blamed for what happened to Kennedy outside the Texas School Book Depository, as perhaps no other American city would have been. There are obvious grounds for this, though they don't strike an outsider as being particularly firm.

The dead President was not universally loved in this city, certainly not by those who set out to control local political opinion. They still hate his brother Bobby and are not ashamed to be heard saying so even now.

Dallas is also by reputation a favoured resort of the Extreme American Right, notably the virulent and muddled inmates of the John Birch Society. When Kennedy fired General Edwin Walker for recommending the Birchite doctrine to his troops, it was to a shabby frame house in Dallas that he withdrew, still shouting, and here he flies Old Glory upside down whenever he sees the nation sliding another few yards towards Communism.

But, the Big Businessmen who run Dallas set out to make the Kennedy visit last week a flawless success. In the first reeling moments after the shots were fired some radio reporters, knowing the Dallas background, leapt to the conclusion that this must be a Rightist act. Now, of course, it is believed that Oswald was 'a hate-spitting Marxist', to use the local phrase. General Walker and some others are satisfied that this clears Dallas of all blame. As he sees it, the shooting was simply a part of the Communist plot, and one of its first aims was to get Texans disarmed and left helpless.

But the odd thing is that although most Americans prefer the quick and uncomplicated explanation of any bewildering event, people do not feel that the city is entirely absolved by this one and keep calling for changes in the nature of the Dallas community as an act of redemption.

Dallas has deficiencies that an outsider may sense. Its ordinary people are kinder in chance encounters with strangers than almost any other except Tynesiders. But the city itself lacks grace and seems soulless.

Nobody could think the entrance to the Triple Underpass a fit place for a great man to die. It has a kind of cheap grandeur – concrete colonnades round an amphitheatre of grass, now patched with wilting flowers. In the background stands the great square box of masonry from which Oswald fired and the nineteenth century county courthouse, like a Teutonic fort, quite terrifying in its ugliness. The whole of downtown Dallas bears a chilling resemblance to Johannesburg, but is, if anything, more desolating because the local black people are subdued and self-effacing.

Dallas is the great financial and commercial city through which the zooming wealth of Texas is processed. It stands on the plain like an ill-constructed computer, the towers of the money moguls rearing beside the old two-storey frontier-type premises such as the Lazy-hour Piano Bar. The place has no old-established working class and no productive roots in its own site. 'The only crop Dallas grows,' said someone, 'is money.'

For twenty-five years this city has been run by a group of rich and powerful businessmen known as the Citizens Council. Stevensonian liberals, offered a rare chance to speak out by the presence of foreign reporters in Dallas, have been trying to establish some kind of mystical link between this group government and the assassination, though, not, of course, a direct one. They have argued that this rule by Boss Men has nurtured 'an atmosphere of hate' in which even a lunatic act of violence might happen. They fervently believe that Kennedy's death at the Triple Underpass will mean the end of Boss Rule in Dallas.

But the Boss Men have foreshortened the democratic process. For years the formally elected rulers have been their choice and their agents. The Boss Men have decided what's good for Dallas and as a result people at the shabby end of town have suffered. Above all they are accused of having used crushing weapons against intellectual and spiritual dissent. Perhaps their worst fault in this horrible context is that they have kept alive in Dallas the old image of America to which the dead Kennedy was opposed.

Cyril Dunn

SLUTS

29 December 1963

This article is dedicated to all those who have ever changed their stockings in a taxi, brushed their hair with someone else's nailbrush or safety-pinned a hem; and those who have not had probably better not read on.

Anyone in doubt, however, can ask herself the following questions. Have you ever taken anything back out of the dirty-clothes basket because it had become, relatively, the cleaner thing? How many things are there, at this moment, in the wrong room – cups in the study, boots in the kitchen; and how many of them are on the *floor* of the wrong room?

Could you try on clothes in any shop, any time, without worrying about your underclothes? And how, if at all, do you clean your nails? Honest answers should tell you, once and for all, whether you are one of us: the miserable, optimistic, misunderstood race of sluts.

We are not ordinary human beings who have degenerated, as people think: we are born this way. Even at four you can pick us out: the little girls in the playground who have one pant-leg hanging down and no hair-slide; at ten we are the ones who look dirty even when we are clean (unlike the goodigoodies who look unfairly clean when they are dirty); and at fifteen, when black stockings are fashionable, we betray ourselves in the changing-room by legs spotted like a Dalmatian's, the inevitable result of using Indian ink instead of darning-wool.

People who are not sluts intolerantly assume that we must like things this way, without realising the enormous effort and inconvenience that goes into being so ineffective: the number of times we have to fill the car's radiator because we don't get it mended, the fortunes we spend on taxis going back for parcels we have left in shops, the amount of ironing occasioned by our practice of un-

179

packing not so much when we get back from a week-end as four days later.

We acquire, it is true, certain off-beat skills: I am much better at holding a bottle of varnish between two fingers than those of my friends who do not paint their nails in the Tube, and they cannot cut their nails with a pen-knife, either; but nothing really makes up for us for the difficulties of our way of life.

However, I am not trying to make a soggy bid for sympathy so much as to work out what we can possibly do to improve our condition. And the first thing, it seems to me, is to inscribe *Abandon Hope All Ye Who Enter Here* over the lintels of all our messy houses; for it is our optimism that is principally our undoing. We keep hoping that we will remember to wash our white collars, or find time to comb our hair on the way to the office, or slide into the building and dump our coats before anyone can see that there are three buttons missing. More, it seems to me, could be done if we could only face up realistically to all the things we never will be able to do.

We can realise, for example, that no power on earth is going to make us look well turned out all, or even most, of the time. We can therefore give up right away any New Year resolutions about fashion: a second pair of little white gloves will simply result in our carrying two right hands; wigs would be a waste of money because those of us who cannot keep our real hair tidy cannot keep our toy hair tidy either. Instead, we can wear reasonably sober clothes normally, go for stacked heels because we know we won't remember to get them re-heeled before they are worn down, have only one colour of accessories, so that we cannot wear the brown shoes with the black bag.

And, having accepted that people are *not* going to say 'she's always so chic', we can concentrate every now and then on really dazzling efforts that will knock our audience sideways. Jane Aus-

ten was right when she said that no beauty accustomed to compliments ever got anything like the thrill of an ordinary looker who was told she was looking terrific *that evening*.

Apart from this sort of grim realism, there are, I think, only two other things that can help up. The first is habit: odd as it may seem, even sluts do occasionally acquire good habits (we clean our teeth, for example, even if we sometimes have to do it with soap) and these, indeed, are all that hold us together. A slut who baths whenever she has time never baths at all: her only hope is to get up into one every morning; if she shops here and there for food there will never be any around, but a Saturday supermarket raid will settle a whole week's hash at one go.

And the second is money: for the only way a slut can really get things done is to get someone else

to do them. Even the most domestic slut will find it worth earning a few pounds to pay for help in the house.

Money, low cunning and a sense of realism may help us somewhat; but it is a hard life all the same. I wrote this article two years ago, but as it was felt that it hardly came well from the pen of a fashion editor, it was never printed. So I thought I had a soft option using it now; except that, of course, I couldn't find it, and have had to write the whole blasted thing again.

Katherine Whitehorn

KATHARINE WHITEHORN *Joined* The Observer *as fashion editor in 1963 after working on* Picture Post, Woman's Own *and* The Spectator. *Won special Press award in 1982 as one of the most accomplished and entertaining columnists in Fleet Street during the previous 25 years.*

THE AUSCHWITZ BUSINESS

5 January 1964

The German judge asks 'May we have your full name please, Herr Kaduk, and your age?'

The accused pays no attention to the court, grasps the microphone and begins to bark some set passages about unlawful prosecution. 'I was sentenced to death by the Soviets,' he shouts, 'criminal proceedings against me here are invalid . . .'

The judge says quietly: 'We know all about that, Herr Kaduk, and shall come to it in due course. Meanwhile we want to know something about yourself.'

The man's hysteria is momentarily punctured. He admits to being Oswald Kaduk, born in Silesia, primary education, 57 years old, butcher, fireman and male nurse by occupation.

Volunteered for the S.S. in 1940? Yes sir. 'What were your reasons?' 'The chess club . . . all the comrades were in the S.S.'

After basic training he was put

through a special NCOs' course, promoted and presently got to Auschwitz.

'Just like that? to Auschwitz?' asks the Judge. 'Had you applied?' Kaduk says he was transferred. The prosecution is expected to call evidence that posting to the concentration camps was highly selective. 'And what were your functions as block guard as Auschwitz?' Kaduk bellows: 'To see there was no sabotage . . . no resistance.'

All the accused here, if the charges against them are true, are direct killers and torturers. These men are said to have taken part in acts, and themselves devised acts so abominable that ordinary human consciousness recoils.

The charges against Oswald Kaduk are dreadful. He is alleged to have trampled a young Jewish boy to death because he had overslept. He is alleged to have made a prisoner stand to attention for a whole day – and when, in the evening, he found that the man had had to foul himself to have thrown him against the live barbed-wire fence. One night, half-drunk, he throttled some elderly prisoners by laying a walking stick across their necks and standing on the stick, it is alleged.

The present trial here is not – and this is a most important thing for the Germans – a war-crime trial, not a political trial, but an ordinary criminal trial for offences against the general West German criminal code, heard before an ordinary criminal court. The preliminary inquiry has already been going on for five years. It was started off by an Auschwitz file, supposedly taken from a burning government building before the arrival of the Red Army by a soldier or ex-prisoner (the story varies), being shown in 1958 to a Frankfurt journalist who handed it over to the public prosecutor, Dr. Bauer, who decided to follow it up.

This cannot have been easy. Too many witnesses are dead, there were not many survivors from those camps. Relevant documents, if not destroyed, are dispersed in the East Zone, in American, Russian or Polish archives. Eventually, 1,300 witnesses, many from outside Germany, were questioned and a huge volume of evidence collected.

After two days out of expected hundreds, the trial, whose moral and technical difficulties will be immense, is still at its earliest stage. After the first shocks and a sense of the utter gap between deeds such as these and human justice, one is led to the slow conviction that the only way in which society can attempt to cope is by conducting as the scrupulously courteous judges of Frankfurt and the three patient young prosecutors are trying to do, a fair trial according to the law.

Sybille Bedford

ALL THIS AND CALLAS TOO

The fascination of Callas: 'A turn of the head; the perception of poetry and dramatic meaning in music.'

26 January 1964

Scorned by the 'pure' musicians, mocked by the spoken theatre, opera lives on faith; on faith that somehow, somewhere, some day, the miracle will happen, and that its warring elements will combine to transcend both music and theatre. It happened last week with Covent Garden's new *Tosca*, and when it does so the spoken theatre is made to seem flat and two-dimensional in comparison. For once the whole preposterous business of opera justifies its own *pretentions*. *Tosca* is a fairly squalid little shocker; effective yet mean in its obsessive concentration on effect. But at Covent Garden it is made to yield all it has to give.

Maria Callas is, of course, the centre-stone of this triumphant evening, Her Tosca is a performance of indescribable brilliance and fascination; no other living singer could come within a mile of it. But what makes Callas unique is not merely her own achievement. Unlike most great *prima donnas*, she sees her own role in the context of the whole work, and she is as inexorably exacting in everything that concerns it as she is about her own performance. The result is not merely a great Tosca but a great *Tosca*.

How am I to describe the full magic of that performance, from

181

the first moment when the eye beholds, not the usual Gainsborough Films lady, not the traditional dowager in a massive robe and a picture hat preening herself before the applause of her public, but a live, tense and infinitely vulnerable creature who flings her flowers impetuously to one side as jealousy and suspicion jostle with joy at seeing her lover?

In her hands, 'Vissi d'arte' does not for once appear as though it had been inserted for no reason other than to provide the *prima donna* with a second-act aria. Unlike the average soprano, Callas does not advance down stage and noisily proclaim her woes to the housetops. On the contrary, she retreats into the anguished self-communing of someone who cannot bring herself to believe that such horror and disaster can have descended on her head. For a moment she is alone with her misery and nothing else exists. It is dreadfully true to life, and the strange absence of applause which greeted an aria that can generally be relied on to bring the house down was itself a testimony to Callas's achievement.

And who will readily forget the murder of Scarpia at the end of the act, the imperceptible stiffening of Tosca's body as she sees the knife, the trance-like manner in which she surreptitiously takes hold of it, and then, as Scarpia advances to exact his price, suddenly wheels round and plunges it into him? It sounds the very essence of melodramatic cliché. Yet the suddenness of that thrust took not merely Scarpia but every member of the audience by surprise.

And once she has nerved herself to the deed, an irresistible flood of hatred and loathing seems to well out of her. The hand that could hardly steel itself to take the knife now cannot drop it as she pursues Scarpia across the room, like some fearful instrument of vengeance. As he struggles to raise himself, she screams 'Die!' and, as though the very force of her hatred had willed it, he slumps lifeless to the ground. In its vividness and dramatic im-

pact it is unlike any performance I have witnessed.

If I emphasise the theatrical aspect of this performance it is that dramatic gifts of this order are rarely given to a singer of stature. But all the dramatic genius in the world would not have made this *Tosca* the occasion it was, had not Callas been in better voice than I have heard her in years.

Admittedly, the voice is still far from conventionally beautiful. But it remains a uniquely splendid instrument that can register a bewildering variety of emotions, and one that is handled with exquisite musicality and immaculate sense of style. Yet in the final resort, the fascination of Callas is not to be analysed. It is the movement of an arm, the inflection of a soft note, a turn of the head, the shaping of a line, the perception of poetry and dramatic meaning in music.

So haunting is her spell that I hope I may be forgiven so wildly unbalanced a notice. For this *Tosca* contains a performance of Scarpia by Tito Gobbi that alone warrants an article to itself. Bland yet menacing, 'a bigoted satyr,' as Cavaradossi describes him, his steely, self-possessed yet lecherous police chief provides a perfect foil to Callas's mercurial *prima donna*, and his singing is as unfailingly assured and pointful as ever.

Franco Zeffirelli's control of the stage and of the two great performers on it is so complete that one ceases to be aware of production as such. For once, music, singing, movement and décor become a seamless entity. It is total theatre.   *Peter Heyworth*

Peter Heyworth (b. 1921)
An outstanding figure in British music criticism. Principal music critic of The Observer *from 1955 to 1978, devoting special attention to opera and contemporary music. Major contributor to 1960s upheaval that shook London's musical life out of its post-Second World War provincialism. Biographer of the conductor Otto Klemperer.*

Michael Caine in Zulu: *'slightly wrongly cast as an upper-class officer but he does it very well.'*

SO BRAVE

26 January 1964

Zulu is going to be a very popular film, and not only with men. It is about an engagement that happened in Africa in 1879 between a tiny contingent of British soldiers and 4,000 Zulu warriors, in which the Zulus ended by retiring and saluting the enemy. Everyone was unimaginably brave, especially us. Even of the British won V.C.s.

Beside the Zulus, blooming with health and thundering fearsomely on shields made of dried animal skins, the actors playing the British look touchingly underendowed physically and much more frightened of death; there is a marvellous shot when they are leaning against the barricades in sheer exhaustion, listening to the Zulus' war songs and wondering how to fight people who don't know the European rules.

The film is nearly all battle, and best when it's most like the *Boys Own Paper*. The liberal lines seem a bit out of period. Every soldier there must have called the enemy the fuzzy-wuzzies at the time, and it's like trying to graft a left-wing leaflet on to the Duke of Wellington to make us accept anything else.

One of the dramatic things about the story is that the soldiers were apparently stuck with a pacifist drunken clergyman who kept yelling sloshed anti-war slogans through the palings of a shed where he was put to shut him up. 'Be quiet now, will you, there's a good gentleman,' says the splendiferous colour-sergeant, played by Nigel Green, through his lush moustaches. There is an interesting actor called Michael Caine who plays Stanley Baker's second-in-command; he is slightly wrongly cast as an upper-class officer, but he does it very well.

Penelope Gilliatt

as his wife went out to buy one: to which she replied bitterly that she would much rather the man thought she was a drug addict.

The most obvious failing of dogs seems to be that they are so often ardent fetishists who take every chair-leg, suitcase, cushion or knee for their object. One man I know said he thought the Government kept the regulations going deliberately just to *stop* people taking their dogs abroad: 'The British are quite unpopular enough already.'

Considering what absolutely rotten public relations pets do for their owners and what a nuisance and expense they are, one finds oneself increasingly wondering why people own them at all (unless they married into them, as I did). Some people keep them to have someone to talk to, I suppose; and they do have some value as a kind of halfway mark between things and people. Yell at a child, and you can kid yourself the discipline is for its moral welfare; yell at a cat, which has no moral sense and no way of getting one, and you know you are simply letting off steam. Some virtues, too, can be practised on animals. Once you have lost a rabbit or two by failing to feed them at regular intervals, you are unlikely to do the same thing to the baby.

And there is, of course, the private colonialism of extending one's control over a wider empire: I know one harassed London kitten who stands in lieu of 10 acres, three horses and a cow to its flat-trapped owners.

They may even, as one Trinidadian put it, 'Fill the gap left by the abolition of slavery', and satisfy the desire to own another life. And I used to think it was this desire to control and dominate that was the main reason people kept pets – pet owners are distinguished from naturalists mainly, after all, by their insistence that the pet shall lead their lives rather than *vice versa*.

The real appeal of pets is simply that they cannot be altogether controlled. To keep a pet is to keep a smouldering fuse that may blow up any time; to retain a piece

JUNGLE ON THE HEARTH

1 March 1964

Since one of my cats has eczema and the other has worms *The Observer* has this week lifted the ban it normally imposes on my writing about pets. Small danger this week, it feels, of a gush of sentimentality about God's Furry Creatures; and they are dead right.

There is probably hardly an animal, now I come to think about it, that is without its revolting side. Goldfish get fungus. Budgerigars are more stupid than one would believe possible – put two virgin birds of opposite sex in a cage together and they *never get*

the message – there was a male who lived in the flat beneath us whose wildest thrill for years was to kiss his female and then run up a little ladder and proudly ring a bell. They finally died, to the relief, of all, by knocking their water-tray over on top of themselves and perishing underneath it.

Ants, of all things, are chic in Paris just now, imported at immense expense from Harrods: the problem is to feed them without letting them out of their (careful how you pronounce it) formicarium. One way is a syringe: 'Be sure you tell the chemist what you want it for,' warned one husband of incalculable jungle in an otherwise ordered existence. The old lady has a parrot because, deep down in her clean, devoted soul, she hopes it *will* speak a rude word in front of the vicar. My in-laws keep vast, intractable dogs in an otherwise respectable suburb: I am convinced they secretly wait for the day when they will go wild and ravage the neighbourhood.

The other evening a man was telling me about his coming of age: downstairs there were debs, flowers, candles, but upstairs their bitch was on heat. His mother was embarrassed by the line of thin yellow dogs panting outside the window and told someone to shoo them away. But the boy who opened the window to flap his napkin at them was borne down by a yelping tide of uncontrollable animals belting upstairs.

I suspect this is what pet-owners secretly hope for, and that the pets we all really want are the Gadarene swine.

Katharine Whitehorn

SLUTS II

15 March 1964

A couple of months ago I owned up in this column to being a slut. It was absolutely splendid: I found that there were scores of us, all struggling away.

There was the woman who had got to be a dab hand at identifying lettuce in the dark, as she never remembered to pick it by daylight; and the one who said she couldn't have a daily help – it was too much effort clearing up before she came. There was one who cited her six children as proof of her sluthood, in one direction at least; and the mother who claimed that (thanks to a scarf in the wrong washing-machine load) her baby was the only one in Ruislip with blue nappies.

Men, too call it 'slob': one wrote in block capitals by candle-light having run out of shillings for the meter, and another said he stapled his braces to his trousers when all buttons failed.

One could go on for ever. No one was able to suggest a way in which sluts could cure themselves of the disease known in my home town as 'doing a Whitehorn' – taking endless trouble to save yourself trouble, so that you clean an oil-lamp rather than walk to the corner of the road to buy a new bulb, or throw cushions at a door for ten minutes rather than get up and shut it.

The only serious spur to tidying up is generally agreed to be visitors – the only drawback being that after they have gone your Pelmanism has to be even better than usual if you are ever to find anything again.

But sluts are good at using memory as a substitute for tidiness – though I absolutely deny that I ever said (as friends allege); 'If you're looking for the tax forms they're under your slippers in the salad-bowl.'

Katharine Whitehorn

The Cyprus agony as recorded by Don McCullin. The island had become independent in 1960 with Greeks and Turks bitterly divided; fierce fighting broke out in December 1963; this woman has just learnt that her husband has been killed. The photograph won a world press award.

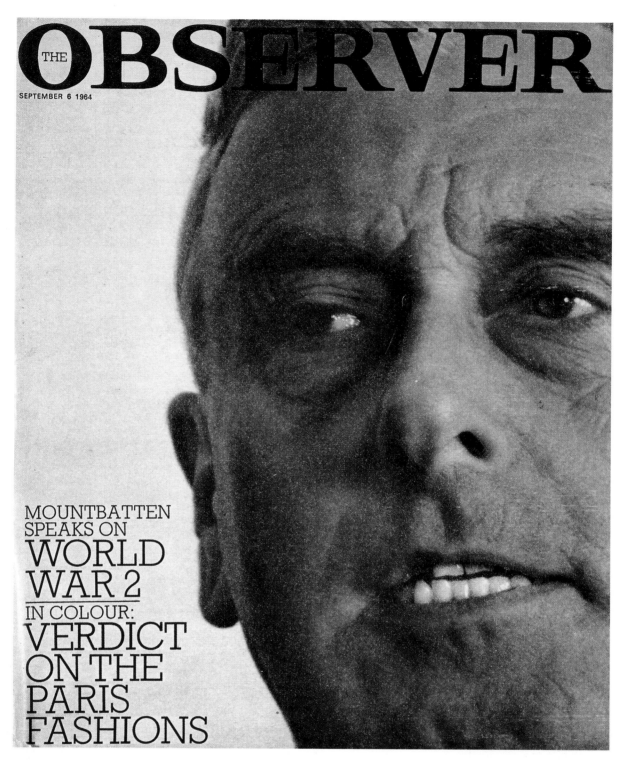

THE OBSERVER

SEPTEMBER 6 1964

MOUNTBATTEN
SPEAKS ON
WORLD WAR 2
IN COLOUR:
VERDICT ON THE PARIS FASHIONS

First cover of Observer Magazine, *launched on 6 September 1964 as a colour supplement to the paper. (Total price, sixpence.)* The Sunday Times *already had a colour magazine; the* Telegraph *launched its magazine later in September but with* The Daily Telegraph *on Friday.*

The month before, David Astor, in a published interview with Kenneth Harris, had explained the reasons for starting a colour magazine: primarily, economics. The growth of the quality Sundays meant there was advertising to be picked up if not by The Observer *then by its competitors. Would dependence on advertising revenue diminish editorial independence? Astor replied 'No, the advertiser is not primarily interested in what we say – he is interested in reaching our readers. It's the confidence of our readers that really matters – that's our real capital.' The spirit and character of the paper would not change. 'If there are more readers like our present ones, it can grow without changing character.'*

The magazine is, of course, still an integral and successful part of The Observer.

WORLD'S FAREWELL TO CHURCHILL

31 January 1965

The procession took that most ancient road that runs from the Palace of Westminster to the steps of the Cathedral of St. Paul. It is a road that half the history of England seems to have taken, on its way to a crowning or to a public and ignoble death, to murder or be murdered, to raise revolt, to seek a fortune, or to be buried. The route was lined with young soldiers, their heads bowed over their automatic rifles in ceremonious grief. The bands played old and slow tunes. The drums were draped in black. The staffs of the drum-majors were veiled. They moved slowly, steadily, at a curiously inexorable pace, and it looked as if nothing could ever stop them. They moved through a tangible silence and the great crowd watched with an eloquent and absolute silence.

It was beautiful in the way that great works of art are beautiful. It

Lord Atlee's farewell to Churchill, sitting on the steps of St Paul's watching the coffin leaving the Cathedral for 'the slow move up the turgid Thames' from Tower Pier.

obeyed secret rules. There was the Earl Marshal walking alone and worried in the centre of a great space like any man lost in a high street, but carrying a gilded sceptre. There was Lord Mountbatten pacing behind the Chiefs of Staff carefully manipulating his sword and, like any trooper, trying to keep pace with the band. There were the officers with their trays of Churchill's medals, held out like ware for sale. There were the heraldic banners of the Cinque Ports and the Spencer-Churchills, too stiff to wave in any wind, carried like trophies before the coffin. And there were the marshals with their batons held on their hips in a baroque gesture that Marlborough would have known.

There was the family looking lost and human and trying to keep up. But the central, the overwhelming fact was the dead body in a box made of oak. It was trundled into the City on a huge and impractical gun-carriage. It was pulled by a great phalanx of lusty young men. It moved, huge and red with the Union flag, past the hotels and the steamy restaurants and the newspaper offices and the pubs, surrounded by this extraordinary silence that could not be broken even by the bands and the rhythmic feet. It was a silence, not of grief but of respect. In fact the City was stopped and was turned into a theatre and it was all performed as a drama that all men understand.

This was the last time that such a thing could happen. This was the last time that London would be the capital of the world. This was an act of mourning for the Imperial past. This marked the final act in Britain's greatness. This was a great gesture of self-pity and after this the coldness of reality and the status of Scandinavia.

But really this was a celebration. And however painful, most

funerals are just that. When a man is buried, those who are still alive crave some gesture of respect that cannot help the cadaver. And this gesture is made over and over again by Christians and Communists and humanists and the unconcerned. It is a proud half-conscious assertion that man is not an animal that dies alone in a hole. It is almost a gesture of contempt to the face of death. And once or twice in a generation a dead monarch or hero is chosen to epitomise a whole nation's assertion of continuity and dignity. And because Churchill at a certain time and in a special way was, for all public purposes, Britain and more than Britain, this assertion was unbelievably eloquent over this corpse.

This was a celebration, then, of our humanity and of the fact of Britain. The ritual, performed to music like a masque for the edification of a king, said things that cannot quite be put into words. The whole country watched the agonised care of the eight guardsmen who carried the box. And vicariously shared their anxious pain. But perhaps most marvellous was the slow move up the turgid Thames. There were things like the gantries of cranes dipping in salute and the music of a host of pipers. There were generals in improbable uniforms and what looked like all the rulers of the world standing on the steps of St. Paul's as if this were a family burial. A whole city looking in on itself as a dead body went by.

It was a triumph. It was a celebration of a great thing that we did in the past. It was an act of gratitude to a man whom we can no longer help or please. The many Heads of State there were appropriate but not important. We were not sad. We knew for whom these bells tolled. We knew the man whose body we removed in such unimaginable splendour. And we did not weep – that is not fitting for great old men – but we saw him off and because he was us at our best, we gave him a requiem that rejected death and was almost a rejoicing.

Patrick O'Donovan

'The overwhelming fact was the dead body in a box made of oak, trundled into the City on a huge and impractical gun-carriage, surrounded by this extraordinary silence.'

How to Help Them Help Themselves

This article was the kernel of E.F. Schumacher's book Small is Beautiful, *published in 1973 and reprinted twice in that year alone. It is still in print; the paperback has had nearly thirty reprints. The Intermediate Technology Development Group he set up as a result of the response to the article is now partly government-funded. Its task, just as he suggested, is going into Third World Countries, 'helping them to help themselves'. There is a Schumacher Society, devoted to propagating his ideas, and an annual Schumacher Lecture. A Schumacher College has just been set up at Dartington.*

29 August 1965

Unemployment in developing countries is most acute in the areas outside a few metropolitan cities; so there is mass migration into these cities. Current forecasts conjure up a picture of towns with 20, 40 and even 60 million people – a prospect of 'immiseration' for a rootless and jobless mass of humanity that beggars the imagination.

The suspicion has been voiced that foreign aid, *as currently practised*, may actually be intensifying this disease. No wonder, then, that there is a widespread search for a new approach.

Central planners take as their decisive criterion the rate of growth of Gross National Product, that is, the developing country's aggregate of money incomes. This is highly misleading. If the rise in GNP, is accompanied by rising unemployment, and an increase in social tensions, the outcome of the enterprise is unlikely to be satisfactory.

The primary task of developing countries now afflicted by mass unemployment and mass migration into a few metropolitan areas would therefore seem to be clear.

1. Workplaces have to be created in the areas where the people are living now;

2. These workplaces must be, on average, cheap enough so that they can be created in large numbers without an unattainable level of savings and imports;

3. The production methods employed must be relatively simple, so that the demands for high skills are minimised, not only in the production process itself but also in matters of organ-isation, raw material supply, financing, marketing, and so forth;

4. Production should be largely from local materials for local use. These needs can be met only;

A. If there is a 'regional approach' to development;

B. If there is a conscious effort to develop what might be called an 'intermediate technology.'

Western technology has been devised primarily for the purpose of saving labour. It has grown up with a vast array of supporting services, like modern transport, accountancy, marketing, and so forth.

This technology, therefore, 'fits' only into those sectors which are already fairly modernised, and that the metropolitan areas, comprising, say, 15 to 29 per cent of the whole population.

The task is to establish a tolerable basis of existence for the 80 per cent by means of an 'intermediate technology' which would be vastly superior in productivity to their traditional technology (in its present state of decay) while at the same time being vastly cheaper and simpler than the highly sophisticated and enormously capital-intensive technology of the West.

Design studies undertaken in India have demonstrated that many products are suitable for 'intermediate technology' production – practically all basic consumer goods, building materials, agricultural implements, and many kind of equipment for the 'intermediate technology' industries themselves – and that these products can be fully competitive with those of Western technology. But 'intermediate technology' is no magic wand. Countries like India need millions of additional workplaces. To provide them with means of an 'intermediate technology' would be possible at any rate within the given and known limits of internal capital formation *plus* foreign aid. It would, to be sure, require a great organising effort on the part of very many people.

Would such an effort be forthcoming? No one can say it would not. The lack of entrepreneurial ability, which the central planners in developing countries so frequently deplore, is itself largely the result of their present fixation on the naive idea that what is best for the rich must also be best for the poor. Most current planning remains outside 'the people's' power of self-help.

This is not to say that all projects on the level of Western technology are useless. Let them continue, although perhaps with rather more caution than has been shown in the past. What appears to be certain beyond doubt is that they will have to be supplemented by a determined effort to reintegrate the jobless millions into the economic process by means of something along the lines of 'intermediate technology'.

Fragments of this 'intermediate technology' exist all over the world, in the advance countries no less than in the poverty-stricken ones. A new approach is needed, a systematic effort to collect them and develop them into practical blueprints for industrial action.

Millions of people in the wealthier countries are today moved by a genuine desire to help those who live in misery, and this elemental force should be capable of overcoming all petty preoccupations. 'Intermediate technology' can help the helpless to help themselves.

E.F.Schumacher

CHARLES DE GAULLE

On the day this profile appeared de Gaulle, aged 75, for the first time in his life faced the French people as a candidate (for a second term as president). He won, but only after a second vote.

5 December 1965

'He is like a man taking his statue for a walk,' a fellow officer said of Charles de Gaulle before the war. The statue still stalks beside the President of France. The man himself has aged, his hair thinned and whitened. Now silver, the wispy moustache is well-nigh invisible. The elephant eyes have sunk into wrinkled pouches behind the huge nose. A big appetite and little exercise have developed a prominent paunch that the tent-like double-breasted suits cannot hide.

The statue, unpromoted and undecorated since 1940, is still that of the acting brigadier who sprang up ready-made at the age of 49 to claim the legitimate leadership of France. Then, with granite stubbornness ('I was too weak to compromise') and through sheer force of character, he saved his country from total humiliation, and won it a place among the world Powers after the war. This alone was enough to put him among the great names of French history. The comparison with Joan of Arc is more than a joke.

De Gaulle consciously fashioned the legendary figure on the lines of the ideal leader he described in *Le Fil de l'Épée* in 1932. He talks about it in the third person as if it has an independent existence. How else can one rationalise the superb cheek of a man who not only speaks for France but for 25 years has calmly assumed he *is* France? Not even the most slavish of his many panegyrists can match the extravagant reverence of de Gaulle on de Gaulle. Of his retirement in 1946, he says in his memoirs, 'With de Gaulle went that wind from the heights, that hope of achievement and that ambition for France which upheld the national soul.'

The most remarkable thing about today's election in France is that de Gaulle has brought the General to the level of politicians, in a contest for the votes of ordinary men and women. It was a hard decision. The risk of damaging his already established historical image, more than anything else, made him hesitate. He has always feared the effects of old age, but weighed the lessons of Marshal Pétain's disastrous senility against Konrad Adenauer's frustration after stepping down.

With this memory and intellect intact, the General decided against a new period of 'bitter solitude.' One of his Ministers said more fancifully: 'The Fifth Republic is his little girl; he wanted to see that she grew up.' So at the age of 75, the rebel of 1940 and the saviour of 1958 is a candidate in a direct election for the first time in his life.

As a candidate, he coolly offers Frenchmen the choice between de Gaulle and chaos. Even in an election he cannot hide his contempt for lesser men and their petty motives. He has always distinguished between France and the French. He offers them no mundane electoral promises, no Government platform, no ideology and no party machine he is ready to call his own. Few people know the man well.

He has mellowed with age. To his habitual old-world courtesy he has added a warmer interest in the personal lives of those around him. He has taken to sending flowers to Ministers' wives when they have babies. He can be quietly humorous at his own expense. Touring the provinces this year, he confided to his entourage 'I'm looking forward to Mass tomorrow – its the only public place where I'm not expected to make a speech.'

He rules France from a gilt desk topped with red leather in a first-floor office overlooking the gardens of the Elysée Palace. Facing him beyond a crystal chandelier is a tapestry showing 'Don Quixote cured of his madness by Wisdom.' There are three telephones on a low table beside his desk, but he hardly ever uses them. When he wants to speak urgently with a Minister, he presses a button and asks an aide to get the man concerned to phone in. He generally sees the Prime Minister privately three or four times a week, the Foreign Minister once. Others may not be called in for months on end.

He is at his desk by 9.45 a.m. and spends most of the day working on written memos. He has daily meeting with his four immediate advisers. These head servants of the inner sanctum are a cross between a brains trust and a protective screen. They are almost a shadow Cabinet of technocrats. They are better informed than many Ministers. All diplomatic telegrams pass through their hands, and they know what's in the General's correspondence with foreign leaders.

They arrange the General's appointments with strict attention to ceremony. In the afternoon, two or three visitors are ushered into the presence for an audience of about half an hour each. More often than not, de Gaulle listens in utter silence, his long arms resting heavily on his desk as if made of lead, the fingers twiching the glasses he hates to be seen wearing. His face is a mask of boredom. But he is a good listener. A banker who recited a laboriously memorised proposal of some technical complexity was staggered when the General gave an informed answer to all 11 points in correct order.

Rolling his cynical, pessimistic eyes over 'the world as it is,' de Gaulle scorns ideology as bunk. He puts his faith in the permanence of sovereign nation-States and the durability of national interests. The guiding principles are simple – to further French prestige abroad and strengthen the State at home. The shock tactics make France appear more powerful than she is. They have won her world attention.

189

Madame de Gaulle, daughter of a biscuit manufacturer in Calais, has remained provincial, petit-bourgeois and narrow-minded. Years of cohabitation with a tall slice of history have taught discretion. Even as wife of the President, she contrives to stay in the background and keep the family out of the limelight. She still does her own shopping unnoticed in a town where staring is instinctive and unabashed. In the whole of de Gaulle's memoirs he mentions his wife only in passing. He once dismissed her from an after-dinner political conversation by simply saying, 'Bon soir, Yvonne!'

There have long been rumours that she has dissuaded the General from promoting loyal followers whose sexual life was not *comme il faut*. There is little evidence to support this. De Gaulle himself has a Gallic broadmindedness, though this necessarily excludes open scandal. He once mildly chided an aide discovered in an illicit bed with 'If you can't cuckold someone in a reasonable manner, then behave yourself.' When gossip about a Minister's adulterous prowess reached his ears he shrugged and said *'Il fait son métier d'homme.'*

General de Gaulle is an attentive father and grandfather. He is naturally interested in the naval career of his son, Philippe. But he is not founding a dynasty, and will leave little property or money behind him. What he does want to bequeath to the world is an untarnished historical image, and perhaps the fourth volume of his memoirs. His greatest achievement to date is his own personality. Historians may be less impressed than his contemporaries by his statesmanship. They will hardly deny his greatness as a man.   *William Millinship*

WILLIAM MILLINSHIP (b. 1929) Paris correspondent from 1958 to 1964, covering the Algerian War and de Gaulle's return to power. Washington correspondent from 1970 to 1973 during the Nixon years. After a period as managing editor became Moscow Correspondent in 1989.

Aberfan disaster, October 1966: 114 schoolchildren died when a giant slagheap engulfed their Welsh village. The Observer's *photographic coverage of such events won worldwide acclaim.*

HOW MAO RIDES THE DRAGON

11 September 1966

Mao Tse-tung does not struggle against his countrymen's sense of history. He moves with it, manipulating them through its flow. His policies, therefore, have been partly dictated by his constant care to present himself to the Chinese millions in the image of the recognisable Chinese hero.

Cunning and unpredictable as the third-century hero Chu-Koliang in his masterly strategies, a bold yet enigmatic dreamer like the peasant leaders of all great Chinese revolutions, he also descended from the misty mountains to overthrow an oppressive dynasty and so change Heaven's Mandate. The scholar-poet with sword in hand, he championed the oppressed,

treated his followers fairly, and 'made a noise in the east, while attacking in the west.' Between swimming the Yangtse and penning poems in Peking, Mao has also remained for millions of his admirers that legendary Chinese figure, the infallible old fox.

For two millennia Chinese loyalty has focused on the ruler rather than the State. Mao's Cult of the Personality continues this tradition. Where men formerly looked up to the Emperor, they now look up to the 72-year-old leader who swam nine miles in 65 minutes; where formerly they were urged to study the Classics as their unerring guide to correct living, today they are urged to study the Thought of Mao Tse-tung. This Thought of Mao makes the rice boil faster, is good for burns, increases the harvest, keeps the road accident rate down, wins international ping-pong matches and 'changes Heaven and Earth.' It is 'the moral atomic bomb which our side alone possesses.'

To the Western observer, with his inflexible dogma of liberalism, China often appears as a monstrous empire of blue ants in which the crushed terrified, half-starved millions crawl through their bitter days, wistfully dreaming of democracy. But that is not necessarily the view from the other side of the looking-glass. China owes her very birth to the iron tyranny of the first Ch'in emperor in the third century B.C. Four out of every five of Mao's charges are poor peasants who will quite happily accept an 'ism' for the sake of peace and quite. Their farming forefathers, who overthrew Ch'in and every decadent dynasty thereafter as if they were sorting out rotten fruit, were the enemies not of despotism but of its abuse. They did not demand democracy but a square deal. There is nothing dismayingly unfamiliar to a Chinese about the Communist legal and police methods that seem so nightmarish to Anglo-Saxons. He is

accustomed to a law that protects the State rather than himself, and if he must suffer the importunities of the Chinese security police, he is at least spared the depredations of secret society thugs.

Chanted slogans and mechanical responses, memorising by rote and the reiterative skills of the parrot and the cuckoo, rewritten history and literature, and brainwashing – the Chinese have long since had to learn to live with these. They may resent the innumerable political meetings they have to attend, but they are not going to start a revolution over any of these things. For they can count their blessings.

They find themselves in a united State at peace with itself. Soldiers are disciplined, taxation is equitable, a man can eat at least two meals – if frugal ones – each day. There is work for all, and there are schools for the children. The establishment of the Communist regime followed half a century of division, unrest and disaster. Today people have food and security and the inalienable right to dream, and this at once means that far more than half of the families of China are better off than they were before the Communist conquest. For the time being at least, the Chinese are thankful for small mercies and are prepared to live by rice alone.

The old may cling to their customs, but the young are like the young everywhere. Some are ready to give whole-hearted loyalty to their country and party, are content to do what others do and only ask not to be sent too far away, but others dream of Beatle haircuts, a bulging bank balance and a book-case full of bourgeois and non-Communist works now condemned as 'poisoned weeds'. Few of these children of the individualistic and go-ahead merchant people yearn for private enterprise on a grand scale, however. The mercantile tradition is not universal. The poor of China never had enough money to run more than the market side-lines in

191

vegetables, poultry and pigs that they are allowed to run today.

The Chinese – ill treated over the centuries, shy and cautious in the presence of a new, stern master – are still of uncertain temper. Democracy and the West they reject, but the uncompromising offer of Communism still sets them mentally dodging and skulking. They know that China has recovered her economic poise since the disastrous days of the Great Leap Forward not because socialist principle was upheld, but because Peking permitted a heretical lapse into capitalism, and peasants were allowed to organise their own private bits of business in the hitherto rigidly regimented People's Communes.

Hang a cage of Java sparrows on a tree, and while those inside will struggle to get out, those outside will struggle to get in. Chinese youth overseas may cla-

mour for Chinese Communism, but Chinese youth at home ask whether the seed is worth the cage.

This is the fear – the fear not of detonation but of dilution – that has thrown up the young 'Red Guards,' who are now rampaging through the cities of China, desecrating Catholic churches and Carnaby Street cult, pushing pork into the mouths of Muslins, burning books and baiting nuns and vilifying all that is foreign, bourgeois, traditional, or just pre-Mao.

The Legalist philosopher Han Fei wrote: 'The beast called the dragon can be tamed and trained to the point where you may ride on its back. But on the underside of its throat it has scales a foot across that curl back from the body, and anyone who brushes against them is sure to die.' Han Fei was speaking metaphorically

of the Chinese ruler, but the Chinese ruler is, and has always been, in the end, the Chinese people. Today Chinese still quote with reverence the saying of sages like Meng Tzu (Mencius) and Lao Tzu (Laocius) who lived long before Christ. The measure of Mao's success in riding the docile yet dangerous Chinese dragon will be whether men still quote Mao Tzu (Maocius?) a thousand years hence.

Dennis Bloodworth

DENNIS BLOODWORTH (b. 1919) Formerly The Observer's *Far East correspondent, Dennis Bloodworth was made an OBE in 1989 for his services to journalism and British cultural interests in South-East Asia. This piece on the Great Cultural Revolution in China was later incorporated in his book* The Chinese Looking Glass.

KEEPING THE LID ON THE WORLD

Robert Lowell in conversation with John Gale.
12 March 1967
Mr. Lowell came into the room quickly, stooping a little to one side. He had a rather sad smile, yet the blue eyes behind the glasses seemed amused. He tended to look down when he talked.

He had spoken somewhere of the danger of the great impersonal bureaucratic machine flattening out humanity. Would he elaborate?

'Once you get that enormous Government machine connected with power and world ambition it's terrifying. And there are a lot of other machines in the world besides America's: Russia is another. I'm haunted by the First World War, when these huge countries, despite inertia – or through inertia – went to war. Nobody could stop it; not even the people running the Governments. We've seen this twice in one century, and it's impossible to see that very much has been done to prevent a third.

'The Kaiser was an unattractive character, but not a villain; most of the heads of State were the same. Even the Kaiser, when he got cold feet, couldn't stop the train schedules when the German trains were going to the frontier.

'Then there's another thing. Isaiah Berlin and I were talking about war, and he said there's one thing worse than war: massacre. I feel very gloomy about the future: the Indonesian massacre and the Hindu-Muslim thing. That seems bound to happen in South Africa and elsewhere.

'I think the best thing – it's a little chilly to me – would be a sort of pax Americo-Russiana: just coming to terms by trying to keep the lid on the world; and Europe might be in this. I think that's a strong possibility. It will be very much 'Two Cheers for Democracy', *faute de mieux* kind of thing: an attempt at peace and just-under-peace. . . .'

Was it true that he often wrote a very gloomy poem when in a very happy mood?

'I write rather slowly, and a lot

boils up and changes in the course of the poem. In a poem you don't try to give the reader distress and disorder: you want to give him something well made and organised, with loveliness to it: and that's exhilarating even with subjects that are apocalyptic. You don't want to be mannered about these things, or else people think they've heard you before you begin speaking.

'I think it should be very hard to say whether life is joyful or tragic: it's all that. Henry Adams's brother, Charles Francis Adams, wrote about the eighteenth-century Frenchman who said he'd had 14 happy hours in his life. Charles Francis Adams didn't know whether he'd had that many, but he was certain that he'd had more than all his family put together.'

Perhaps he would rather not say any more about Vietnam?

'It's peculiarly hideous and useless right now. It would have taken a million years for North Vietnam to have done as much harm to us as we've done to ourselves. Our whole life is torn by it. And our students are about to be drafted. It absorbs conversation, and the cost and brutality are appalling.

'I suppose it's a small minority in America that's disgusted with the war. But it's almost universal with intellectuals. Kennedy has changed and grown, I think. You're not sure of any person in power. He could take a very bad turn. He's about the best we could

hope for, I think; he's about as open morally as a politician could be. I don't mean that if he was elected we wouldn't object to a great deal he did. But it would be an enormous relief. Of course he has odds against him. But it does look more likely; and I think the country as a whole is sicker of the war than they know; the ugliness and unsuccess.'

A last question. He had once spoken of the 'sheerness' of

America. Could he say any more?

'I've got a phrase out of that interview I used later in a poem: the "monotonous sublime." It can get too sheer in that way. It has something to do with our character. It's probably harder in America to be a first-class minor poet. Most people are ruined. They feel immoral not doing what the national genius expects. They've got to do something on a big scale.'

South Vietnam, 1967, American GIs and Vietnamese: 'It would have taken a million years for North Vietnam to have done as much harm to us as we've done to ourselves.'

IN THE MORRIS MANNER

19 March 1967

Two very different styles of life are defined by the two styles of architecture which seem most pervasively influential in our time – the austere classicism of Mies van de Rohe and his followers on the one hand, and the currently more fashionable informality of Charles and Ray Eames on the other.

It's not easy to know which to aspire to. So I think it's worth saying that there is a *third* lifestyle, fundamentally different again, which has been developed over the years by our friends Horace and Doris Morris and indeed our good selves. All we lack at the moment is an architecture to put around it.

In the Miesian canon, if I understand it, the overriding goal is perfection of form. The skin of the building is the most formally perfect solution possible of its function, expressed (usually) in terms of glass to keep the weather out and steel to hold up the glass. The contents are as important to the form of the whole as the transparent skin; so they, too – furniture, carpets, pictures, the lot – are as strictly located by the architect as the drains.

I see the attractions: four days out of seven I should like nothing better than to have an authoritarian architect design my life for me. But then I see the attractions of the opposite conception, too, as developed out of the Mies tradition by Mr. and Mrs. Eames, and enshrined in the house they have built for themselves at Santa Monica, in California.

According to Geoffrey Holroyd, in *Architectural Design* recently, 'the house is filled with a huge collection of toys – objects of indigenous Santa Fé folk culture, tumbleweed, driftwood, desert finds of great variety – placed everywhere . . . Mies wants all glass and no clutter; Eames wants clutter, 'functioning decoration.' The house is also full of Eames chairs – 'the first chairs which can be put into any position in an empty room.'

This bald description makes the Eames life-style sound superficially rather similar to Horace and Doris Morris's and our own. The concept of *clutter* is certainly very special to our thinking. Our houses contain huge collections of toys, mostly broken, together with a random precipitation of pieces of wood, pebbles, old tin cans and cardboard boxes, broken chalk, dolls' legs, scattered heads, empty bottles, and torn envelopes with examples of indigenous child-art on the back. Our chairs, too, are arranged all kind of anyhow.

But a glance at photographs of the interior of the Eameses' house shows that their clutter is clutter only on the loosest sense; it's not clutter in the strict sense that we and Horace and Doris Morris mean at all. The Eameses' tumbleweed has tumbled neatly on to rows of hooks on the wall. The driftwood has drifted into an elegant complex just outside the garden door. The objects of indigenous Santa Fé folk culture have arranged themselves on a square board squared off with a square table, and the chairs have rained down from heaven into positions of the most geometrical exactitude.

The general appearance, in fact, places Charles and Ray Eames pretty firmly in the tradition of our good friends Christopher and Lavinia Crumble, whose extensive collection of folk junk and *objets achetés* has also arranged itself about the living-room with an effortless casual elegance which is entirely alien to the Horace and Doris Morris style.

A completely different approach to the organic development of the clutter is involved. When Christopher Crumble finishes reading a book, for instance, and tosses it casually down on the coffee-table, it lands squarely on top of 'Giovanni Battista Piranesi and the Origins of Op Art' (Limburger & Brie. 7gn.), the edges parallel, the diagonal extending the diagonal of the alabaster lamp-base standing at the golden section of the table. When Horace Morris or I toss a book down, however, it behaves in a much more radically casual fashion. It hits an abandoned Wellington boot standing in an empty soup bowl, perhaps, loses its jacket, and comes down half-open, halfway into an ashtray which is teetering half off the table and half on, kept in balance only by being half-covered with a pair of old trousers which have been put out for mending.

Later, one throws down the daily paper, half-open, on top of the ashtray, the book, the boot, the trousers, and all the rest of it, whereupon half the paper slides down the side of the heap, and wafts away to fetch up along with the book jacket, half under the sofa and half out.

One's wife comes tramping through the broken chalks, pebbles, and amputated dolls' legs, carrying a large cardboard box marked Heinz Spaghetti with Tomato Sauce, and full of old bills and grey woollen socks. With unthinking deftness she half folds up the half-open newspaper to half make room for it, so that the box forms, some days later, an attractively unstable podium on which to rest the load of old colour supplements which have finally slipped off the top of the television set.

Within a week or two one is hacking one's way down to table level again, hefting the sliding sea of colour supplements up by the armful and dumping them into a Sainsbury's Australian Pear Halves Box, which one shoves into the kitchen while one tries to think what the hell has happened to a Wellington boot and a book which have mysteriously gone missing. And didn't one once have a spare pair of trousers . . . ?

It's a style of life all right. All we need is a style of architecture that makes sense of it.

Michael Frayn

THE AUTOBIOGRAPHY OF BERTRAND RUSSELL

19 March 1967

There is no contempory to whose memoirs one naturally turns with greater expectation and eagerness than to Bertrand Russell's. His outstanding intellectual gifts, the variety of his interests and enthusiasms, the vast social changes his long life has spanned and his notable part in shaping some of them – all this made me agog to open the first instalment covering the years 1872 to 1914.

As I read on I must admit to feeling a certain disappointment. The narrative is witty and entertaining; some of the many letters quoted are most interesting; the characters – such as his grandmother, the dowager Countess of Russell, his first wife, Alys, sister of Logan Pearsall Smith and sister-in-law of Bernard Berenson, the famous Lady Ottoline Morell with whom Russell had his first taste of adultery, amusingly described with a nice touch of astringency – emerge with the utmost clarity. Yet something one feeds is lacking.

What? I can find no better way of expressing what I mean than to say that, for me, Russell is the original of the legend of the man without a shadow. His brilliant intellect; his proneness to moral earnestness even about what used to be, and sometimes still is, regarded as immorality, or at any rate a-morality; his fidelity to a splendid family tradition of Radicalism – all this and more, yes. A scholar, a wit, an amorist, a martyr, a philosopher, a polemicist, a demagogue even on occasion, but somehow lacking substance; if you like, lacking a soul.

It is not an accusation I should expect Russell to take amiss. Indeed, in the light of my few encounters with him (on one such occasion he bet me £20 that Senator Joseph McCarthy was bound to become President of the United States, subsequently paying up, I am glad to say), I imagine him as rather priding himself on a condition of soullessness, and being decidedly indignant with anyone who suggested the contrary. He has a fine eighteenth-century aristocratic contempt for nebulous concepts like the soul, and is in consequence capable at times of what to sentimental bourgeois eyes like mine looks uncommonly like callousness.

Take, the case of the Bryn Mawr girl who got to know Russell in Oxford, and then spent a night with him when he was a guest in her parents' house in Chicago, her two younger sisters obligingly keeping guard outside to ensure they were not interrupted. It was arranged that she should join Russell in England, but by the time she arrived there with a view to living with him, the First World War had begun, and Russell felt that the pacifist campaign he proposed to mount would suffer if his private life had any public irregularities.

The Bryn Mawr girl stayed in England, and, Russell writes, 'I had relations with her from time to time, but the shock of the war killed my passion for her, and I broke her heart.' Later she went hopelessly insane. 'If the war had not intervened,' Russell concludes, 'the plan which we formed in Chicago might have brought great happiness to us both.'

It is impossible not to admire the extraordinary candour with which he recounts this sordid little episode, of a kind which arises all too frequently in the police courts up and down the country. At the same time, one cannot but marvel that it should never seem to occur to him that his behaviour was in any way reprehensible, and that he, and not just the war, might be to blame. In the light of these revelations I find it in a macabre sort of way exceedingly funny that Russell should be widely accepted as a discerning expert on marriage and relations between the sexes.

To me he is an example of one of the great puzzles of our times – how it is possible for human beings intelligent to the point of genius in one direction to be so exceedingly silly in others as to constitute a public danger. This did not matter much when intellectuals were regarded as harmless loonies who could safely be relegated to celibate fellowships at Oxford and Cambridge and remote vicarages. Now that they air their views to millions on television and radio programmes, get elected to Parliament, and are generally held in respect as oracles, the matter is more serious.

Malcolm Muggeridge

TWO WRONGED PEOPLES

4 June 1967

The Six Day War began on 5 June 1967

This is the second week of the crisis of Israel. The threatened blockading of the Gulf; the assertion by President Nasser that, if Israel attacks, his objective will be 'the destruction of Israel'; and the feeling that any clash might lead to world war – all this is sickening reminiscent of Europe some 30 years ago. Once again, it is the Jews who are in the position of chief victim – this time, in many cases, the children of those who were done to death in Europe.

In the thirties, although Germany had frontier grievances and mass unemployment, the situation in Europe was relatively calm and normal. By contrast, the *status quo* in the Middle East during the last 19 years has been exceedingly unstable. Israel's frontiers have not been formally recognised, guerrilla warfare has been endemic; there has been a

195

Victorious Israelis. 'An offensive strategy and an attempt at peace through victory would be disastrous. A defensive strategy aimed at negotiations would have good hope.'

continuous state of semi-war. Israel has maintained its existence only by watchfulness on all frontiers, reserves kept constantly at the ready, violations of frontiers usually accepted with stoic calm, but sometimes answered by retaliation.

These differences between Europe in the Thirties and the Middle East today have significance both for the objectives that it is sensible to pursue and for the means of attaining them. A comparison between Israel now and Czechoslovakia in 1938 is apposite.

Czechoslovakia's only aim was to retain its *status quo*. Israel's aim must be to improve a scarcely tolerable position. The Czechs would have done better for themselves by precipitating a general

war as soon as they were touched: their only hope against Hitler lay in that course. But would Israel, which has virtually been living at war for 19 years, be likely to attain its different aim (of an improved local situation) by reacting to the blockade of the Gulf and to Nassar's threatening speeches by taking the offensive?

To answer that question, the nature of Israel's actual situation must be considered as unemotionally as possible. And the basic fact of Israel's situation is that this little State was created where Arabs had lived.

That the Jews were more than morally justified in seeking a territory of their own cannot be questioned. But that the Arabs of Palestine should have been obliged to give up most of their

homeland to accommodate them was, obviously enough, unjust. A conflict between two deeply injured peoples has thus grown up. It is not a clash between the right and a wrong claim (as was the European conflict of the Thirties) but a conflict between two wronged peoples. Unless it is appreciated that the Arabs have seen Zionist immigration as the solving of a Christian problem at their expense there is no chance of discovering a means of improving Israel's situation among the Arab States.

An improvement of Israel's situation means one thing only: gaining political acceptance by the Arab States. In practice, it is a choice between seeking peace through military victory or seeking peace through indefinitely protracted holding operations and, ultimately, through negotiations. It is here that the irrelevance and hazards of reasoning by reference to Czech or other analogies becomes evident. For in the actual situation of Israel today, an offensive strategy and an attempt at peace-through-victory would, in all probability, prove catastrophic. Whereas a defensive strategy aimed at ultimate negotiations would – without being certain of success – have good hopes.

An offensive peace-through-victory strategy, whether conducted by Israel alone or by Israel and her Western friends, would certainly provoke among the Arab States an anti-imperialist reaction. This is because the Arabs do not feel like the Germans of yesterday, but like what they are – the still-humiliated Arabs of today. Whereas Nazi Germany could be defeated and made sober, defeated Arab States, feeling even more wronged, would become increasingly bitter and dangerous.

Moreover, the Arab States have means of frustrating an Israeli or Western military victory. First, Egypt can close or sabotage the Suez Canal. Second, the Arab States can call upon the Russians to support their resistance. The Russians could paralyse the situation: they could make an attack on an Arab State a risk of escalation into world war. But, supposing Israel and its Western friends opted for the more promising course of a defensive strategy, what hope is there of negotiations being ultimately successful? Would the Arabs, indeed, ever agree to negotiate? Could common ground one day be found?

Clearly, the pre-conditions of success are that Israel should have demonstrated itself to be undefeatable, unaggressive and willing to bargain. Any bargain would, obviously, have to leave Israel fully viable, both economically and militarily. But it would also have to make some concession to the perfectly reasonable sense of grievance felt by the Arabs. Is that compatible?

It is never wise to argue another man's case for him: we would, therefore, be foolish to tell either Israelis or Arabs that they could safely make a compromise. What can be asserted, though, is that if no compromise is possible, then peace in that area is impossible.

It certainly appears possible to imagine concessions that could be offered to achieve the inestimable blessing of a peace settlement. Some Palestinian refugees could be taken back, although all the Jews who have come to Israel from Arab countries might have to be deducted from the number of Arabs with a claim to return. The de-militarised zones, particularly on the Syrian border, could be internationally policed and minor frontier adjustments might be negotiated.

In the atmosphere of today, few Jews can believe that the Arabs would ever accept such concessions in settlement of their grievances and thereafter agree to live on good terms with Israel. But it is, at least, certain that they would be more likely to accept, eventually, a peacefully negotiated agreement of this kind than that they would ever settle down peacefully after a further military struggle – particularly if the Arabs suffered more initial defeats.

In spite of the deeply-depressing dangers that beset the State of Israel, it has never been more important than today that its leaders should think like strong men, capable of restraint; like men of peace, who can understand the needs of others and who abhor war.

David Astor

Fleeing refugees. 'Few Jews believe that the Arabs would ever accept concessions in settlement of their grievances and agree to live on good terms with Israel.'

PRIVATE COLLECTIONS

10 September 1967

I wish people weren't so coy about showing their slides and films and snapshots. You have to drag the stuff out of them, as though it were their first efforts at poetry.

They let themselves be frightened off by the convention that one's snaps are boring to others. But the truth is more or less the opposite. It's oneself who is likely to be bored, since one has seen it all before; to others they're almost certainly fascinating.

At any rate, they are to me, in any reasonable moderation. I find the prospect of sorting a huge muddled parcel of somebody else's snapshots over the carpet on a winter's afternoon, or of sitting in the calm after-dinner darkness watching the brilliantly coloured images of someone else's life succeed one another on the screen, a distinctly cheering one.

I don't mean so much the pictures of the Baptistery at Pisa, or the barefoot boy driving goats on Naxos, or the Hopi initiation ceremony in New Mexico (though I must admit I enjoy these too). I mean the really basic stuff – the pictures taken by our old friend Horace Morris of his wife Doris, with the sun in her eyes and a telegraph pole growing out of her head; the pictures of Horace by Doris where he is striking a humorous attitude on top of a rock, with this feet bigger than his head, half his head missing, and the horizon at 10 degrees to the horizontal.

I suppose it's partly plain curiosity about how other people live their lives when one's not around to watch. But there's more to it than that. I think one is perhaps soothed to have some nagging unconscious solipsism stilled by this evidence of the world's independent existence.

'The mystical thing,' wrote Wittgenstein in the *Tractatus*, 'is now *how* the world is, but *that* it is.' And since the arrangement of things in these pictures is unimportant, we are brought face to face with this fundamental aspect – the sheer fact that there was a moment in the history of the world when Doris Morris stood in front of a telegraph pole, and screwed up her eyes against the sun; that whatever was or was not, a rock with Horace Morris on top of it was.

The moment has gone. The state of affairs that united Horace and rock has disappeared beneath a thousand million succeeding states of affairs, and minute by minute grows remoter still. Horace will become to old to climb upon rocks; the rock will be worn down to sand by the sea; the photograph itself will fade and disintegrate. But nothing will ever destroy the fact that it recorded for long enough to be appreciated – that at one particular moment this one particular state of affairs did obtain.

I suppose newspaper photographs and television images say no less. But I suspect that we don't entirely believe them. We accept them, as we do the accounts given by physicists of molecular structure, but we don't intimately feel the reality of them, as we do of the things which touch upon our own existence and identity. If we registered all those pictures of suffering, wealth, and action as anything more than a sort of factual fairyland, they would overwhelm us.

But poor old Horace Morris I know. My total belief in his reality might falter if I saw him on television, discussing the country's economic situation. But to the top of that only too probable rock, to a position 10 degrees out of the vertical, with too much foot and too little head, my belief will follow him unquestioningly.

And on, by extension, beyond him, to the world outside the frame of the picture. To the cigarette packet lying half-buried in the sand, just seven feet to the right. To the two men who walked by, three minutes earlier, gazing down at the sand as they talked, the one absently swinging at pieces of seaweed with a child's plastic spade, while the other said, 'That may be so, I don't dispute that for a moment'.

I like the modesty of snapshots – the fact that they make no claims, imply no principles, demand no reactions. They don't, like news photographs, claim to show anything typical, or illustrative, of matters outside themselves. They don't, like advertising pictures, attempt to suggest attitudes or courses of action.

They make a counterpoise to art, too. For the convention of all art is that things can be arranged, or selected, or lighted, or simplified, or emphasised, to bring out some significance within or beyond the objects themselves; or that events can be represented as falling out in such a way that they cast some special illumination upon human behaviour; or that men can be driven by the pressure of extreme circumstances to some special self-knowledge or self-revelation.

One accepts this as the convention which makes art possible. But so universal it is that it comes to seem more like a natural law. And what *that* suggests is that there really is, in the external world, some special 'truth' which the everyday appearance of things conceals; and that the real significance of these appearances is that they can be manipulated by the artist to reveal this truth.

The snapshot, however, reminds us that the world is not like this – that things are what they are, and that they are significant in themselves, for their own sake. Horace Morris, on his rock, stands for nothing, except Horace Morris on a rock; typifies nothing except Horace Morris on a rock; purports to reveal no truth about the nature of Horace Morris or the rock, except that at this particular moment of time the one was standing on the other, and that together they looked thus and so.

Horace for Horace's sake – a good working principle.

Michael Frayn

INTRODUCING PEANUTS

Charlie Brown and Snoopy, the main figures in the 'Peanuts' strip, joined The Observer *in 1967. Penelope Gilliatt talked to its creator Charles M. Schulz.*

31 December 1967

Even more than America loves a film star in politics or a young father talking to his kids from a space-craft, it loves Charlie Brown and Snoopy. Charlie Brown is the beset little boy in 'Peanuts' and Snoopy is his dog, an amusing, trauma-riddled hound with a fantasy about being an air-ace. Since the Peanuts cartoon started seventeen years ago it had grown to syndication across the continent in about seven hundred papers and spread across the Atlantic in a dozen languages. The book reprints sell in millions. American children's bedrooms seem to be awash with Snoopy gear; Snoopy shoe-bags, toys, and flying goggles.

The creator of 'Peanuts' is a cartoonist called Charles Schulz, a nice gentle man of 45, vaguely alarmed by the public life of his creatures. Cartoon strips often seem knowing and brutalised, but Schulz's are simple and drawn with affection. Charlie Brown himself is a baldish child with no shoulders, bat ears, jelly-baby arms, and a face that has, so girls tell him, no character. If he apologises for being late, he is the sort of boy who gets told that no one even realised he was coming. Charlie Brown has his beaten-down moments, and Snoopy suffers from a massive neurosis about being despised by wild animals; but when either of them is backed into a corner his instinct is generally to stick up for number one and get the hell out.

The little girls in the strip are beasts, calculating beyond their years, with the chill self-assurance of nursing sisters shaking the ill awake to smooth the bed. Lucy, the chief gorgon, is a toddler with an old soul and hair that looks permed. She has a Mussolini chin and a ready temper, and any pre-

tence of talk on an equal footing between Charlie and herself is exposed as a rubbish at once. She has him on toast. Charlie wonders, but Lucy always *knows*.

The only chink in her steel-clad ego – Schulz calls it 'a serious flaw' – is her love for the piano-playing Schroeder, a dedicated little boy whom she dopily hopes to con into marriage by battering the reputation of his beloved Beethoven. No one else impinges on her at all. Charlie's chum Linus, the intellectual of the group – a credulous grieving child with large anxieties and a blanket that he hangs on to wherever he goes – receives the true Lucy treatment when she firmly says she has cut a piece out of the blanket to make a quilt for her doll. 'Perhaps if you went deeper into Lucy,' says Schulz in his infinitely benign voice, 'you'd find she was even more awful than she seems.'

In the long span of Peanuts drawings her character has matured subtly for the worse.

Schulz deeply enjoys drawing and employs no helpers to do it,

unlike most cartoonists so busy. He was interested by a question about what strip-cartoons can do that films can't: 'Violent action, I guess. The characters can emote in really wild manners. Flip over backwards and do grotesque things.' And in Schulz's hand, the jump-cuts of a strip can have effects of energy or deliberate bathos or instant stoicism that live cinema can't match without seeming gadgety.

Schulz quite recently decided that Snoopy was a beagle, not because of any physical evidence but because he likes the word. 'When Lucy says, "You stupid beagle," it sounds right. "You stupid bassethound" wouldn't be funny.' (' "Beethoven" is a funny word. "Brahms" isn't. "Ophthalmology" is, "Optometry" isn't.')

Like the line of his drawings, which is pure and sweet, the dialogue in Schulz's work is oddly delicate for a strip. He doesn't go in for '*EECH*!!!' and '*WHAM*!!!' In private life he hates swear words 'because they're ugly'. One of the elements contributing to his prodigious syndication across

Charles M. Schulz and Charlie Brown, 'a baldish child with no shoulders, bat ears, jelly-baby arms': still loved by millions.

199

The Observer's *first Peanuts strip, featuring Charlie Brown and Lucy – 'a toddler with an old soul
and a steel-clad ego'. Snoopy followed soon after: they are all still with us.*

America is undoubtedly his genuine puritanism, for the fireside-hearted nation is sated with shock-art and warms to any re-emerging glimmer of its historic native decorum. Schulz has practically put 'Good grief!' back into usage: and 'Rats!' Schulz says: ' "Rats!" will take care of everything.'

He has never been to England, and an English word like 'Blighter' makes him laugh. He wanted to know if it sounded funny to an English ear, too, seemed relieved to hear that it did, and then withdrew. 'I'm on dangerous ground here. I'm a strictly uneducated mid-Westerner. I do a lot of things without thinking about them and if I started making guesses I couldn't draw. That's all I do, really, I just hunch over the drawing board and do these figures all the time. I would make a very poor political cartoonist. I'm the kind that if the Governor took me out to lunch I wouldn't be able to draw him ever again.'

PROMISED LANDS

7 January 1968

Israel's Prime Minister, Mr. Levi Eshkol is this weekend in the United States for talks with President Johnson and will later see Mr Wilson in London. The main subject is the prospect of peace or war between Israel and the Arabs. Is a settlement now possible?

One effect of the Middle East war has been to set the Israel-Arab problem more clearly than before into three widening circles: Israel and the Palestine Arabs; world Jewry and the Arab world as a whole; and the Great Powers. As far as Israel and its immediate Arab neighbours are concerned, one is struck by the profound psychological gulf that still exists between them, so that to look for an early reconciliation would be optimistic. But a second impression is the realistic long-term aims of the moderates on each side are now much nearer to each other.

They are based on the assumption that secure coexistence is both more essential than territorial expansion to the Israelis and more important to the Arabs than a new attempt at reconquest or annihilation.

If this assumption can be firmly established, it is no longer impossible to think of a programme of peace which might lead eventually to a more formal peace treaty and even one day to a closer link, such as a confederation between Israel and Jordan or more than one Arab State. But the process is bound to be long and gradual with outside forces – the Great Powers and the wiser elements of world Jewry and the Arab world – needed to give confidence at every step.

The central problem is basically simple: if two nations claim the same land, either one drives the other out, or they agree to drop their claim to exclusivity and enjoy it jointly, or they divide it. In an ideal world the second solution would be the most sensible, and one day may come. But it implies a radical change in the nature of both Jewish and Arab nationalism that seems unattainable as long as each nation is dominated by the desire to assert its separate identity and not be subject to the rule of another.

Moreover, there are special factors which make the idea of a mixed Arab-Jewish State, even a federation, as difficult now as it has always been. One factor is the difference in cultures and social and economic development. Another is the dynamic nature of Zionism, which claims through immigration to extend potential Jewish nationhood to many more people throughout the world than are already in the State of Israel. This would make a mixed State – unless its immigration were limited – unstable from the Arab point of view, while the much higher Arab birth rate would make it unstable for the Israelis.

But if the idea of one side driving the other out has been abandoned and a mixed State does not yet seem practicable, there has to be some form of partition even if mitigated eventually by some confederative measures, such as an economic and security agreement.

The heart of the problem is, what kind of partition will give both Jews and Palestine Arabs a reasonable physical security and economic viability? And what help is needed from outside to ensure the security and viability of the Jewish and Arab States? For despite all Israel's brave talk of relying on itself alone, the fact remains that both it and the Palestinian Arabs depend in the last resort on outside support in money, arms and ultimate military and diplomatic protection.

So the key point of a settlement – frontiers, including the status of Jerusalem, the refugees, and transit rights – have to be approached in a way that help, in the first instance, the creation of both a

secure Israel and a viable and effective Palestinian State on both sides of the Jordan. The first cannot exist without the second. A secure Israel cannot be built on the ruins of Jordan. A Palestinian State burdened with nearly a million refugees cannot be viable with *less* cultivable land than before.

In securing the political settlement the two crucial questions are likely to be the status of Jerusalem and the problem of the refugees. There has to be some compromise over Jerusalem if the ancient yearning of the Jews is not to be simply replaced by a new irredentist passion of the Arabs. One possibility might be a change in the frontier which gives Israel control of the Wailing Wall and of access to Jewish Holy Places in the Old City, while creating some international supervision for the Old City as a whole. Practical unity of the city might be maintained by co-operation between Arab and Jewish municipal bodies.

The Wailing Wall: 'There has to be some compromise over Jerusalem if the ancient yearning of the Jews is not to be simply replaced by a new irredentist passion of the Arabs.'

201

But in discussing apparently rational political formulae, it has to be borne in mind that one is dealing with two sets of highly sensitive human beings in a unique situation. Palestine, alias Israel-Jordan, is, alas, an unforgettable country: alas for peace and sanity, for under the tense bright sky that spans its fertile plains, its dreamlike hills and legendary towns of golden stone, it is easy to see why it has been so fought over, why it has haunted the Jewish memory for 2,000 years and why the Palestinian Arabs who have known its reality for 1,300 years cling to it so passionately, and in exile have already developed something remarkably like a second Zionist movement.

A human and historical problem which has remained unsolved for 50 years (or 2,000, according to your point of view) is unlikely to be finally settled in six days of war, however spectacular, or six months of diplomatic argument.

There is at least now a slender chance that wise diplomacy could turn the trend of events and thoughts nearer to reconciliation than to destructive defiance. It remains to be seen if the Great Powers can seize it.

Robert Stephens

ROBERT STEPHENS (b. 1920)
Close to David Astor's thinking and renowned for his grasp of foreign affairs, especially of the Middle East, where he began contributing to The Observer *in 1946.*

SALUTE TO FONTEYN

25 February 1968

The great are the critic's bane. It's ridiculous to keep repeating the virtues of Bach and Rembrandt; yet to ignore them may imply that young Mr. So-and-so is in the same bracket. It's easiest to give them a regular passing touch of the forelock – but that's not always fair or wise, or helpful either. There are occasions for the 21-gun salute.

The return of Margot Fonteyn to Covent Garden after a long absence is one of them. We have had some fine performances while she has been away, but seeing her back puts them immediately into perspective. With her we are no longer in the canary-fancier's corner, rating one artist against another. We seem to move out into an altogether larger, calmer, freer world. It's not that she brings any qualities we don't know already. She doesn't jump any higher, spin any faster, balance any longer, have more elegant legs. The reason she astonishes is simply the truth of her dancing. It strikes home with a quiet finality, like a great painting seen after a long, anxious time. Yes, you feel, that's how it is. Everything is all right.

Of her three interpretations in the past two weeks, her *Giselle* was perhaps a shade more beautiful than her *Swan Lake*, where the virtuoso requirements now and then revealed the prodigious technical work which she normally hides under those movements which seem to flow so naturally and limpidly. But to both she brought her special gift – economy, tact, harmony, the purest of lines and a kind of inner dramatic sense which informs her every step and phrase, lending conviction to the total role. She never forces or woos: why should she? We are all up there with her already. Her pauses are a wonder; she dances as eloquently when she is standing as when she runs and flies. There is a stillness at the heart of her every movement.

Watching her now and remembering her career, you can see how she has not only broadened her attack and style in recent years, but immeasurably developed here interpretative gifts. Maybe it's because of this that she now excels in *Giselle*, a ballet in which she never used to look quite happy; and why the best of all her new performances was in *Romeo and Juliet*.

Here another element enters – Nureyev. He, too, must usually be content with a brief note of appreciation, or even (for it is the fate of all master-figures to set their own standards and then be judged by them) of disappointment. But while discussing Fonteyn we can acknowledge the enormous debt she owes to his consistently tactful and positive partnering, and also his own pre-eminence. Singly, they are irreplaceable; together they are incomparable.

Nureyev's Romeo, which also lacked consistency in the early days (the roles were originally written for two very different dancers, Lynn Seymour and Christopher Gable) has jelled into an interpretation in which dance and character blend with blazing vividness. He turned the rather niminy-piminy ballroom solo into a mating-display with an Elizabethan richness of vocabulary; he rocketed round the market-place as though his high spirits were bursting their buttons; and in the big balcony duet they came together with passionate abandon. It was a revelation to watch, as the tragedy rolled forward, the purity of her style, the power and richness of his. She moved like a girl holding fast to a vision; he danced like a young man in love, a torch to her steady taper.

Alexander Bland

ALEXANDER BLAND
The pen-name of two people: Nigel Gosling, The Observer's *Art Critic from 1962 to 1975, and his beautiful wife, the former dancer Maude Lloyd, a leading ballerina with the Ballet Rambert and one of the outstanding British dancers of her time. It was her expertise and technical insight that underpinned his deft descriptive talent and interactive intelligence. Nigel Gosling, who died in 1982, was universally loved and very wise. 'There are no rules in art,' he once said to a colleague who was sounding off about some ultra-provocative example of modern sculpture, 'there are only risks.'*

Fonteyn and Nureyev rehearse Giselle*: 'There is a stillness at the heart of her every movement . . .*
Singly they are irreplaceable; together they are incomparable.'

BEHIND THE MOON

22 December 1968

The emotions aroused by Apollo-8, which is to culminate with three astronauts looping the loop round the moon on Christmas Day, will be more mixed than usual. There is simple awe in the face of an historic and fantastic adventure; there is schoolboy pleasure at a lavish display of monster fireworks, with spectacular electronic conjuring, and the prospect of daring space-artists chatting nonchalantly from out of a dizzy void on our fireside goggleboxes. But there is also despair and sadness that such dedicated skill and such lavish resources should be poured into a pantomine, a huge exercise in technolo-

gical show-biz which looks garish, insensitive and meaningless beside the anxious and hungry realities of life at ground level.

The whole enterprise is essentially irrational. At one time, American generals were trying to sell the moon as a strategic base: 'The nation that controls the moon will control the earth.' But not much is heard of this now. A more serious argument is that man is the most versatile and critical scientific instrument that can be sent to explore unknown regions. While it is just conceivable that the astronauts may make some totally unexpected observation, few scientists would rate this possibility very high.

A more sophisticated justification of the space circus is that it has stimulated advanced technology and scientific education, as well as demonstrating American determination not to be put in the shade by Soviet sputniks. One weakness of this argument is that defence research, which is on a much larger scale, is in any case forcing the same technologies. But a more serious charge is that the effort diverts resources, attention, and above all, talent, from more urgent problems. There is some reason to think, in fact, that several modern technologies have been advancing *too* fast. Not only do techniques and equipment become obsolete before they have been fully exploited: the pace of industrial and economic change is put-

'To look down at the wild and empty wastes of the moon will be a truly historic moment in human evolution.'

---

ting social and political evolution under the most serious strains.

Mr Nixon's line on space is still obscure; quite soon after taking office he will have to decide whether NASA is to have a genuine future (only minimum funds have yet been voted to keep the organisation going after the first moon landing next summer). Probably a circumlunar triumph now will make it harder to be mean to NASA next year, whereas coming second yet again to Russia (who may also be about ready for a moonshot) would deflate prospects still further.

However this may be, there is no ignoring the fact that Apollo-8

is very dodgy indeed. To begin with, NASA had to take a gamble on Saturn 5, its monster booster, which on its previous (unmanned) flight last April developed a violent and potentially hazardous 'pogo stick' vibration, while its second stage did not function properly and the third stage failed to restart.

But beyond this lie hazards of a new order. During flights in earth orbit the astronauts could always make an emergency re-entry. But by setting off to manoeuvre round the moon, the possibility of rapid return to earth is gone. For 45 minutes on each moon orbit they will be hidden behind the moon

and out of radio contact.

In itself, there is nothing wicked about taking risks. Pioneering of any kind is inherently risky, and the astronauts are chancing their lives by their own choice. What does not smell so nice is the suspicion that on this occasion they have been asked to take risks in the interests of an organisation concerned with self-preservation, and for motives of political rivalry which are largely bogus (the propaganda impact of space spectaculars has become increasingly feeble and ephemeral).

None of this need prevent us respecting the courage and sharing the wonder of this unprecedented experience. For three men to look down at the wild and empty wastes of the moon, and then look up and see the earth hanging in the black sky, a brilliant blue globe veiled delicately with clouds, will be a truly historic moment in human evolution. Perhaps the one truly honest justification of the space race is that it arises out of that aspect of human nature which drives us to do very difficult things, which can lead to crude ambition, but also to high idealism.

The notion of voyaging in space may well have roots in some of the deepest and oldest ideals of all. It is not so very long ago, historically, that the moon's orbit round the earth was thought to embrace all that is fallen and corrupt in the universe, while beyond it lay the realms of the heavenly spheres. Modern rational man can expect to see only a starlit blackness behind the moon. But then, Apollo is not a wholly rational enterprise.   *John Davy*

IS THIS WHERE I CAME IN?

In this Farewell column as a regular contributor to The Observer, *Edward Crankshaw compares the Brezhnev invasion of Czechoslovakia with the Stalinist coup of 1948.*

22 December 1968

It is just 22 years since, to my surprise and gratification, I was invited to write about Russia for *The Observer*. Tempted, I fell: about a year of it would, I imagined, be enough. Too much, thought quite a number of readers, to judge by their letters to the Editor. But here we still are, and in the act of detaching myself from day-to-day involvement it is worth looking at

some of the differences between then and now. The more so because the invasion of Czechoslovakia made many people feel that nothing can have changed.

The very manner of that invasion in itself showed radical change. When Stalin gathered up Czechoslovakia in 1948 it was

Prague, 1968. Students were among the foremost in defying Brezhnev's brutal invasion – some, indeed, stood in the way of tanks. Most, however, could only demonstrate forlornly, as pictured here.

part of a calculated pattern. It was to complete his broad defensive *glacis*, which could also, if desirable serve as an offensive base. He was engaged in creating a new European situation and he saw that it was good. He set about it with remarkable economy of means. He had, for all practical purposes, already annexed Poland, East Germany, eastern Austria, Hungary, Bulgaria and Romania by the simple expedient of transforming armies of liberation into armies of occupation. Czechoslovakia was secured through the agency of a handful of traitors without the use of Soviet troops at all, save as a threat in the background.

How spare and elegant compared with last summer's operation. When Brezhnev moved, it was in a panic reaction to restore the system of his old master, which had hopelessly broken down, by means he did not want to use. There was a military plan – trust the soldiers – but no coherent political plan. Neither Brezhnev nor any of his colleagues knew what they would do next (there are few signs that they know now).

When I speak of Brezhnev I mean the ineffable collective, working either together or at loggerheads: Podgorny, Andropov, Shelepin, Suslov, Mazurov, Voronov, Shelest. Old Uncle Tom Cobleigh and all. The supreme government has lost its identity. All it could think of last year was the jubilee of the Revolution. All it can think of now is the coming centenary of Lenin's birth. Talk about a country that has lost is empire and cannot find a role. The Russians have not lost their empire, yet. But the leading party has lost its role, both as the ark of the covenant of a great international movement and as the received authority within the Soviet Union.

It took the Collective just nine months to break Malenkov for trying to get on top. It then contrived for another four years to bridle Khrushchev himself, a man whose extraordinary skill and conviction can only now be measured. Even when he broke through in 1957 he never made it entirely. Even when he was behaving like an emperor, the Collective got him in the end. We may take it for sure that none of the gentlemen listed earlier will let Brezhnev or anybody else at present in sight get the power of life and death over the rest of them.

They are not merely living with one another. They are also living with the Soviet people getting on for 250 million of them, who now count and have to be reckoned with. What do they count for?

It is the hardest thing to tell. There is a strong and numerous managerial class, forming, with the party bureaucracy, a new bourgeoisie. There is also a new intelligentsia. When Stalin imposed his pattern on a society, which was decapitated and extremely raw, he had neither of these forces to deal with (force is force, even when inert). To begin with, also, he had the enthusiasm of the young on his side. The young are not enthusiastic now.

What of the masses? In the 1930s they were hungry, illiterate and cold. Most now have enough to eat, many have television. Almost all can read. This does not mean that they are enlightened. It does mean that discontent with continuing insufficiencies tends to be cancelled out by fear of losing what has been gained. With all their wonderful warmth, most Russians are not deeply interested in opposition. They want freedom to live their own intense lives with as little interference as possible: they want a tolerable standard of living.

The vast majority of the new bourgeoisie, nineteenth-century parvenu philistines in mood, are still more of a conservative force; they have now something to lose. They want snugness, smugness and tranquillity. They were brought up under Stalin in terror and in corruption. Too often they react with immediate subservience to the least touch of the whip, with eager alacrity to the hint of a bribe. Not a very stimulating picture? No, indeed.

It is not the whole picture. Except for about 20 years under Stalin there has always been an opposition in Russia. It is the intelligentsia – by definition the opposition. The intelligentsia are not what we understand by intellectuals (though they include intellectuals) but simply people who try to think for themselves. They may be writers and artists of all kinds, obviously; scientists, teachers, doctors, engineers, technicians. They form not a political movement but a sort of freemasonry of questioners.

We shall hear much more of them. Brezhnev, for the moment, is subduing them and encouraging the yahoos. But he evidently does not want to suppress them absolutely, even if he could. He needs their minds to keep the highly complex economy functioning at all. He balances, as Khrushchev did, but dully and without inspiration, between the dead but indispensable mass of the Party functionaries and their hangers on and the new forces which have to be harnessed unless the Soviet Union is to die.

The mood of the leadership is Khrushchevism without conviction, without attack, without a sense of purpose. It is simply trying to hang on. It is also highly conscious of its image. Its attempt to restore that image, after the crass ugliness of the Czechoslovak affair has been little short of abject. Not all the proud naval display in the Mediterranean (which has now been reduced in case the Arabs and/or the Americans took it too seriously), not all the abuse hurled at Britain in an attempt, without risk, to show how strong and angry they can be, can hide the underlying indeterminacy or put Humpty-Dumpty together again.

Edward Crankshaw

*E*DWARD *C*RANKSHAW *(1909-1984) Began writing on Russia for* The Observer *in 1946. Doyen of Cold War Kremlinologists, responsible for* The Observer's *great scoop: securing the secret text of Khrushchev's historic denunciation of Stalin in 1956.*

TIME OFF IN LEBANON

5 January 1969

Because they detect a humidity in the air, which we would identify as delicious heat, the local lay-abouts go to the mountains in summer and the coast in winter (unless they are skiers), which is the opposite of what most visitors will want to do.

It is not really necessary to follow their example, as a light wind blows much of the time, which takes a lot of the steam out of the heat. March-May, when there are marvellous flowers, and October-November, are the ideal months, especially if you want to visit the antiquities – Phoenician ruins, Roman ruins, Crusader ruins, Arab ruins, and all those cedars, which are practically monuments themselves.

Beirut, half-way up the coast being a free port in every sense, is a great place for stocking up on things you can't possibly do without: drugs, gold bars, precious stones (some of which are precious only in the eye of the buyer – you need a long purse to shop with the Lebanese), Scotch twin-sets and girls. Oil Sheikhs, if they can't summon up the energy to make the journey in person, send their central buyers here to stock up for a thousand and one nights on the Gulf (if you take a job here as an *au pair* meet the family first).

Beirut has a powerful night life which throbs and wobbles (big belly-dancing centre) from dusk to dawn in dozens of cabarets, night-clubs, stereo clubs and bars, some of them saucy, some downright lugubrious. For the out-of-door pleasures there are well-tended beaches.

Far nicer than any of this is the coast, one of the loveliest and most interesting anywhere in the Mediterranean. North is ancient Byblos and the island of Ruad, where the caiques were built until recently with timber floated out from the shore; and Tripoli, which has marvellous *souks*. There are a lot of non-pay beaches. South of Beirut are the Phoenician seaports of Sour (Tyre) and Saida (Sidon), the latter in its time the richest in the world. It's worth staying in both of them.   *Eric Newby*

ROYAL RINGMASTER

Kenneth Harris talked to the Duke of Norfolk, Earl Marshal, Hereditary Marshal and premier Duke of England when he was planning the Investiture of the Prince of Wales at Caenarvon on 1 July 1969.

15 June 1969

The Duke: Sit down and have a drink. Do you smoke? Curious, all the cigarette boxes have disappeared. (*Rings bell: butler appears.*) Rawlings, have we been burgled?

Rawlings: Not that I am aware of, your Grace.

The Duke: All the silver has been removed.

Rawlings: It is being cleaned, your Grace.

The Duke: That's much more satisfactory. Thank you, Rawlings. (*Turning to me.*) Now, you wanted to know what exactly *is* a State Occasion?

Harris: Yes: and who says it is.

The Duke: It is an occasion which the Queen, in consultation with her Prime Minister, decides will be a State Occasion. Not all great occasions are state; Gladstone's funeral was imposing but it was public, not state.

Harris: What was the first you heard about the investiture?

The Duke: I was listening to the radio a few years ago to find out what the weather would be like for cricket and I heard that the Queen had made a speech in Cardiff and said she was going to present her son to the people of Wales at Caernarvon as Prince of Wales at a future date.

Harris: What was your reaction?

The Duke: Rather pleased. Up till Sir Winston's funeral my father and I had done four state occasions each. Sir Winston's funeral put me ahead. The investiture gives me a clear lead. I do not claim to be a statistician, but I can tell you that my father and I as hereditary Earl Marshals have been doing these jobs for one hundred and eight years between the two of us.

The Investiture of the Prince of Wales: the Queen presents her son to the people of Wales at Caernarvon.

Harris: To what extend does the Queen decide how the occasion will go?

The Duke: A large extent. It is, after all, *her* occasion; she likes to know exactly what is going on. I list the matters on which I need her direction, reduce them to Yes and No propositions, wait till I have enough to make it appropriate to ask for thirty minutes of her time, then ask for an audience. Sometimes she will ask *me* questions, sometimes make suggestions. She knows her own mind. If I were not giving satisfaction I imagine I would be the first to hear of it. Recently she said, 'You are getting quite good at this.'

Harris: Will the relatively constricted area at Caernarvon present you with a special problem?

The Duke: We shall have enough room. There are only five peers involved in the actual ceremony of the investiture, handling the mantle, and the sword, and so on. But the lords-lieutenant have to be there, and the mayors with their maces – some have two. Then there are the processions – we're going to have twelve processions representative of Welsh life. One wants not only to have processions but to make them significant and interesting.

Harris: If something goes wrong on the day -

The Duke: Something will go wrong on the day. That is the essence of planning – to be able to cope with what might go wrong.

Harris: What kind of thing has gone wrong in the past?

The Duke: Nothing serious. We had to alter our plans for Winston's funeral because when Harold Macmillan discussed it with me several years previously he had been quite certain that Winston wanted to be buried at Chartwell, in Kent. This meant that we could take the coffin down the river to Gravesend.

It turned out, however, that Winston wanted to be buried at Bladon, near where he had been born. We still used the river, but went to Waterloo instead of Gravesend. You have got to be flexible.

Harris: Are you influenced at all by, for example, the theatre or the film, or other art forms when you produce these state occasions?

The Duke: I do not produce. I reproduce. My job is to reproduce history. What time is your train?

Harris: 3.20, I must go.

The Duke: Would you like to come and see the cricket ground? We shall pass it in the car.

Harris: Yes, I would. I'm told it is one of the most picturesque in the country.

The Duke: I like to think so. It has a cathedral and a castle nearby, and fifty-four varieties of trees around the edge, so it begins with certain advantages. But come and judge for yourself.

Kenneth Harris

KENNETH HARRIS (b. 1919) Joined The Observer *after going down from Oxford, serving inter alia as Pendennis columnist, labour correspondent, Washington correspondent and star interviewer. Achieved an indelible place in the paper's history when in 1976 he was responsible, through his friendship with the American journalist Douglass Cater, for Atlantic Richfield's purchase of* The Observer *at a time when Rupert Murdoch seemed about to become owner.*

UNDER DERRY'S WALLS

In the late 1960s a Civil Rights movement began to form in Northern Ireland, dedicated to ending discrimination against Catholics, especially in jobs and housing. It included Protestants, but it aroused Protestant fears and drew down the repression of the Protestant-controlled police who, in October 1968, broke up a civil rights march in Londonderry with batons and water cannons. The IRA began to infiltrate the movement though its hard men had not yet taken over. Acts of sectarian violence began to multiply and in August 1969 troops were stationed in the province to protect Catholics. Serious violence broke out, again in Londonderry, Mary Holland, who had reported the 1968 march and its break-up, was there.

17 August 1969

The architecture of Londonderry forms a backdrop for a Jacobean tragedy – battlemented and black. The old city is built on a hill guarded by stout 17th century siege walls. Here in cramped terraced houses live the Protestants. On Tuesday, as they prepared for the annual Apprentice Boys' Parade around the walls – to celebrate the Protestant colonists' victory in the siege of 1688 over the Catholic Irish natives – their streets were gay with red, white and blue bunting and newly painted wall pictures of Prince Billy at the Boyne. There were bonfires for the kids. They were the first fires in a conflagration which was to set Derry City alight.

Outside huddled under the sheer drop of the walls, is the area known as the Bogside. Here, in a cheerfully squalid mess of dilapidated terrace houses and new sky-scraper flats, live the Catholics. It is a natural battlefield. All the natural weaponry of rioting – building materials, bricks, lead piping – lie conveniently close to hand. Most important of all, there is a block of skyscraper flats which look down over the both main entrances of the Bogside from the centre of the town. Last week they were the instruments of victory against the Royal Ulster Constabulary. From Tuesday afternoon young boys, some of them only 10 years old, gathered on the flat roof. Whenever the police managed to disperse the men on the barricades the youngsters lobbed down a merciless volley of flaming petrol bombs and forced them to retreat.

As late as midday on Tuesday, it still seemed that the Apprentice

Boys' Parade might, just possibly, miraculously pass without real trouble. The early part of the march did pass peacefully.

The incident which transformed it into something very different took place at about 7 p.m. Most of the Protestant marchers had gone home sensibly and quietly, but some had stayed behind, still wearing their silk collars and their red and white 'remember 1690' rosettes. They stood together with the police and together they hurled bricks and stones at the Catholic crowds who were, of course, doing the same to them. As far as I could see, the police made no attempt to stop them, nor to push them back. Still, the alliance was not yet formalised. But at 7 p.m. the police charged with batons flailing into the Bogside and, right up beside them, armed with lead piping and hurling bricks, were the Protestants.

It seems clear that this charge was made by the police on the spot in defiance of their commanding officer. When the Catholics saw the police apparently leading the Protestants in to attack them, it was though a dam broke in the collective tribal feeling. Always before, the majority of the Derry Catholics has drawn back from the appalling abyss of sectarian strife. At 7 p.m. last Tuesday all that was changed, utterly. The Catholic community, priests, politicians, people, fused together in a will to fight.

Walking along the narrow streets of the Bogside that night, one kept stumbling over groups of women and young children gathered around the tin baths which had been brought out from the houses with no bathrooms. The baths were full of petrol. The children were cutting up rags and old clothes to make fuses. The women were filling empty milk bottles with petrol and sand.

It was the gas that clinched the situation. It came at midnight on Tuesday, billowing in white clouds through a sky alight with petrol bombs and burning buildings. It blinded the eyes, tightened the chest, dragged the guts

Derry's battleground, photographed by Tony McGrath, part of an award-winning series.

into helpless retching. Strong men collapsed and lay crying like babies on the sides of the street. Next day, when it penetrated into the flats and children could be seen with eyes like raw meat from weeping, it seemed to the Catholics that they had now become involved in something quite different from the protest movement of the civil rights campaign.

On Wednesday morning the gas seemed stronger. It was being used almost continuously, and canisters were being fired at individuals. Catholic reactions were stronger too. One kept being stopped by people saying, 'By Jesus, miss, they must not beat us now.' I'm convinced that it was the gas which finally kept the Catholics at the barricades through Wednesday. It was an apocalyptic night of burning factories and shops and cheers went up from both sides whenever a new building was set alight.

After the pyromania of Wednesday, Thursday seemed almost an anti-climax. There was sporadic fighting between Catholics and the police, and one spectacular charge in the early afternoon when the police were beaten back out of the Catholic area. Soon afterwards the young soldiers of the Prince of Wales Own Regiment appeared at the bottom of William Street and threw a barbed wire entanglement across the street. As the police disappeared something close to jubilation broke out. The police might admonish journalists, 'Don't you be saying now that we were defeated. We wanted to stay and finish the job', but to the Bogside the result was clear. The enemy had been beaten, the people had won. The British troops, at least for the moment, are the living symbol of that victory.

Mary Holland

209

Anti-neo-Nazi riots, Nuremburg: Bryn Campbell's photograph captured the essence
of the violence and despair and won the first prize in the News section of
the British Press Picture Awards.

A PHOTOGRAPH'S ONLY A PHOTOGRAPH

18 January 1970

Jane Bown has been a photographer on *The Observer* for exactly 21 years. In that time, in a quiet and determined way, rather like a golden hamster crossed with a rosy apple, she has photographed some of the most interesting people and things of the age. By 1950 she was seeing in a new way and was well known for a style that was her own, though much imitated since.

She would probably treat an old gardener more gently than a Prime Minister, but she has been rough with no one. No one that has been photographed by her has forgotten her. A well-known playwright remarked on being introduced: 'I've always wanted to meet you. I heard of you years ago and of how you carried your cameras in an old shopping basket.'

Though so experienced, she treats every job, even the smallest, as though it was her first, and thinks nothing of going off in a grimy train below zero at four o'clock on a January morning. She has a very special eye and she loves what catches it. In the early years it was things rather than people. To Jane, both have their own life. Her best work has humour and mystery; to her, a man's back may say more than his front; the things left unsaid in her pictures are often very loud. She can make a pumpkin look like a Matisse; she can make a bishop look pretty funny.

How did she become a photographer? 'I don't know,' she once remarked. 'I was eligible for a two-year grant after the Wrens and there was a long list of things that I could study; and the only one that jumped out and seemed the least bit interesting after my fabulous Wren life was photo-graphy.' As a young girl, one of her first trips for the paper was to Paris, and she nabbed Cocteau and several others in a few hours just by being herself.

She tends to distrust intricate equipment and shuns any lens that distorts. Sometimes she asks: 'What is photography? Oh dear, a photograph's only a photograph.' She would love to go back to a Box Brownie, believing that if you can take a photograph with that, you are a photographer.

For many years Jane Bown has been Mrs Martin Moss (her husband is managing director of Simpson of Piccadilly) and she has children of 14, 11 and seven. She loves the country and making jam and feeding cats, and she is a true housewife; even so, cold trains at dawn and the scent of a good story still draw her. She loves her friends and they love her. *John Gale*

210

Cowes week 1969 as seen by Jane Bown. 'In those days,' she said 'if you were sent to Cowes Week you came back with something different.'

HALF IN LOVE WITH DEATH

Malcolm Muggeridge was one of The Observer's most distinguished regular contributors, whose witty and perceptive book reviews and essays first appeared in the early 1950s. This extract is taken from a feature on one of his favourite subjects – death.

22 February 1970

I come in for a lot of mostly good-natured reproach and ridicule for talking about dying. This is considered to be somehow sick or morbid. Death has replaced sex as the forbidden subject.

Curiously enough, my own feelings about death were finally crystallised in an unlikely suicide attempt. Pretty well everyone, I should imagine, has at one time or another envisaged the possibility of suicide, but as between the person who actually pulls it off and all the various degrees of attempting and failing, there is a wide chasm.

How serious was my intention? It is impossible to say, especially as there was the complication of my being at the time, as a wartime counter-intelligence agent, engaged in a ludicrous espionage charade into which an attempted suicide fitted rather well. For fugitives from themselves espionage is a more effective recourse than even marijuana or LSD, which may help to account for the popularity today of spies and spying, in fiction and in life.

The fact is, anyway, that on a sultry, steamy African night, with a good deal of stale booze washing about inside me, and a stronger than usual sense of the futility of most human endeavour, especially the fringe activities in waging a war, I decided to make a once-for-all exit by swimming out to sea and never coming back. I cannot remember feeling particularly het up as I drove to a remote beach; I left no notes to anyone because I calculated that, as a known inveterate bather at all hours of the day and night, my death would be assumed to have been accidental. It just seemed a rather ordinary, sensible thing that I was doing; like taking a suit to the cleaners or extricating oneself from a sleeping embrace; slipping away, softly shutting the door behind one, and treading alone the grey dawn pavement outside.

211

It was a very low tide that night, and I had to wade, as it seemed, for miles and miles, through soft, dark mud before the water even came up to my waist. There is always an intrinsic absurdity in any theatrical act or gesture, and, if anyone had seen me, I must have looked quite ridiculous as, naked and muddy, I made my way so laboriously to the sea. The water, when at last I began to swim, was tepid and treacly, with heavy moonlight falling leadenly upon it. There were sharks about as I well knew, but in the circumstances it seemed foolish to give them a thought. I swam on and on until I began to feel drowsy; a precondition of drowning, as I had read somewhere. A rather nice end, I decided – falling asleep in the sea.

Then I decided to have one last look at the shore, and turned over on my back for the purpose. How very far away it seemed! I could just see the lights of a café I had sometimes been to, kept by a Greek; called Peter's Café, or some such name. The place was always ready to stay open indefinitely as long as there were customers buying drinks. So there must be someone there, I decided; easily imagining the scene – the scruffy waiter half asleep, a party of drinkers out on the terrace overlooking the sea, maybe playing dice or cards, Peter the Greek himself seated stonily behind the bar.

It was these drinkers, the rattle of their dice, their screwed up eyes as they looked at their cards, Peter's hard, avaricious face, that beckoned me back. I realised with a kind of ecstasy that the earth was my home, and they and all men my fellow-internees. The wonderful sleep I had almost fallen into would come later. It was something to look forward to – as Bakunin's sister put it to him on her deathbed: 'It's lovely to die, Michael; to stretch oneself out.' Words I have often and often said over to myself.

As I struggled back to shore, fighting off the somnolence and weariness now instead of surrendering to them, I felt a great joy at

Malcolm Muggeridge, self-confessedly 'half-in-love with death', died in Sussex on 14 November 1990 at the age of 87.

returning. It was a joyous homecoming; even after I had finished with the water, and was struggling, exhausted, through that seemingly endless waste of black, soft mud. Thenceforth I have never doubted that every life must be lived out to the end, just as *King Lear* must be played to the end; that to interrupt or terminate the performance is to rob it of its point.

The following day, to cover myself, I cyphered off an account of what had happened as though it had been a carefully planned and executed Intelligence stratagem. Back in London, my report went first to Graham Greene, who, with his novelist's eye, saw at once that I was covering up for life with a legend. The head of the department, Kim Philby, on the other hand, readily accepted the legend, being even then engaged, as we now know, in spinning his own infinitely more variegated one. Truly, fiction is stranger than fact.

It is difficult today, without appearing a humbug or a fool, to explain that death is neither a misery to be evaded, a fate to be dreaded, nor an outrage to be endured, but a joy to be welcomed. That each moment of life, whatever the circumstances, is made more precious because it passes. That it is precisely because we die that living is so wonderful a gift – whether for a minute or a full lifetime, sick or well, crazed or serene, in pain or in delight, no matter; still wonderful.

As I write these words, I look out of my window at a wintry landscape. Yet I know that already the earth is stirring, buds pushing out. Soon it will be spring. One more spring, and then another, and then another. For me, not so many now. Maybe ten, maybe not even one. Thinking so, the bare twigs seem to glow with an inward light and the bare earth to shine visibly with the promise of fruitfulness, and Donne's splendid words ring in my ears – Death, thou shalt die.

Malcolm Muggeridge

DAVID HOCKNEY: NO DUMB BLOND

22 March 1970

David Hockney has one of those faces which seem to be drawn with halfpennies, bland round-eyed features from which candour and wonder shine out with egregious transparency. With his straw-coloured thatch and cheerful North Country vowels, he is the epitome of that pastoral myth, the country lad come up to town. Soft and fresh as butter, he is preserved from urban infections by the sheer density of his innocence. He looks like the hero of Voltaire's *Candide*. A blue-eyed simplicity impregnates his whole personality. He knows what he likes, says so, and feels no need to rationalise or excuse his tastes. He is as little fussed about his sex life as he is about his love of travelling, good restaurants or films. He has preserved the infinitely rare capacity to relish a cliché.

As every schoolgirl knows, innocence has to be nurtured like an orchid, and the puzzle about Hockney is how far his attitudes are self-induced. He has been accused of posing, of playing the false naïf. There must be something contrived about such stainless purity clinging to such a knife-sharp intelligence but it would be wrong to regard him as a hypocrite. Hockney seems simply to have become aware of this quality in himself early on and realised its value. He clings to his innocence with the tenacity of a child who won't let go.

Hockney's friendly accessibility, photogenic appearance and the amusing unexpectedness of his views, have made him a popular interviewee on all kinds of topics, from mini-skirts to moral-

ity. He doesn't mind, but he sometimes feels that the mainspring of his life, his painting, gets overlooked. This may partly be explained by its nature. It reflects an almost undeviating mood of enjoyment which is easily confused with flippancy. He likes to crystallise strongly felt situations into trim tableaux as stiff as scenes in a puppet theatre, and this seems a natural expression of

his temperament. He gets involved but not committed, he remains cool but never cold. You might call him semi-detached.

Hockney had the kind of instant success typical of his generation. While he was still at college in 1961 somebody gave him a huge canvas and he cast round for 'something important' to fill it. He was reading the Greek poet George Cavafy and remembered

David Hockney: a face 'drawn with halfpennies, from which candour and wonder shine out with egregious transparency.'

the tragi-comic worthies in *Waiting for the Barbarians*. The result was *The Procession*, which made a sensation in that year's Young Contemporaries Exhibition – a row of figures looking more like dolls and guys than patriarchs and dignitaries, pathetic lay figures propping up their grand costumes. The compassionately mocking spirit has haunted his work ever since.

This was the show which launched British Pop Art. But Hockney is very far from being a Pop artist. He seldom if ever uses mass media images culled from advertisements, television, cartoons or conveyerbelt production. He works much from photographs and model-books, but the poses are fused with real characters in real situations. He pulls everything back into his own experience. The swimming pool and the chintz settee, the Hollywood home, the shower-curtain, the open window showing palm trees on the Los Angeles skyline – all seem intensely personal, almost private. You feel that even the cushions he uses as patches of colour are the ones he has sat on.

This violently individual flavour is the most immediately noticeable quality in his work. A Hockney is strongly like all other Hockneys and strongly unlike anything else. You can analyse its elements down into its components, but it is the overall attack which strikes you, the controlled, witty delivery of the born storyteller.

Nigel Gosling

CRAFTSMAN, ARTIST, GENIUS

Igor Stravinsky died on 6 April. W. H. Auden was co-author of the libretto of The Rake's Progress.

11 April 1971

I must leave it to others, better professionally qualified than I, to estimate Stravinsky's achievement as a composer. I can, however, I think, speak with some authority about Stravinsky as a paradigm of the creative artist, a model and example from whom younger men, be they composers, painters, or writers, can derive counsel and courage.

First, let them pay attention to this conception of artistic fabrication. 'I am not,' he said, 'a mirror struck by my mental functions. My interest passes entirely to the object, the thing made.' An artist, that is to say, should think of himself primarily as a craftsman, a 'maker,' not as an 'inspired' genius. When we call a work 'inspired,' all we mean is that it is better, more beautiful, than we could possibly have hoped for. But this is a judgment for the public to make, not the artist himself.

Where art is concerned, Valéry was surely right when he said: 'Talent without genius isn't much, but genius without talent isn't anything at all.' The difference between a pure craft, like carpentry, and art is that when the carpenter starts work he knows exactly what the finished result will be: the artist does not know what he is going to make until he has made it. But, like the carpenter, all he can or should consciously think about is how to make it as well as possible, so that it may become a durable object, permanently 'on hand' in the world.

As an illustration of Stravinsky's professional attitude, let me speak from personal experience. When Chester Kallman and I were offered the opportunity to write the libretto of *The Rake's Progress*, we felt, of course, immensely honoured, but at the same time rather alarmed. We had heard that Stravinsky had on more than one occasion expressed the view that, in setting words to music, the words themselves do not matter, only the syllables.

We were afraid, particularly since Stravinsky had never set English before, that he might distort our words to the point of unintelligibility. But from the moment we started working with him we discovered that our fears were groundless.

Going through our text, Stravinsky asked for and marked into his copy the spoken rhythmical value of every word. In one instance, only one, he made a mistake. He thought that, in the word 'sedan-chair,' the accent in 'sedan' fell on the first syllable. When we pointed this out to him, he immediately altered his score.

Second, Stravinsky's life as a composer is as good a demonstration as any that I know of the difference between a major and a minor artist. In the case of a minor poet, A. E. Housman for example, if presented with two of his poems, both of equal artistic merit, one cannot, on the basis of the poems themselves, say which was written first. The minor artist, that is to say, once he has reached maturity and found himself, ceases to have a history. A major artist, on the other hand, is always re-finding himself, so that the history of his works recapitulates or mirrors the history of art. Once he has done something to his satisfaction, he forgets it and attempts to do something new which he has never done before. It is only when he is dead that we are able to see that his various creations, taken together, form one consistent *oeuvre*. Moreover, it is only in the light of his later works that we are able properly to understand his earlier.

Last, and most important of all, in his attitude towards the Past and Present, Tradition and Innovation, Stravinsky has set an example which we should all do well to follow. All of those whom we think of as the founders of 'modern' art, Stravinsky, Picasso, Eliot, Joyce, etc., reached manhood before 1914. Until the First World War European society was in all significant respects still what it had been in the nineteenth century. This meant that for these artists the need they all felt to

Stravinsky, creative artist, 'from whom younger men, be they composers, painters or writers, can derive counsel and courage.'

widespread error is the exact opposite of Plato's, namely to take political action as the model for artistic fabrication.

To do this is to reduce art to an endless series of momentary and arbitrary 'happenings,' and to produce in artists and public alike a conformism to the tyranny of the passing moment which is far more enslaving, far more destructive of integrity and originality, than any thoughtless copying of the past.

Once more, Stravinsky: 'What, may I ask, has become of the idea of universality – of a character of expression not necessarily popular, but compelling to the highest imaginations of a decade or so beyond its time?'

This, as we all know, his own compositions have achieved. If any young artist hopes to do the same, let him begin by forgetting all about 'historical processes,' an awareness of which, as the Master has said, 'is probably best left to future and other kinds of wage-earners.'

W. H. Auden

make a radical break with the immediate past was an artistic, not a historical imperative, that is to say, unique for each one of them. None of them would have dreamed of saying: 'What kind of music or painting or poetry is "relevant" to the year 1912?' Nor did they think of themselves collectively as the avant-garde, a term of which Baudelaire, who was certainly himself a great innovator, quite rightly said: 'This use of military metaphor reveals minds not militant but formed for discipline, that is for compliance: minds born servile.' What each of them felt, I believe, was rather: 'It is only by creating something "new" that I can hope to produce a work which in due time will take its permanent place in the tradition of my art.' They were also lucky in their first audiences, who were honest enough to be shocked. Those, for instance, who were scandalised by *Le Sacre du Printemps*, may seem to us now to have been old fogies, but their reaction was genuine. They did not say to themselves 'Times have changed, so we must change in order to be "with it".'

In times of rapid social change and political crisis, there is always a danger of confusing the principles governing political action with those that govern artistic fabrication. Thus Plato, dismayed by the political anarchy in the Athens of his time, tried to take artistic fabrication as the model for a good society. Such a theory, if put into practice, must, as we have learned to our cost, result in a totalitarian tyranny, involving, among other things, the most rigid censorship of the arts.

Today in the so-called 'free' societies of the West, the most

DREAM IN A PERSIAN MARKET

Peter Brook's production of A Midsummer Night's Dream *made theatre history. The Observer's theatre critic, Ronald Bryden, interviewed Brook in Stratford.*

20 June 1971

Ever since last August, when it opened at Stratford-on-Avon, the fame of Peter Brook's production of *A Midsummer Night's Dream* has been rumbling round the world, growing in volume. Everyone else seemed to know at once that theatrical history had been made.

An Australian drama don I know hopped on a plane from Sydney in the second week of its run simply in the hope of procuring a ticket. (Disappointed, he returned straight home without attempting to see anything else.)

David Merrick snapped it up instantly for New York, where Clive Barnes called it 'without any equivocation whatsoever the greatest production of Shakespeare I have seen in my life'. In a 14-week tour of North America, it was seen by 200,000 people and lowered our sterling deficit by well over a million dollars.

Everywhere the word was the same. Peter Brook had pointed the theatre's nose in a new direction for the next decade, and was 'one of the greatest, most imaginative directors in the modern theatre'. Now it is London's turn.

I interviewed Brook before the Stratford opening. He seemed far less interested in his forthcoming first night than in the rehearsal he'd held before an audience of children: 'The perfect audience – they crystallise things without judging as adults do.' He talked about a recent trip to Iran on which he'd seen some ancient Persian folk-plays, like Old English sagas played by the medieval mummers, he said.

It wasn't until I caught up with his production of *The Dream* three months later that I realised he'd been telling me all about it. The moment his cast marched, to a roll of drums, on to Sally Jacob's white squash court of a set, wearing the baggy trousers and gaudy satin nightshirts of oriental acrobats, it was clear that this was to be a supra-national translation of what he'd found in those Persian folk-plays.

As they launched into Shakespeare's story, miming and dancing through an imaginary Athenian wood of dangling wire coils, halting to address Shakespeare's poetry straight into the auditorium, they ranged effortlessly between avant-garde group improvisation and the formalised speech and playing you look for in great classical ensembles like the Comédie Française.

Argument will go on, probably for years, whether it is really the finest thing he has done. John Gielgud for one is convinced that his *Dream* has ushered in a new era in Shakespearian production.

Ronald Bryden

Magazine Fashion – sweaters designed by four artists, worn by Julie Christie. below, Elizabeth Frink sweater, beside Frink's bronze bird; right, Patrick Hughes' design.

A SENSE OF FEAR IN GREECE

In 1967 a Greek military junta took over the country and set up a highly repressive regime. Torture was rife. It lasted till 1974, when Greek officers in the Cypriot National Guard caused an international crisis by trying to overthrow Archbishop Makarios and replace him with the terrorist Nikos Sampson. Turkey invaded the island and in Athens the junta relinquished power. In 1972 C. M. Woodhouse who, as a 26-year-old colonel in the British Army had led the Allied Military Mission to the Greek resistance against the Nazi occupation, visited Greece.

20 February 1972

'Go anywhere you like, ask anyone you like; you will find everyone perfectly contented.' This was the advice given to me by Brigadier Pattakos, the Deputy Prime Minister three years ago. On my most recent visit to Greece, I thought it might be worth while to test the Pattakos doctrine in a modified form, subject to certain firm conditions.

One condition was to avoid Athens entirely and to travel in the provinces by public transport. In Athens everyone knows what everyone is going to say about everything. The small towns and villages are less predictable. For exactly the same reason, I tried to avoid old acquaintances – another motive for avoiding them was their own protection. When I was last in Greece, every old friend I met was questioned by the police; and at least two (a general and a judge) were soon afterwards arrested and deported without trial.

I sat beside a schoolmaster on a bus crossing the Metsovo pass from Epirus to Thessaly. He assured me that there was no dictatorship. That was a myth of the Scandinavians, 'who hate us because we fought the Germans and they didn't.' Other passengers round us nodded approval: no one said a good word for the Scandinavians. Nor did anyone except me pause to read the slogan painted on the wall we were passing: 'No more victims for Communism!'

Communism, the civil war and the resistance are no more than unhappy memories, but they are memories that are assiduously kept alive. War memorials and cemeteries are a concrete index seen every day. In Grevena, a memorial to the Turkish wars of 1912 to 1922 bears eight names; another to the civil war of 1946 to 1949 bears 56. On the outskirts of Kastoria stands a cemetery with 477 graves of men killed on the neighbouring hills in those latter years.

To most Greeks, the constraints do not seem positively oppressive. There are compensations: 'Every bad has its good,' as their saying has it. The agricultural community is pleased by the cancellation of debt, as well as by the extension of roads, electricity and machinery to their villages. (But the professional and business community grumbles at having to foot the bill.) The politicians are unemployed, but the Civil Service is said to be more efficient and helpful. When they look back, and especially when they look abroad (for example, at Northern Ireland), the Greeks find much to be thankful for.

If, as some think, the present Government is playing for time, it is doing so successfully. The prospect of any alternative authority grows steadily more remote. The former political leaders, whether in exile like Karamanlis and Andreas Papandreou, or isolated at home like Kanellopoulos and Mavros, are fading from the public consciousness. The Communist Party is hopelessly fragmented and impotent, however useful it may be as a bogy for propaganda purposes. A few politicians still have a high reputation in their own localities, but that is all. Organised labour is a tool of the Government.

And yet . . . and yet . . . I am in no doubt of the incompleteness of this picture. The Pattakos doctrine is certainly not the whole truth. For one thing, the silence is abnormal. Never before have I found half the Greeks I met so reluctant to talk. Nor could one fail to notice that those who praised the 'set-up' invariably did so in the hearing of other Greeks. The atmosphere of fear is unmistakable. 'Never ring me up except on an automatic phone'; 'If you write me a letter, make sure to seal the envelope tight from corner to corner': such warnings are probably unnecessary and certainly pointless, but they are regularly made. Moreover I recalled that for the past four and a half years, whenever I had received a letter from an opponent of the Govern-

ment in Greece, it was invariably posted from abroad.

I attended by chance a semi-public dinner in one of the larger provincial cities. Afterwards a young man came up to me. 'What do you think of it all?' he asked. Following the Pattakos doctrine, I said that everyone seemed prosperous and contented. 'It may interest you to know,' he said, 'that 90 per cent of them detest the Government.'

I asked why. 'It's a question of human dignity,' he replied. 'We Greeks cannot endure being told what to do by people we never invited to sit on our necks – just like the German occupation.' (He was, incidentally, too young to remember the occupation.)

I tested his judgment on another guest. 'That's an exaggeration,' was the reply. 'I wouldn't put the opposition higher than 80 per cent. But he's right about human dignity. There's nothing on earth so strong as Greek *philótimo*.' *Philótimo*, which is so feebly translated 'self-respect,' will need no explanation. To offend *philótimo* is the ultimate crime.

The Greek mood is boredom, frustration, hopelessness and fear. To anyone who doubts that conclusion, I offer this advice. Go there; travel and sit around; listen. The first day you will hear nothing, or nothing but good cheer. The second or third day you will sense another mood. The fourth or fifth day you will detect fear. By the end of the week, unless you are very insensitive, you will feel fear yourself.

C. M. Woodhouse

THE RIGHTS AND WRONGS OF EUTHANASIA

14 January 1973

The concept of euthanasia is probably as old as civilisation; certainly the Greeks (Pythagoras, Aristotle, Plato, Epictetus) and Romans (Cicero, Seneca, the younger Pliny) wrote about it. So, in *Utopia*, first published in 1515, did Sir (since 1935 Saint) Thomas More:

'If the disease be not only uncurable, but also full of continual pain and anguish, then the priests and magistrates do exhort the man that he will ... either dispatch himself out of that painful life, or else suffer himself willingly to be rid out of it by others ... And because in the act he shall follow the counsel of the priests, that is to say, of the interpreters of God's will and pleasure, they show him that he shall do like a godly and virtuous man.'

In 1873 there was a plea in the *Fortnightly Review* that euthanasia should be made legal, and in 1936 the Voluntary Euthanasia Society was founded by Dr C. Killick Millard, former Medical Officer of Health of Leicester. (The word comes from the Greek *eu*, meaning 'good,' with the association of 'easy,' and *thanatos*, 'death.')

The society's aim is to promote legislation allowing physicians to give euthanasia to an adult patient of sound mind who, in the words of a Bill debated in the Lords in 1969, 'is thought on reasonable grounds to be suffering from an irremediable condition of a distressful character, and

who has, not less than 30 days previously, made a declaration requesting the administration of euthanasia in certain specified circumstances.' (Similar Bills were debated in the Lords in 1936 and 1950; there was a Commons debate in 1970.)

Euthanasia has always been a highly contentious matter. What is stoking up the controversy now is awareness that medical advances have given doctors unprecedented power to fend off death, without ensuring that the extra life won for the patient is really worth living. 'Frightful things are done where there's a lot of technology,' said one doctor.

Opponents of euthanasia complain that its supporters argue unfairly when they back their views with horror cases of 'prolonging life artifically.' However, the worst horror story I heard came from a caring doctor at a terminal-care hospital, who strongly *opposed* euthanasia. He told of a patient who was given antibiotics to cure him of pneumonia, only to let him go on enduring the cancer he already had. 'To let him die, while making him as comfortable as possible,' the doctor insisted, 'would not have been euthanasia: it would merely have been good doctoring.' He went on: 'There is good doctoring and over-treat-

Newmarket, 1972, by Chris Smith, twice named Sports Photographer of the Year.

ment, and good doctoring and euthanasia, and both are opposites.'

There are many moral and religious arguments against voluntary euthanasia. But the main basis for opposition to is the so-called 'wedge' argument: the danger that legalising the taking of human life, however desirable in one individual case or another, would, if raised to a general line of conduct, encourage moves towards all sorts of other forms of euthanasia – for deformed children, the mentally handicapped of all ages, psychotic criminals – thus opening the way to a terrifying degradation of society. One hears the words, 'slippery slope,' and the slope they mean is the one down to Auschwitz.

The practical problems too are formidable. I talked with a hospital doctor who formerly supported the idea but now saw why his fellows 'would find the whole business of bringing the law into the sickroom cumbersome and distasteful.' He agreed that relatives, whether because they were unscrupulous or because they simply could not cope any longer, might put pressure on sick old people to sign a declaration requesting euthanasia. Again, feelings of guilt, always an important aspect of bereavement, might well become unbearable for the relatives of a person who had asked for euthanasia, however devoted they might have been.

However . . . He then told this story. A patient, in his forties, had had a stroke. 'When I first met him he could talk, just, and he begged me not to let him go on living if he got worse. Then he had another stroke which left him completely paralysed except for his eyes. When I came into the room his eyes used to follow me, filled with hatred. In the end I had to tell him he was not going to get any better. I said, "If you want to die, close your eyes." He closed them. I then put it to him the other way. Again he made it clear that he wanted to die. I talked about it with the consultant, and he agreed that we should help him to go.'

Doctors opposed to euthanasia simply deny that patients want it. A peer said in the 1969 debate: 'For 17 years I was in charge of a geriatric department consisting of 120 beds in one of the London hospitals. So far as I remember not one patient of mine ever said, "Will you please put me out of my misery or pain".'

Against that a National Opinion Poll survey in 1964 and 1965 among 1,000 GPs showed that 48 per cent had at some time been asked for it.

There is another, more positive argument against euthanasia: that dying need not be an ordeal. I visited a hospital primarily concerned with terminally ill patients, a hospice, as such hospitals are known. It gave me above all an impression of serenity. Its doctors agreed about the problem of pain and other types of distress but insisted that they have developed techniques to deal with them. One is the anticipation of pain. Regular administration of drugs ensures that the patient has no reason to fear its onset.

Such institutions are wholly admirable, but their capacity is limited. In many if not most Health Service hospitals, care of the dying cannot, with the best will in the world, measure up to the standards of the hospices. All this poses a daunting moral problem. What is needed is information, not assertion and counter-assertion. The late Bishop of Durham, Dr Ian Ramsey, who died last autumn, aged 57, was against euthanasia, but not dogmatically so, as he made clear in the Lords in 1969. His arguments were almost entirely based on practical grounds. His suggestion was that there should be an inquiry by a 'consultative group' into all the moral problems faced by doctors dealing with death. This should not be a committee that would merely reach a majority decision, but a body representing all the various disciplines and professions involved which, he felt, could reach 'a creative decision.'

It is difficult to see anything against this proposal.

John Silverlight

Now That the GIs Have Gone

Fighting in Vietnam escalated into a major war in the early 1960s. When it ended, the Americans had lost 55,000 dead with more than 300,000 wounded. The Vietnamese, North and South, numbered their casualties in millions. Here are extracts from a report on Vietnam in the first week after the American withdrawal.

1 April 1973

At last, the great American khaki wave has trickled away. The uncouth, hairy horde, so loud, so short on dignity, has vanished like another age. Lilliput – the small, beautiful, quicksilver world of Vietnam – has re-emerged. Poorer, grubbier, but too old to be deeply changed. Normal life seeps painfully back like feeling returning to a damaged limb. At last you can travel. Touch wood, even the Government's lyrical tourist posters, once so grotesquely inappropriate ('Big Game Hunting at Dalat,' 'Yachting at Nha Trang') may be valid fairly soon. In a Saigon drawing-room, a European wife said to me: 'I hear the VC are quite friendly.' She spoke tentatively, like someone confiding a belief in ghosts. But at last, indeed, you can meet the Vietcong.

In the shadow-line between Government and Vietcong territory, a solitary reed stands up in the dust bath. It has a message tied to it, like an arrow in Red Indian country: 'Soldiers, let us put aside vengeance. We need reconstruction now, and friendship.' A little further on, another one in childish peasant scrawl: 'Soldiers, please do not shoot at us and frighten our animals.' As we read, a salvo of heavy mortar shells crashes out from an army post we can see silhouetted on the road.

The Vietcong arrive silently, six men in single file, in dark green uniforms, guns balanced on

A South Vietnamese soldier amid the rubble of Quang Tri city. Desolate though much of Vietnam was, Gavin Young, who took this photograph, found grounds for hope.

shoulders. Their officer gives me a thin priestly smile. I ask the youngest what his medal is for. 'For killing 12 Americans,' he says. Their leader has been in the National Liberation Front for 17 years. Captured in 1958, he did eight years in prison. He was once a primary school teacher. He speaks of 'President Thieu's indiscipline' and 'truce violations,' but adds: 'Some soldiers are less hostile than others. If we can stick this period out, perhaps conciliation will grow.' That remark means hope.

In Saigon, President Thieu's wife is opening a new hospital. We stand in heavy heat; journalists, diplomats, Vietnamese Ministers, their wives. Various foreign Governments are said to have given money for the hospital. Diplomats had an impression it was for the Vietnamese man in the street. They come out baffled. 'There seems to be only one public ward. All the rest are large private rooms. Damned if I know who can afford it, or who will staff it,' someone in the British Embassy says. Is there a serum against official myopia?

Up in Hué, in the American military compound, the few remaining GIs sit around their makeshift air-conditioned bar drinking up the remaining cases of liquor. A tawdry, end-of-term look has begun to encroach on the nearly abandoned buildings, the ramshackle cinema with its 'Perfume Picture Palace' sign, the sandbags where I saw an American colonel direct mortar fire into Hué in the 1968 Tet offensive.

Not far away, the front rooms of Madame Dinh's house on a bustling Hué street are rented to a tailor. A small army of apprentices pedal away at their sewing machines. I first came here in 1965. In the dark back of the house, with its sparse, dark furniture and the bullet holes in the walls, Madame Dinh, a strong, tiny woman, stitches a bow for her grand-daughter. 'Is it really going

221

to be peace?' she asks. 'We'll see. How can one trust anything?' She talked about her eldest son, killed in action in 1967. 'He died so far away, near Quang Ngai. I went down there to bring him back for burial here. It was very difficult. He was so . . . scattered.' She was near tears. 'The Army gave me a plastic shroud. In the end I still couldn't find one arm.'

We visited the tomb, one of many in a soldiers cemetery. Under the yellow Buddhist swastika, an inscription says simply: 'Died for his country 7.6.1967.' Madame Dinh lit some incense sticks, put her hands together and bowed several times to her son. By now she was quite calm. Then we came away.

Bitterness hangs in Vietnam's air like tear-gas. With an old friend called Chinh, I walk through a camp of a quarter of a million refugees. The squalor is terrible. Nine families crowd into one stench-filled hut. On the door is an old stencil-mark: 'No Vietnamese allowed in this hut.'

Chinh has a sad, gentle face. He is a dreamer, and works with munitions in the Army. His family is nearly penniless. I look at the refugees and say: 'Incredible.' Chinh says with great force: 'What's incredible? Only foreign-

ers are shocked by these refugees and beggars and cripples. Vietnamese feel no shock or horror or anger or even pity any more.' He added: 'My brother was killed last year, as you know. Did you know we couldn't find a single fragment of his body? Perhaps these wretches are the lucky ones.'

Later, Chinh said furiously: 'You know, all foreigners, English too, are only tourists here.'

'Chinh, I don't feel heroic being in Vietnam.'

The bitterness went. 'I know that,' he smiled.

At some levels South Vietnamese soldiers and Vietcong are getting on moderately well, though the scars of war are indescribably deep.

The one overriding danger is connected with face – the face of non-South Vietnamese of any faction. If the leaders in Hanoi decide that they cannot live with failure – they have not won here, as they assure their people they have – the temptation of yet another offensive may prevail.

I watched Madame Dinh and her daughters walking in their trailing ao dais through clouds of tiny butterflies by the river outside Hué. Here, in the gentle confusion of vivid green fields, water, temples, the royal tombs of

Annam, is something much nearer the essence of Vietnam than the loudspeaker vans of Hanoi or Saigon. Something indescribably valuable, that conveys, I believe, to the Madame Dinhs and the Chinhs: 'Peace and conciliation are all that matter. Here among this beauty is common sense. All the rest, from North or South, is a corruption.'

This face of Vietnam persists. It may be doomed. It has no political power. It may be crushed again between armoured forces of inexorably selfish international idealists, of Right or Left, whose idealism can lead to the machine-gun burst in someone else's stomach, and to a woman on a remote battlefield scooping chunks of her son into a plastic bag.

Gavin Young

GAVIN YOUNG (b. 1928)
Joined The Observer *in 1960, reported 16 wars including those in the Congo, Angola, Nagaland (walking for nearly three weeks through the Burmese jungle to get to that forbidden territory) and the Middle East. Spent two years in Vietnam, and was the only foreign reporter present at the birth of Bangladesh in 1971. Won International Reporter of the Year award in 1972 for his reporting of the collapse of East Pakistan.*

EXIT A MAN WITH A TALENT TO AMUSE

1 April 1973

One night in the spring of 1959 I sat down to dine at Sardi's, the New York theatrical restaurant. Crowded before the Broadway curtains rise and after they fall, it is usually empty in between, and was on this occasion. Suddenly I looked up from the menu and froze. Noël Coward, also alone, had come in; and that very morning the *New Yorker* had printed a demolishing review by me of his latest show, an adaptation of Feydeau called *Look After Lulu*.

I knew him too well to ignore his presence, and not well enough

to pass the whole thing off with a genial quip. No sooner had he taken his seat than he spotted me. He rose at once and came padding across the room to the table behind which I was cringing. With eyebrows quizzically arched and upper lip raised to unveil his teeth, he leaned towards me. 'Mr T.', he said crisply, 'you are a cunt. Come and have dinner with me.'

Limp with relief, I joined him, and for over an hour this generous man talked with vivacious concern about the perils of modishness ('There's nothing more old-

fashioned than being up to date'), the nature of the writer's ego ('I am bursting with pride, which is why I have absolutely no vanity'), the state of the theatre in general and of my career in particular. Not once did he mention my notice or the play. It would have been easy to cut or to crush me. It was typical of Coward that he chose, with an almost certain flop on his hands, to amuse and advise me instead.

I first met Coward in the early 1950s, during his cabaret seasons at the Café de Paris, and heard him exploding with mock-outrage when he found in 1954 that the place had been completely redecorated in honour of Marlene Dietrich's impending début. 'For Marlene,' he said, 'it's cloth of gold on the walls and purple marmosets swinging from the chandeliers. But for me – sweet f*** all!' To describe his own cabaret appearances, I went back to his boyhood and wrote: 'In 1913 he was Slightly in *Peter Pan,* and you might say that he has been wholly in *Peter Pan* ever since.' The young blade of the 1920s had matured into an old rip, but he was as brisk and energetic as ever; and if his face suggested an old boot, it was unquestionably hand-made. The qualities that stood out were precision of timing and economy of gesture – in a phrase, high definition performance. After a lifetime of concentration, he gave us relaxed, fastidious ease.

The style he embodied – as writer and performer alike – was the essence of high camp. He was one of the brightest stars in the homosexual constellation that did so much to enliven the theatre between the wars. Coward invented the concept of cool, and may have had emotional reasons for doing so. At all events, he made camp elegant, and wore a mask of amused indifference – 'Grin and rise above it' – to disguise any emotions he preferred not to reveal. From the beginning of his career he was a shrugger-off of passion and a master of understatement – queerdom's answer (you might say) to Gerald du Maurier, the matinée idol of his day. It was du Maurier who led the attack on Coward's first hit, *The Vortex,* on the grounds that it was a dustbin drama.

In 1964 we decided to put *Hay Fever* into the repertoire of the National Theatre and to ask Coward to direct it. Nobody alive knew more about sophisticated comedy, and I remembered Coward's remark to Rex Harrison: 'If you weren't the finest light-comedy actor in the world next to me, you'd be good for only one thing – selling cars in Great Portland Street.' Coward himself was astonished by the invitation. Soon after it was issued, I was walking along a Mayfair street when a Rolls pulled up at the kerb. The electric window zoomed down and Coward peered out. 'Bless you,' he said, 'for admitting that I'm a classic. I thought you were going to do nothing but Brecht, Brecht, Brecht.'

When he arrived to start rehearsals with a company led by Edith Evans and Maggie Smith, he made a little speech that began: 'I'm thrilled and flattered and frankly a little flabbergasted that the National Theatre should have had the curious perceptiveness to choose a very early play of mine and to give it a cast that could play the Albanian telephone directory.'

Kenneth Tynan

Noel Coward photographed by Jane Bown. 'If his face suggested an old boot, it was unquestionably hand-made.'

ARABS FIGHT FOR THEIR SELF-ESTEEM

The so-called Yom Kippur War broke out on 6 October 1973. It ended effectively on 24 October.

14 October 1973

People here crane their necks to cheer the Syrian MiGs and boo the Israeli Phantoms overhead like a young audience watching Peter Pan battling with Captain Hook. I have met many cautiously joyful Arabs this week, but none with much hope of straight military victory. That for them is not overridingly important. This has been a war for Arab self-esteem and this is also a looking-glass war. Hold a mirror up to the Six-Day War of 1967 and several aspects repeat themselves, though back-to-front. The Israelis now are crying 'foul' because the Arabs started this war, just as the Israelis fired the first shots in 1967 and 1956.

Arab newspapers have shown stills from Egyptian television films of Israeli prisoners, sitting crouched, hands locked over their heads. No doubt Egyptian viewers are laughing as Israeli viewers joked about Egyptian prisoners in 1967, particularly as the Egyptians were often obliged to strip to their underpants.

However frivolous these things may seem, to Arabs, the butt of so many cruel jokes since 1948, they are not frivolous at all. Arabs are deeply resentful of what they consider to be the provocative tone with which Israel's leaders habitually address them. What Arabs hear is a deeply patronising voice, half amused, half contemptuous. It repeatedly includes phrases like, 'Show the Arabs what the game is all about'. Those phrases have been much in use this week: Israel the stern schoolmaster, the Arabs the truent adolescents.

The Arab world is galvanised with the excitement of battle and success. Success may peter out, or give way to tragedy and ultimate failure. But something has been done: honour is served: an enemy has been made to suffer, too.

Gavin Young

THE NO-DAY WEEK

In the winter of 1973-4 miners went on strike and paralysed the country by picketing power stations. The Heath Government ordered a three-day working week and called a general election. The Conservative slogan was 'Who governs Britain?' Labour won. The Conservatives did not return to office until 1979, when Mrs Thatcher became Prime Minister.

3 February 1974

Lord Carrington, the Minister of Higher Explanations, as we call him in our house, has warned that we must face up to the prospect of a two-day week. Maybe even a one-day week. Well, I'm ready. Face up, Crosby, I say. Never let it be said that a Crosby shirked the onus of taking five days off. Or even if pressed, six.

'It'll be a great shock to my nervous system, all that leisure,' I said to my wife. All I got out of her was a hollow laugh. She claims that I've been on a two-day week for 20 years. She is a living example of Christopher Morley's old saw: 'A writer's wife will never realise, not if she's been married to him for 40 years, that the writer is working when he's staring out of the window.'

Meanwhile, I have been warming the cockles of my heart by reading stories in the foreign Press telling me how cold I am. I love all those pictures in foreign magazines showing me lighting myself to bed with a candle like Charles Dickens. Of course, not all of the foreign comment is that kindly. It's been Let's Be Beastly to the British Week in the foreign

Edward Heath: he lost the general election.

bladders, and I must say I have thoroughly enjoyed it.

David Dimbleby flew across the Atlantic for the BBC to discuss Britain's image with distinguished American thinkers. They said the things Americans usually say about the British, but which the British usually don't pay any attention to.

Lazy coves, you limeys. Class warfare. All that. Eric Sevareid, of the Columbia Broadcasting System, muttered disapprovingly about those signs telling the tradesmen to deliver in the rear. My goodness, you don't see those any more, Eric. Nothing to deliver to the rear any more. Everyone's on strike all the time.

Anyhow, back in England Dimbleby then discussed – or tried to – Britain's image abroad with a studio audience united only in agreeing that the Americans were full of blather. The audience then erupted into what my six-year-old son calls an argue and had a fierce argue about what was really at the root of Britain's ills, Dimbleby having a terrible time keeping them from all talking at once.

I thought a class war was going to break out right there in the studio, a real television first if it had. 'This is the only country in the world that pays strikers while they're on strike,' shouted one fellow. Dimbleby swiftly retorted: 'This is the only country in the world whose television goes off at 10.30 p.m. Goodnight.' That's one way to quiet a studio audience – just turn the station off. And they did.

Professor D. H. Fodor, a Prague psychologist, was quoted as saying: 'Your country is a quarter of a century behind the rest of Western Europe and the need to catch up is producing great strains.' Now look, I didn't

say it. He did. That Czech over there.

Just to round out the week the Shah of Iran spoke up from the snowbank into which he had just fallen at St Moritz. 'Permissive, undisciplined society on the verge of bankruptcy.' quoth the Shah, of Great Britain.

I asked an American correspondent who, like myself, has lived here for years, to sum up the British plight. 'It's quite simple,' he said. 'The workers don't work, management doesn't manage and the investor doesn't invest.

British capital hasn't invested in Great Britain since 1912.'

'Very succinct,' I said to him. 'But you and I know that's precisely why we live here.' And we both laughed immoderately. Because, of course, it is. Britain has many splendid qualities, but a love of hard work is not one of them, thank God. And you shouldn't delude yourself that it is. Lord Thomson, once said: 'There must be something wrong with this country if it's this easy for me to make money in it.'

John Crosby

In 1974 Alan Road went to Indonesia with photographer Bryn Campbell for The Observer Magazine. *They found the way of death for the Todadja tribe a unique relic in a fast-changing country.*
Above, *Toradja family graves.*
Left, *alongside, the villagers have cut shallow galleries and placed in them lifelike effigies 'Looking,'* Alan Road wrote, *'like theatregoers in some exclusive royal box, they stare out across the terraced valley.'*

225

THE ETERNAL CRISIS

KNOW THYSELF ON EVEREST

1 December 1974

It is eight years since *Cathy Come Home* awakened Britain to the human misery that lay behind its housing scarcity, and since Shelter was launched to keep the reality of that misery in the forefront of public attention.

Last week I looked back on the first leaflets Shelter produced in 1966. Words like 'crisis' and 'scandal' were freely employed; they still are in every newspaper today.

In those eight years there have been countless reports on every aspect of the housing problem. Whichever political party has been in oposition has made it a major political issue. There has been a vast number of newspaper, radio and television 'shock reports' and 'exposés.' In any word association test taken by anyone who could listen or read, the word 'housing' would automatically be linked to 'crisis' or 'scandal.'

It is not just a question of better policies, because over the past eight years we have achieved many policy successes. Our overall housing policy is not unsound. It is certainly not a question of lack of awareness. What it comes down to is resolution. It may be a painful judgment on the society we live in, but in eight years of constant acquaintance with housing problems, and other minority causes, I have become convinced that the resolution is not there simply because there's not enough in it for someone – not enough votes for the politician, not enough money for the businessman. The solution to the housing problem, like so many other minority problems, has always lain with resources, the switch of public and private resources from an electorally or economically profitable area to one with less return. Yes, that does call for idealism, resolution, sacrifice. No, they have not been forthcoming.

The spirit that carried me into Shelter, held me together through the five years' endurance test of that campaign, and has been the basis of the quarter of a million-odd words I have written about minority causes, like housing, has been a spirit of optimism. I have to admit today that it is a spirit I find harder and harder to maintain.

I have lost my fundamental belief in the will of most people to want to be confronted with the truth. I never cease to be amazed at our ability to rationalise our inability to act in the face of suffering.

I've never yet met a man on £5,000 a year who is willing to – even believes he can – take a cut. There's always a reason why he needs every penny, has to travel first class, has to eat in the best restaurants, stay in the best hotels. He – we – can always rationalise self-indulgence.

I've done it myself – countless times, to my discredit and shame. So have you. We'll give our hearts, our words, our applause, a little time, a tiny bit of action, even other people's lives, and sometimes – in a minority of cases – even a little of what we have . . . but not much. Resolution stops short at resources.

That's why we haven't solved the housing problem. Because it always called for money and land and it always will, and we would, and probably will, never give it. That's why our minorities will remain minority causes.

As my mind runs back to those earlier days with Shelter, I recall a poster I sanctioned in the face of a lot of criticism: it showed a homeless family on the steps of a slum and it said: 'Christmas – you can stuff it for all we care.' Damn it, that was the right note, the right spirit.

Damn you, Britain, for your complacency, your hypocrisy and your selfishness, for your weakness and your greed. Damn you because you will do nothing. Damn you because you will soon be worth nothing. Damn us all because this column will achieve nothing.   *Des Wilson*

Dougal Haston and Doug Scott were the first to climb Everest by the south-west face. Tragically, Mike Burke, from the same British team, died on 29 September while attempting a second climb – and expeditions to Everest have continued unabated since 1975.

28 September 1975

In mountaineering parlance it is called 'winding your neck right out' and it carries with it an acceptance of the fact that your neck may well be chopped off. That is the risk that Doug Scott and Dougal Haston took last Wednesday.

They went on climbing the final summit pyramid of Everest well beyond the time that, by all the normal tenets of mountaineering, they should have turned back to reach some sort of shelter. Instead, they went on to gain the summit at six in the evening and then survived a bivouac at over 28,000 feet.

It is irrational, irresponsible and yet wondrous.

The assault has a touch of the Charge of the Light Brigade about it: crazy and horrifying, but one would be a poor human being if one did not feel a moment of jubilation, a lift of the spirit. Man has become what he is because there have always been some members of the species who have taken risks and reached beyond their grasp.

Dougal has always been such a man. I will long remember his answer to a question which I threw at him across the cliffs of Orkney while he was being televised pitoning his way up an unclimbed route on the Old Man of Hoy. I asked him simply why he climbed, and his reply was, 'To know myself.'

At the time, Dougal had only recently graduated from Edinburgh University where he read philosophy. Since then, he has de-

Sherpas and climbers struggle towards Camp 2 on one of the many (too many?) Everest expeditions since the historic first climb of the south-west face by Haston and Scott. Photograph by Doug Scott.

voted himself to the mountains, making his base in Switzerland, and using some desperate expeditions as a journey into his soul. Surely he reached the end of that journey as he crouched, chilled beyond human comprehension, through that long night.

Having survived it, and the climb down and across the most exposed traverse in the world to the comparative safety of the fixed ropes that led from Camp Six, one might think that he would be tempted to know himself to be a superman, able to withstand winter on the Eiger and autumn on Everest. But I believe that he will feel very humble because he, among all men, will have lived longest with the thought that it needed only the faintest stirring of the weather, a whisper of wind in the valley 12,000 feet below, to create a raging torrent of icy air at 28,000 feet – a wind that would have killed them both.

The successful assault on the south-west face will undoubtedly bring in quantities of money to the expedition coffers. The 1953 Everest Expedition produced a surplus of £90,000 which was invested and put under the mantle of the Mount Everest Foundation. Over the years the MEF has distributed £190,000 to help British expeditions all over the world and, such is the way of modern finance, they still have £90,000 left – although, of course, a much deflated £90,000.

The present expedition has cost between £120,000 and £150,000, a figure which shocked many British mountaineers, especially those who know what is happening in the high valleys of Himalaya. It is, for instance, more than the total sum ever spent on the education and health of the Sherpa people, on whose backs every Everest expedition has climbed.

Now the south-west face of Everest ('an attractive route up a pile of rubble,' as one member of the present expedition put it) has been climbed many people hope that we have seen the last of these vast and expensive caravanserais which are so ludicrously out of place in the pitifully poor villages of the Himalayas.

May this one, therefore, be the last, and may the profits from it be used for the benefit of the Sherpa people who have lost so many of their finest men on the high peaks around their homes.

And may this expedition return safely home and not succumb to the very natural desire to put as many people on the summit as possible. After all, 47 men and two women have now stood on the summit of Everest and there can now be little point in risking the lives of sahib and Sherpa to make that figure into a half-century.

Christopher Brasher

An Editor Looks Back

David Astor ended his twenty-seven-year editorship at the end of 1975. In this piece he questioned himself on points in the paper's evolution.

28 December 1975

Q: What was *The Observer* like when you began?

A: Much the same as now, in some ways. Particularly in its treatment of the arts and of books. And sport – the paper always fancied itself for sports writing.

But politically *The Observer* had changed its position in 1942. Till then, it had always been a Tory paper, although an irregular one under the 34-year editorship of J. L. Garvin. After his time, it declared itself non-party – at that time an unusual stance, now one claimed by almost all papers.

Q: What was the motive?

A: A belief that a non-party paper might get a better hearing for sensible liberal ideas and a new look at international relations.

Q: And where were the ideas to come from?

A: They were to be generated by a little bunch of writers of various sorts, drawn together by the wars and the Thirties. We imagined we could see some of the lessons of that bloody period.

We weren't any kind of movement. Indeed, one agreed notion was the importance of tolerating disagreements – unlike the two totalitarian camps which had dominated the nightmare of the Thirties. One formative contributor was Arthur Koestler. George Orwell, who wrote for the paper long before he was well-known, probably had the greatest political influence on me. Incidentally, it was his idea that the paper should concentrate on ending British colonial rule in Africa without delay (unlike the long-lingering British Raj in India) regardless of the political mistakes the Africans might then make.

Orwell influenced me in avoiding cliquishness in book reviewing, by recommending who should *not* be our literary editor. He himself set an example in writing so as 'to make your meaning inescapable.'

Q: What were the paper's domestic politics at that time?

A: It had no platform, but attempted to apply rationality and a humanist morality to the real world – which it tried to describe without prejudice. Its particular attitudes can only be sketched. One was that a mixed capitalist-socialist economy is not just a tolerable compromise, but the most efficient and humane of economic systems and the one most compatible with an unregimented society.

From that it followed that the moderate wings of the two large parties were our allies, but the extreme wings of both were regarded as self-deceived in believing that they contained a special truth. The Liberals were viewed not as the repository of a unique revelation, but as able to offer an independent stimulus to the moderates of Left and Right.

Q: What about the paper's role at Suez?

A: That was a case where we went beyond strictly reasonable argument. The mistake that we thought the Government was making and the deviousness of its methods were such that we used emotive terms, such as 'crooked,' of Government policy. This attracted both more support and more hostility than we have ever had.

Q: Did the paper suffer commercially and, if so, would you do it again?

A: Yes, there was a sustained loss of advertising, both from those who felt we had let this country down and those who believed we had abandoned Israel, a country we had backed since birth.

But, yes, I think I would do it again. The Suez attack was an attempt to put the clock back. This just could not succeed and the longer it was persisted in, the greater the harm it must do. You couldn't keep quiet.

Q: Did the paper habitually make itself notorious then?

A: I hope not. That would have been a shade adolescent and there's always plenty of that about. We no doubt shocked by using the word homosexual when advocating law reform, and again by printing that famous offending verb in the Lady Chatterley case before its publication became standard practice.

But we equally offended the usual givers of offence by not being for legalising pot or taking seriously stage nudity, student revolutionaries, and other such items.

Q: What has been your special field of interest in journalism?

A: Talent spotting and foreign policy. Writing talent will always be as rare as gold and will always turn up in unlikely places. Finding it – and being allowed to employ it – doesn't become easier. It's to me the most thrilling part of the job.

As to foreign policy, I long ago arrived at the view that peace-keeping wouldn't happen through general disarmament or by sheer luck, but just might through some concentration of power behind some agreed system of war prevention. As the world includes two unchallengeable super-Powers, the only effective basis of peace-enforcement obviously can only be whatever these two are able to agree about. Successful examples of this are the division of Europe and the precarious, but effective way in which the Middle Eastern wars have been contained.

Q: What is your view of man's future?

A: You tell me.

Q: Well, what about *The Observer*'s future?

A: I think the paper's in very good order. What's more, its readers are faithful and they continue to be the best and brightest readers in the country. So, long may their transaction with the paper continue.   *David Astor*

SUNDAY BEST

4 April 1976

Placid Sunday seems a silly name for this vivacious, ardent Spanish singer, regarded by many as the finest tenor since Björling or even Caruso. I first met Placido Domingo in 1970 when, as an unknown, last-minute import from the New York City Opera, he replaced Franco Corelli and made his British debut in a sensational Verdi *Requiem* conducted by Bernstein for London Weekend Television. With dark complexion and articulate, canny maturity, he appeared well into his thirties then; but he swears he was only 35 last January. Age matters: 'The best years for a tenor are between 33 and 40'.

Domingo is tall for a tenor, with broad shoulders and a wide chest span occasionally increased by the temptation of pasta. (Caruso had a private chef, primarily for macaroni.) His hair is naturally black and springy, and one of his dark brown eyes contains a keyhole flaw in the iris. (Sign of genius, they say. Churchill had one, didn't he?)

Domingo's memory is extraordinary. He memorises phone numbers casually and whistles the tune a violin played in a hotel restaurant in 1970. He reckons he could remember as many as 25 roles without rehearsal; and another 25 with a couple of days for revival. A large number of these operas were studiously accumulated during his early twenties, when he spent a couple of years with the Tel Aviv Opera. He sang Turiddu in *Cavalleria*

Placido Domingo in the title role of Otello. *'Domingo's intensity during performance is less a matter of technique than a test of the artist who believes passionately in today, and tonight.'*

Rusticana at least 50 times there. Other Tel Aviv achievements included Pushkin in Hebrew, with Lensky in Tchaikovsky's *Eugene Onegin*. Domingo now speaks English easily, with clipped Spanish inflection and occasional twinges of American. He often says 'sing-ging', and things like 'becoz my plane leave at faw-thirrdy'.

Domingo's intensity during performance is less a matter of technique than a test of the artist who believes passionately in today, and tonight. Born in Madrid, the only son of a couple of Spanish zarzuela (operetta) singers who emigrated to Mexico when he was nine, Placido is largely self-taught, and represents a triumphant antidote to the strict regimes of singing teachers. At 16 he was obliged to earn his living, playing the piano in nightclubs, singing in zarzuelas and musical comedies – *Brigadoon*, *The Redhead*, and *My Fair Lady* – until he started to sing with the Mexican National Opera.

At that time he was a baritone. He changed his mind after singing the baritone's prologue from *Pagliacci* in an interpretation class with Carlo Morelli, who laughed and said, 'You don't have the top notes, but you're a tenor'. The dark, elegant, velvety voice still contains baritone colours, and has become noticeably richer and heavier since 1970.

I recall a record made in 1968, shortly before his debut at the New York Metropolitan, also replacing Corelli. This record includes the fiendish aria 'Il mio tesoro' from *Don Giovanni*, sung with supple lightness and such sustained breath control that the very long cadenza is taken in a single breath where other tenors sneak several. He looks pleased. 'I can do it today, you know. During the rehearsals for *Otello*, in Hamburg, when everybody was saying "Oh, Placido, be careful!" I would vocalise in my room, and sing "Il mio tesoro" with the voice light, and no problems with the coloratura.'

We tread carefully around the suggestion that he is singing too much, doing too much, mortgaging the future. Ideally he would like three days between performances. One to recover, one for normal life, and one for quiet preparation. Even if that were practicable, it would be characteristic of Placido to interrupt the scheme and visit his two young sons at home in Barcelona, or his teenage son who lives near Guildford; or hop over to Stuttgart for a Tosca. The voice is in its prime now, so naturally he wants to sing everything. 'Well, everything I can manage, without hurting my voice.'

Eventually he hopes to transfer his career to a new one as conductor, and has already conducted a handful of operas (mostly Verdi's) in New York, Barcelona and Germany. Perhaps aptly, his next conducting engagement, in May with the Hamburg Opera, is *La Forza de Destino*.

Gillian Widdicombe

WORSE AND WORSE

1 May 1976

My choice of a title and subject for this column will surprise that trifling number (if any at all) who have the faintest flickering interest in my character or personality. I am known to that number as an incorrigible optimist.

On 3 September 1939 mine was the loudest voice in proclaiming the certainty of victory and its speed. I have retained a sanguine view about situations regarded by most people as beyond hope. I entertain hopes even about the Government. I was convinced that *The Observer* would remain in business, contrary to the sepulchral voices of its cormorant competitors, and now look.

I maintained a continuing belief that the tiny and weak sprouts of civilisation emerging from an unwatered soil would preserve the Arts and even cause them to burgeon. Every time the Philistine armies closed in I was

present in the ranks of the tiny platoon of defenders and somehow emerged unscathed, even though I maintained the belief that the 3p per week per person contributed by an enlightened Government to support all cultural activity might one day – and who knows, aided by inflation – become 4p.

Why then is my sabbath contribution to *The Observer* readers the lugubrious declaration that everything gets worse? It is because it is a simple fact, or nearly so, and it will not, I hope, diminish their determination to sustain the human spirit. In fact, a recognition by stranded Arctic explorers that the ice will get still colder, the seals less edible, and the rescue date further removed, is a better way to secure the survival of the resolute and determined than by false hopes of early rescue. It is only when one has acquired age and approaching

senility that one can assess how bad things have got – and with philosophical composure.

There is more crime. There are fewer policemen, who are smaller and seemingly less equipped to deal with the increasingly ferocious criminals, whose profession is about the only growth activity that the Government can boast of. There is now, for practical purposes, no public transport in London. I cannot pretend that I make frequent use of it – I am, I believe, the prototype of the passenger who when asked for his destination by the bus conductor said '43 Portland Place.' But the long and patient queues that I observe from my modest motor car can cause only grief to a sensitive heart.

The streets are dirtier. The cinemas, which in my youth made available front seats at sixpence – the old sixpence – are now nearly all closed and can draw audiences only by febrile displays of feminine nudity which, having exhausted the postures of conventional love, now devote themselves to the more esoteric perversions. The good old days when I could go and see Tom Mix and W. D. Hart and Lilian Gish and Clara Kimbell-Young and the hundreds of others whose names trip off the tongue of recollection have wholly vanished.

For practical purposes bread has disappeared from England. I am never quite sure what it is we chew but those delicious little rolls, the soft cut loaves that those (then) benefactors of mankind J. Lyons delivered in their little

vans, the bathbuns that made an annual outing to Wimbledon one of the great joys of mankind, all have vanished for objects of dessicated sawdust.

And the theatres. Blessed with enlightened parents there was hardly a week when I did not trail off to some West End establishment, where in the upper circle (5s 9d) I could sit in comfort and watch an intellectual progression from *Mr Wu* and *The Garden of Allah* to *Saint Joan* – the original Sybil Thorndike production – and *The Enemy of the People* and *The*

Father, and a sequence of delights that opened a new world and will continue to sustain me throughout the increasing miseries of our present lives.

In a word, however bad things will get it can never be altogether dark if we have a sufficiency of reserves. That is why every generation has a right to claim the 4p so as to redeem with a few imperishable treasures the continuing vulgarities, imbecilities and cruelties of a world that for the time being gets no better.

Lord Goodman

APARTHEID REAPS THE WHIRLWIND

Police in Soweto, near Johannesburg, opened fire on black rioters on 16 June, killing six and injuring 60. On 17 June 39 people were killed. By 25 June deaths had risen to 176, including many children; more than a thousand were injured.

20 June 1976
In Alan Paton's memorable book *Cry the Beloved Country* the victim of black anger is a white liberal who devoted himself to helping Africans.

The passage from Paton's novel was enacted in real life last Wednesday. The first white victim of mob violence was Dr Melville Edelstein, a 55-year-old sociologist, whose working life was spent in trying to improve the lot of black people, and who tried to warn white South Africans about what could happen unless they reached out a hand across the colour line.

Protests against the teaching of Afrikaans in schools had been smouldering in Soweto for several weeks before Wednesday's riot. Earlier last week, Councillor Leonard Mosala, of the Soweto Urban Council, warned that teaching through the medium of Afrikaans could result in another Sharpeville.

His prophecy came true at 9.30 a.m. on Wednesday. A small group of police tried to stop a protest march of between four and

five thousand black schoolchildren. When the police intervened, the children began hurling stones at them. They opened fire, killing 13-year-old Hector Peterson. A general riot developed. Dr Edelstein, who was the Chief Welfare Officer in Soweto, was dragged from his car by enraged black schoolchildren and hacked to death.

At 10 a.m. an official of the West Rand Administration Board, the body which administers Soweto, was clubbed to death. A black municipal policeman who was with the white official was knocked unconscious. The vehicle he was in was set alight and he died in the fire.

At 11 a.m. the police called for reinforcements. Ammunition and supplies were flown in by helicopter as the violence began to escalate. A number of vehicles were then set alight and by 2 p.m. a number of buildings were burning. By 4.30 p.m. the police were having difficulty keeping track of the fires buring and it became clear that the situation was rapidly getting out of control.

Any one of a score of grievances could have triggered off the violence that engulfed Soweto. It was purely accidental that the spark should have been ignited by the anti-Afrikaans protest.

The most alarming feature of the violence was the fury and hatred shown against all whites.

No white person – no matter how liberal or pro-African – was safe.

Dr Edelstein, for example, was a man who played a leading part in the lives of the Africans in Soweto. 'He helped schoolchildren and the old, and solved many of our problems.'

The immediate physical targets were the institutions built by the Government – even where they served the interests of the black community.

Three of Soweto's schools were burnt down and every Government building was damaged. As the violence spread farther afield, the targets of attack were the hated symbols of apartheid. In Zululand the administration block of the blacks-only university was gutted, and an attempt was made to burn down the non-white Medical School in Durban.

It is still not clear how far the chain-reaction of violence will spread from Soweto before it is finally brought under control. But what is already clear is that the deceptive security of the Republic has been shattered.

South Africa never fully recovered from the impact of the Sharpeville shootings in 1960, which made apartheid a hated word throughout the international community. The aftermath of Soweto is already more serious than anything that happened at Sharpeville.

Colin Legum and David Barritt

231

The singlehanded Transatlantic Race was sponsored by The Observer *from 1960, when Francis Chichester's* Gypsy Moth *won from only five boats, to 1984. In 1976 the race 'went mad', with 125 starters, the longest 236 feet, and maximums were imposed of 100 starters, and 60 feet.*

THE CATCH 22 WORLD OF CABINET SECRECY

7 November 1976

No doubt I am more ignorant of the processes of government than I should be, but it has fully dawned on me only during the past week – reading Crossman's *Diaries* and Sir Harold Wilson's new book *The Governance of Britain* – that it is impossible to find out how we are being governed.

This sounds absurd. Let me demonstrate its truth. Crossman's *Diaries* are peppered with references to Cabinet Committees and how they run (or fail to run) the country. Sir Harold has a whole section about the Cabinet Committee system, and how its use 'has increased' and 'is increasing.' He stresses particularly the Committees' power to take decisions independently of the Prime Minister, and the Cabinet itself. He adds: 'The Government does not publish the names or number of Cabinet Committees.'

Why not, I wondered?

Thinking vaguely that Mrs Shirley Williams might be the sort of liberal-minded Minister who would feel that the voters had the right to know what her job was, I rang up the Department of Education and Science and asked which Cabinet Committees Mrs Williams sat on.

'Hold on, will you?' Long pause. 'Well, we're not allowed to tell you.'

Why not? 'I don't know. Have a word with the Cabinet Office.'

I rang the Cabinet Office.

Mr Stephen Wall. 'No, we don't reveal that information.'

Why not?

'Well, Cabinet Committees are sort of set up by the Prime Minister out of a particular need or requirement, to – obviously – provide advice. It's certainly the custom not to reveal anything about them. Whether it's laid down anywhere I don't know.'

'How can I find out?'

'Hang on a second.' Pause. 'I think it's custom, rather than rule.'

'Sir Harold Wilson, in his new book, says there are about 25 Cabinet Committees. Can you confirm that?'

'Well, I'm afraid your questions are getting into territory I don't feel prepared to say any more about.'

Next, I spoke to the head press officer of one of the biggest Departments. Having confirmed that he too would not tell me which committees his Minister sat on, he told me, on condition I didn't print his name, that the convention 'has always struck me as daft.' It was the Cabinet Office, he added, that 'writes the rules.'

I next discovered that the Cabinet Office goes to extraordinary lengths to keep the Cabinet Committees secret. Every now and again, apparently, to confuse outsiders and make leaks more difficult, the Secretary of the Cabinet, Sir John Hunt, changes the names and identifying codewords of committees. There used to be a group of Cabinet Committees called 'MISC' for 'Miscellaneous.' Not long ago, Sir John cunningly changed 'MISC' to 'GEN,' for 'General' – a stratagem known in the Royal Navy (Sir John was an RNVR officer during the war) as 'laying down smoke.'

Next, it occurred to me to wonder about the attitude that backbench MPs adopted towards the smokescreen. Mr Cranmer in the Table Office, which deals with parliamentary questions (the bastion of our liberties), was helpful. Having dug about in his files, he came up with the Report of the Select Committee on Parliamentary Questions, 1971-72. An appendix by the Table Office, drawn up with the approval of the Speaker and accepted by the House, notes that successive Governments had refused to answer questions about Cabinet Committees.

'The point is,' Mr Cranmer told me, 'that when successive Governments refuse to answer questions on a subject, the refusals ultimately build up into case law, and we stop accepting questions about it. We wouldn't now accept questions about Cabinet Committees.'

There has not been a squeak of protest from any MP since 30 April 1968, when Mr Jock Bruce-Gardyne (a journalist) asked the Prime Minister whether he would now answer questions about Cabinet Committees. The Prime Minister (Wilson) said he would not.

Mr Cranmer thought it might be something to do with the Official Secrets Act. The Home Office are in charge of the Official Secrets Act, so I rang them.

A Mrs Sims said it didn't seem to be a question of the Official Secrets Act; more of a convention. But I'd have to ask No. 10.

Back to the Cabinet Office. 'I don't know. I can't answer that, and no one else will either, on account of that's for the courts to decide.'

The Home Office rang again. A man. Mr Grant. 'I'm a little bit puzzled to know what you're driving at'

'It's very simple. If someone in government told me the names of the members of a Cabinet Committee, would he be contravening the Official Secrets Act?'

'It's nothing to do with the Official Secrets Act. The Act bites on unauthorised disclosure. This is a convention.'

'But does not the convention impose a ban on disclosing anything about any Cabinet Committee?'

'You're saying it's a rigid blanket thing. We don't reveal a lot of what goes on. But the existence of Cabinet Committees is *known* and constantly talked about all the time.'

'Could you give me an instance.'

'Oh dear. It's done all the time, perhaps not as *Committees*, but as groups of Ministers. Your lobby colleagues understand it. You can't expect it to be revealed what's being discussed in government.'

'But I'm not asking to know what's being discussed. Only what the system of government actually is. My point is that I cannot discover the names of the people who are governing us now, and how they are doing it. That's secret.'

'It's not *secret*.'

'Well, if I ask you the names of the Committees your Minister is on, you won't tell me.'

'It's not *secret*. It's just that the membership of Cabinet Committees is confidential.'

I said that no one seemed to know *why* there was a ban.

'I can think of a dozen reasons why.'

Could he give them?

'One. Most of them would cut across individual Ministers' spheres of responsibility. It would be an invitation to pressure groups to get at the chairmen of the Committees. That's surely well-known and understood.'

'Well, it's not well-known and understood by everyone I've talked to.'

'Two. If people outside knew what committees existed and who was on them they could discover what was current.' He paused.

'That's two reasons. Ten more to go.'

'Well I'm not going to give them. The place to ask is the Cabinet Office.'

Flummoxed, I then thought that – obviously – the people with the answer would be the specialist academics. Who was the best-known and most authoritative?

Perhaps Lord Blake, the historian and biographer of Disraeli, and the author of a book, quoted approvingly by Sir Harold Wilson himself, on 'The Office of the Prime Minister.'

I found Lord Blake at Queen's College, Oxford, where he is the Provost. Could he tell me why the existence and membership of Cabinet Committees was kept secret?

'Well, it is odd, very odd,' he said. 'On the face of it, it's hard to see any reason. The history is a bit obscure; the first mention I've come across, when writing my life of Disraeli, was in 1858, when a Cabinet Committee was set up by Derby to consider drafting of the Reform Bill of 1859.

'I don't see how the secrecy over Cabinet Committees can damage the process of government. Ministers might be lobbied, I suppose. Why don't you try the ex-Prime Ministers? They ought to know. Or Sir John Hunt; it's not unreasonable, I think, to ask why something is secret. It's always been a surprise to me.'

I asked Mr Heath's office whether he still thought it necessary to keep secret the existence and membership of Cabinet Committees; and, if so, why? Two days later I received the message that 'Unfortunately, Mr Heath is unable to help you.'

Accordingly, I asked a supplementary: 'Can Mr Heath not help me (a) because he is too busy, (b) because he does not know the answer, (c) because he does know the answer but does not want (or cannot) reveal it, (d) some other reason.'

I also put my original question to Heath to Sir Harold Wilson's office, but got no answer at all from there.   *Michael Davie*

MICHAEL DAVIE (b. 1924)
Writer of the weekly back-page Notebook. Began contributing to The Observer *as an undergraduate at Oxford. Was successively reporter, sports writer, news editor, sports editor, magazine editor and deputy editor. Spent four years as editor of* The Age *in Melbourne. A versatile and graceful stylist. Journalist of the Year in 1976.*

*I*n November 1976 The Observer *was acquired by the American oil firm Atlantic Richfield. Donald Trelford had taken over at a critical time. The cost of newsprint had been going up inexorably. More damaging still was the greed of the production staff and the bully-boy tactics of the unions in enforcing their pay demands. The Trustees decided to make new financial arrangements and cast around for a suitable prosperous proprietor. One such indicated that it would be his intention to change the editor. The journalists solidly refused to serve under anyone but Trelford, which disposed of that would-be owner, and satisfactory arrangements were made with Atlantic Richfield.*

RED RUM TAKES A LEAP INTO HISTORY

3 April 1977

There were enough sentimental tears to make an extra water jump at Aintree yesterday as Red Rum, the most popular horse British racing has ever known, galloped inexorably away from his shattered pursuers to become the first steeplechaser in history to win three Grand Nationals.

Even the ranks of Ladbroke's and Hill's could scarce forbear to cheer, although the 12-year-old bay gelding's 25 lengths victory represented perhaps the worst result the bookmakers have had in the race.

Charlotte Brew, the first

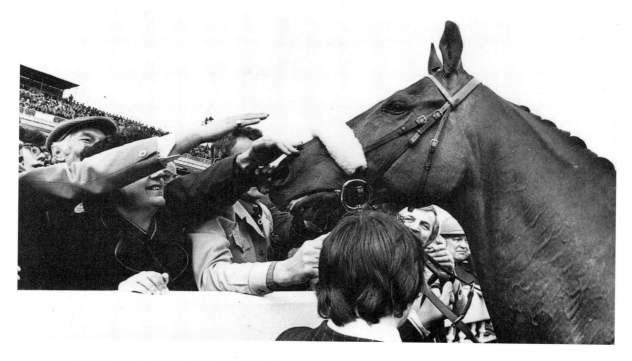

Red Rum wins the Grand National for the third time. 'The old horse loved all of it. He seemed to know the cheers were for him and to reckon he deserved them.'

woman rider in the Grand National, surprised many by going as far as the 27th fence where her horse, Barony Fort, refused. By that time, however, the sweat was almost drying on the hero of the day, Red Rum.

The public has been in love with him ever since he first came out of Ginger McCain's extraordinary little racing stable behind a car saleroom on a busy street of Southport to tackle the Nationals, and he has repaid their affection and their betting support by winning at his initial attempt in 1973, doing a repeat in 1974, then running bravely into second place in 1975 and again last year.

'Rummy' has had the toughest working life any racehorse could experience, starting with two-year-old events and selling plates on the flat and carrying on without respite through a long jumping career until now he has competed for money around 90 times.

Some of his most dedicated admirers felt that it was just too much to ask the old hero to cope once again with the four-and-a-half-miles and 30 fences against what was considered a good class field. But, though he had to give weight to all his 41 rivals, Red Rum proved that there are only two classes in the National, while he is around – one for him and one for the rest.

He was always going beautifully in yesterday's bright sunshine, before a fan club of 51,000 at Liverpool and millions elsewhere. The bookmakers let him start at 9 to 1, with Andy Pandy from the great stable of Fred Rimell at 15 to 2 favourite. Andy Pandy showed that those odds were not wildly flattering by going into a decent lead before the field went to Becher's for the second time, but on landing beyond that daunting obstacle he crumpled.

'That was my most anxious moment of all,' said Tommy Stack, the Irishman who was winning his first National on Red Rum, as he wiped tears from his eyes in the unsaddling enclosure. 'I had to yank the horse to the right to avoid being brought down. Then a loose horse came up on my inside going to the Canal Turn, and I had to race him to that fence to be sure he did not come across me.'

That contest with the loose horse was to be the most dramatic phase of the race from that point, and when Red Rum won it to jump the Canal Turn unhindered he was in marvellous shape to resist the one remaining challenge, from Churchtown Boy.

'The horse is an absolute marvel,' said Stack. 'He is so intelligent, always looking for open spaces, always alert to loose horses and other dangers. He loves the challenge of Aintree and jumps like a cat'out there.

'Looking towards the winning line, where the crowd seemed to converge to make a chute, a kind of corridor of faces and deafening noise, my one fear was that I would fall off or that we would suffer some other disaster like Devon Loch's.

But the old horse loved all of it. He seemed to know the cheers were for him and to reckon he deserved them.'

Hugh McIlvanney

Hugh McIlvanney (b. 1934)
The Gibbon of the prize ring.
First journalist to win the
Journalist of the Year prize in the
British Press Awards five times.

TIGHTROPE ACT WITHOUT A NET

President Sadat of Egypt's historic visit to Jerusalem, when he acknowledged the State of Israel for the first time and put forward proposals for peace in the Middle East, resulted in the Camp David peace treaty in September 1978.

20 November 1977

Sadat, one is told in this still-bewildered city, always wanted to be an actor. Today, however, he is the act, high above the Arabs who are watching him with that expression of expectant horror reserved by crowds for the tightrope walker who spurns a safety net. This villager's son from the Nile Delta has launched an astonishing enterprise, one that even the great Nasser at the height of his histrionic powers would have found hard to surpass.

Egyptians, notoriously slow in expressing their inner feelings, are reluctant to say whether it is the daring of a brave or a reckless man.

The shock of Sadat's decision to go to Israel is reverberating. No one had said anything about Jerusalem until it popped out in a long and boring speech to the People's Assembly here 10 days ago when he suddenly dropped in his now famous phrase about 'going to the Knesset to search for peace'

What impelled Sadat to make this extraordinary move? Frustration at the stagnation of Egyptian political and economic life is one reason. The familiar stultifying effects of a 'no war, no peace' situation, despite the boost of having the Suez Canal and the Sinai oilfields back in Egyptian hands, are sapping the frail Egyptian economy.

At the same time, Sadat's war option is virtually crippled whatever Israel's chief of staff might say. The Egyptian Army is, it seems, in no shape to fight a major war. The shortage of spare parts is acute and a number of countries like India, China and Czechoslovakia that use Soviet equipment are being scoured for replacements.

The reopening of the Canal and the reconstruction of its towns mean that the country has that much more to lose should war with Israel break out again. And, for the moment anyway, much of the Egyptian Army is facing west confronting a hostile Libya rather than looking eastwards to its traditional foe.

Another clue to Sadat's motivation can be found in his character. In his early days when he was fighting the British, he displayed a taste for taking risks, often in an impetuous way (though when it comes to urban guerrilla operations, it has to be said that Begin was by far the more effective operator).

But Sadat also had a highly developed sense of survival and the patience of the *fellah* – 'Sadat,' one Egyptian who knows him well told me, 'is the sort of man who, on entering a room immediately checks the exit.'

He is still a gambler, a loner and a conspirator. But, many Egyptians are asking, where is his sense of survival, the calculation behind the risk, when he talks to Israel's Prime Minister?

For there are no illusions here that Sadat will, by the mere act of going to Jerusalem, not be handing over several important Arab concessions on a plate. Egypt will have recognised the State of Israel and the City of Jerusalem as its capital – something not even the United States has done – and, whether it is Sadat's intention or not, he will have driven a wedge into the broad Arab alliance supporting the Palestinian cause.

Judging by Mr Begin's firm line on the substantive issues of occupied Arab territory and Palestinian claims, it would be hard to imagine his making major concessions at this stage.

Where the Israelis could perhaps be more flexible would be over a separate deal with Egypt built around returning virtually the whole of Sinai, including Sharm es-Shaikh.

The overall impression from here is that this time Sadat has not checked his exits too well. That is not to say there will be a popular revolt against him if he brings nothing back. However, a cleavage in the intelligentsia has already taken place. There is a growing scepticism and doubt about the President's motives among students, professional people and civil servants.

The Army, as ever, is the critical factor. General Gamassy, the man credited with planning the 1973 Suez Canal crossing, believes in keeping out of politics as much as possible. He is a low-keyed man but as nationalistic as any Egyptian. If things go terribly wrong he will probably exercise the maximum restraint against military intervention, although some of his younger officers may not be as cautious.

The more likely outcome if Sadat's daring bid to bring peace fails is an accelerating erosion of his power base within the country, coupled with increasing hostility from the Arab countries. 'Our Watergate will have begun,' said an Egyptian journalist with a gleam in his eye.

Much is at stake, but there is no open hostility yet, although Sadat may have touched a raw religious nerve with countless Egyptians as he prepares to worship in one of Islam's great shrines under the humiliating protection of Israeli guns. In general, there is goodwill. 'Let him try to bring peace,' a shopkeeper said. 'We've had enough war.' A Coptic taxi-driver called Ted took the longer view. 'Sadat is going to Israel because he wants to enter history.'

The inevitability of this aspect of the affair is not in doubt. But what remains highly dubious is whether Anwar Sadat's historical passage will be stately and splendid or degenerate into the inglorious and bathed descent that all actors favour.

John de St. Jorre

Prince Edward Emmanuel, of the Jamaican Rastafarians, who claims to be the Black Jesus Christ,
with two of his younger followers. James Fox wrote about the movement in the Colour Magazine on
9 April 1978. This photograph, taken by Colin Jones, was on the cover.

This photograph of Li Chen Shi was Sports Photograph of 1978, taken by Sports Photographer of the Year, Eamonn McCabe.

WAITING FOR THE CAVALRY IN BEIRUT

8 October 1978

Camille Chamoun, octogenarian Lebanese politician, leader of the National Liberal Party, feudal Maronite chief known as 'The Tiger,' sits in a padded swivel chair in his basement talking on a red telephone to the American Chargé d'Affaires. The last seven months of a conflict between the Christian militias and the Syrian Army appear to have finally reached a Wagnerian climax. The sounds of exploding shells and rockets merge into one another. Fires start in shattered homes and blacken white stucco finishes. Cars lie on their backs like stranded beetles. Sometimes, above the dull explosions, comes the sharp cracking sound of automatic rifles being fired as fast as the magazines can be changed.

For over a week, 12,000 Christian militiamen have taken on the vastly superior firepower of the Syrian Army. They have gambled on an offensive in the hope that the Israelis, who have previously promised they will not stand by and watch their friends massacred, will intervene. Both sides have something to gain from Israeli intervention. The militias would get a breathing space. But it is the Syrians who are in the heads-I-win-tails-you-lose position. The military price they would undoubtedly have to pay, if the Israelis came to the Christians' rescue, would be enormously offset by the political dividend of undermining the Camp David peace agreement, which they regard as a hopeless sell-out.

When I arrived at Chamoun's headquarters last Sunday morning, a ceasefire had been in force since the previous afternoon. In bright sunlight, dazed civilians picked their way around the rubble-strewn streets. Unexploded shells were collected in the back of a Land-Rover. A yellow bulldozer removed debris covering the bodies of an elderly blind couple.

A few hours later the ceasefire began to crumble, then exploded. Over a hundred hours of continuous shelling later, the Christians were still waiting for the cavalry.

During this period I came to know some of the militia quite well. Like most frontline soldiers, they were usually very young. The youngest was Paul, who was 14 and still had acne on his cheeks. He was used mainly as a runner and was the only one I knew to get hurt – some minor shrapnel wounds in his left arm. Then there was Jo, blue-eyed, half-French and a former medical student, who, as well as his rifle, carried a huge Magnum revolver under his left armpit. He has been fighting on and off for three years. On his ammunition pouches he has written his blood group and the name of the hospital he should be taken to.

Raymond was studying business administration and intended to work in an Arab country when he graduated. 'That's where the money is.' He went off to attack a Stalin Organ rocket launcher with a heavy machine-gun mounted on the back of a Jeep and was quite astounded when they fired a whole salvo back at him. Charles, who had been issued with a modern British helmet, gave me the telephone number of an English girl he had once walked out with. 'She's getting married next week. Please give her my best wishes and tell her I'm OK.' The others were mostly Maronite mountain boys, fresh from the villages, who sang Arabic love songs long into the night, the sort that sound like a fly in a bottle to untuned Western ears.

There were also two very cool young female secretaries with Chamoun, who spent a lot of time doing crosswords. During the Syrian bombardment in the early hours of Monday morning, when the drum roll of the Stalin Organs was booming above our heads, one of them asked: 'Are you afraid? I'm not and I'm a woman.' Her main task was manning the radio, powered by a brace of car batteries, which kept them in touch with the militia's artillery in the hills above Beirut. Once a gunner's retort on the amplifier mike made everybody laugh. 'That's good, take it down,' Chamoun ordered. 'He said, "The next one is for your beautiful eyes".' In the circumstances one could not but admire the old man's sense of public relations. *Colin Smith*

COLIN SMITH (b. 1944) Joined The Observer *in 1968. Successively Middle East correspondent, chief foreign roving reporter, Asian editor and defence correspondent. Authority on international terrorism. Covered 20 wars for the paper including the post-Black September aircraft hijackings in 1970 and the Yom Kippur War in 1973. Imprisoned while covering the Katanga rebels' invasion of Zaïre in 1977 and ambushed during the Turkish invasion of Cyprus. International Reporter of the Year 1974 and 1984.*

GIFT OF GOD AND SCOURGE OF THE SHAH

21 January 1979

The revolution in Iran must count as one of the most extraordinary of modern times. An unarmed mass rising, climax of a year of protest and agitation, has been able – so far at least – to impose its will on an absolute monarch supported by one of the strongest armies in the world. Iranians, who are mostly mild-tempered and tolerant by nature, are proud that relatively little blood has been shed on the losing side. Perhaps most astonishing of all, the millions who repeatedly risked death to strike or march peacefully through the streets did so in the name of an elderly Muslim divine living thousands of miles away in a suburban bungalow near Paris.

Ruhollah Khomeini was born into a family of Muslim divines in Khomen, in central Iran. His father, elder brother and maternal grandfather were all ayatollahs (the title means Gift of God). He is now seventy-eight years old, a tall, stooping man with a white beard. His craggy face has an expression of unbending seriousness. He rarely smiles. He has shown that he is able to mobilise spiritual forces for political ends

Ayatollah Khomeini photographed in Paris in 1978, just before returning to Iran. 'An expression of unbending seriousness.'

on a Gandhi-like scale. His ability to do so is a product of his personal reputation and of Iranian history. But his movement is also part of a wider resurgence of Islam as a political and social force throughout Western Asia, visible in different forms in Pakistan, Turkey and parts of the Arab world.

As in most Muslim countries, the dominant trend among the Islamic establishment in Iran has been towards compromise – under pressure – with the modernising forces of the State. But for fundamentalists like Khomeini, religion and politics are as naturally indivisible as they were in seventeenth-century England. This is particularly true of the Shia branch of Islam. Dating back centuries to a dispute over the succession within Islam that led to defeat and schism, Shi'ism has always been concerned with the legitimacy of leadership and linked with the national identity of Iran itself. It has a millenarian and tragic character.

During the Mussadiq period of nationalist government, from 1951-53 (when the Shah was briefly exiled), Khomeini was politically quiescent. He did not emerge as a public figure until 1963 when he was arrested for his opposition to reforms, especially those concerning land and women's status, in the Shah's so-called 'White Revolution'. Khomeini's arrest led to riots in the religious city of Qum which were suppressed by the Army with hundreds of dead. A year later he was exiled, first to Turkey, then to Iraq. There he taught, wrote and maintained contact with his supporters inside Iran.

The present opposition campaign began with the protests of intellectuals and professional men – journalists, writers, artists, lawyers and judges in the summer of 1977. But they lacked political organisation. The Shah's secret police, SAVAK, had created an atmosphere of terror among the middle-aged intelligentsia who would normally have been politically active. The result was a vacuum of power with only a few

fossilised politicians left to fill it.

By last autumn it was clear that the secular political leaders of the opposition had lost all power and had to fall into line with Khomeini's religious movement, which was also given organisation and financial backing by leading merchants of the Tehran bazaar. His presence began to embarrass the Iraqi Government so he settled in France at Neauphle-le-Chateau, 25 miles west of Paris. Here, among the ramshackle chalets, small orchards and children's

swings of Paris surburbia, he set up his headquarters in two small rundown bungalows facing each other across a back road. Dressed in a black robe and turban, sitting on a rough brown blanket in a small living room empty of furniture and with the floor covered with Persian carpets, he received a steady stream of journalists and other visitors. At midday and early evening he would come out to lead prayers in the big blue striped tent in the garden that served as a mosque. He was

usually accompanied by his son and two grandsons, and by his only wife, Khodsi.

Khomeini denies that he wants to put the clock back in Iran. One of his books, *Islamic Government*, shows that he regards religious minorities in Iran as of doubtful loyalty, and that he approves of the corporal punishment recommended by the Islamic Sharia law and still practised in Saudi Arabia, such as the cutting off of limbs for theft, flogging for drink and fornication and stoning to

death for adultery. He has said that after the removal of the last vestiges of the 'illegitimate' monarchy he would hold a referendum on the establishment of an Islamic Republic. The segregation of the sexes in schools and universities would probably be restored and the law liberalising abortion for women revoked, but it is unlikely that an attempt would be made to enforce the wearing of the veil. There would probably also be a ban on alcohol.
Robert Stephens

The Rape of Amazonia: Norman Lewis's report on the destruction of the rainforest was published in the Magazine in April 1979 and, with Colin Jones's dramatic photographs, showed clearly the horrifying scope of deforestation in Brazil. The report brought home to British readers the extreme gravity of the situation and alerted the public to its disastrous consequences.

Below, *a typical shot by Colin Jones of the devastation.*

SIR HAROLD, MR TOAD AND HISTORY

Dr Conor Cruise O'Brien's books include To Katanga and Back, United Nations: Sacred Drama, States of Ireland *and* Passion and Cunning. *He resigned as Editor-in-Chief of* The Observer *in order to be able to spend more time with his family in Dublin.*

18 February 1979

'As a historian, Conor, do you think . . .'

This promising opening hung in the air, or rather, in the smoke. Sir Harold Wilson – for he it was who thus apostrophised me – is a master of the prolonged pause, his pipe his instrument.

Flattered and attentive, I wondered what historical conundrum I was to be invited to consider.

Sir Harold went on:

' . . . do you think that one who owes as much to History as I do' – puff – 'owes something to History in return?'

I took in my breath as I gazed into the abyss of Sir Harold's conception of his personal relationship to History. Victor Hugo, on Napoleon III, wrote:

'To the Horses of the Sun, you hitch your *cab*.'

The Horses of the Sun, for Hugo, were the great battles of the First Empire. The equivalents in the twentieth century are the two world wars, one among the minor historical consequences of which was indeed the political emergence of Sir Harold Wilson. The problem about which he was consulting me was whether he should now offer to these apolcalyptic beasts a handful of sugar – in the shape of another volume of his memoirs – in consideration of their exertions in conveying him safely to Chequers, where our conversation took place.

When effrontery assumes cosmic proportions, one can only bow before it, as I now did. I muttered something to the effect that History did seem to deserve some kind of a tip, and we went in to dinner.

The occasion was a conference of Socialist Leaders. I was not really a Socialist Leader, but the actual Irish Socialist Leader of the day preferred walking his dogs along Wexford Pier, on a fine Saturday afternoon, to going to listen to Harold at Chequers. Some of the other Socialist Leaders, that afternoon and evening, must have wished they had taken some form of the Wexford alternative. It was a distinguished gathering: Willy Brandt was there, Bruno Kreisky, Olof Palme, François Mitterrand, everybody who was anybody in the Socialist International. (This column will not shrink from name-dropping. Readers who feel nervous about that should wear a hard hat.)

It was a good dinner, in its own way. The distinguished guests, I rather imagine, thought they were going to have a general conversation, exchange views and so on. What we got, however, was an uninterrupted monologue, from Sir Harold, about Sir Harold, for Sir Harold. He told us about his debut in public affairs. Lord Woolton, it seemed, had rung up the Vice-Chancellor of Oxford University to ask him for the name of the most brilliant of the recent graduates of that seat of learning. 'For some reason,' said Sir Harold, 'he gave him my name.' He spoke of his family. His father had been an unlettered man, but a mathematical genius. He could extract, in his head, the cube-roots of ten-digit numbers.

Harold Wilson photographed by Jane Bown. 'Over a glass of excellent Burgundy I thought his appearance was changing.'

According to Sir Harold, people came from all over Lancashire to witness this feat. 'That particular form of genius,' said Sir Harold, 'skipped my generation. But my children have it.'

And so on, and on.

Sir Harold's boasting is easy, affable, good-humoured, and incessant. As I listened to him, and watched his bemused (but still Socialist) guests, I had to remind myself that the man was the Prime Minister of Great Britain and – slightly to his embarrassment – Northern Ireland, and that his silent audience were among the leaders of Western Europe.

The evening passed, the wine went round, Europe was hushed, and still Sir Harold boasted on. Watching and listening, over a glass of excellent Burgundy, I thought Sir Harold's appearance was beginning to change. Surely his nose had got flatter, his eyes poppier, his person more dumpy. I could hear a distant murmur of foliage, a pit-pat of little feet along a river-bank. The wind was in the willows.

This was not Chequers but Toad Hall, and here was Mr Toad himself, singing for his guests 'the most conceited song that any animal ever composed':

The world has held great Heroes
As history-books have showed
But never a name to go down to fame
Compared with that of Toad!

Sir Harold was supremely happy that evening, and some at least of his happiness seemed to spill over on his bewildered dinner-guests – the moles, rats and badgers of the Socialist International.

Sir Harold should not trouble himself about his place in history. In reality, Sir Harold has *had* his place in history. All that bothers him now is how he will *look*, to future generations, in his niche in the Hall of Fame. That is his idea of a place in history.

I think he has got all this a bit wrong. There are two kinds of history, in the mnemonic sense of that word, the sense that preoccupies Sir Harold. The first is popular history, the history of song and story and major television features.

You do not get into that sort of history by having been Prime Minister umpteen times and then writing your memoirs. You get into it by being a hero, or a God, or a martyr, or a monster, or a royal courtesan. Jesus Christ is there, and Nelson, Adolf Hitler, and Mrs Langtry. Sir Harold is not there.

The second kind of (mnemonic) history is that of the history-books, written by: *the clever men at Oxford* . . .

Sir Harold thinks he will somehow win that lot over with his memoirs. In the same way, certain African villagers believe that they can win the Sacred Crocodile round to their way of thinking by staking out a young goat. Reality remains other.

Crocodiles eat goats; historians eat memoirs. That is all. Goat and memoir eaten, crocodile and historian remain the cold, sullen, implacable creatures they were before.

The memoirs will be checked against all other relevant sources, and in the case of conflict, other sources will be preferred.

Sir Harold knows best what kind of historical comfort that process is likely to bring him.

But he has had a splendid run for his money, and he has enjoyed himself hugely, God bless him.

In the words of Georges Fourest's epitaph on a forgotten French poet:

Your poor ambition only dreamt of Glory
But God, more clement, gave you happiness.

Conor Cruise O'Brien

CONOR CRUISE O'BRIEN (b. 1917) *Irish diplomatist, academic, Labour politician, critic, essayist, polemicist and scrapper. One of the most brilliant newspaper controversialists of the post-Second World War period. Had contributed to* The Observer *intermittently for many years before becoming editor-in-chief from 1978 to 1981 and regular leader-page columnist.*

THE PRIDE AND THE GLORY

Earl Mountbatten was murdered by the IRA, with his grandson and his 17-year-old boatman, on 27 August as he and his family set off on a fishing trip in the harbour of Mullaghmore, County Sligo.

2 September 1979

Lord Mountbatten was murdered at much the same age as Gandhi, and he too was the victim of politico-religious fanaticism. But the man who killed Gandhi at least had the courage to do his wretched deed in the open, accepting the consequences for himself, whereas the cowardly maniacs who killed Mountbatten actually boast of having done it by remote control. Moreover they did it in such a way as to kill or maim women and children as well.

At the time of Gandhi's death, the poet Sarojini Naidu said: 'What is all the snivelling about? Would you rather he had died of decrepit old age or indigestion? This was the only death great enough for him.' As an Admiral of the Fleet, Mountbatten was still on the active list, and he died on a day when 18 other members of the British Armed Forces were slaughtered by the same vile enemy.

Never indifferent to fame, Mountbatten died in a manner that is sure to enhance still further the historical interest and glamour of his career. If only he could have died alone, without the tragic involvement of others, including members of his family, he would hardly have wished for a more appropriate death.

He was born with almost every advantage except material wealth. Handsome, intelligent and royal, he also had the driving ambition without which even the most privileged cannot succeed.

Wealth was added when, in 1922, he married Edwina Ashley, who inherited a large fortune

243

from her maternal grandfather, Sir Ernest Cassel. On her father's side she inherited Broadlands in Hampshire, the estate in Ireland where Mountbatten was killed – and a tradition of philanthropy.

By the time the Second World War broke out Mountbatten had made quite a reputation for himself in the Service. In 1939 he was a captain commanding a destroyer flotilla, and in 1941 was awarded the DSO. In May of that year his ship, the Kelly, was sunk under him off Crete.

Then Churchill put him in charge of Combined Operations, and in March 1942 he was given a permanent seat on the Chiefs of Staff Committee. It was the all-important break in his career.

Mountbatten fully deserved his luck and vindicated Churchill's choice. He was an outstanding success at Combined Operations, and many of the techniques later used to good effect in the Allied invasion of Europe were developed on his initiative or under his direction.

When the post-war Labour Government reached deadlock in its attempt to solve the Indian problem, Attlee turned to Mountbatten. But before accepting the vice-royalty in March, 1947, he insisted that he must have absolute *carte blanche*, and that there must be a precise time-limit for the transfer of power.

Thus, in a very real sense, the key decisions of his vice-royalty were taken before he left England. He arrived in India as a plenipotentiary, with complete freedom to negotiate and, if necessary, to impose a settlement by June 1948 at the latest.

In fact, he wound up the British Raj and transferred power to the two successor States of India and Pakistan by mid-August 1947. It was a prodigious achievement, but he has been criticised for forcing the pace too hard, for partitioning the country perhaps unnecessarily, and for failing to prevent the appalling massacres that accompanied partition.

These criticisms are very largely unfair. At the time Mountbatten knew that morale in the Army and Administration were cracking, and that any serious delay in transferring power would lead to chaos.

The atrocities in the Punjab might conceivably have been mitigated if people at the centre, including Mountbatten himself, had been free to give their full attention to warnings from officials on the spot. But turmoil and carnage on a large scale were inevitable, granted the necessity for partition.

One of the conditions on which he undertook the vice-royalty was that it would not cost him his chances of promotion in the Navy, because he was determined to follow in his father's footsteps as professional head of the Service.

In 1955 he realised this ambition, and during the next four years presided over a drastic modernisation of the Fleet. Later, he became the second Chief of the Defence Staff. He retired in 1965.

As an ageing man (when I got to know him) he retained the essential characteristics of his youth and prime. His mind was astonishingly quick, clear and incisive, but geared to action rather than reflection. He was impetuous, and he could be obstinate, but he was never down-hearted or at a loss for expedients.

He would always try to get his way by persuasion, but a moment might come when he would lose his temper and his pleasant voice would then become a harsh bark, his fine face almost ugly. The moment would pass, and he was not given to rancour.

He excelled as a public speaker, whether he wished to inspire, instruct or merely amuse.

An American attached to Combined Operations said of him: 'Dickie acted the democrat, but he was always royal underneath. It was an act.' Indeed he was a most accomplished showman, and he was a very proud man at heart, however easy and familiar his manner. But the touch of hubris in his nature was combined with so many glorious qualities that even the gods should forgive him.

John Grigg

WORDS

One of the first of John Silverlight's light-hearted Words *articles. What was unusual about the column was that he included readers' letters in it so that almost from the start it became something of a dialogue. Indeed, a leader-page piece he wrote about it was headlined 'The Column the Readers Created'.*

11 November 1979
Cosmetic. A substance used to enhance one's looks; there is cosmetic surgery; a cosmetic change is superficial rather than one that goes to the heart of the matter – all rather ordinary, even, in the last sense, faintly pejorative. But the word 'cosmetic' has associations with one of the most tremendous concepts ever formulated: the music of the spheres.

It comes from the Greek *kosmos*. My abridged Greek lexicon gives the first meaning as order, then good order, then an ornament, then 'the world, or universe, from its perfect *arrangement*.' It was Pythagoras (*fl.* 540-510 BC) who first used it in that last sense. Pythagoras believed in metempsychosis, or transmigration of souls; he was also one of the great pioneers in mathematics – he discovered the mathematical ratios that determine the principal intervals between musical notes – and astronomy. He maintained that the bodies of the Universe, including Earth, were spheres, revolving around the central body and giving out musical tones that produced an harmonious chord, though one that was not, alas, audible to mankind.

Sir Thomas Browne wrote in *Religio Medici* (1642): 'For there is a musick wherever there is a harmony, order or proportion; and thus far we may maintain the music of the Spheares; for those well-ordered motions, and regular paces, though they give no sound unto the ear, yet to the understanding they strike a note most full of harmony.'

John Silverlight

Eamonn McCabe's haunting picture of a scene in Soweto Township, South Africa, 1979.

IN DEEPEST DALLAS

9 December 1979

More fascinating than ever in its current series, *Dallas* continues to offer its uniquely Texan combination of wealth, family conflict and sumptuous, scantily draped females. The men wear Astroturf haircuts topped off with ten-gallon hats. Marginally more *simpatico* this time, J. R. Ewing has a new haircut which changes colour from shot to shot and a hat-band composed of what appear to be crushed budgerigars. In the normal course of events he is an easy man to loathe, but lately he is having a prarlm with his wife. A prarlm is something difficult to solve.

Sue Ellen has had a baby, of which J.R., all unbeknownst to him, is not the father. She used to have a drinkin' prarlm, but quit. Now she has a different prarlm: she hates J.R. 'if we trah, really trah,' J.R. tells her, his hair changing colour and his hat-band fluttering in the wind, 'we can solve all our prarlms.' Sue Ellen sneers at him and doffs her robe preparatory to a dip in the pool. J.R. eyeballs her fair form and declares himself lustful, as well he might, because Sue Ellen is beautiful enough to make a man break down and crah.

Spurned by Sue Ellen, J.R. climbs into his powerful convertible and drives off to lernch. A meal taken in the middle of the day, lernch is when characters in *Dallas* get together to discuss the plot. It transpires that Sue Ellen's baby may well be sufering from neuro-fibrowhosis, a rare disease which attacks children who have been written into a long-running series and may have to be written out again later. Sue Ellen, it is agreed, must not be told. 'Sue Ellen's already so guilty about the baby this could put her over the edge. Don't you understand she's *not well emotionally?*'

Not well emotionally, Sue Ellen climbs languidly out of the pool. She looks quite well in other respects. Beads of chlorinated water cling to her peachy epidermis. But just when you were thinking that no woman could have a more attractively lopsided contemplative smile than Sue Ellen, her sister Kristin comes back. Kristin has been away. That is why she has come back. In order to come back, she had to go away in the first place. Kristin wants J.R. She and Sue Ellen engage in a lopsided contemplative smile competition.

The third beautiful woman in the cast is the level-headed even though lovely Pamela. For a cattle man who's had a hard day at the computer terminal, coming home to discover one or more of these ladies lying around the pool sure takes a weight off his mind. Removing his hat would take even more weight off his mind, but there are limits.

Clive James

CLIVE JAMES (b. 1939)
The Observer's *TV critic from 1972 to 1982. Writer of songs, literary criticism, verse and autobiography. Writer and presenter of TV programmes. In 1982 he was chosen as the British Press Awards Critic of the Year.*

THE IRON LADY

27 April 1980

In her moment of triumph Mrs Thatcher stood outside the door of No. 10 Downing Street and quoted St Francis of Assisi.

Where there is discord,
  may we bring harmony;
Where there is doubt,
  may we bring faith;
Where there is despair,
  may we bring hope.

It has not turned out quite like that. Nor, given the determined character of Britain's first woman Prime Minister, was it likely to. Mrs Thatcher has had an extraordinary impact: her climb to the top of the greasy pole, as Disraeli called it, marked the arrival of the most forceful and aggressive political leader since Winston Churchill.

Two budgets, three rounds of public expenditure cuts and many Cabinet rows later, her colleagues acknowledge her determination to pursue her 'politics of conviction.' Mrs Thatcher may not be much loved, but even those colleagues who find her difficult, divisive, and at times almost impossible, respect her resolution and phenomenal capacity for work. 'Her initial instincts are almost invariably wrong,' said a senior Minister. 'But if you can get to her before she has time to voice them publicly, there is hope.'

In foreign affairs, the impact of the Thatcher personality has been no less felt. From the triumph of the Commonwealth Conference at Lusaka to the impasse of the European Summit at Dublin, the Iron Lady (a nickname she likes) has engaged in full-blooded personal diplomacy. The other Heads of Government have found it as difficult to adjust to this new phenomenon as the Foreign Office. The West German Chancellor, Helmut Schmidt, is said to have compared her, in a moment of extreme irritation, to a rhinoceros – a description which Labour's Shadow Chancellor, Denis Healey, seized on in the Commons:

'She has,' he told MPs, 'an impenetrably thick hide, she is liable to mount charges in all directions, and she is always thinking on the trot.'

A charcteristic of the rhinoceros which Healey did not mention is that it goes straight for its target. On her way to the Commonwealth Conference, Mrs Thatcher told Lord Carrington, as the RAF VC-10 circled over Lusaka, that she feared the proceedings would be very rough and that the Commonwealth might break up. The Foreign Secretary tried in vain to reassure her. On the Prime Minister's lap lay a pair of dark glasses with huge lenses. 'You know why I have taken these?' she said quietly. 'I'm afraid I'm going to have acid thrown in my face.' As the VC-10 touched down, the Prime Minister's party were alarmed to see a vast crowd of gesticulating, chanting black faces surrounding the plane. It was impossible to tell whether they were friendly or hostile. Without a second glance, Mrs Thatcher went down the steps into the crowd, leaving her dark glasses on the seat. 'She has got guts; no one can deny that,' said a colleague.

The extraordinary outbursts of semi-public fighting within the Cabinet stem mainly from deep political divisions, but they have not been helped by Mrs Thatcher's personal style of leadership. Without perhaps realising it, she can be extremely rude in argument. In meetings she interrupts constantly, she browbeats and she hectors. 'She treats her colleagues abominably,' said one observer. After a particularly bruising encounter at No. 10 one Minister retired in tears to her Department and had to be comforted with a glass of whisky. The sharpest division in Cabinet is not between the Wets and the Hawks, but between those, like Prior, who stand up to the Prime Minister and shout back, and those who allow themselves to be pecked to death.

Mrs Thatcher's abrasiveness is not confined to her colleagues. Her visits to every major department – something no Prime Minister has done before – have sent shockwaves through Whitehall. 'She gives the civil servants hell,' said one observer. 'She writes these brusque, caustic notes accusing them of woolly thinking, and they are absolutely terrified of her.' Those who do best are those who answer back. At the Department of Industry, when Mrs Thatcher launched into her familiar attack, John Lippitt, a deputy secretary, said quietly: 'That's absolute rubbish, if I may say so, Prime Minister.' There was a moment's appalled silence in the serried ranks of deputy and under-secretaries, kow-towers to a man. The Prime Minister, amazed, stopped dead in her tracks, but she made it clear afterwards that she was delighted to be taken on.

As Prime Minister, she conforms to no previous rules. It is not just that she is a woman; that is perhaps the least part of it. She knows she became Leader of her Party by an accident. And she knows she will be given only one chance. As a politician, she prides herself on her caution, but it is her boldness that commands attention. 'What have you changed?' she was asked shortly after becoming Conservative Leader. 'I have changed everything,' she replied. That boast is far from being fulfilled, but few doubt the strength of her political convictions and her instinct to test them to the limits. Whatever else it is, her period in office will not be dull.

Adam Raphael

*ADAM RAPHAEL (b. 1938)
Joined* The Observer *from* The Guardian *in 1976 as political correspondent. (1973 British Press Awards Journalist of the Year, and also Granada Awards Investigative Reporter of the Year). Became political editor in 1981. Transferred to TV in 1987 as presenter on Newsnight, returning in 1988 as editor of the Open File investigative column and subsequently executive editor.*

BOUNCING RAINDROPS

29 June 1980

The first week of Wimbledon starred Harry Carpenter and his famous Rain Commentary. During the opening days there was hardly any tennis, but there was more than enough rain for Harry to perfect his commentary, if perfecting was what it needed.

It has been years now since Harry began calling Wimbledon Wmbldn. Later on he contracted to Wmbldn. to Wmin. This year it is back to being Wmbldn, possibly because Harry's lockjaw has been loosened by the amount of rain demanding commentary. 'Covers still on the outside courts. Thousands of people waiting, hoping against hope ... Not a pretty sight is it?' The cameras zoomed in elegiacally on the canvas covers as the raindrops bounced. 'Still, we're pretty cosy here in the BBC commentary box under the Centre Court, and what's more I've got Anne Jones with me.' Obviously it was a Beatrix Potter scene down there in the burrow.

The downpour lifted long enough for Borg to demolish El Shafei and his own racket, which exploded. To be more accurate, it imploded, since it is strung to a tension of 80 lb. As we saw in *Borg*, the young champion strings his rackets so tightly that they go 'ping' in the night thereby waking up his manager. Borg runs a taut ship. He likes his headband tight too, to bring his eyes closer together. He likes them touching. 'Do you think it's going to make any difference to Borg's play, when he gets married? somebody asked Gerulaitis. 'I hope so,' was the sad reply.

Like a Volvo, Borg is rugged, has good after-sales service, and is dull. There is no reason to begrudge him his claim to the title of greatest of all time, although it is not only Australians who believe that Rod Laver would have won Wilbledon 10 times in a row if the absurd rules against professionalism had not kept him out during the best years of his

career. But Borg's role as chief mourner in a Bergman movie becomes positively treasurable if you compare him with Nastase, as it was possibly to do when the rain briefly stopped on a later day.

I turned on the set hoping to see more rain, but instead found Nastase on his hands and knees banging his head against the turf. Then he got up and pretended to skate. Then he got back down on his hands and knees and had a lengthy conversation with the electronic eye, a machine which threatens to crab his act, since he

will be able to dispute no more line calls. Imagine how exhausting it must be during those terrible few mintues in the morning when there is nobody to show off to except his own face in the shaving mirror. You can imagine him drawing moustaches on himself with the foam, sticking the brush in his ear etc.

'There's a drain down both sides of the court, where the water can escape,' Harry explained. 'Brighter weather is apparently on the way. But it's going to be some time ...' More rain next week.
Clive James

Bjorn Borg's fierce concentration captured by Eamonn McCabe.
'He strings his rackets so tightly they go ping in the night.'

247

In 1979 the Transglobe Expedition set out on the world's first polar circumnavigation. (Magellan's East-West circumnavigation began in 1511.) It reached the South Pole in December 1980, the North Pole in 1982.

Bryn Campbell photographed the expedition for The Observer's *exclusive reports – here is the arrival in Antartica (Colour Magazine, 27 April 1980). It was led by the explorer and author Sir Ranulph Fiennes, who is pictured right with the 'ice-group' nearing Ryvingen after their 240-mile Ski-Doo journey from the coast.*

FOND FAREWELL
TO A YOUTHFUL PRODIGY

3 August 1980
Kenneth Tynan, theatre critic, died in California at the age of 53

New Year 1977. Hollywood. The house of a director who had had three important, as they say, successes in a row, swiftly followed by a triad of failures which meant that soon he would have to leave town or start all over again or both. *Almost* everyone was at the party. Kenneth Tynan and I stood at the far end of the flag-

stoned ('fag stoned,' I hear Ken whispering in my ear) drawing-room. Since I thought that Ken was rather hurt at being made so little of, I said, to be consoling: 'Have you noticed how, no matter what you say, no one ever listens?' Ken nodded. 'They don't even,' he said, 'way-way-huh *wait* for me to stop stammering.'

We met a quarter-century ago in London. Ken was the country's leading drama critic. I was writing a film in England. Ken wore a

plum-coloured suit. Held that fatal cigarette between middle and ring fingers. Talked Marxism with passion at the Mirabelle, where we drank Musigny Comte de Vogüé, courtesy MGM, my studio. 'Money ought not to breed money,' he declaimed as the dawn broke over Curzon Street.

We went back to his flat in Mount Street. One wall was covered with a more than life-size reproduction of Hieronymus Bosch's *Garden of Earthly Delights* triptych. In one corner lived, upside down, a deeply discouraging sloth. That night the sloth, in very slow motion, crawled down the arm of a demented American novelist and, with slow deliberate speed, as the US Supreme Court might say, sank its teeth into the novelist's plump wrist. Screams in Mount Street.

In the Fifties, Ken surfaced in New York. Broadway was made for him; he for it. He even made an occasional sortie into the intellectual world. With awful fervour, he would preach Marxism to battle-scarred former Stalinist-Trotskyite-Henry Wallace-ite Republicans. Finally, an editor of *Partisan Review* turned to him and said: 'Mr Tynan, your arguments are so old that I've forgotten what the answers are.' Ken had the good grace not to join in the merry laughter.

In the Sixties, Ken, Elaine Dundy and I went on an eating tour of France. I drove. Ken did not. But he read the map marvellously well. 'Just the place to write a novel,' he murmured, as we arrived at the Hotel de la Poste in Avallon, where whatever money that had been bred was taken from us. At Annecy we rowed on the lake. Ken's long tubular white body (are they grown anywhere but in England? like the marrow?) grew very pink in the sun. We recalled passages from E. Nesbit. Later, the Marquis de Sade.

As is well known, England's youthful prodigy insisted that he would be dead by 30. But 30, then 40, came and went. When 50 came, health went. Even so, Ken was quite ready to soldier on. Yet once he had created, launched and left the National Theatre, I'm not sure that he quite knew what it was that he ought to do. I suggested politics but he said, no – wrong temperament.

Ken was made for public occasions. Performance was everything to him. He could make one feel the excitement of an audience on a certain night; show us the sweat bubbling beneath the make-up of an actor who has managed to make bright the air within the proscenium arch.

Ken left England in order to live longer. He left New York City for Hollywood for the same reason.

I saw a good deal of him in Hollywood. He would be in splendid if rather fragile form for an hour or two; then he would lose his breath. If he was in my house, he would go, shakily, to his car where he would inhale oxygen from a cylinder that he was obliged to travel with. At night, he slept with tubes in his nostrils, feeding oxygen to a pair of lungs that did not work at all except for a quarter-inch which, finally, last week, shrank to nothing. But he could be jaunty about his curtailed life. 'I live like the sloth,' he said. 'I move very slowly. And it suits me. I never liked running about. I prefer,' he lied, 'life in slow motion.'

The last time I saw Ken he was working on his autobiography. He was enjoying himself. but he wondered if he would be in good enough health to get the book done this years. Death was not mentioned. As he talked, I studied his face. He looked very thin and curiously young, the way people often do in the last lap. I noticed that when he mentioned his illness, there was a sudden gelid glare in those gooseberry eyes: rage, pure rage. He will live to finish it, I decided. That was last winter. I have a hunch that fury saw him through to the end.

Gore Vidal

DREADFUL SECRET AT WOOH CORNER

21 December 1980

'I've lost it,' said Howie-the Wooh. 'I thought I had it. But it's gone.'

'Lost what?' said Niglet, who was easily excited.

'Well, that's just it,' said Wooh dolefully, 'I'm not quite sure what it is.'

'What what is?' squeaked Niglet.

'You know,' said Wooh. 'The Money Thingummyjig that She's always going on about and asked me to look after. It's around here somewhere but I just can't seem to put my paw on it.'

'Oh,' said Niglet, who imagined that it was a dangerous animal like the Rampaging Staflation or the dreaded State Interventionism-prism, or whatever it was called.

'We must track it down and find it,' he added eagerly.

'Well, the trouble is that it does seem to move about an awful lot and it keeps flying away like a bird. It's sort of . . . '

And he hummed to himself a little song he'd been making up while thinking where he would start looking:

There's not enough honey
And far too much money.
But I don't know how to control it.
I've put on a squeeze
And put up the fees,
But I don't know how to control it.
I've thrown men from work,
Rates have soared with a jerk,
But I don't know how to control it.
Some say it's the inflow;
They all say that they know;
But still I cannot control it.

And he gave a little jump to show how pleased he was with it, when his mood was suddenly brought down by Niglet squeaking:

'But you can't have lost it. She told you it was important. It's the Most Important Thing in the Whole World, more important than people.'

Naturally the first thought was to go and see Joseph Eeyorperhaps, who had believed in the Money Thingummyjig before anyone else. They found him puzzling over two sticks lying side by side. 'Don't interrupt me,' he snorted without looking up. 'I am considering what is before me.'

'What is that?' asked Niglet. 'That,' said Eeyorperhaps, 'is an equation. Why, I was reading only the other day the question of whether equations were really infinite parallels or parallel infants or whether . . . '

At which point Wooh interrupted: 'But we've come to ask you about Money Thing.'

'Oh,' said Eeyorperhaps. 'At the centre, that. Explains all our Problems.'

'But it's not at the centre, wherever that is. The trouble is that it's nowhere. At least it isn't here.' Wooh said – slowly, because he knew he only had a Little Brain and therefore had to go cautiously, step by step, as if he was crossing some stepping stones and couldn't turn round, as he once did, which caused him to fall in the water.

Suddenly along came Nott A. Rabbit out of the bushes.

He was called Nott A. Rabbit by Christopher, because when they had first met, Christopher had said, as seemed right and polite, 'Hello, rabbit.' But Nott A. Rabbit replied: 'I'm not a rabbit.'

'Well, what's the matter?' asked Nott A. Rabbit with an air of importance.

'It's our Money Thingummyjig,' said Wooh. 'Weve lost it, or at least it's escaped.'

'Ah, that's bad,' said Nott A. Rabbit , who liked to seem wise although he could never quite make others believe it, not even Her, whom he tried so hard to please.

'Yes,' said Wooh, anxious not to be made even smaller than he was already feeling.

'But perhaps it's a question of Definition,' he added more brightly. 'Maybe we should sort of describe it better.'

'Quite, quite,' said Nott A. Rabbit, not wishing to be caught out by this new word. 'Absolutely right.' And anxious to seem already ahead of Wooh, he added quickly: 'But I don't have time for that. You will have heard about my Great Programme. I'm freeing everything and selling everything. I'm a most radical rabbit.'

Wooh hadn't heard about the Great Programme at all, but didn't like to say anything in case he hurt Nott A. Rabbit's feelings. anyway he didn't like radishes.

Meanwhile, Niglet couldn't resist saying: 'The only thing you seem to have freed, Wooh, is the Money Thingummyjig.'

Wooh wondered somethimes about Niglet's friendship. but he decided that wondering only got a Bear of Little Brain into trouble. So he said instead, in a firm voice: 'We must go and see Owl, then.'

They found Buffin Owl sitting in his tree looking distinctly sad in an owlish sort of way.

'Oh Owl,' said Wooh, looking upwards, 'do help us. We've lost our Money Thingummyjig.'

'You have, have you?' Owl said in an understanding and wise tone. And he looked across the fields.

'From where I'm sitting,' he said, 'I can't see it. Indeed, I've been wondering,' he said 'whether it's really worth hunting at all.'

'What?' said a genuinely astonished Wooh. 'You can't say that. It's very, very Important. She's told us so.'

'Maybe,' said Owl. 'But from where I sit I can only see the plants dying in Eeyorperhaps's field. Perhaps it isn't worth all this suffering,' he said, remembering the phrase from the day he flew into a church in pursuit of a mouse.

'But that's terrible,' said Wooh, in a voice so alarmed that Owl felt he had to say something to calm him.

So he said, with an air of great authority: 'But then There Is No Alternative.'

Wooh brightened and immediately a hum came into his head.
Whatever they say, tiddely pom,
There's no other way, tiddely pom,
There's no other way, tiddely pom,
To start growing.

And Wooh was feeling much better when along came Christopher.

'I though I'd find you here,' said Christopher pleasantly. 'What have you been up to?'

'Well Niglet and I have been chasing the Money Thingummyjig,' said Wooh. 'Eeyorperhaps, Nott A. Rabbit and Owl all say it's frightfully important but they

can't tell us where it's flown to.'

'Oh, I wouldn't worry about that,' said Christopher.

'But we have to.' Wooh went on. 'She says its Very Important and She'll never forgive us when she finds that we haven't got it trapped and in a cage.'

'Well,' continued Christopher, 'I've just come from Nanny and she says that all this Money Thingummyjig doesn't matter any more. Indeed,it may never have existed.'

For the first time in his life, Wooh could think of nothing to say, nothing at all.

'Yes,' said Christopher. 'She says that the main thing was never the Money Thingummyjig. It was whether the sweet shop was charging too much and whether the valet knew his place, and the parlourmaid curtseyed to the nanny and the nurserymaid was tidy and the butler served the wine without asking for more wages. And she says that all those things are coming right. So we can forget the Money Thingummyjig. Only we mustn't tell because silly people would say silly things like she had Changed her Mind or Reversed her Course. And that would never do for a person in her station.'

'But ... but ... ' exclaimed Wooh. And he thought how people would find out and how they would blame it on him, who wasn't to know because he was a Bear of Little Brain. And anyway he was only following orders and perhaps She wouldn't trust him with the money box any longer, but give it instead to Nott A. Rabbit or Patrick Jackass or even to Niglet. And he couldn't even think of a hum, although Christopher didn't seem in the least surprised by it all.

Adrian Hamilton

ADRIAN HAMILTON (b. 1944)
Son of the late Sir Denis
Hamilton. Joined The Observer
1977 as Industrial then Business
Editor. Joined The Times *1981 as*
Business Editor and Assistant Editor,
returned to The Observer *in 1983*
as Assistant Editor, became Foreign
Editor 1986; now Deputy Editor.

HERO OF THE LENIN SHIPYARD

*Lech Walesa –
'always a bit of a rebel'.*

28 December 1980

Like many of the best heroes, there was something mysterious about Lech Walesa's first appearance. On 14 August 1980, the early shift at the Lenin Shipyard in the Baltic port of Gdansk went on strike demanding higher wages. Strikes had broken out all over the country, but most of them had been settled easily enough with promises of more money. Gdansk was different. The authorities knew that workers there were angry about bad living conditions. They also knew that the memory of the workers killed on the Baltic during the suppression of strikes in 1970 gave that anger a special bitterness.

Not the least of the Government's worries was the fact that later on that August morning a man in a nondescript grey suit, open shirt and sandals had climbed over the shipyard wall. He was at first glance not a daunting figure, rather slight of build and with a heavy moustache hiding a withdrawn lower lip. But when he climbed on to an excavator to interrupt the shipyard director who was trying to get the men back to work, he was immediately accepted as the leader.

Few people in Poland had then heard of Lech Walesa. He became a public figure and a budding hero only 17 days later, when he appeared on Polish television for the signing of the Gdansk agreement, which recognised Polish workers' right to free trade unions.

There is no questioning his working class credentials. He was born in 1943 and left school at 16 to become an electrician. He seems always to have been a bit of a rebel. When he was eight a priest warned him he would end up in prison. Since that time, he says, 'when I have seen something wrong, I have fought.' But this strong character fits into Catholicism as though it were the most natural thing in the world. His bodyguard, a benign-looking bruiser who fought in the wartime Resistance, wakes him up at six every morning so they can attend early Mass.

He was working at the Lenin shipyard at the time of the December 1970 strike and shootings and was a junior member of the strike committee set up then. Fighting against the erosion of the concessions made then to the workers eventually cost him his job at the shipyard. He was sacked from two more jobs, because he was too active and outspoken. Six months ago he was, for the Gdansk police, a jobless trouble-maker. Today, he is the leader of two-thirds of Poland's 12 million blue and white collar workers.

His life has become bizarrely hectic. His wife, with six children to look after, finds that he brings home handfuls of strangers to breakfast after Mass, though these days he is often travelling round the country attacking crises with the (so far) wonder-working dash of a comic strip hero. His wit and skill at story-telling help here, but so do his appeals to patriotism. 'Every one of us is first a Pole and only second a member of Solidarity.' A Walesa meeting usually ends with singing the national, and then the Polish Church, anthem.

Walesa is often criticised for his lack of interest in organisation, which did not matter in the dramatic days but arguably does now that the union is trying to consolidate. He is the sort of man who either breaks off a conversation after five minutes or talks for two hours, chain-smoking cheap 'Sport' cigarettes. He seldom stays put when chairing a meeting. Secretaries despair of him. Colleagues have to fight for his attention. And without developed ideas of his own, how can he guide Solidarity? What Walesa does have is a very human common sense that is almost startling in a part of the world where the drums of ideology have been beaten so long and so hard.

'It is not a question of being Communist, or Socialist or Capitalist. What matters is that each system should be human, should be for the people and with the people.' There are the makings of a quiet revolution in that remark alone.

Mark Frankland

*O*n 25 February 1981, for the second time in five years, ownership of The Observer *changed hands. The American oil firm Atlantic Richfield, which had taken it over from the Observer Trust in 1976, sold it to Lonrho, headed by Mr. R. W. ('Tiny') Rowland. Lonrho has made a substantial investment in the paper, which has allowed expansion of editorial coverage, including the introduction of a separate business section.*

Lord Carrington in his seventeenth-century Manor House, at Bledlow, in Buckinghamshire, in 1980, when he was Foreign Secretary. He was speaking to the Colour Magazine in the first of the series 'A Room of My Own', in which people talk of a favourite room. Others include Paul Eddington, and Nigel Hawthorn, of Yes, Minister, *Felicity Kendall and Salman Rushdie.*

THE POISONING OF OUR CHILDREN

The Observer *placed special emphasis on environmental issues for decades before they became fashionable – articles by Julian Huxley in 1960 led to the foundation of the World Wildlife Fund. It is the only national newspaper to have had a full-time environmental correspondent for some 20 years.* The Observer*'s two-year campaign against lead in petrol led to the level of the toxic metal being cut by two-thirds in 1981, then to the decision in 1983 to phase it out.*

12 April 1981

Nearly 2000 years before the internal combustion engine, Pliny warned of the dangers of breathing lead fumes, but, curiously, he advised that wine should be stored in lead vats.

Too many Romans may have taken his advice, for Roman skeletons often contain high levels of lead. Some scholars have seriously suggested that the Roman Empire declined and fell because the effects of lead poisoning sapped the abilities of its people.

Meticulous research shows that we have about 500 times as much lead in our bodies as our primitive ancestors. Children are particularly vulnerable to the poison, partly because their brains are still growing and partly because they absorb it at least six times as easily as adults.

Successive governments have, nevertheless, insisted there was no evidence that the relatively low exposure to lead pollution was doing children any harm. But study after study in the 1970s suggested that children were suffering brain damage from relatively low levels of lead.

They indicated that the most brilliant children would become less able than they otherwise would have been, and many dull children could be condemned to idiocy.

Unfortunately, almost all these studies had serious flaws. For example, they measured lead in children's blood, which shows up only recent exposure to the metal, not the longer term contamination which would affect their brains. Then, relatively few children were studied.

Dr Herbert Needleman, of the Children's Hospital in Boston, measured lead in teeth – a much more reliable indicator of long-term exposure – from over 2,000 children. He found that the children with the highest level of lead in their teeth had lower IQs than those who were least contaminated. The effect of this is to double the number of mentally retarded children in the highest lead group. Even more shocking, these most contaminated children had lead levels much lower than earlier studies had suggested were harmful – levels common among urban children.

Dr Needleman went even further. He collected teachers' assessments for all the 2,000 children. These assessments set beside results of chemical tests clearly indicated that the children's abilities progressively fell with the amount of lead in their bodies, so that all children, except those with the very lowest levels, were harmed in some way.

Research in Birmingham suggests this might mean that 95 per cent of Britain's city children could be affected to some extent.

The DHSS now estimates that lead in petrol, directly or indirectly, is responsible for 40 per cent of the contamination of children. What is at stake is the health and happiness of almost every child in a British city. As a civil servant said: 'It's about your child and mine.'   *Geoffrey Lean*

THE GREATEST SHOW ON EARTH

2 August 1981

With camera shutters crackling around her like an electrical storm, Lady Diana Spencer, as she then was, had a little crisis. Off she went in tears with the world's media in pursuit. Perhaps the whole deal was off. Perhaps she would become a nun.

Next day in Windsor Great Park Prince Charles told ITV that it was all nonsense about his betrothed not liking polo. 'Not much fun watching polo when you're surrounded by people with very long lenses pointing at you the entire time.' The place to be in such circumstances, it was made clear, was on horseback. 'Well, Sir,' asked Alastair Burnet, 'what makes you play polo?' With the first chukka awaiting the swinging thwack of the royal mallet, Prince Charles was eager to be away, but he gave the question his serious consideration, 'I happen to enjoy horse activities because I like the horse.'

An hour or so of horse activities duly ensued, apparently for the specific purpose of mystifying Mrs Reagan. 'Prince Charles with the ball . . . Prince Charles out on his own . . . playing for England against Spain just three days before his marriage . . . typically British . . . you can't get anything more British . . . and it's there! Prince Charles has scored for England.'

It became increasingly clear that Prince Charles had scored for England, Britain, the world, the solar system and the galaxy. Every human frailty manifested by Lady Diana only increased the universal conviction that the entire script was being written by the Brothers Grimm and that the heir to the throne had picked himself a peach. 'Are you looking forward to Wednesday?' the Beeb asked Mrs Reagan. 'I certainly yam. Isn't everybody?' The possibility was small that she would have said: 'I certainly yam not, it's just another wedding,' but the enthusiasm was plainly genuine.

The Royal Fireworks (BBC1) were laid on in Hyde Park by Major Michael Parker, First Gentleman of the Rockets and Sparkler in Waiting. Raymond Baxter supplied the commentary, excelling even Prince Charles in the strain he put on a certain vowel, or veil. 'The Queen and 20 craned heads from other lands . . . bonfire built by Boy Skates . . . the Boy Skates, Sea Skates and Air Skates . . . the fuse darts ate across the grass.' Up went the rockets, but not so as to take your breath away. billed as 'the most tremendous fireworks display since 1749,' it looked a bit sedate.

Both channels evoked a huge dawn security operation featuring underground bomb-sniffing Labrador dogs at large beneath

'A universal conviction that the heir to the throne had picked himself a peach.'

the city, but already it was apparent that ITV, with a less elaborate studio set-up and more flexible outside coverage, had the legs of the Beeb, which was interviewing boring old buskers while the other side had successfully tracked down the people who had made The Dress. Plainly they would reveal nothing even under torture, but it beat looking at a man with a mouth organ.

On ITV, Andrew Gardner was with Barbara Cartland. 'What I believe in, of course, is Romance.' Twin miracles of mascara, her eyes looked like the corpses of two small crows that had crashed into a chalk cliff. They were equalled for baroque contrivance by the creation decorating the top lip of the BBC's next guest, Sir Iain Moncreiffe of That Ilk and That Moustache.

Sandy Gall tuned in from Hyde Park Barracks, where the Blues and Royals of the Escort were already providing a formidable example of horse activities. Prince Charles was Colonel of every regiment in sight but actual power resided in the glistening form of Regimental Corporal Major Lawson, who would be the senior NCO on parade. 'The majority on parade,' rasped Corporal Major, 'will never ever see a parade of this enormity.' Filling the close-up, the hirsute extravaganza adorning the Corporal Major's top lip made That Ilk's paltry ziff look like a dust-bug.

With fine young ladies poised beneath them, big hats were floating into the Cathedral like pastel Frisbees flying in slow motion. 'I think it's going to be the most amazingly chic wedding of the century,' burbled Eve Pollard on the Beeb. 'It's because *she's* such a knockout . . . endless huge hats.'

But Tom Fleming, the Beeb's chief commentator, ploughed on. 'Queen Elizabeth, like Prince Charles, loves horses.' The Queen's carriage left the Palace accompanied by the cheers of the multitude. 'There they are, all waving their flags,' said Tom Fleming as the people waved their flags. 'Hats,' he said, as the screen filled with hats. Lady Diana was

dimly visible through the window of the Glass Coach. Tom was ready. 'A fairy-tale sight . . . that shy smile we've grown to know already . . . these bay horses look hale and hearty.' Lady Diana alighted to mass agreement that she looked like a princess in a fairy tale. 'Ivory pure silk taffeta!' cried the Beeb's Eve in triumph, her predictions fulfilled. 'Isn't it a fairy tale?' asked Judith Chalmers rhetorically.

At least one viewer thought that The Dress had been designed to hide the outstanding prettiness of its occupant's figure as thoroughly as possible, but to say so would have been treason and anyway the lady had only to smile in order to remind you that she would look good in a diving suit.

With all those present in the Cathedral and 700,000,000 viewers throughout the world dutifully pretending that her father was guiding her instead of she him, the bride headed down the aisle towards the waiting groom, Charles Philip Arthur George, shortly to be addressed by Lady Diana as Philip Charles Arthur George, a blunderette which completed the enslavement of her future poeple by revealing that she shared their capacity to make a small balls-up on a big occasion.

Spliced at last, the Prince and Princess headed for the door with Tom Fleming's voice helping you master the details. 'The capholder appears with cap and gloves,' said Tom as the capholder handed Charles his cap and gloves. Off they went down Ludgate Hill in the landau. Tom didn't want the horses to feel left out. 'These horses . . . certainly not reacting to the cheers . . . and yet perhaps . . . ' ITV snatched the best shots of the bride. The policemen who were all supposed to facing outwards spent a lot of time facing inwards. It would have taken a saint not to drink her in. 'And so, slowly,' intoned Tom, 'the horses find their way home.'

As the only clean train in Britain set off on its journey, the Beeb's Tom was ready with the words whose solemn gravity so exactly failed to sum up the occasion. 'Throw a handful of good wishes after them . . . from the shore as they go . . . may they carry these memories . . . to cheer them on their journey into the unknown.'

But the people were less frivolous. Having put off the tone of portent until the inevitable day when it would come in handy, they were dancing in the streets.

Clive James

SHANKS FOR THE MEMORY

Hugh McIlvanney pays tribute to the memory of one of football's great managers and characters, that pugnacious romantic, Bill Shankly.

4 October 1981

Opponents of Liverpool Football Club would be rash to assume that they have done with Bill Shankly. Once Bill's ashes have been scattered on the pitch at Anfield any visiting forward who is setting himself to score an important goal is liable to find suddenly that he has something in his eye.

Certainly Shanks would want us to believe in the possibility. Even after the results were in the

paper, showing a scoreline against his men, he always refused to give defeat houseroom. Maybe we should follow his example and regard his death as just an ugly rumour.

To those who knew him well his loss is about as sore as any could be. But there is some easing of the grief in the knowledge that few men ever had such a capacity for warming and delighting their fellows without being physically in their company. For many of us he really will always be there.

Most of the thousand and one Shankly anecdotes, the tales of his doings and his utterances, are distorted and diminished in the telling, but he communicated such a

Bill Shankly in 1949. 'Maybe we should regard his death as just an ugly rumour.'

◆

strong sense of himself that enough of what was unique and marvellous about him is bound to survive. Nearly everyone connected with British football has tried at one time or another to impersonate the accent and the mannerisms he brought out of the South Ayrshire coalfield as a teenager and guarded against even the tiniest erosion through half a century in England.

Few of the impersonators get within touching distance of the reality but nobody minds. The Shankly legend is the living, genuine article and the smallest fragment of it can spread laughter in any group of football people.

Clearly, however, he needed far more than earthy, utterly original wit to make the impact he did. His unshakable attachment to the ordinary supporters of football ('I'm a people's man – only the people matter') was a big help but his real strength was, perhaps, drawn from something even more unusual.

With his drill-sergeant's hairstyle, his boxer's stance and his staccato, hard-man's delivery he did not fit everybody's idea of a romantic. But that's what he was, an out-and-out, 22-carat example of the species. His secret was that he sensed deep down that the only practical approach to sport is the romantic one. How else could a manager persuade grown men that they could find glory in a boy's game. Shankly did that and more.

Looking into the faces of some of his outstanding former players in the last few days, men like Ian St John and Ronnie Yeats and Kevin Keegan, we could see how much they felt they owed to the Boss. He gave them more than a share in trophies, nothing less than a wonderful dream.

He fed it into their spirits by many means; by humour, dedicated example and that romanticism that insisted on talking defeats away as if they were fleeting embarrassments that a malevolent and dishonest fate had inflicted on his teams without regard to their true worth. His performances in that line were like those of a witch doctor, full of blind faith and incantations. They worked so well that his players never allowed defeat to become a habit.

Of course, he had learned plenty about the nuts and bolts of the game in his long career as a player with Carlisle, Preston (where he developed a bottomless admiration for Tommy – never Tom – Finney) and Scotland, and his management years at Carlisle, Grimsby, Workington, Huddersfield (where he had a brief memorable alliance with the young Denis Law) and from 1959 at Liverpool.

His Liverpool won the Second Division championship in 1962 by eight points and by the time he retired prematurely in 1974 they had taken the League title three times, the FA Cup twice and the UEFA Cup once. It is no diminution of the splendid manager who succeeded him, Bob Paisley, to say that Shankly left behind a foundation that contributed hugely to the subsequent domination of Europe by the club.

He also left behind a great deal of himself and the pathos of his self-precipitated conversion into a peripheral, haunting and sometimes embittered figure at Anfield was painful to his friends. But he was never reduced in the eyes of those who knew him best. No manager ever gave more to the folklore of a game than he did.

'Me havin' no education,' I once heard him say, 'I had to use my brains.' He used his heart, too. It was as big as a town.

Hugh McIlvanney

255

'*Great Rivers of the World*', *one of the Colour Magazine's most acclaimed series. In 1981 Paul Theroux travelled 1,500 miles down the Yangtse with photographer Colin Jones. Theroux wrote: 'The Yangtse is China's main artery, the source of many of its myths, the scene of much of its history. On its banks are some of its greatest cities. It is the fountainhead of superstition. It provides income and food to half the population. It is one of the most dangerous rivers in the world. It represents both life and death. It is a wellspring, a sewer and a tomb; depthless in the gorges, puddle-shallow at its rapids. The Chinese say if you haven't been up the Great River, you haven't been anywhere.'*
(Colour Magazine, 3 January 1982.)

No Tears for Galtieri

20 June 1982

An episode that began three months ago as farce, with the landing of Argentine scrap dealers among the penguins of South Georgia, has ended in a mixture of triumph and tragedy, with the British recapture of Port Stanley and the sacking of General Galtieri after the loss of a thousand lives.

No tears will be shed for Galtieri, a brutal and stupid man who brought shame, death and despair to his long-suffering people. The conduct of the Falklands campaign itself redounds greatly to the credit of the war Cabinet, especially Mrs Thatcher's decisive leadership, and to the courage and professional efficiency of our fighting forces. Now that the campaign is won, however, public attention will shift towards the origins of the crisis and to what kind of future the Falklanders can now expect.

An inquest is necessary for three main reasons. First it is owed to those who died or otherwise suffered in the crisis. Secondly, the operations of the task force have raised serious questions about our defence policy, equipment and capabilities. And, crucially, an inquiry may put the whole episode into a fuller historical perspective and thereby, one suspects, remove or modify some prevailing myths which may have sustained the public in war but lie across the path to a satisfactory peace.

Mrs Thatcher has so far publicly ruled out any further talks about the future of the islands, at least for the time being. She believes that British public opinion, after the war losses, would not now understand any deal involving an Argentine share in sovereignty over the islands, and that it would be unthinkable now to ask the islanders themselves to accept such a change. Looking further ahead, however, it is already clear that it will not be easy to get the co-operation of other countries in establishing an international security umbrella over the islands unless there is Argentine participation in a political settlement. Without a settlement, without international security guarantees, without foreign economic aid, the financial burden of maintaining a Fortress Falklands policy could become formidable.

To this must be added the broader political and economic effects of a continued state of tension in the South Atlantic. It would damage our relations with other Latin American States and reduce our outlets for trade in those countries. It would also mean either a reduction in our contributions to NATO or a substantial increase in our defence budget, which is already too high for a country with three million unemployed.

Mrs Thatcher may be right in her view that public opinion in Britain would not understand or tolerate any immediate move towards the Argentinians. But the British public can see clearly enough that the islands are a long way from home and barely viable, and that we cannot afford to fight a war for them indefinitely. Our people have learned to accept the long retreat from empire.

The logistical landing ship Sir Galahad, which was bombed at Bluff Cove in the Falklands on 8 June 1982.

THE CHOCOLATE SOLDIER

11 July 1982

He was in Port Stanley buying chocolate in the supermarket when I saw him again, a shy para lieutenant who was 22 years old and looked 17. The last time we had met had been on *Canberra*, four weeks and a small war before. 'They tell me you're a hero now,' I said; he looked both pleased and embarrassed.

Three paras were pinned down by Argentine machine gunners on Mount Longdon and the lieutenant had led an attack to knock out the position. Now there was talk of a medal.

The lieutenant made a slightly surprising hero. On the way down he had been regarded as the baby of the unit and butt of some mild joking. His transformation, though, was just another example of the dramatic difference between the way things appeared on the journey down and how they turned out to be in fact.

Despite the mental bracing that had gone on throughout the voyage, nothing could have prepared us for the experience of being on a ship on Friday 21 May in San Carlos Water. On *Canberra* it started with a scene of bizarre innocence with the ladies of the P&O crew (girls from the purser's office and medical staff) strolling around the Promenade Deck to get their first sight of the Falklands, rather like inquisitive nineteenth-century memsahibs docking at Bombay. An hour later they were lying flat on the decks while the Argentine air force tried to sink the ship. The civilian crew behaved with incredible sangfroid, in contrast to the marine major who dived into a strongroom slamming the door behind him every time the planes arrived.

For the marines and paras, waiting for the action appeared more nerve-wracking than the fighting itself. The night that 42 Commando were due to go up Mount Kent they prepared for battle with the deliberation of matadors, dressing with slow ritual. First their Arctic underwear, then camouflage trousers, quilted Mao suits and windproof smocks. With the final application of black camouflage cream, the transformation from avuncular jovial types into fighters was complete. They wrote last letters to their wives and families then struggled into their kit. Some of them were carrying so much that they had to put it on sitting down before being hauled upright. Another image came to mind: medieval knights before a joust. 'Hey, I've always really fancied those binoculars of yours,' said an officer who was staying behind. 'Can I have them if you don't come back?' It was an old joke in keeping with the black humour all the Services used.

By the time we got to Stanley, everyone was too weary for celebrations and the fantasies of drink and rapine talked about along the way went unrealised. It was all talk anyway. Everyone discovered, with increasing concern, that one of the first casualties of the war was the libido.

Many of my memories of the war are already receding; the cold, the wet and the fear seem distant now. It is the smells that are easiest to recall: the hot, eye-watering blast of aviation spirit exhaust that hit you every time you got on and off a helicopter, the powdery tang of artillery smoke, and the acrid smell of a hexamine stove fuel block. Some memories are too strong to fade. I remember the awful stillness of a dead Argentine I nearly trod on while wandering around the back of a house in Stanley, and the sight of a row of survivors from the *Ardent*, their expressionless faces smeared a ghastly white by Flamazime anti-burn cream, lying on the floor of the Ajax Bay field dressing station. They lay silently, not moaning.

As wars go, it was not a bad one. It was short, decisive and surprisingly cheap in lives. During the slack middle period we listened to World Service reports of the Israeli attack in the Lebanon and at first envied the astonishing speed of their advance. We changed our minds when we heard the casualty figures. Perhaps, we reflected, if wars have to be fought at all, it would be best if they were all like this one.

Patrick Bishop

ISRAEL'S PENITENCE

In 1982 the Israelis invaded Lebanon, destroyed Palestine Liberation Organisation (PLO) bases and occupied East Beirut, from which they shelled and bombed the main PLO force in West Beirut. The PLO evacuated the city and the Israelis introduced Phalangist (i.e. Christian) militiamen into two Arab refugee camps to clear out guerrilla nests. The resulting massacre of several hundred non-combatants, including women and children, provoked an international howl of protest, nowhere fiercer than in Israel itself. Prime Minister Begin was forced to set up an inquiry which, in February 1983, charged the Defence Minister with indirect responsibility and called for his resignation.

26 September 1982

Tonight is Yom Kippur, the most sacred event in the Jewish calendar, and the culmination of a period of moral stocktaking and introspection known as the 'Ten Days of Penitence.' This year Jews both in Israel and the Diaspora have greater cause than usual for such stocktaking, and the feelings of many of them were well summed up by Hanna Semer, editor of the Tel Aviv *Davar*. 'The Prime Minister,' she wrote, 'can go to synagogue three times a day all the Ten Days of Penitence, but if there is a God in Heaven . . . he will not be forgiven for his sins, and the dreadful slaughter which has climaxed a period of moral bankruptcy extending now for over three months.'

People had reservations about the invasion of Lebanon, but they were willing to believe that it was necessary for the peace of Galilee. They had the deepest misgivings about the siege of Beirut, but they were told that Israel's northern borders would never be secure until the PLO was expelled and Lebanon was at peace. But what of Sabra and Chatila? At first Mr. Begin disclaimed any knowledge of it at all. Later he said it was a matter of 'goyim killing goyim,' and that it was a 'blood libel' to suggest that Jews were involved. As a rule when Mr Begin is cornered, he invokes the Holocaust. By invoking the blood libel he has gone further back in history to a period when Jews were accused of using Christian blood for religious rituals.

The attitude of Jews to Mr Begin is and always has been complicated. Every Prime Minister of Israel begins with a fund of goodwill which in the case of Mr Begin was augmented by the fact that he was ostentatiously more Jewish than his predecessors. He knows how to engage their loyalties if only by provoking their fears. And by harping continuously on the Holocaust, the Inquisition, blood libels, and on every misfortune in Jewish history, he has strengthened their belief in fortress Israel as the one secure refuge for Jews.

He is also a good man in the simple sense that his private life is above reproach and such is the strength of Jewish puritanism that there is a general feeling that a man who is blameless in his private life cannot be entirely wrong in his public actions. There is also the natural tendency of Jews to rally round Israel and its Prime Minister whenever they are the subject of universal opprobrium, and, indeed, *because* they are the subject of universal opprobrium, for the simple reason that they begin to feel better themselves. This tendency has withstood many a crisis, including the siege of Beirut, but it has not survived Sabra and Chatila.

Many individual Jews, and whole groups of academics and writers, have not infrequently criticised Israel openly and vehemently, but up to now representative Jewish institutions, whatever reservations they may have had in private, have always acted as if Israel could do no wrong. All this has now changed and even an organisation like the Board of Deputies of British Jews has publicly expressed its anguish to Mr Begin at the massacres. This does not mean that a chasm has opened up between Israel and the Jewish people, for there can be few places where the feelings of revulsion at events in Beirut are stronger or more widespread than in Israel itself. A spontaneous demonstration (which was swiftly and brutally put down by the police) was held outside Mr Begin's home soon after the news appeared on television, and massive anti-Government rallies held up and down the country. The Knesset was brought into emergency session to debate the issue and people went about their work with transistors to their ears, as if they were following the final exciting overs of a Test Match. The debate could also be followed in hotels, restaurants and public vehicles. A thin, elderly lady, with whom I shared a taxi, shouted as Begin was speaking. 'Has he no sense of shame?' she asked. 'None,' I told her, 'only self-righteousness.'

The tragic events of the past 10 days have opened the eyes of the Jewish people, both within Israel and without, to the man he actually is: petty, vindictive, remorseless, xenophobic and mendacious, whose statecraft has rarely risen above the level of low cunning. He has, like Nixon, tried to avoid an inquiry, and like Nixon, he has now been compelled by public opinion to have one.

Israel is still basically itself: resourceful, vivacious, compassionate and progressive. The Lebanese invasion was a foreign adventure which tragically misfired, and many of the people one encounters are once again prepared to think small, and one senses a yearning for the days when Israel was a cherished member of the comity of nations, instead of an outcast, and Jews were able to approach their festivals with hope instead of foreboding.

Chaim Bermant

THE WORLD ACCORDING TO SPIELBERG

21 November 1982
Steven Spielberg's films have grossed approximately $1,500 million. He is 34, and well on his way to becoming the most effective popular artist of all time ... What's he got? How do you do it? Can *I* have some?

'Super-intensity' is Spielberg's word for what he comes up with on the screen. His films beam down on an emotion and then subject it to two hours of muscular titillation. In *Jaws* the emotion was terror; in *Close Encounters* it was wonder; in *Raiders of the Lost Ark* it was exhilaration; in *Poltergeist* it was anxiety; and now in *E.T.* – which looks set to outdo them all – it is love.

Towards the end of *E.T.*, barely able to support my own grief and bewilderment, I turned and looked down the aisle at my fellow sufferers: executive, black dude, Japanese businessman, punk, hippie, mother, teenager, child. Each face was a mask of tears. Staggering out, through a tundra of sodden hankies, I felt drained, pooped, squeezed dry; I felt as though I had lived out a year-long love affair – complete with desire and despair, passion and prostration – in the space of 120 minutes.

Steven Spielberg – 'a pretty regular guy' – with E.T., 900-year-old alien, box-office miracle.

Spielberg is unco-ordinated, itchy, boyish: five foot nine or so, 150 pounds, baggy T-shirt, jeans, running-shoes. The beard, in particular, looks like a stick-on afterthought, a bid for adulthood and anonymity. Early photographs show the shaven Spielberg as craggy and distinctive; with the beard, he could be anyone. 'Some people look at the ground when they walk,' he said later. 'Others look straight ahead. I always look upward, at the sky. This means that when you walk into things, you don't cut your forehead, you cut your chin. I've had plenty of cuts on my chin.' Perhaps this explains the beard. Perhaps this explains the whole phenomenon.

E.T. is all Spielberg, essential Spielberg, and far away his most personal film. 'Throughout, *E.T.* was conceived by me as a love story – the love between a ten-year-old and a 900-year-old alien. In a way I was terrified. I didn't think I was ready to make this movie – I had never taken my shirt off in public before. But I think the result is a very intimate, seductive meeting of minds.'

Despite his new-deal self-discipline, Spielberg decided to 'wing *E.T.*', to play it by ear and instinct. (He brought the movie in on the nail anyway, at $10 million.) 'If you over-rehearse kids, you risk a bad case of the cutes. We shot *E.T.* chronologically, with plenty of improvisation. I let the kids feel their way into the scenes. An extraordinary atmosphere developed on the set.' *E.T.* is, after all, only an elaborate special effect (costing $1.5 million – 'Brando would cost three times that,' as Spielberg points out); but 'a very intense relationship, developed between E.T. and his young co-star, Henry Thomas. 'The emotion of the last scene was genuine. The final days of shooting were the saddest I've ever experienced on a film set.' Little Henry agrees, and still pines for his vanished friend. 'E.T. was a person,' he insists.

Later, while scoring the film, Spielberg's regular composer John Williams shied away from what he considered to be an over-ripe modulation on the soundtrack. 'It's shameless,' said Williams, 'will we get away with it?' 'Movies are shameless,' was Spielberg's reply. *E.T.* is shameless all right, but there is nothing meretricious about it. Its purity is utopian, and quite unfakeable.

You can ask around Los Angeles – around the smoggy pool-sides, the oak and Formica rumpus-rooms, the squeaky-clean bars and restaurants – in search of damaging gossip about Steven Spielberg, and come away sorely disappointed. There isn't any. No, he does not 'do' ten grand's worth of cocaine a day. No, he does not consort with heavily set young men. In this Capitol of ambition, trivia and perversity, you hear only mild or neutral things about Spielberg, spiced with many examples of his generosity and diffidence.

Spielberg, it appears, is a pretty regular guy. Apart from his genius, his technique, his energy, his millions, his burgeoning empire, he sometimes seems almost ordinary.

'I just make the kind of films that I would like to see.' This flat remark explains a great deal. Film-makers today – with their target boys and marketing gurus – tie themselves up in knots trying to divine the Lowest Common Denomintor of the American public. The rule is: no one ever lost money underestimating the intelligence of the audience. Spielberg doesn't need to do this because in a sense he is there already, uncynically. As an artist, Spielberg is a mirror, not a lamp. His line to the common heart is so direct that he unmans you with the frailty of your own defences, and the transparency of your most intimate fears and hopes.

Martin Amis

SEDUCTIVE MAHATMA

5 December 1982

At the centre of this week's major movie is a small, bald, bespectacled figure who has walked with crowds and kept his virtue and talked with kings without losing the common touch, an astute politician with a steely sense of destiny, yet renowned for his modesty and revered by his followers as an almost saintly person. He is, of course, Sir Richard Attenborough. His honourable, honestly affecting, carefully crafted film, *Gandhi*, opened on three continents last week.

Ben Kingsley's performance as Gandhi, ageing 50 years in three hours, from dapper, status-conscious lawyer to emaciated ascetic in a loin-cloth, is likely to take its place among the cinema's great historic portraits. Around him some famous Western actors and some little known Eastern ones lend presence, if not depth, to a variety of real and composite personages.

We first see Gandhi in 1948 at that fateful prayer meeting when he was shot down by a Hindu fanatic, and as millions gather for his funeral in Delhi and the world's leaders make their lapidary tributes, the film flashes back to a chronological account of his life, beginning with his arrival in South Africa in the 1890s aged 23. Firmly in possession of a first-class ticket, he is thrown off a train in the middle of the night by an irate railway guard at the behest of an indignant white passenger.

This is the first personal lesson learnt by an ambitious conformist. Thereafter each scene of this didactic movie involves learning and teaching as Gandhi develops his ethical system, beginning by encouraging a handful of Indian immigrants to defy the police in a dusty South African township and ending up trying to unite the teeming millions of the sub-continent in passive resistance against the British Empire.

For instance, when Gandhi comes home to India in 1915, he is advised by his mentor, Professor Ghokale, to spend a year seeing the country, and he does so, travelling third-class (to the eloquent accompaniment of Ravi Shankar's music). On his return he urges the middle-class intellectuals at a Congress Party rally to go to the villages and begin a grass-roots mass movement.

Later, in introducing his fellow Congress leaders to the idea of non-violence, he demonstrates, through his treatment of Jinnah's house-servant, that they themselves act towards the lower orders the way the British treat India. 'Forgive my stupid illustration,' he said, 'but I want to change their minds – not to kill them for weaknesses we all possess.'

Back in 1939, John Gunther called Gandhi 'an incredible combination of Jesus Christ, Tammany Hall and your father,' and all three aspects are brought out by Ben Kingsley. This isn't a pious portrait. There is much sly humour and human warmth in this man, and his relationships with his illiterate wife, Ba (Rohini Hattanady), and his friend, the Anglican priest Charlie Andrews (Ian Charleson), glow.

But the film deliberately leaves out his eccentricities, presumably to prevent the viewer attempting any glib psycho-analytic reading of his character, and has little to say about his religious or political ideas. Much of what made Gandhi controversial in his life and death is hardly touched on.

Attenborough has produced a very beautiful-looking movie that is maybe a little too seductive for its own good. Almost the only touch of real poverty is a ragged mother breast-feeding her child, whom Gandhi sees from the carriage bringing him through the streets of Bombay on his return from South Africa.

But Attenborough shows once again his skill in managing the big set-piece, and here he involves us in the very idea of non-violence during the march on the Dharasana Salt Works, and he denies us any pleasure in his three major action sequences – the massacre at Amritsar, the assault on the police station at Chauri Chara by Gandhi followers who lose their heads, and a clash between two columns of refugees moving in different directions during the partition. We watch with mounting horror as a peaceful scene turns ugly, then violent, and finally explodes in senseless slaughter.

Philip French

Gandhi, played by Ben Kingsley, mingling with a crowd. 'He was an incredible mixture of Jesus Christ, Tammany Hall and your father, and all three aspects are brought out by Kingsley.'

TELEVISION TIME WITH BETJEMAN

20 February 1983

At the start of *Time With Betjeman* the camera moved obliquely down the Poet Laureate's bookshelves and picked out a cloth-bound Victorian volume called *Dear Old England*. Fifty minutes later, was there a viewer left in the kingdom who wasn't snuffling sentimentally into his hanky and murmuring 'Dear Old Betjers'? I doubt it.

The Laureate's charm and humour have ensnared us for decades; his playful, relaxing manner even used to put Michael Parkinson at his ease. But there's also a roguishness about him, as if he's daring the viewer to take his modesty at face value.

Some years ago he was tackled by a perky Parky on one of literature's Big Questions. 'I had W.H. Auden on t' show a while back,' revealed Mine Host, 'and he said t' function of poetry was t' protect t' language.' 'Oh I say,' replied the Laureate bashfully, as if the debate were already way over his head, 'that's *frightfully* good.' And he lapsed into bemused silence, leaving us to guess who exactly was being taken for a ride: Auden, Parky, the viewer, or all three.

The first chunk of this seven-part tribute contained another such teasing moment. A clip from his 1968 film, *From Marble Arch to Edgware*, showed the poet (in a curiously prophetic imitation of Guinness's Smiley) nervously dodging juggernauts as he crossed the Edgware Road. Once safely on the far pavement, he explained how much he hated lorries, but added that he had recently equipped himself with a spotters' guidebook which told him their trade names.

His surmise was that learning what the foul monsters were actually called might help him learn to love them. What exactly did he mean? And where precisely did whimsy end and the joke begin? With Betjeman, the saintliness is usually laced with mischief, just as his supposedly safe, cosy, jolly poems are stained with terror, hatred and despair.

Time With Betjeman adopts a loose, scrapbooky format, with clips from Sir John's old TV-films, chats with chums and snug huddles round a viewing screen. There's a bit too much sitting around waiting for the old boy to come up with a gem, or at least a bit of sparkling paste.

Even so, it's revealing to compare this series with Malcolm Muggeridge's recent TV reminiscences. St. Mugg similarly sat around a lot in the cutting-room, groaning at the sight of his old clips and flagellating the younger self for its vanity, arrogance and folly. Good Old Betjers, by contrast, is entranced by his own footage; he simply thinks his programmes are rather good.

And yet of the two it is Muggeridge who comes across as self-obsessed, and Betjeman as transparently modest. How does he do it? At one point he was busy praising Harrow for being an unpushy establishment with splendid school songs, when producer/chatter-up Jonathan Stedall pointed out, 'But you sent your son to Eton?' 'Yes, that was snobbery,' replied the Laureate wistfully, as if it were only years after the event that this fragment of insight had come to him.

Betjeman photographed by Jane Bown on his favourite cliff walk in Cornwall, 1972: 'Saintliness laced with mischief.'

Julian Barnes

Mrs Thatcher's Dual Monarchy

3 June 1983

During the 1979 election, I went with the Press on Margaret Thatcher's campaign plane to Scotland. I went on her plane again to Edinburgh this time and was among those who followed her around on a bus watching her visit factories etc., first in the Highlands, and then in north-west England. In between the experience of 1979 and that of 1983 I had seen the lady only on television, which is not quite the same thing. I found her changed, of course. She was attractive and impressive then, Heaven knows, and she is impressive and attractive now. If the adjectives have changed places, it is not so much because she is less attractive, it is because she is more impressive. Significantly more impressive: almost portentously so.

I nearly wrote that in 1979 she never put me in mind of royalty, but in fact she did; I found myself writing about the Snow Queen. But this time I was reminded of *real* royalty. In Bolton I asked a bakery worker (who happened to be an *Observer* reader) how he felt about her visit. 'Very excited,' he said. 'We had Princess Alexandra here before.' I don't think his association of ideas was unrepresentative. In those parts of her tour where she was in the midst of her supporters – which was most of the time – she clearly attracted a kind of loyalty, not unmixed with awe, that mere politicans do not excite. Voices at Edinburgh, behind me, as if in pain: 'She's beautiful. Oh!' And she herself consciously cultivates such feelings, both by her language and her increasingly regal demeanour. She does not merely lead, she symbolises the virtue of the nation. She has made it known who her heroines are: great, past Queens of England, Elizabeth, Victoria. And in a moral and spiritual sort of way, she feels herself to be in that succession, preparing the renewal of such glories. At Edinburgh, in the peroration of a splendid speech, she said

Margaret Thatcher at her most regal. 'She feels herself to be in the succession of great, past Queens of England.'

serenely: 'We've surprised even ourselves. Those who spoke of decline didn't know the British people.' As she spoke the last three words, her features lit up with a radiant smile of conscious incarnation, and her worshippers almost swooned.

Something odd is happening to the Prime Minister. As I watched I found myself remembering the lines in which Victor Hugo describes the metamorphosis of Napoleon during the last years of the Consulate. 'The brow of the

Emperor, through many places, was breaking the narrow mask of the First Consul.' Putting it another way, if Mrs Thatcher's government, after these elections, should propose the creation of a new post of Mayoress of the Palace, I think the Queen would be justified in treating such a proposal with a certain amount of reserve.

Not, of course, that Margaret Thatcher is capable of harbouring any conscious unconstitutional thought. It is just that the force of her personality and temperament, her convictions and her ambition, is enough to create, and is creating, a new style of politics in this country, which must lead to a new type of institution: plebiscitary, charismatic, revivalist politics leading towards the emergence of a Presidential-style Prime Minister, an executive Monarchy, parallel with the ceremonial one. You doubt that, I shouldn't wonder. But you should consider the style and language which the lady is *already* using, while contesting – if that is the right word – a democratic election. At Edinburgh – in making the point that it is for business, not for Government, to create jobs – Margaret Thatcher, in the unscripted part of her discourse, said: 'Look at my Ministers – *they* haven't created jobs.'

'My Ministers . . . ' But that is language proper to the Queen, is it not? Mrs Thatcher and her Cabinet colleagues are all alike Ministers of the Queen, in constitutional theory. But in Mrs Thatcher's heart and mind, these people are already *her* Ministers, just as the members of President Reagan's Cabinet are the President's Ministers, removable at will by him. Nobody batted an eye, in the great hall of George Watson College, Edinburgh, when they were asked to look at the Prime Minister's Ministers. I suppose a certain type of Prime Minister might use that language altogether inadvertently, without meaning anything in particular. But this is a lady who means what she says, and she does mean that they are *her* Ministers, or else no Ministers at all.

Mrs Thatcher didn't have it all her own way in the North. There was quite a large, aggressive demonstration against her (outside a brewery in Southport) which she handled circumspectly. (The rougher patches of the hustings are tricky for a quasi-royal persona. Queen Victoria didn't have to fight Midlothian.)

It's not true that she goes on a lot about defence. Generally, she relies on her opponents to bring that up, and make a mess of it.

Outside the building where she spoke in Edinburgh, the CND had a placard about 'the nuclear election.' In so far as CND can make it that, they are putting Mrs Thatcher in. As Mr McGeorge Bundy wrote recently . . . 'Fear of the bomb itself has always been less powerful than fear of an adversary bomb.'

Under Bundy's Law, the more Mrs Thatcher's adversaries exploit 'fear of the bomb,' the more Mrs Thatcher benefits from the more powerful fear. As a defender, she inspires confidence.'

Having watched her in action – in regions very unfavourable to her, by every social and economic index – I think she is going to get the 'unusually large majority' she is looking for. And what then will she do with the 'unusually large authority' she is also looking for? Nothing spectacularly awful, I should think. She is no Fascist, nor about to become one, nor is she likely to dismantle the National Health Service, or do anything else – if she can help it – which could damage her prospects of being again re-elected. All the same, there are some grounds for reaonable apprehension; hubris level is already dangerously high, and about to get higher. Government is likely to grow increasingly personal, poisonous acolytes increasingly in demand, and as for critics: 'Out, out, out!'Such conditions, historically, have always clouded the judgment of princes.

The lady is very clever indeed, but not even she can be quite as clever as she thinks she is. 'He is wrong – not surprising,' she said at Edinburgh, and added: 'I was right – not suprising either.' Just a shade disquieting, perhaps, coming from a lady who has announced herself in quest of an 'unusually large authority.'

It will all be very interesting, not least in its cryptic quasi-constitutional implications. It seems to me that, although Austria-Hungary is no longer with us, the conception of a Dual Monarchy has not altogether perished from the earth.

Conor Cruise O'Brien

THE UNSUNG HEROES OF CHERNOBYL

18 May 1986

'The Soviet news coverage of Chernobyl was late, meagre but not untrue. The Western coverage was fast, massive and misleading.'

The speaker was Dr Hans Blix, director of the International Atomic Energy Agency. The audience was the International Press Institute, a body composed mainly of editors from the non-Communist world, and Dr Blix – just back from Moscow, Kiev and Chernobyl itself – was addressing the IPI at Vienna. A peremptory, even authoritarian figure, Dr Blix is concerned to keep the Soviet Union co-operating with the IAEA, rather than to pillory Soviet failings over Chernobyl.

Understanding that, I still felt he was far too kind to the Soviet media. Nobody would excuse a fire brigade that was 'late and meagre,' but which poured a trickle of genuine water rather than petrol on the embers which it finally turned up. For a population showered with deadly radiation,instant information is a matter of life or death. Some of the first Tass information, in good faith or bad, was indeed untrue.

The crass, defensive silence in Moscow, however, allowed full resonance to the terrific scream of jubilation that burst from the Western media – the Anglo-Saxon, above all. The Murdoch Press, for example, gave inimitable tongue, from the *New York Post's* reports of over 20,000 dead through the *Sun's* 'Red Nuke Disaster' – '2,000 Dead Riddle' down to the merely absurd *Sunday Times* picture of a 'radiation cloud' over Kiev.

Television in Britain, on one memorable night, was able to assure the nation that a full-scale core melt-down was actually taking place at that moment, with

The young Marilyn Monroe, photographed on the beach at Malibu by her friend Bill Burnside. The pictures were published for the first time in Britain: a scoop for The Observer Magazine.

Heysel Stadium, 1985. The ghastly scene as rival fans fight and die during the Juventas v. Liverpool match. Eamonn McCabe's chillingly brilliant picture won the News Photograph of the Year Award.

180 tons of molten uranium descending through the Chernobyl foundations to reach the water table. In Washington, officials blithely speculated about a Ukranian apocalypse until their own agonised nuclear industry pointed out the damage they were doing at home. The European Community imposed a quite unnecessary total ban on East European produce. In West Germany the State Government of Hesse declared a radioactivity threshold for milk eight times lower than that of the Federal Government. Austria told parents not to let children sit on the grass. Sainsbury's in Muswell Hill, London, ran out of bottled water and Long Life milk.

None of this tale of exaggeration, however, is meant to underestimate what happened. As the invisible plume waved slowly across Europe, something said by a few people for a long time became – I think permanently – recognised as wisdom. The release of radioactive material into the environment is a crime against humanity. Those responsible for the release – planners, corrupt contractors, bungling engineers, servile managers – are criminals against humanity. Some would say that those who accept any use of nuclear energy are criminals too. I don't agree. But this disaster is universal, and to say: 'Red nukes are bad; ours are good' is more dangerous than any melt-down.

So Chernobyl has been not just a catastrophe but a missed chance – missed so far, at least. Its effect has not been to make manifest a common interest in the survival of life. Instead, it has sharply intensified the mutually hostile images of East and West.

It did not have to be like that. Arrant nationalism dances on the frontiers of technology, and yet there is still a feeling among ordinary people that physical discovery, with all its risks and its unknowns, should unite rather than divide. When Challenger exploded and its seven men and women perished, there was – so friends in Moscow tell me – a spontaneous wave of horror and sympathy in the Soviety public.

Why has there been almost nothing like that in the West over Chernobyl? In part, it's a matter of presentation. The fearsome film of Challenger's disintegration was given to all the world to see, more powerful than hours of ideological footnote. The long, long silence of the Soviet Government over Chernobyl changed fear abroad into wrath and came to seem like a hostile act – which in effect it was, as Mr Gorbachov now seems tardily to grasp. The propagandists of the West were given the issue of the decade, and they used it.

We know now that, in the horror of Chernobyl, scientists at the other reactors on the site stayed at their posts. It also came out that technicians from all over the Soviet Union have been entering the intense radiation of the stricken Chernobyl IV to fight the fire and secure the controls. They go for brief spells, in relays. A casual answer to a journalist's question revealed that they are volunteers.

A few Western newspapers and broadcasts speculated on the awful courage of these men (and possibly women), and on what could be happening to their bodies. I don't think that I am misreading the mood in this country, at least, to say that many people would have been glad to have read or heard far more about them, and to have had confirmed their feeling that beyond the curtain of political hostility there still live individuals as brave, generous and reckless as Russians always have been.

Blame Soviet paranoia and secrecy, blame Cold War oportunism in the West: for both reasons, the chance that their acts might make Chernobyl something to unite rather than divide was lost. All the same, the invisible thing they fight, as it comes out of the reactor, is the mortal enemy of us all, not just of the Soviet Union. So was that other enemy, in 1941. And – then as now – if they lose, we lose.

Neal Ascherson

NEAL ASCHERSON (b. 1932) Specialist in Central European affairs, also reported extensively from Latin America and Africa. A writer of great polish and perception, won the 1981 Granada TV Reporter of the Year award for his dispatches on the Polish crisis.

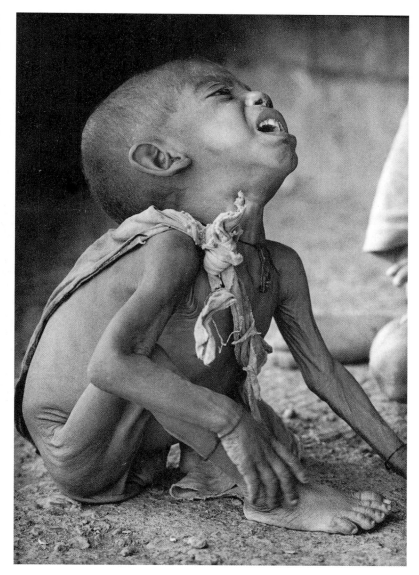

The horror of famine, Ethiopia 1984. Tony McGrath's harrowing photograph helped to spark the subsequent Live Aid campaign. Made into a poster it raised over £20,000 for famine relief charities. It also won the British Press Photograph of the Year Award.

THEY DID IT THEIR WAY

18 January 1987

If you thought that *Twelfth Night* began with music being the food of love and somebody whose name you can never quite remember playing on, think again. Declan Donnellan's dark, witty and moving production for Cheek by Jowl begins with a clattering and cacophonous carnival of music and smoke from which emerges Viola (Patricia Kerrigan) clutching her lost brother's jacket and fearfully demandig

'What country, friends, is this?'

It is not only Illyria, it is the country of those maddened by love: no one escapes. When the inhabitants have been introduced to the newcomer (and us) we revert to the familiar beginning of Osrino's languid request: the food of love is blowsily dished up on a saxophone by the actress who will play Maria as a cross between a night nurse and pouting masseuse in a kinduvabrooklyn twang.

Maria is a sulky slut who

adores Sir Toby and knows as well as the rest of them that the fearful eructations that hurl him into the ground in agonies of dyspepsia presage a fatal attack from booze and pickled herrings before long. Keith Bartlett plays Toby as MCC-shabby, but murderous when tempted to smash a bottle over Malvolio's head: he reacts to the news that youth's a stuff that won't endure with a speed and dismay that show he too has been thinking that way for some time.

There is a slight scorch of mortality upon him. His days in the Long Room are numbered.

Aguecheek, by contrast, is a tumescent jack-rabbit from the boondocks of Middle America, juddering and whooping with fantasies of valour in combat and sexual prowess – making, indeed, no distinction between the two. Instead of the usual catch that brings their nocturnal revels to a pitch of disorder and rouses Malvolio from his bed, Sir Toby and Sir Andrew lead Feste and Maria, with inebriate completeness through all the verses of 'My Way.'

The audience, of course, loves it, and were this all, Cheek by Jowl would not be one of the most exhilirating things to have happened in English theatre over the past three years, but merely a bit of fun. There are those who still think them a scream, a hoot, but in some way evasively vulgar and limitingly camp.

But the point, I take it, is to follow the RSC's pioneer lead in chamber-Shakespeare and perform the classics of world theatre (Racine, Corneille . . .) in a manner acknowledging that television and the cinema have altered our physical perception of them for good, to do this in an intimate space, and to look as though you enjoy doing it. Among the means to achieve this is the shock of anachronisms which scribble across received notions of the play like graffiti and clear the spectator's mind for a fresh and faithful view of the text. It is the tough and heartfelt uses to which Donnellan puts these mischievous shock-tactics that make him one of the most inventive and intelligent directors of Shakespearean comedy around.

Hugh Ross plays Malvolio with hysterical calm in a virginal toupee and shiny choirboy smirk employing an accent as crisp as the green apple to which he takes a paring knife for lunch.

The inventiveness of this chilling performance continues until the final image of the play when the most deceived of servants ends by taking us all in. Having forgiven his deceivers with disconcerting bonhomie and speed, he raises his arms with a brittle grin, cuts off the last verse before it is done, and like a malevolent Prospero, throws the switch on the revels and plunges the stage into black. Malvolio's revenge has begun. Cakes and ale are off.
Michael Ratcliffe

THE JOURNALIST AS PATRIOT

8 February 1987

When this newspaper first revealed the banning of the BBC's Zircon film three weeks ago, we little thought it would provoke such a fit of national hysteria.

There were three strands to the story in our minds. There was the question of censorship. There was the banned revelation itself – that Britain was building a spy satellite to eavesdrop on the Russians. There was the claim that the £500 million cost had been illegally kept from Parliament.

It was hard to form an instant view on these matters. The country might need such a satellite, after all, and it might well need to keep its existence secret. Perhaps we could afford the additional defence burden; perhaps not. The BBC may have been acting responsibly and on the best advice in first commissioning and then stopping the programme. Or not, as the case may be.

These were not matters for us to decide. As journalists, our job was to present the facts to the public as we knew them, taking care not to stumble around clumsily in areas of ultra-sensitivity.

We were urged at first not to identify the project as an intelligence satellite, for example, and we didn't.

Since then the so-called scandal has taken on many new forms, according to one's political perspective and capacity for outrage:

The Speaker's initial ban on MPs seeing the film in the House of Commons;

The distribution of bootleg videos around the country;

The Special Branch raid on the *New Statesman's* offices;

The raid on Duncan Campbell's house;

The raids on the BBC offices in Glasgow;

The roles of the Attorney-General and the Scottish Lord Advocate in authorising these raids;

The Government's failure to act much earlier, before the film was even made;

The BBC's decision-making procedures;

And – always at the root of it all – the Official Secrets Act.

Howard Simons, managing editor of the *Washington Post* at the time of the Watergate affair, was in London last week. He was astonished and appalled by the attacks on the British media, and even more by the muted public reaction. 'If the police had gone in to the *Post*,' he told me, 'they'd have found Kay Graham [publisher of the *Washington Post*] lying in the doorway to stop them.'

Meanwhile, where were our society's self-proclaimed defenders of Truth, Freedom and Democracy? Not lying across doorways to protect the media, that's for sure. In a piece that was wild even by his own trigger-happy standards, Paul Johnson went so far as to link the BBC's use of investigative reporters – 'a low form of journalistic life' – with share ramps in the City. He described the 'Secret Society' series as 'possibly the most damaging breach of national security for many years,' ignoring the fact that the satellite project had been revealed last year in Press hand-outs by British Aerospace.

Another rabid Left-to-Right convert, Lord Chalfont, branded the 'muck-raking journalist' as a 'traitor' – 'ill-intentioned and irresponsible people making their own decisions about what is secret and what is not.' He also claimed, however, that 'Campbell's story was of very little real importance' – which made one wonder what he was getting so excited about.

If a government's job is to keep secrets, part of a reporter's job is finding them out. An editor's job is deciding whether to publish them or not. In doing this he may take advice and withhold a story in the name of national security (by using the D-notice system, for example, which seems to have been curiously inoperative over the Zircon affair). Or he may go ahead and publish anyway, on the grounds that the public ought to know. He may turn out to be right or wrong either way.

But what makes a journalist think he's entitled to decide about a state secret when nobody elected him to do that? The best answer I know to that common charge is contained in the remarks of an American judge in the Pentagon Papers case, quoted in an address by Howard Simons to the American Society of Newspaper Editors:

'Security also lies in the value of our free institutions. A cantankerous Press, an obstinate Press, a ubiquitous Press must be suffered by those in authority in order to preserve the even greater values of freedom of expression and the right of the people to know.'

Governments, especially this one, fail to recognise that expressing a view about the national interest in a peacetime democracy is a matter for anyone. National security in time of war involves different considerations, and may require some curtailment of this liberty by mutual consent.

Secrecy is not a simple concept. It is not just a reserved, adult body of knowledge to be kept from children. It goes very deep in human nature, for secrecy is at the core of power. To be keeper of secrets confers status and identity. It was part of the divine right of kings. Elias Canetti, the Nobel Prize-winning writer, said: 'It is the privilege of kings to keep their secrets from father, mother, brothers and friends.'

In this primitive system of values, power must be impenetrable. To let the public know is seen as a mark of weakness, a sharing or dissipation of power. In Britain there is still a presupposition in favour of secrecy where, in a fully democratic society, there should be a presupposition in favour of openness.

It took the public grilling of Sir Robert Armstrong by Mr Malcolm Turnbull in Australia to bring this important truth painfully home.

Journalists live with secrets all the time. In a society like ours, where far too much information is classified (as the Franks Committee reported 15 years ago) you can hardly investigate anything at all without bumping into something supposed to be a secret. Even the Government's own lobby briefings to the Press are a secret and officially never take place.

This is a useful reminder that journalists don't invent secrets: secrets are given to them. Many of these leaks are deliberate, which journalists need to be wary about. As for giving things away to the enemy, there is nothing to compare with the record of the security services themselves, both here and in the United States. Traitors and defectors have left a far more deadly trail of havoc than a hundred Duncan Campbells could ever do.

This is why the security services have to be watched, too, and why journalists take an interest when they learn of defence programmes that by-pass Parliament and, in the Peter Wright case, of our intelligence agents playing dirty tricks on allied countries and plotting against the elected Prime Minister.

A week that exposed the thin skin protecting our much-vaunted freedoms ended with two ironies. A Bill of Rights was voted out by MPs – and the Foreign Office had the nerve to invite 35 countries to London for an international conference on freedom of information.

Two, at least, of the countries would be impressed by our record in the Zircon affair: the Americans with Duncan Campbell and the Russians with our Special Branch.

Donald Trelford

ON THE PRESENT STATE OF AFFAIRS

27 December 1987
Having mislaid my optick Glasses, and with logarithmick Fluxions of the Phases of the Moon rendered full of Errour by reason of the great Advances in Natural Philosophy, I will, in this short Paper, desist from making my customary Predictions, that would have been for the Year 1988; but will, instead, give an Account of the present State of Affairs, beginning with Mris.

Thatcher, her Ministry.

This was chosen for a third Term (as the cant Phrase in the publick Prints expresseth the matter)some half-year pass'd, although the precise Particulars, and all the surrounding Circumstances of the Event, I have not forgot; except that the chief Credit for the Enterprise belonged to the Chancellor, Master *Lawson*, the great Oeconomist, rather than to Mris.

Thatcher, the principall Minister, who, to say the Truth, spent most of her Time in assuaging the Feelings, and arbitrating upon the Disputes, of divers low Persons then in Employment, altho' some of 'em are now out of Favour, *viz.* my Lord *Young*, Master *Tebbit*, Signor *Saatchi* (that is a Levantine), not to mention Master *Tim Bell*, who hath an Eye for the Ladies and hangs loose upon Society, living off the Crumbs

269

*Jorge Donn, acclaimed Argentian dancer of great athleticism, caught in mid leap as he dances the lead
role in Maurice Béjart's ballet* Bolero *for London Festival Ballet at the Coliseum. This striking
photograph by Richard Mildenhall won him the BP Art Photographer of the Year Award.*

that fall from the Tables of great Persons and mighty Corporations, which Position in our Polity he hills on account of his Agility with short Words, and his many ingenious Scheams to maintain the present Ministry in Office.

Nevertheless, the Controversies surrounding these Persons (concerning which a Book has been writ, or so I am informed) were but a diversion from the Great Events taking place; for, as the small Streams make the loudest Noise, so it is the silent River that carried Goods and Merchandise to their Destination in distant Ports.

Master *Lawson*, his Scheam, was to put money in the Pockets of the People, which hath ever been the favour'd Device of Chancellors of the *Tory Faction*, while Attempts to emulate their Conduct by Chancellors of the *Labour Faction* hath met with small Success or, in some Cases, with a Run on the Currency, or a Fall in the Stocks, or both of 'em together; as Examples of which, I will cite Master *Callaghan*, that is now a Lord, and Mr Secretary *Healey*, that is now retired to a Life of Contemplation and Repose, and Master *Roy Jenkins*, that is still a great Figure in the Land, as Chancellor of *Oxford Univ.*, and is Lord *Jenkins of Hillhead*, in Scotland.

The *Scotch* put out Master *Jenkins* (who had formed a *New Faction*, now fallen into utter Ruin) and likewise showed no Gratitude towards Master *Lawson*, his Disbursements; as a Consequence of which they are known in the Ministry as a surly Lot for whom nothing can be done, a similar *View* being held of the *Welsh*, who in a like Fashion raised their Voices and cast their Votes against the present Ministry; with the Difference that no Gratitude hath ever been expected from *them*. but in *England* 'twas a different Story altogether, the Result being, that there is now an *English Faction* as well as a *Tory Faction*, with Mris. *Thatcher* at the Head of both, as *Lord* (or, as some would express it) *Lady Protector*, or *General-for-Life*.

In such a Case, one would expect her to be surrounded by Sycophants, Place-seekers and others in search of Employment, as a Cheese is infested by Maggots; which, to tell the Truth, is very far from being so, although, in perfect Candour, I must make an Exception for several *Stock-jobbers*, or *Men of Business*, who are Maggots that are grown into fine, fat Bluebottles, making a Buzz around Mris. *Thatcher's* Ears, and alighting from Time to Time upon the Body Politick to suck its Blood, to their infinite Nourishment, and the consequent Impoverishment of the Citizens of the Commonwealth, who compose that Body of which I speak.

Master *Lawson*, of whom I writ earlier, is full of Impertinencies, as a Pudding is filled with Raisins, some spilling out on to the Plate, which Tit-bits are taken up by Scribblers and pass'd from one to another before being swallowed, to universall Merriment.

The Minister that was before Master *Lawson* at the Treasury, Sir G. *Howe*, who now traverses the Globe in the Interests of his Mistress, and for his own Improvement, hath made a Call for Compassion and Responsibility; which, on a loose Translation, is a Proclamation of his Intention to seek the highest Office at the most opportune Moment.

I will now tell you more of this Sir G. *Howe*. He is a Welsh-man, son of a country Notary, from *Port Talbot* in *Glamorganshire*, as another Man of Ambition, Master *Heseltine*, is from *Swansea*, in the same County. Now this *Sir Geoffrey* (to set out his Christian name and Title) was, in his youth, at *Trinity Hall* in *Cambridge*, where he was distinguished in the Law and afterwards practised his Trade or, as some would have it, Profession in the *Temple* by *Fleet-street* and the *Law Courts* in the *Strand*.

However, I am bound to say, at this Juncture, in the Interests of perfect Truth, that young *Geoffrey* cut a greater Figure in Politicks, being Chairman of the *Bow Faction* and wielding a mighty Pen in the Cause of Liberty and rational

Conduct by Government, not to mention Reason and Compassion; his chief Contribution being, a Piece with the Title of *Whither the Social Services?*, which appeared twice-yearly, without fail, either in the *Crossbow* sheet or in the *Daily Telegraph*, that was then maintained by my Lord *Hartwell*.

There is another Master of Arts from *Cambridge* that I will mention, *viz.*, Master *Douglas Hurd*, who was at *Trinity Coll.* His father was a Farmer and Scribbler (Agricultural Correspondent, so call'd for *The Times* sheet, in the Days before Master *Murdoch*, and sat as Member for *Newbury* in *Berkshire*, as his Grandfather, the good *Sir Percy*, sat first for *Frome* in *Somerset* and afterwards for *Devizes* in *Wiltshire*. Master *Douglas* was, in his hot youth, a Familiar and drinking Companion of Master *Heath*, that is now in Disgrace, and is exiled to the Cathedal-close at *Salisbury* in *Wiltshire*, although still able to give pert Orations from Time to Time in *Westminster-hall*. Another of the same Kidney is Master *Kenneth Baker*, who concealeth his inordinate Ambition behind an agreeable Expression.

Of all these Ministers and great Figures, Master *Heath* and Master *Heseltine* are out of Employment; whereas the others of whom I have writ must needs make a nice Calculation of where their true Interests lie, and whether they will be secured by catching hold of Mris. *Thatcher*, her Skirts; or, as an alternative Course, by turning on her, as Beasts of the Jungle do kill and devour their Mates when they grow old, and of no further Utility. God Save the Queen.

Alan Watkins

*ALAN WATKINS (b. 1933)
Joined* The Observer *as political columnist in 1976 after working for the* Sunday Express, Spectator *and* New Statesman. *His citation as the British Press Awards Columnist of the Year in 1982 praised 'the elegance of his style, the wit and good humour of his approach and the congenial manner with which he illuminates the political scene.'*

Afghanistan, August 1987. A woman and her three children suffocated in their cellar, huddled together like the corpses at Pompeii, after Russian planes attacked their village. Photograph by Radek Sikorski declared World Press Picture of 1988.

LEAVING OUR OLD CURIOSITY SHOP

17 January 1988

The Observer is leaving its offices at Blackfriars this week, and moving to a new building at Battersea in South London. Newspapers have been written and printed on this site for just two centuries. Printing stopped last year, and now the writers are departing as well.

Do I feel nostalgia? Not really. This is an ugly building, without character, and for all the years that I have spent in it, I shall leave without regret. It used to be *The Times* building, before they moved to Gray's Inn and then to Wapping. To construct it, however, the *Times* people pulled down a lovely, early nineteenth-century house around the shady courtyard of Printing House Yard, with the *Times* emblem glowing on its pediment across the Thames. Graham Greene described working there, in the old sub-editors' room where the

only sounds were the scratching of pens and the noise of burning coal settling in the grate. I still see that building, and miss it.

And I am sorry to leave this little part of London between St Paul's and the river. Until redevelopment began a few years ago, it was an early Victorian precinct, a jumble of tiny offices and warehouses raised along streets laid out by King Alfred on the ruins of Roman London. Shakespeare worked here, off Carter Lane, and in the shadow of the old Blackfriars Monastery, his actor friends used to kidnap little boys and train them to play his female roles.

When I first saw this place, the river was just across the road. In Puddle Dock, beside his new Mermaid Theatre, Bernard Miles lived in a Dutch barge which listed sideways on the beach when the tide went down. Blackfriars

Station, on its facade, still offered tickets to Baden-Baden, 'Leipsic', and St Petersburg. All that has gone, replaced by huge new office blocks and a motorway.

And this has been a convenient quarter, too. All around Fleet Street and Blackfriars, there grew up hundreds of tiny enterprises: pubs, coffee shops and stationers, but also blockmakers, designers, specialist mechanics and electricians, translators, freelance journalist agencies, inkmakers and all the rest. They were the ancillaries of the newspaper industry. Now, as the papers move out to the Isle of Dogs, Wapping or Battersea, they are withering away.

We, the journalists, are going to a handsome white building between Battersea Park and the old Power Station, a place of space, light and computer screens. Others, who we used to know so well, will not be coming. I went downstairs, and looked at the enormous, darkened hall, as empty as a ballroom, where the ranks of clattering linotype machines used to stand and where the compositors whipped type from wooden boxes to metal formes as the paper was made up on the 'stone'. Down in the basement stand the printing presses, two stories high, the size of an old cruiser's engines. Too costly to dismantle, they will be left to the wreckers.

After more than 400 years, the printers of the City of London are finished. They used to have the right to walk home with swords, printing being a nocturnal trade. It ended in the great war between the newspaper proprietors and the print unions, which the unions finally lost at the battle of Wapping. There was protection and overmanning, some extortionate wages, 'Spanish practices' which were less than honest. Less than honourable, all the same, was the part played in the printers' defeat by journalists, who took their jobs.

Even if the printers had been saints, the new technology meant that their trade was doomed. But I will miss them: often eccentric, kindly, sometimes inflammable, they helped to keep our feet on the ground. Journalism is a trade at one remove from reality, by definition; these men worked with their hands at machines and saw life and labour directly, not through the reporter's periscope. Looking at the long rows of basins where they used to clean up, it occurred uneasily to me that their kind of dirt was easier to wash off than ours.

Printing, by any standards, is part of 'heritage'. Benedict Anderson has argued that the 'print revolution', by stabilising vernacular language and spreading the idea of an imaginary community of readers, made the modern nation possible. So I can predict a little steam tram, in the City of the future, carrying tourists to watch compositors and machine-minders pretending to make hot-metal newspapers. Perhaps it will all make a return on investment, and have a 'high workforce profile,' and sell souvenirs – like the nameplates in looking-glass type the men downstairs used to cast for my children. But I don't think I will care to buy a ticket.

Neal Ascherson

'We, the journalists, are going to a handsome white building between Battersea Park and the old Power Station, a place of space, light and computer screens.'

SLEEPING DOGS LIE

7 February 1988

The Freud retrospective is at the Hayward. From first to latest this is a show of how Freud himself has been affected over the past 40 years.

Freud's early, graphic images – the dissolute cacti, the bubbles on the gooseflesh of the half-plucked chicken dunked in a bucket – were wonderfully rakish and odd, bound to get up the nose of Sir Alfred Munnings, one would think. The drawings extended beginner's luck into downright candour bordering on plain insolence. They still seem provocative, even when the handling suggests devoted scrutiny of a love object.

The kitten held by the neck – 1947 – is perfectly relaxed, whiskers restive, paws dangling not clawing, yet people keep identifying it as the first of Freud's victims. The pet is seen as representing what its equally wide-eyed mistress feels as, squeezing gently, she holds on, she herself also waiting to be let go. Both, it's assumed, are being sacrificed to the young master's ambition.

The idea of Freud the cruelty man, exploiting those close to him, exposing them and enjoying their unrest, is attractive because it enables the commentator to switch to a trenchant mode without further thought. Freud, they say, picks on women and subjects them to merciless examination unsparing in his accounts of sag and flab and on-going wrinkles. What a brute. How they must hate him.

It's just possible that this retrospective will put an end to such interpretations, for no one surely could fail to be affected by the way Freud has set himself challenges and has come to see that the one task is to make the image a true presence, naked or otherwise. There is no humiliation involved, and certainly no degradation. Those who pose for Freud lend themselves to the purpose of realising a kind of apparition; what he sees them to be.

In the course of the 40 years themes circulate, coming in for different treatments and altered circumstances. The sleeping dogs, once a bull terrier but recently whippets, demonstrate total, abandoned relaxation. You are made aware that to paint a cyclamen or a sinkful of buttercups isn't altogether separate from dealing with fur or hair or flesh. After all, the paint's the same and the concentration needed to establish what's there vividly and weightily is only slightly modified when nobody else is involved.

Studies of foliage shrivelling brown under his gaze, and views through the studio window of mattresses slumped beneath the buddleia and broken glass along the top of a wall catching the light are excursions for Freud. He becomes fascinated with the difficulties of painting intricacies of form and void, such as the heaped rags he wipes his brushes on or a mass of Creeping Jenny.

He paints his mother repeatedly, lingering over the patterning

Lucien Freud, by Jane Bown: 'Freud has come to see that the one task is to make the image a true presence.'

on her dress, showing dispassionately (anything else would be Mama Mia or mawkish) her apprehension, her ageing.

The others he paints, Frank Auerbach, head bowed, doing his duty, the 'Big Man' with his massive hands and strained trouser seams, and the women too, are Freud's references, answering to him and answering his purposes. Baron Thyssen, in a fine chair with gilt swans' necks on which to rest his arms, is presented as a rare specimen, positioned alongside a turbulence of smirched rags. The hands are splayed on

his knees; his face is a study in disquiet. What if he suddenly forgot who he is?

Freud's women sit or lie, either on the baggy couch or on the bed, sharp-shadowed most of them because of the artifical light. Collectively they seem to float, Baroque yet modern, taken out of themselves.

Freud paints women for what they are. Their privacy, which he shares at the time, is preserved in that he shows the individuality; so much so that, after a while, the state of nakedness or of being fully dressed becomes hardly a con-

sideration. The person counts most. The paintings get better and better, each a proof that true art explores where others have gone before and yet makes discoveries and renews.

William Feaver

WILLIAM FEAVER (*b. 1942*)
Joined The Observer *from* The Sunday Times Magazine *as art critic in 1975. Critic of the Year 1983. Organiser of the 1979 Thirties exhibition at the Hayward Gallery (among others) and author of books on John Martin, caricature and pitmen painters.*

THE BIG HEAT

The Observer *has been in the lead in warning about the greenhouse effect – one of the issues that will dominate the 1990s – and in campaigning for Government policies to tackle it.*

3 July 1988

There is now a scientific consensus that, unless urgent action is taken, the world faces an unprecedented disaster in the lifetimes of today's young people.

So far this decade, the world has experienced the four warmest years in a century – 1980, 1981, 1983 and 1987. The last three were the hottest since reliable records began. So far, 1988 looks like being even warmer.

Britain's appalling summer last year does not invalidate these global averages. Climatologists say that the weather goes to extremes when big changes take place – so some areas will have unusually miserable weather even during a general warming.

Research at Cambridge University shows that British plants and trees, including the oak and the bilberry, have already begun to change as a result of the greenhouse effect. Australian research has established that three quarters of the world's beaches are eroding. And American scientists have found that the Arctic permafrost has warmed by up to three degrees centigrade over the last 100 years.

These are just some of the first early warnings of an impending global crisis. The threat is twofold: the size of the likely climatic change, and its speed.

The climate that has allowed the growth of civilisation and agriculture – and to which all our crops, customs and structures are adapted – is virtually certain to disappear. The world may even become warmer than at any time since the emergence of humanity on Earth. This threatens to take place over the next 40 years.

Humanity will find it hard to adapt, particularly in a world fragmented by national boundaries and competing interests.

At the end of the last century, Svante Arthenius, the great Swedish scientist, coined the phrase 'the greenhouse effect'.

Carbon dioxide in the atmosphere acts like glass in a greenhouse.It lets the sun's rays through to the Earth, but traps some of the heat otherwise radiated back into space. If there were none of this gas in the atmosphere the Earth's temperature would on average, be a bleak 18 degrees centigrade below zero. Natural levels of the gas keep it at a comfortable 15 degrees C.

As more reaches the atmosphere, the hotter the world becomes. We emit about 5.4 billion tons every year from burning oil, gas and coal.

Cutting down trees, as in the tropical rain forests, makes things worse. Living trees mop up carbon dioxide – when they are cut down and burned they release it.

Top scientists now agree that the Earth has already warmed by about half a degree centigrade over the past 100 years. They also agree that unchecked it is likely to add another 1.5 to 4.5 degrees centigrade by the 2030s.

This is beyond civilised man's experience. The Middle Ages were warmer than today – vines grew in Southern England, Greenland truly appeared green to its Norse discoverers, and the warming may have helped kill off the Mayan civilisation. But the temperature was only half a degree higher than today.

The last equivalent temperatures were at least 125,000 years ago when the climate was 2 – 2.5 degrees warmer, and elephants, lions and hippopotami roamed the Home Counties as freely as today's property developers. Less than 100 years from now, if present trends continue, the Earth could be a massive 8.6 degrees warmer. Rising sea levels are the most predictable result – water expands as it heats up, and snow and ice melts. Again, there is a scientific consensus: the rise would be between 8 inches and four-and-a-half feet by 2030.

A rise of just a foot would erode most sandy beaches on the US Gulf and Atlantic coasts, causing massive property damage. A

275

three-foot increase would flood a sixth of Egypt's arable land, making eight million people homeless. Fifteen million people in Bangladesh would lose their homes and livelihoods. New Orleans, Shanghai and Cairo would be flooded. The glories of Venice and the toxic horrors of Canvey Island would be imperilled. And many of Asia's best rice growing areas, on low-lying plains and deltas, would be ruined.

A study prepared before the Thames barrier was built to show the effects of a London flood gives some idea of the consequences for a major city. Forty-five square miles of the city would be affected it said, and 1.3 million people put at risk.

Flooding, though, will probably be much less damaging than changes to the world's winds, rains and ocean currents. The Earth will heat up unevenly, the poles warming faster than the tropics. This will probably make the weather much stormier. The best scientific estimates suggest that the great grain-growing regions of the world, the American Mid-West and the Soviet grainlands, will become much drier, leading to sharp falls in crop yields. Harvests are expected to fail in Central Europe, too.

The rains are expected to move North to Canada, Siberia and Scandinavia. Yet these areas have poorer soils and so will not be able to replace the world's present bread-baskets. Famine would increase in the dry parts of Africa, and could well spread to Western countries.

Britain's weather, as ever, seems particularly hard to predict. One scenario suggests that the country will get warmer; wine growing would flourish but the Cox's orange pippin would die. Skiing in Aviemore would cease for lack of snow and the bitter debate over the afforestation of North Scotland's Flow Country would finally be settled. It would be too warm for the conifers and too dry for the wildlife, so both would disappear.

Another scenario suggests that Britain and much of Western Europe would actually get colder, as the Gulf Stream veers away from our shores. Wildlife would be devastated all over the world, because habitats could not keep up with the changing climate.

Coping with the greenhouse effect is likely to be enormously expensive. Building just one mile of sea-wall can cost about £1 billion; the Netherlands spends a higher proportion of its wealth keeping out the sea than the US does on defence.

Poor countries will not be able to afford to; rich ones could end up spending trillions of pounds. By one estimate, coping with a 2.5 degree rise could soak up a crippling 3 per cent of the world's economic output each year.

There is one more depressing scientific consensus: that the warming is now 'inevitable'. A study by the World Resources Institute in Washingtron shows that even a determined effort to fend off the greenhouse effect would 'only' postpone the warming expected by 2030 by some 30 to 60 years.

But that time is worth buying. It gives us some chance to adapt, to breed drought-resistant crops, to prepare for the rising sea. This would mean cutting back on the burning of fossil fuels.

More nuclear power brings its own dangers and is unlikely to be developed fast enough. Renewable energy, like wind and solar power, are more attractive environmentally, but are not well enough developed yet.

The best hope is strict energy conservation. Japan, the world's most successful economy, uses half as much energy per head as the US – and could do even better. Stopping the felling of forests and planting new ones to soak up carbon dioxide would help. Unless action is taken fast, it will be too late. *Geoffrey Lean*

Unbelievably, Pitsford Reservoir, Northants, the result of drought in Britain: 'Early warning of an impending global crisis?'

Andy Warhol's Final Sale –
Observer Magazine *story on
Warhol's extraordinary collection of
arts and artefacts which went on
show at Sotheby's, London, before
the Manhattan sale. Preview by
Peter Watson, photographs by
David Gamble.*

Andy Warhol (above) *died in
February 1987, aged 56. He was
an obsessive collector – furniture,
jewellery, pictures, all kinds of
junk.*
*Left, Coke bottles and cassettes
jostle a landscape frieze painted by
his former companion Jed Johnson.*
*Below, some of Warhol's
possessions at Sotheby's. 'Let's go
shopping for masterpieces,' he used
to say.*

PRACTISING GENIUS ON THE HIGHEST PLANE

24 July 1988

During the past week we have constantly been told that Severiano Ballesteros is back. Admittedly the occasions are increasingly frequent these days when I have to telephone home from Charing Cross station to ask where I am supposed to be going but I had not noticed that he had been away.

Since he won the Open at St Andrews on that unforgettable day in 1984 he has won the world match-play championship twice, the Irish Open twice, the French Open twice, the Spanish Open, the Dutch Open, the Sanyo Open, the British Masters, the Monte Carlo Open, the Suze Open, the Lancome Trophy, the New Orleans Open, the Westchester Classic, the Mallorca Open and twice played the major role in winning the Ryder Cup for Europe.

He has never claimed to be the greatest player in the world, conceding that these days there are a number of great players of whom he likes to think he may be considered among the top five. The statistics bear out this assessment for he has never been outside the leading five in the Sony world rankings during his absence.

With any other player in the world those four barren years would be seen as an impressive record. In the case of Ballesteros he is regarded as having been away, such is the international perception of golf's only practising genius.

Only in that highly refined sense can he be said to have made a comeback by his glorious victory at Royal Lytham and St Annes. He said afterwards in his euphoria that his last round 65 was the best it was possible for this game to be played. That

might have been stretching things a touch but I did not think I would live to see golf again of the quality played by Jack Nicklaus and Tom Watson in their duel at Turnberry in 1977.

Ballesteros and Nick Price produced it and for the same reason: the Open came down to a match-play confrontation. The record books will show that Ballesteros won by two strokes but the real result was a victory by one hole. Price's long putt to tie the scores was his final thrust, a typically daring attempt and his missing of the return putt was immaterial. The Open was over by then and those two last strokes had no more significance that practice putts.

It is possible to imagine that Ballesteros might have won by seven strokes, as seemed on the cards after his brilliant opening round, but it is hardly conceivable that he could have scored a last-round 65 without being inspired to it by the courage and virtuosity of Price.

In 1982 at Royal Troon Price lost the Open. This time he never

Severiano Ballesteros escaping from The Belfry, Ryder Cup, 1989, the photograph that made Mike King Sports Photographer of the Year. Ballesteros 'has never claimed to be the greatest player in the world. He likes to think he may be considered among the top five great players.'

faltered, played a winning last round and was beaten. There is a Grand Canyon between those outcomes and Price did not need the victor's generous tribute to realise that he has what it takes to win a major championship. He knew it already and that knowledge will surely bring its reward in due course.

We must also save a portion of the glory for Nick Faldo, who put up a great defence of the title. He looked to be frustrated and at odds with himself when things did not happen for him but he kept plugging away for his honourable third place.

Sandy Lyle, by contrast, seemed to be back to his old days of feeling that there was no point in taking pains over his putts because he knew very well that the ball would not drop no matter what he did. Pity. At least we may be spared more of those absurdly premature tributes by the greatest British golfer of all times. His potential is immense but he still has two Toms, a Harry, a John H, a James and a Henry to overtake.

There was some consternation among the tradespeople of St Annes over a rumour that this was to be the last Open at Royal Lytham. The club does have particular problems at the best of times and this year it faced the added appalling difficulties of the weather and a washout, a challenge to which it rose quite magnificently.

Once again the American professionals failed to come to terms with Lytham. It was not that they were unable to handle the course or the weather, they could and did for individual rounds, but not one of them was able to maintain that form over four rounds.

Although he holds a British passport, Price is essentially an American Tour player and as such he proved that there is nothing much wrong with the current standard of American professional golf. It took Ballesteros in his most compelling mood to uphold the fragile supremacy of European professional golf and he will have to maintain his revivial at the same suprememe level if he

is to achieve his goal of claiming the American PGA championship next month. By then Greg Norman will be fully restored and the Americans will be out for blood.

Historically, last week's triumph will last for ever but for practical purposes it will not mean much in a month's time. After his previous major championship it took Ballesteros four

years to sort out his priorities. We must hope that he can stay on his single-minded track and go on to achieve the rich potential of his remarkable talent.

And let us further hope that our other heroes, Nick Faldo, Sandy Lyle, Ian Woosnam and Bernard Langer, are there to make it tough for him, or perhaps for one of them to do the business himself.

Peter Dobereiner

KEEPERS OF SECRETS, TELLERS OF TALES

11 September 1988

There is a Western European democratic nation, according to an impressive series of reports published last week, where the very concept of liberty is under attack by the Government. It is a country in which freedom is being curtailed, sacrificed or even abandoned if the political, commercial or administrative price rises too high. Where those who publish a vulgar poster depicting a political leader in suspenders and carrying a whip can be prosecuted under a wide-ranging Public Order Act. Where even universities are under threat because of a Prime Minister who suffers from 'cultural bossiness' and resents any potential centre of power or influence which could loosen the grip on national life of the ruling party.

It does not sound a happy place. It is a country in which values once thought to be self-evident are now regarded as hopelessly old-fashioned, if not downright unpatriotic. It is a country named Britain.

According to *Index on Censorship*, which has long championed the cause of the oppressed, censored and silenced across the world, Britain now merits a special issue devoted entirely to its own failings. It is the first time in the magazine's 15-year history that it has turned the spotlight in this way on a Western democratic country. 'If freedom is diminished in the United Kingdom, where

historically it has deep roots,' writes the editor, Matthew Hoffman of the *Independent*, which helped prepare the special report, 'it is potentially diminished everywhere.'

Freedom of information is a fundamental human right. To be able freely to choose who shall govern us, it is first necessary to know how those we put into power behave. Governments, naturally, wish to be well thought of; they will try therefore to conceal anything which might detract from the respect, acclaim and adulation to which they feel rightfully entitled. 'This is so palpable,' John Stuart Mill remarked, 'that a man must be either insincere or imbecile to deny it.'

Yet Britain today, sadly, would leave Mill much perplexed. Where was the outcry over the proposed new Official Secrets Act, which would effectively make the security services unaccountable to Parliament or public and beyond the reach of the law? Over an Education Act which gives central government a degree of power and control uparalleled in recent history, especially in universities, where funding is being squeezed relentlessly? Roy Jenkins, humane and liberal Home Secretary, now Chancellor of Oxford University, writes that the Government's clear aim is to ensure 'that in future decisions about what the universities teach, by what methods and to how many students in each category, shall be decided more by officials in London under the direction of Ministers and less by the universities themselves.'

Where, indeed, was the outcry over the emasculation of a public service broadcasting organisation suffering from political pressure so intense that it led, three years ago, to a strike by journalists at both the BBC and ITV? It is an unfortunate truth that those who complain most loudly about curtailed freedoms are those who suffer most directly. It is scarcely surprising that journalists feel strongly about restraints on press freedom (restraints which are imposed not only by Government but also by the steady concentration of press ownership in the hands of fewer and fewer corporations).

Yet governments are surely wrong if they think it is journalists alone who care. There is widespread public mistrust of untrammelled authority, even if not all newspaper readers would necessarily regard their chosen journal as an adequate safeguard against the misuse of power. The basic lessons of the *Index on Censorship* survey are easily stated; 1, knowledge is power, therefore accurate and complete information (no more mandarins who prefer to economise on the truth) is a vital prerequisite in a healthy functioning democracy; 2, the dimunition of one freedom is a threat to them all; and 3, that freedoms which have been hard to win are equally hard to keep.

'There has long been a tension between freedom of the Press and the secrecy of the governors,' says the survey's introduction. 'It is the considered belief of the writers in this issue . . . that this tension is in danger of being resolved in ways that favour the keepers of secrets over the tellers of tales.' As tale-tellers who believe that most, though not all, secrets are best out in the open, we shall continue to struggle both to find the tales which need telling and then to tell them.

THE WILSON PLOT

Peter Wright's book Spycatcher *was published in the US in 1987. British newspapers were not allowed to reveal what was in it. In 1988 the Law Lords ruled against the Government's attempts to suppress the information.*

16 October 1988

As we were saying before we were so rudely interrupted, some lunatic elements in MI5 were plotting to bring down a British Prime Minister in the crazed belief that he was an agent of the Soviety KGB . . . Now that the House of Lords has restored to the Press and the rest of the British public the right of free speech over the Peter Wright affair, we can finally evaluate the claims made in his book.

In 1986 *The Observer* disclosed that this senior MI5 officer was prepared to admit in his unauthorised memoirs that there had been a plot of some kind in the previous decade against the Labour Prime Minister Harold Wilson – something long suspected, not least by Wilson, but never proved. As the Government's lawyers said, it was 'the first publication aywhere in the world' of this claim. We set out to investigate so grave an allegation: what kind of men, what kind of secret organisation, could do such things in a democracy and get away with them? One might have expected the Government and its law officers to be equally concerned at such iniquity. But no.

The next two years were a costly diversion – albeit a constitutionally important one – as this newspaper and a number of others, along with Wright's publishers, fought off worldwide attacks from lawyers to prevent us finding out and publishing the truth. Why the Prime Minister, the law officers and MI5 behaved in this way is a matter between Mrs Thatcher and the taxpayers, who are some £3.5 million worse off as a result.

Today, after this long interruption, we are now able to publish the results of David Leigh's investigation. This discloses in convicing detail just how Peter Wright and his charmed but uncharming circle abused their secret powers and fell into a world of prejudice and paranoia in which they betrayed the democratic values they existed to serve. If Wright was a wicked person, he was not made so by newspapers and publishers: he was a creature of MI5, an organisation the Government still plans to place above the law.

ORPHANS OF THE EARTHQUAKE

18 December 1988

One terrible detail stands out from the multiple horror of the Armenian earthquake; out of a school of 500 children, a single child survived. What will happen to that child? And what will happen to all the other children who have survived, perhaps while their parents or their whole families have perished?

These are questions loaded with political implications and the weight of Armenia's tragic history. Haig Vartanian, of the Aid Armenia Committee, notes that after the Turkish massacres of Armenians in 1915, 'there was a fight over the orphans. American missionaries took over their care, and the Armenians were at the time so dazed and stunned that they didn't realise what was happening. It was only after two or three years that they started saying: What are our children doing in foreign hands? Then they started building orphanages themselves.'

In the present tragedy, things have moved faster. When Mikhail Gorbachev, visibly moved, witnessed the extent of the disaster in the Armenian cities, he pledged that any child who needed treatment would be given the best medical care in Moscow. Twenty-five children are now being treated in Moscow hospitals.

The Armenians on the British committee do not question Gorbachev's compassion, but his action struck a raw nerve, and 20,000 women from Yerevan demonstrated to stop any more children being taken out of Armenia. At a press conference under the glittering chandeliers of the Dorchester Hotel's Orchid Room (given free by the management to help the Aid Armenia Committee), speakers insisted there was no danger that orphans of the Armenian disaster would be taken from their homeland. But the subject was still difficult.

People disagreed about how many orphans there were. One Committee member said 10,000; another, 50,000. A third quoted the representative of Soviet Armenia in Moscow, who in a telephone conversation had broken down and said that all he knew was that because the earthquake occurred in schooltime, 85 per cent of the school-age children in the devastated cities were dead.

Rosalie Kerbekian, a child psychotherapist who works with the Unit for the Study of Trauma and its Aftermath at the Tavistock Clinic in London, is the child of an Armenian father orphaned at the age of four in the Turkish massacres and separated from his surviving sister. 'At the age of 77, he feels he has never recovered from the pain of being orphaned,' she said, urging that children affected by the disaster should be kept with surviving family members wherever possible. If a whole extended family were lost, they should remain in Armenia with an Armenian adoptive family.

'These children are already traumatised by the destruction , and they will be even more psychologically damaged if they are separated from people they know and trust at a time of profound stress,' she said. They needed not only food and clothes and shelter, and not only the kindness of neighbours who would take them into their homes.

'We have learnt from Zeebrugge and King's Cross and the Middle East that in disasters it is vital to get some psychological first aid to the families and the children quickly. I am concerned that Armenia should be rebuilt materially, but I am even more concerned that people's lives must be rebuilt, and the psychological damage repaired.

'If it isn't, and if these children's emotional difficulties are not treated, they will carry them into their adult lives, and the damage can go on for generations.'

Psychological injuries are already beginning to show in the earthquake survivors.

'Rescue workers cannot get people to leave the wreckage of their homes. They sit there, hoping a relative or child may yet be brought out alive. They try to stop the Soviet army from taking away the corpses. They want to bury their own dead,' said Haig Vartanian.

He predicted that 'the reaction of our people to this disaster will be to care for the children and to try to make them forget the past. But I agree that there will be a psychological aftermath, for which they may need special counselling and help.'

Janet Watts

A Bad Girl's Book of Beasts

26 March 1989

Once upon a time there was a journalist of Burmese extraction called Little Brown Susan who was asked one day to talk about censorship at the Children's Book Circle conference. The hall was full of big white delegates talking loudly about Important Intellectual Things like Fertile Imagination versus Frail Psyche and the Principles and Pressures of Book Selection in the Public Sector, and Little Brown Susan's psyche felt so frail and flustered in front of all these clever librarians and teachers and publishers and authors bent on safeguarding our children's interests that she almost ran away and hid in the nice warm tea room of Fortnum & Mason next door. 'I am not here as an expert,' Little Brown Susan

reminded herself. 'I am here as a mother of five reading, or about to read, children.' This made her feel much better.

There were three speakers before Little Brown Susan – Little White Imogen, a publisher who spoke very well and rather fiercely about the editorial balancing act (with slides), Lithe White Toby, an Anglican priest and author of two teenage books, who talked about the importance of language, and Plumpish White James, another author, whose address was entitled 'Youth at the Sharp End'. How the delegates loved them – especially Father Toby, who said that contemporary writers were too scared to use adult words in children's books which was Very Silly since children in real life used them all the

time. Lithe White Toby told lots of funny stories containing naughty four-letter words which made everyone in the audience, especially two fat pink ladies, laugh and laugh in that half-pleased, half-embarrassed way that ladies do when off-duty priests in thick-knit jerseys use four-letter words to make a serious point.

Then it was Little Brown Susan's turn. Up she jumped in her smark silk jacket, her straight linen skirt and her beautiful navy shoes with the pointed toes and the shiny high heels she had bought at the Russell & Bromley Winter Sale and told the delegates that she didn't mind in the least if her children read the Famous Five or Biggles or Little Black Sambo, or indeed any of those other books children aren't supposed to read, for she honestly believed that if there was one thing that encouraged children to read at all it was a ripping good story. Furthermore, though she knew it was fashionable for children these days to read the Mister Men and Postman Pat and Thomas the Tank Engine, her own brood seemed to prefer the adventures of Sambo, Quibba, Quasha, Mingo et al, because on the whole stories about wicked tigers, crafty crocodiles and indescribably evil snakes curled round the trunks of mango trees are more interesting than stories about level crossings and postmen.

Suddenly there was a terrible *ROAR* from the front row and Big Black Mike, Senior Inspector for Multi-ethnic and Anti-racist education in ILEA, jumped up and cried in an angry voice that Little Brown Susan had a Facile Appreciation of the subject in hand and a Poor Grasp of the very serious issues; in short, that she was a racist. At this all the small, medium and large pink-and-white delegates who had laughed so heartily at Father Toby's dirty jokes sat very still and shocked. Poor Little Brown Susan.

She had put her beautiful navy shoe with the pointed toe and the shiny high heel that she'd bought at the Russell & Bromley Winter

Sale well and truly in it. She tried (somewhat feebly, it has to be said, for the wrath of Big Black Mike was disconcerting) to explain that being half Burmese she was well used and well-nigh impervious to being called a wop, a chink, slit-eyed, Susie Wong and Kowloon Lucy the Sailor's Friend, and that the British attitude to racism pretty much passed over her head. She wanted to tell them that she regarded Little Black Sambo as neither more nor less racist than Little Red Riding Hood or Snow White or that all-time children's favourite, Tin Tin, who, if you recall, in that thrilling story about the Blue Lotus refers to his

THE FAYED BROTHERS EXPOSED

The Observer's long campaign from 1985-90 to reveal the truth about the Fayed brothers' purchase of the Harrods stores group, House of Fraser, incurred severe government displeasure, complex legal actions and a great deal of public attention, not all of it flattering to the newspaper's reputation, since it appeared to serve the interests of its proprietors, Lonrho. It is worth recalling the background to what is now publicly acknowledged as the exposure of a major fraud.

Lonrho had already taken a substantial holding in House of Fraser four years before it acquired **The Observer**. But the two issues became connected in the public mind in 1981, when Lonrho faced separate inquiries by the Monopolies Commission: should it be allowed to bid for control of the Harrods stores group? Was it in the public interest for Lonrho to own **The Observer**? They lost on the first and won on the second.

In late 1984 Lonrho's 30 per cent stake was acquired by the Fayed brothers, who launched a cash takeover bid in March 1985,

valuing the company at £615 million. The House of Fraser board recommended acceptance. Lonrho was still waiting for release from the ruling not to bid. Their hands were tied.

The Observer – whose previous coverage of the affair had demanded delicate judgment in view of its Lonrho connection – decided the time had come to take a more positive stance and on 10 March 1985 published an article entitled 'The Bloody Harrods Battle', written by its City Editor, Melvyn Marckus.

The question was: how substantial were the Fayeds' resources? Who was behind them? Who were the Fayeds? Marckus and his colleagues talked to numerous contacts, who invariably described Mohamed Fayed as a ruthless middleman of humble origins, not the fabulously rich Pharaoh dabbling with inherited wealth as generally portrayed at the time. Estimates of the Fayeds' assets were in the region of $100 million. Even doubled, that was not much in the context of a £615 million bid which, according to the

Fayeds and their advisers Kleinwort Benson, was being funded entirely out of the Fayeds' resources.

Mr R.W. 'Tiny' Rowland, chief executive of Lonrho, had alleged that the Fayeds' bid was being financed by the Sultan of Brunei and had called for a referral to the Monopolies and Mergers Commission. On 14 March Norman Tebbit (then Trade and Industry Secretary) chose not to refer the bid.

Then a writ arrived from the Fayeds in respect of 'The Bloody Harrods Battle' article. In Marckus's words: 'This was the first of many attempts to silence us. After Tebbit's decision, Lorana Sullivan, a dedicated unraveller of complex fraud, busied herself to locate the Fayeds' shipping fleet: to little avail. Michael Gillard, a highly experienced investigative journalist, was also flexing his muscles. Peter Wickman, former correspondent of **Stern** eventually joined the team.

In the summer of 1986 **The Observer** published Wickman's article, 'In Search of the Fabulous oriental assailants as Yellow Scum and filthy yellow chinks. But this did not seem to be the time or place for such opinions.

Other delegates joined the debate. A middle-sized white lady bookseller declared that she had been forced to withdraw Little Black Sambo from her shelves after several complaints. Little Brown Susan, by now fully repentant of her inherent racism, offered to run home right away and burn her children's much-thumbed copy of the hateful book whereupon a slender white girl in the second row replied, with just a hint of a smile – the only one since Father Toby's merry speech – that this might be unwise since

the book was out of print and could be valuable. Big Black Mike, however, was not smiling one bit but continued to chase Little Brown Susan's racist views round and round so furiously that in the end, like the tigers chasing each other round the tree, he completely disappeared, leaving nothing but a small Logical Conclusion.

Afterwards at tea, the only delegate brave enough to speak to the disgraced Little Brown Susan was a pretty girl from the Bodley Head who said it was refreshing to hear a different point of view. Alas, this comfort was short-lived. When I got back to the office I found a letter complaining

that my remarks about Indian restaurants and curried cat were nothing short of racist. I have nothing more to say on this distressing subject, except perhaps to draw your attention to the winning entry in the under-18 category of the BBC 'Today' programme's mini-saga competition. It's by Kathryn Clarke aged 15:

'Come and meet my friend on Sports Day, Mummy.' Sports Day came. 'Where's your new friend, Paul?' 'He's sitting on the front bench.' There were 10 on the front bench. 'He's wearing red shorts.' There were three boys with red shorts. 'His hair's curly.' 'Oh, the black one,' said Mummy.
Sue Arnold

Pharoahs,' which not only exposed the myths surrounding Mohamed Fayed but also made a mockery of the coverage of the House of Fraser affair by rival newspapers.

'We often likened the Fayed saga to the Emperor's New Clothes. Tebbit, the Office of Fair Trading's Sir Gordon Borrie, Kleinwort Benson, lawyers Herbert Smith, the Daily Mail, The Times, Sunday Times *and* Sunday Telegraph *all marvelled at Mohamed Fayed's wealth and assets. The* Observer *was the little boy who shouted "Look at the Emperor . . .". It was a lone stand. The so-called inquiries carried out by rival Sundays and their daily brethren appeared to throw up only one fact: Lonhro owned* The Observer.

'Privately, I had always argued that the myths surrounding Mohamed Fayed were so open to question that financial journalists would eventually change their editorial postures. In late 1985, I realised I was wrong: it was far more fun to describe The Observer *as Lonhro's mouthpiece than do battle with Fayed's lawyers – who by now had showered us with writs and complaints to the Press council.*

'In November 1985 I wrote an

open letter to Tebbit's successor, Leon Brittan. I stressed that, should it ever be proved that the Fayeds' takeover was financed entirely out of their own resources, I would tender my resignation to my Editor, Donald Trelford. But it was not until the spring of 1987 that Paul Channon, Brittan's successor as Trade and Industry Secretary, finally appointed DTI inspectors to investigate the matter.

'It was during The Observer's *evidence to the inspectors that the quality of the investigative work carried out by Gillard, Sullivan and Wickman became clear. We had consistently asserted that the Fayeds had not purchased House of Fraser with their own funds and had misrepresented their wealth, their origins, even their date of birth.*

'Much was made of the Editor's decision to publish key extracts from the House of Fraser report in a special Observer *midweek edition on Thursday 30 March, 1989, a date which coincided with Lonhro's AGM. The truth is that we had little choice. This was our chance to prove the paper's stand had been justified. Rowland was in possession of a copy of the report and was intent on informing shareholders of the inspectors'*

findings at the AGM; any such statement from Lonhro would inevitably have brought about an injunction from the DTI which would have meant that on Sunday 2 April The Observer *would have been unable to refer to the fact that the newspaper had been vindicated.*

'It was not until 7 March 1990 that the DTI's findings were officially made public. Had we not published our leaked version of the report, it might never have seen the light of day. The principal conclusion said it all: "The Fayeds dishonestly misrepresented their origins, their wealth, their business interests and their resources to the Secretary of State, the Office of Fair Trading, the Press, the House of Fraser board and shareholders, and their own advisers."

Marckus concludes: 'Let the inspectors have the final word: "Most newspapers and magazines considered that discretion was the better part of valour and preferred to write about other things than get involved in an expensive libel action with a rich man. As a result of what happened, the lies of Mohamed Fayed and his success in 'gagging' the Press created . . . new fact: that lies were the truth and that the truth was a lie".'

Magazine Feature, April 1989: most loved and most loathed buildings. Norman Parkinson was photographed by David Gamble in front of his favourite building, Brighton Pavilion by John Nash. He hated most Basil Spence's Household Cavalry buildings in Hyde Park.

REVENGE OF THE OLD GUARD

Jonathan Mirsky was in Tiananmen Square during the bloodbath of the weekend of 5 June, and was badly beaten up by the police. These are extracts from his article.

11 June 1989

On the Friday night before the Saturday massacre when thousands of poorly uniformed young soldiers came trotting down Changan Avenue, a few hundred yards from the square, they were surrounded by sleepy Pekingers in their underpants and pyjamas, who stripped them of their packs, scattered the meagre contents on the pavement, and lectured them as if they were naughty children.

The scolding went on for hours,

but even when the soldiers were cowering in bushes along the Avenue, they were in no danger. At dawn, these country boys with closely-cropped hair and tattered khaki gym shoes had been sent packing.

Indeed, even after the great killing had begun most of those surrounded in their lorries, who had not yet used their guns, were not dragged out and killed, but remained the targets of outrage and moral exhortation.

If the masses of Peking maintained order, discipline, and good humour matched only by that of the students, and confined their resistance to a non-violent determination worthy of a Quaker organiser, why did senior leader

Deng Xiaoping, President Yang Shangkun, and the rest of the geriatric thugs now in control order them to be gunned down that Saturday night?

It is possible that the 27th Army, blasting its way through the roadblocks west of Tiananmen, crashing into the square, and showering everyone in it with semi-automatic and machine gun fire, truly believed that the figures it saw moving about in the smoke and flame were not students and working poeple, but hoodlums who were intent on overthrowing the government and the State and Communism itself.

To soldiers from remote regiments, who had been told that on Friday night other soldiers had been kidnapped and beaten by 'bad elements', shooting the moving figures in the square might have seemed their patriotic and military duty.

But last Sunday morning, in the warm dawn and the growing heat, why did the soldiers continue to shoot? Frantic parents of those who had been gunned down and bayonetted the night before clustered around the roadblock in front of the Peking Hotel, a couple of hundred yards from the square. There they could see the massed tanks, with their guns depressed and aimed straight down Changan Avenue towards the agitated crowds.

Soon they saw soldiers trot out and fire a volley over their heads. The crowd retreated, hesitated, and reassembled. Then the soldiers fired again, but straight into the crowd. Many were killed and wounded. Soon two ambulances appeared, and doctors and nurses, in flapping white gowns ran among the bodies, kneeling down, feeling for wounds. The soldiers fired again, and now there were white-clothed bodies, too.

So, again, why have Deng, Yang and the rest of the Gang done it? Deng had featured on magazine covers as a man devoted to the modernisation of China, and so devoid of ideological commitment that he had said, 'Who cares what colour a cat is as long as it catches mice?' He was the man who had shaken hands with Mrs Thatcher and the Queen and was hailed as the originator of the Hong Kong settlement formula intended to assure the inhabitants of the teritory that their future was safe in Peking's hands.

Devotion to Party discipline, the conviction that the Party and the Party alone stands between the Chinese people and chaos, is the key to Deng's character and to the bloodshed of last week. From his resumption of power after Mao's death Deng planned and ordered the Four Modernisations in agriculture, industry, defence and science. But he also regularly suppressed anything that looked like a challenge to Party supremacy.

Most telling of all, Deng has confessed that the two greatest mistakes of his life were the appointments as Party general secretary, of Hu Yaobang and Zhao Ziyand. In 1987, Deng forced Hu's resignation for failing to stop campus demonstrations for more democracy, threatening to expose high-level corruption, and advising Deng to retire.

Some time during the last three weeks Deng struck again, to remove Zhao – also for encouraging dissenting students, admitting that his own sons were corrupt, and daring to disagree with the Supreme Leader on whether the students were hoodlums and traitors. Only this time Zhao refused to go quietly, like Hu, and had to be forcibly removed from the scene. He is certainly under arrest, and by now could be dead.

His supporters and disciples are now being 'investigated' as counter-revolutionaries, a deeply serious crime in China. As the murderous days drag on, they face imprisonment and perhaps execution.

The soldiers real task was not to crush the students but to secure Peking against a possible counter-coup by the followers of Zhao Ziyang.

Yang is the other arch-criminal, as deeply committed as Deng. He is known to have insisted on the removal of Hu Yaobang, and to have opposed Zhao as his successor.

The rest of the aged gang,while they may not have approved the mass killing of last weekend, in their speeches created an atmosphere of emergency and alarm which could be used to fire up the PLA for the job they were given in the square.

These old men are convinced of one thing: they are the Founding Members of the Firm. We entered the Party 60 years ago, they remind one another, we survived the Long March in 1935, the Japanese, Chiang Kaishek, the early years of land reform when we killed hundreds of thousands of landlords and class enemies.

We endured Mao's Cultural Revolution. This is our country and our Party and no one is going to take it from us, certainly not that rabble in the square, provoked and misled by Zhao Ziyang.

This is the attitude which explains the rumours running through Peking in late May that Deng had said, 'Two hundred thousand deaths are not too many to ensure 20 years of stability,' and, 'What are a million deaths in a population of one billion?'

Government announcements warned everyone to stay at home to avoid harm, and by Saturday afternoon the soldiers had begun to use teargas. 'Why are they doing this?' I asked an elderly man.

'Haven't you seen today's *People's Daily*?' he asked. 'It says there is 'planned turmoil'. That means they can do whatever they like to anyone, no matter what size, age or sex they are.' And anything is what they did on that Saturday night, and what they kept on doing all last week, even if, as it appeared, parts of the army were consumed with guilt, revulsion and horror.

But do we learn then, as we secretly feared in our racist youth, that the Chinese are unusually cruel rat-eaters who slide bamboo under finger nails, kill with a thousand cuts or with countless drips of water? Are their leaders, as a British diplomat said recently, just a bunch of thugs, who sometimes murder in the dark, one by one, or in the daylight in heaps which are then stacked up in hospital morgues or burned secretly at night?

There are such Chinese. They gave the orders for the Saturday night massacre. They drove the tanks which clanked over the students in Tiananmen, they fired the AK-47s which knocked over the doctors and nurses, and they tortured the wounded and bound students. Such men are intellectual terrorists, too, who wish to crush the intellects of the dissidents.

But then there are the non-cruel Chinese, the great mass.

These have emerged during the last months as politically sensitive and in their great numbers so non-violently disciplined that they could have been trained by Quakers. They brought into Tiananmen the statue of Liberty of the Goddess of Freedom, explaining that whereas the Statue of Liberty holds her torch with one hand, the defence of freedom in China is tougher and therefore requires two.

There were the members of the Autonomous Workers Federation, in their tents in the square – almost the first over which the tanks rolled – who made hundreds of people laugh with their comic dialogues between Mao and Deng meeting in Heaven. There were the doctors and nurses who piled out of the ambulances last Sunday morning on Changan Avenue, after the soldiers had shot down the parents of people who had been

killed in the square a few hours before, as they knelt among the dead and dying. There were others who risked execution for letting BBC cameras into a morgue. And there were the people who tried to persuade me to leave Tiananmen when the soldiers began firing at us, and patted me kindly after the police had slugged me half-senseless with their truncheons.

Finally, there is the singer from Taiwan, Hou Jedian, a pop idol in Peking, and very rich, who came to Tiananmen to start a hunger strike with three companions. He had composed a song about the protests which he taught the crowd and which it rapturously sang.

He also composed a statement, which I listened to him discuss at dinner. It said that he was coming to the Martyrs' Memorial to show the Li Peng Government that the Chinese had for too long listened

and not spoken; that it was not a small handful opposing the regime, but the people themselves; and that Hou and his comrades were giving up food not for death but for life.

Hou was lucky to escape at the last moment, but it is true, none the less, that what happened in Tiananmen, beginning in mid-April and continuing until the massacre, was indeed for life. This is what the old men could not stand, and it is what they will continue attempting to snuff out in the dark period ahead.

Jonathan Mirsky

JONATHAN MIRSKY (b. 1932) Specialist in Chinese politics and culture. Began writing for The Observer *in 1974 after university teaching at Columbia, Cambridge and Pennsylvania. Voted International Reporter of the Year 1989 for his brilliant dispatches on events in Tiananmen Square.*

In the Yawalapiti tribe of Upper Xingu, in Brazil, women are equal to men. Children are never beaten. Huka-huka keeps them fit. This photograph (Colour Magazine, 18 June 1989) helped to win Peter Lavery the Design and Art Direction Silver Award.

NEW WAVE ARK

25 June 1989

Julian Barnes's new book *The History of the World in 10½ Chapters* is not a history but a fiction about what history might be: 'just voices echoing in the dark; images that burn for a few centuries then fade; old stories that sometimes seem to overlap; strange links, impertinent connections.' Overlapping stories, strangely linked, is what we're given, a post-modern, post Christian series of variations on the theme of Noah's Ark.

Barnes is in his *Flaubert's Parrot* mode, only more so. In this vein he's like a wordly secular reincarnation of a medieval glosswriter on sacred texts and what he offers us is the novel as footnote to history, as subversion of the given, as brilliant, elaborate doodle around the margins of what we know we think about what we think we know. This is fiction as critique, which is its limitation as well as its strength, because for all its high intelligence and formal elegance it proceeds (except for one brief, redeeming parenthesis) from the brain rather than the heart.

There's no denying the ingenuity, though, and at its best Barnes's *History* offers much high and some low comedy as well. There's a woodworm's-eye view of the Ark story, featuring a drunken Noah who thinks of his menagerie as a 'floating cafeteria' and eats many species into extinction, and a God described as an 'oppressive role-model' who drove poor Noah to drink.

The playful irreverence of this chapter would make instructive and no doubt shocking reading for some of today's hard-line religionists. (Sorry, Julian.) The woodworm crop up again in the hilarious proceedings of a medieval French court; this time they're the accused in a surreal trial, charged with eating a Church until it falls down.

A church, being a ship of souls, is also a sort of ark, and the Titanic was an ark, and so, for Jonah, was the Whale, and so was the raft of the survivors of the Medusa that Géricault painted. And just as Noah ate his animals, so the Medusa's survivors turned to cannibalism and there is the woodworm, as is suggested in the Géricault picture's frame. The stories proliferate and Noah's tub becomes an ever more protean image. We are all, it seems, riders of Barnes's lost ark.

Not all the stories convince, however. In particular, 'Upstream', the epistolary account of the making of a film something like *The Mission*, told by a notably self-regarding actor and containing a notably self-indulgent, in-jokey reference to the author's buddy Redmond O'Hanion, is a real turkey.

And several times the connections between the tales offer no enrichments. In chapter six, a religious zealot, Amanda Fergusson, dies on Mount Ararat in 1839; in chapter nine, another religious zealot, an astronaut who believes he has been spoken to by God when he was on the moon, goes to Ararat to find Noah's Ark and, finding Amanda's skeleton, claims to have discovered old Noah himself. You get the point but not the message.

The key to this strange, ambitious novel lies in the ½ of its 10½ chapters. Here the author gazes at us directly, like El Greco staring out of his masterpiece *The Burial of Count Orgaz*, and talks to us about love. Barnes's view of history (voices echoing in the dark, near-meaninglessness upon which we try to impose meanings) is just too thin to support the whole fabric; but his view of love almost saves the day. His idea is that history 'is ridiculous without love', that 'love teaches us to stand up to history', to reject its stupid, martial terms. Love, too, is a kind of ark, he says, on which two people might just be saved. I don't know if this is any truer than Auden's 'We must love one another or die'; but the idea that *the opposite of history is love* is worth hanging on to, like a lifebelt, like a raft.

Even here, though, one wishes that Barnes the essayist had stepped aside for Barnes the full-blooded novelist; that instead of a disquisition on love, we could have been given the thing itself. 'Don't talk of love,' as Eliza Doolittle sang, 'show me.'

Julian Barnes has written a book that is frequently brilliant, funny, thoughtful, inventive, daring, iconoclastic, original, and a delight to read. What more, he might legitimately inquire, could anybody ask for? I can only reply that, for me, the bits didn't quite add up; that, although they possess in abundance the high literary virtue of lightness, they fail to acquire the necessary weight: it being the paradox of literature that you need the pair of them on the voyage, weight and lightness, and, as with lovers and animals, you can't afford to leave half the couple off your ark.

Salman Rushdie

MARX AND THATCHER: GOODBYE TO ALL THAT

12 November 1989

When the first signs of the collapse of Communism in Eastern Europe became apparent, there was rejoicing in many quarters. In the camp of Mrs Margaret Thatcher, Prime Minister of all Britain, the news was received with extra relish. Perestroika, and the courtship of Mrs Thatcher by one or two East European leaders, came when Thatcherism itself was running into trouble. These new developments appeared to offer the Iron Lady a new lease of life. Could not events in Eastern Europe be interpreted as the final triumph of Thatcherism? Was not the whole world emulating the British Revolution?

Well, not exactly. I would submit that while East European-style Communism is most certainly in the process of collapsing, Thatcherism has already done so. The German nationals fleeing in their tens of thousands from East to West Germany prefer capitalism to communism. The mistake Mrs Thatcher has made is to assume that Thatcherism is the only alternative to communism.

In fact, Thatcherism is – or was – a bastard form of capitalism from which, as the opinion polls demonstrate, even the British public has already distanced itself. In maintaining that 'socialist' ideas are finished, Mrs Thatcher and her acolytes make one good point and one bad one. The idea that East European-style state planning, combined with the absence of political freedom, could satisfy people's needs for consumer goods was a chimera. Gorbachov's principal contribution to economic history is to admit defeat in this matter. But to extend this judgement to the belief that all, or even most, state provision is bad is manifest nonsense.

Even with the more modified form of market liberalism, the belief in a general bias against state provision is also misguided. An example of bias against public sector provision is provided by the Thatcher Government's housing policy. This has been to sell the existing public sector housing stock to the occupants and largely eschew public provision for the homeless.

A frightening picture of hundreds of thousands of homeless people in Mrs Thatcher's Britain has recently been painted by the charity organisation Shelter and a grim report by the *New Statesman*. There is in Britain an acute housing shortage, which the private sector has failed to satisfy. And the bias against the public sector in favour of the private has also served to aggravate the problems, besides housing, of education, health and transport. Such neglect, and insufficient state spending on research and training, has also aggravated the problems of the private sector in whose interests the public sector cuts were putatively made.

The cumulative effects begin to look devastating. If one adds the present Government's bias against alleviating the problems of the poor, including the many beggars on the streets of the nation's capital, one sees that the public squalor of modern Britain owes much to the deliberate imposition of the Thatcherite heresy.

Public opinion in Britain is telling the Government that however helpful the market may be in the allocation of consumer goods, the other half of the nation's spending requires more careful handling. Left to itself, the market system suffers from two obvious deficiencies. It encourages all manner of sharks and charlatans and, therefore, requires regulation. And there are many areas, ranging from transport and roads, through clean air and unpolluted water, to education and health, where the mass of the people cannot easily acquire what they need or want. 'Public goods' are best provided centrally (or by public authorities locally).

Mrs Thatcher's battles with the rest of the European Community are not just about sovereignty and the wisdom of economic and monetary union: they are about whether the pragmatism for which the British were once renowned, but which is now more prevalent in Continental Europe, should give way to the Thatcherite way of doing things. The French and Germans are not interested; nor are a majority of Britons.

Communism is an extreme version of planning, just as Thatcherism is an extreme version of market liberalism. The East Germans are fleeing to a country that practises a form of capitalism much more modified than Thatcherism, and even has regional equality built into its constitution.

It is one of the great ironies of our time that the economy which is peacefully conquering the rest of the world, namely Japan's, has more personal freedom than the discredited. East European communist states, but is also essentially a planned economy. The other great irony, of course, is that the two powers defeated in the Second World War, namely Japan and Germany, are the two most devastatingly successful economies of our time.

Then there is the awful embarrassment that the European Community, which was conceived as a means of keeping Germany under control, now finds that it is dominated by Germany.

The implications of events in East Germany for the European Community are going to be worked out before our very eyes. I agree with Timothy Garton Ash, Foreign Editor of the *Spectator*, that fears of too dominant a united, or confederated, Germany could be assuaged by a move to a more Federal Europe – just the kind of thing Mrs Thatcher most dreads. I also think it more likely that the East Germans are fleeing towards social democracy than to a Fourth Reich.

Both Japan, the planned economy that seems to work, and West Germany, the model social democratic economy, were greatly assisted by massive US aid after the war. There may be a moral here for those who are struggling with the question of how best to help Gorbachov and others in East Europe, to say nothing of the Third World. The most obvious candidates for contributions to such a modern Marshall Plan are, of course, Japan and West Germany.

William Keegan

WILLIAM KEEGAN
Joined The Observer *as Economics Editor in July 1977. His column* 'In My View' *began shortly afterwards, when the Labour government under James Callaghan was still in office, but became mainly noted for its opposition to the economic policies of Mrs Thatcher and her Chancellors. Keegan attacked both the deflationary policies of Sir Geoffrey Howe and the over-reaction to these under Nigel Lawson.*

GOODBYE TO THE COLD WAR

12 November 1989

The dominoes are falling with dizzying speed. In all the years of learned speculation about how the Cold War would end, nobody ever suggested that the regimes that have ruled Eastern Europe for more than 40 years would ring down the curtain by abdicating. The world has little experience of Communist governments who admit they have failed and come out with their hands up. Yet that is exactly what is happening.

Even a month ago it was unimaginable that East Germany, the heir to Prussian discipline, would crumble so fast. Could the old dogmatists of East Berlin be taught new tricks? Faced with the exodus of their people and the huge demonstrations clamouring for reform, they are performing somersaults. Free elections have been promised and the Berlin Wall, hated symbol of the jailer state, has been opened up.

On Friday the Bulgarians joined the fun, ousting their leader Todor Zhivkov in a palace coup. The germ of reform is virulent, and spreading so fast it is impossible to control. What its progress has revealed is the patent lack of political legitimacy of the ruling regimes of Eastern Europe. By what right did they impose their doctrines on their unwilling citizens? By force, or threat of force, backed up by the grizzled old bear in Moscow, tugging at its leash at the first sign of non-conformity.

Once that threat lost its credibility, the carefully-constructed image of government, party and people in harmony was revealed to be a sham. Communist parties in Poland, Hungary and East Germany are now struggling to retain even a share of power, remaking themselves as democratic organisations just as if their history of coercion and bad faith could be instantly erased.

The West has been reduced to the role of a spectator, watching open-mouthed as impossible events take place. It now seems perfectly reasonable to imagine Germany reunited, the European Community stretching seamlessly from the Atlantic to the Soviet border, a continent made whole again after the long nightmare of division and mistrust. Bliss was it in that dawn to be alive.

In a few weeks' time, President Bush and Mr Gorbachov meet on the Mediterranean for their first summit: from Yalta to Malta, as the Soviet spokesman put it. It will be an opportunity to probe the Soviet leader about his intentions towards his allies, but not a moment to draw up ambitious plans for the future of Europe. The lesson of the past few weeks is that Europe, both East and West, is outgrowing the dependence on the superpowers which has determined its history since 1945. The war is over, finally over; and Europe is ready to take its own future in its hands. It is a wonderful prospect.

Dawn, 10 November 1989. Bill Robinson captured the moment when the Wall – 'hated symbol of the jailer state' – started to come down. 'Faced with the exodus of their people and huge demonstrations demanding reform, East Germany's rulers are performing somersaults. Free elections have been promised.'

THE CHILDREN'S REVOLUTION

26 November 1989

Let us begin with the square and the people who in growing numbers poured into it each afternoon until a leadership that was as stubborn as it was blind at last found the grace to resign. Neither Wenceslas Square, nor the inhabitants of Prague, are ideally suited for such heroic demonstrations. Like a plank a kilometre long thrown across the city, the square begins at the steps of the National Museum and reaches almost to the Tyl Theatre where Mozart's *Don Giovanni* received its first performance. On Thursday – a vital evening because the demonstrators had to show strength to the Communist Central Committee which was to meet the next day – one man hung like a spider in the middle of a defunct neon sign high above the crowd.

But enthusiasts for revolution were not the only ones on the move that evening. On the opposite side of the square, in a bar on top of a department store, a trio dressed in red Cossack shirts were playing Latin American music. Two middle-aged couples, plain of face and dress, scampered on to the dance floor as though the quarter million people standing in the biting cold below did not exist. Vaclav Havel spoke. Somehow in this inconvenient square a quarter million voices kept rhythm as they sang the national anthem. The four dancers did not even break their step. The rumba was revolution enough for them.

This is a nation that has in the last 20 years been forced to accept humiliation upon humiliation from a regime which understood their people's lack of taste for risky resistance. People knew they were lied to. Last week, when the students launched their campaign to get the workers' support, the regime used the same old weapons. It promised whatever it could think of, like free holidays to exotic places, to stop workers joining the general strike called by students for tomorrow.

Government and people have co-existed in a cynical marriage whose offspring has been mutual contempt. There have been attempts to break it up. Ten years ago the writer Ludvik Vaculik published in *samizdat* an essay on heroism. 'Heroic deeds,' he suggested, 'are alien to life.' The most valuable resistance to the regime lay in something more modest: 'The integrity of the ordinary man.' As time passed, though, many in the opposition came to wonder if that amounted to much.

For older Czechs the miracle of the last week has been the emergence of a new generation of students who by their own efforts have freed themselves from this system of connivance and contempt. 'Parents,' reads a poster on the side of the monument to St Wenceslas, 'come with us. We are your children.'

When the students gathered to lick their wounds after the anti-terrorist squads had savagely broken up their demonstration on 17 November they had little notion of what had happened to them. But a historian, a signatory of Charter 77, had recognised that 'some very potent national symbols were coming into play without anyone giving a signal.' On 27 October students had gone to Vysehrad Cemetery to mark the death of Jan Opletal, a student who died in 1938 after demonstrations against Hitler's move into Czechoslovakia. The police broke up this march too, but it was on 17 November (the anniversary of Opletal's funeral) that their violence overstepped all bounds. No one knows how many students were hurt, for many dragged themselves home fearing arrest if they showed up at hospitals.

Supported or on their own, the students could not stop. That day's events, one of them said, 'acted like a bomb. For the first time I began to lead a political life.' The theatre students at Damu took the first step. The next day they called a strike, and demanded an investigation into the police action. By that evening the Prague theatres had come out in support. On Monday all the university faculties of Prague declared an occupation strike.

And though they did not know it yet, the students were no longer on their own. A wary, bitter nation was opening its heart to them. 'The Czechs have a need for martyrs,' the historian said quietly, as though thinking aloud. 'Masaryk [the much-loved pre-war president] often criticised them for it. Their attitude changes completely when blood is shed, because blood is so precious here.' By earning through their wounds the right to articulate the long-suppressed bitterness of the nation, the students were taking their place in an apostolic succession. It was police brutality against students in 1967 that provided similar fuel for the Prague Spring the following year.

The students threw themselves into the business of making a nation begin once more to talk among itself. As the week went on declarations, statements and appeals appeared in ever greater quantity stuck on shop windows and above all the walls and platforms of underground stations.

The fear, though, lasted almost until Friday. Knowing little of what was happening outside Prague, the young men and women living in their lecture halls were swept by rumour and at times panic. Several faculties used the same brave slogan: 'If not us, who? If not now, when?', but Tuesday was a very queasy day. Tanks were reported in the outskirts of Prague. Buses brought new units of the hated People's Militia from Moravia. The fear of violence was palpable. 'We don't want violence,' the slogans cried obsessively from the walls, and Czechs are not people to take fright at imaginary ghosts.

What was going on was a struggle for the workers. The students had the intelligentsia's support, but as a woman who has lived

Prague, November 1989. 'The miracle has been the emergence of a new generation of students who have freed themselves from this system of contrivance and contempt.'

through all the dramas of post-war Czechoslovakia remarked, 'Intelligentsia has become a dirty word in this country.' Every day the faculties have sent out delegations to factories in Prague and the Bohemian countryside beyond. Many were turned back at factory gates. Some were arrested. But others got through and on Friday the meeting on Wenceslas Square heard that almost 700 enterprises and organisations were supporting the Civic Forum.

Although the students do not know it, they could not have behaved as they did without the 1,000 brave men and women who signed Charter 77 twelve years ago. The chartists, isolated and persecuted, were sometimes compared to early Christians in the catacombs, but they set an example of what Havel liked to call: 'Living within the truth.'

One must assume that the Communist bosses still do not realise how discredited they are, for they too have lived too long in isolation, gazing at themselves in only the most flattering of mirrors. As for the opposition, its work is just beginning. The astonishing sight of Alexander Dubcek and Havel falling into each other's arms on the stage of the Magic Lantern Theatre on hearing of the Politburo's resignation may not often be repeated. Dubcek, the leader of 1968, still talks the old socialist language, though ordinary people are attracted by his simple, human manner.

The Czechs are the only nation in eastern Europe to have proved their democratic skills this century, and their chances of making democracy work again are better than anyone else's. Pictures of Masaryk, the scholar-president, are going up everywhere. No other nation in the Soviet bloc has a democratic leader to look back to: from Hitler to Hungary's Horthy they were dictators to a man.

Czechs are connoisseurs of repression. The baroque buildings that are the country's glory are evidence of Rome's attempt, largely successful, to eradicate Czech Protestantism. Hitler did his best, in the cellars of what is now the Ministry of Foreign Trade, to exterminate the Czech intelligentsia. The caution thus instilled is a useful democratic skill. Coming back from the joyful square on Friday evening I passed a new poster. 'If we have learned to fly like birds and swim like fish, then we can also learn to live like people.' Not like heroes, or romantics, or revolutionaries, but like normal people, some of whom will always find the rumba more seductive than any revolution.

Mark Frankland

LETTER FROM BUCHAREST

Viorica Butnariu, a 21-year-old student of tourism at Bucharest University, witnessed the fierce clashes between the army and forces loyal to deposed dictator Nicolae Ceaucescu. By candlelight she wrote a letter, in English, to an American friend, describing her horror at the bloodshed and the joy of final triumph. Here is her remarkable account.

31 December 1989

Dear Kathy, I write in this hour of despair and hope. Ceausescu ran away a few hours ago. You should have seen the joy, laughter and tears that came then.

Right now the cannon and guns are playing a frightful melody. I'm afraid, afraid that we might lose what we have gained with so much blood and tears. I'm transfixed, staring out of the window as cannon go off on both sides of the house. I can see tracer-bullets whistling past. No doubt I'm a sitting target. I feel so desperate: I must write to you now in case it's my last chance.

The radio and television send desperate calls every five minutes. It's nearly midnight on Friday 22 December, a day we'll all remember. This morning I went to the office *Viorica works as a part-time translator in a watch factory* only to find out we're on strike. Oh, these cannon, I wish someone could stop the noise. It's a nonsense of course: the army fights for us. Oh, God bless them. They refused to open fire against the people.

If only we can make it through the night. I have a terrible headache. I was on the streets all night yesterday with my student colleagues, asking for our rights and freedom. You know how they answered.

I was horrified. The boys tried to protect us, but we had only our bodies against the bullets. They died under my eyes: people I didn't know, and some I did. And they were all so young. It was dark and they fired at random. A girl whom I talked to a few minutes ago was dead at my feet. A boy – I don't know his name – took my hand and we began to run. I was running and crying.

Some fortunate God protected us and a man opened a door. The boy wouldn't stay there in safety.

He went away, back to the fighting, and he did not return. I don't know what happened to him. I swear we weren't doing anything wrong. Kathy, I saw blood, and dead bodies, and bullets, and things that seemed to be taken out of a horror movie. Oh Kathy, it's war, these cannon make a terrible noise. You know what Ceausescu did before he left this unfortunate city? He infected the water. We have to boil the water. The hospitals are full of dead and most of them are young like me and my brother or even younger.

I can't stop the tears thinking of my unfortunate friends, my brave and generous generation. With their lives they paved the road to freedom. I was there, and I tell you, most of them were under 26.

My radio is on so I can hear the news. The general committee of the city sends orders every few minutes. Bucharest is torn to pieces by street battles. And what an afternoon of glory we have had. I thought it was enough. But the bastard wants more bodies. He ordered this killing, brother against brother.

I was at the Presidential Palace with my brother when Ceausescu left by helicopter. My brother went inside, and when he came back in his hand he had a bullet. I couldn't follow him: the crowd was like a wild monster with a hundred mouths against Ceausescu. The crowd would have torn him to pieces and devoured him.

I don't know how everything will end. Kathy, when you read this give a thought to those who died.

The fighting is closer than it was. My brother just left to defend the radio station. The radio appealed for help. I hope he will come back safe and sane.

Maybe I'll go too. I feel like a coward sitting here while my friends are there.

What happened last night happened today, too. I'm afraid, but I feel I must go. It's just that I can't stand seeing mother cry. She's like a ghost. She almost lost me last night. This morning, going to the office before the general strike was announced, she had to wade through our blood – they had tried to wash down the streets but the water and blood just mixed in large puddles. Right now I have found out that a very nice girl friend of mine is also dead. Her body was identified this morning. Her mother just called. Now I know I must go. Kathy, when you're in church this Sunday think of the students crushed by the tanks.

Saturday 23 December. I can't stop crying, but no tears are coming. I prowl restlessly about my room. I was out last night but all I could do was help the doctors give a drink and a piece of bread to the wounded. There were thousands of our people. Poor kids who couldn't aim a shot, bravely faced these skilled murderers.

I finally quit in the morning because I couldn't help them in any way. Daylight brought some peace, but they wrote on the walls: 'We'll come back tonight.' Now it is night and they've kept their word. They're back. The palace square is on fire. They're trying to destroy the palace and the Central Committee building, now that our people have taken it over.

There are not many terrorists left, but they're trained for this job, fanatics who destroy buildings and kill people for a dead cause.

Ceausescu and his family are caught and they know it. Still no sign of surrender. They break into houses, kill the inhabitants and open fire from the windows. Among them seem to be Libyan mercenaries.

Our killers are now dressed like us, and behave like us and are hardly noticed. The only differ-

Writer John Sweeney and photographer Mike Goldwater went to Romania after the revolution. Their report was published in the Magazine in February 1990. They followed the stories of three ordinary Romanians: a Butcher – died in Palace Square in the revolution; a Baker – lived in terror of dreaded Securitate and lost a foot trying to escape; a Candlestick-maker – killed by Securitate sniper in the revolution.

Left, *the Butcher's family visit his grave;* below, *his widow holds up their wedding picture.*

ence between us is that they have a hidden gun.

Like many others, I will go this night, too. There's little I can do. Still, when I see groups of young-sters going there, laughing and shouting 'Get up and come with us' I realise that I am afraid no more.

I had such a wonderful feeling last night, walking beneath the dark sky while cannon boomed on my right and guns on my left . . . the feeling that I could change the world only by being there.

I'm happy you and the kids aren't here. It's not a town for foreigners any more. Some of them have been wounded. But as a friend said, I'm happy to be here now, this moment, while history is being written. Once in a life-time you see such a thing. It's a Christmas that we will never for-get.

At the university, where some of us were killed on the 21st, people placed candles against the walls. Candles and fir branches. Ceausescu the killer will never pay enough for their lives. I'm deeply touched by the friendship and help ordinary people are giving the youth.

Ceausescu has no friends. Now our battles prove to the people that we are not cowards.

Poor soldiers, they look so tired, their faces grey, deep shadows under their eyes, lips dry, but ready to die for us. We are worn out. I haven't been sleeping for the last three days and nights for more than one hour, but I'm not tired and I feel very light. I don't know what'll happen this night but I'm sure in the end we'll make it.

From my window I see the fire. The flames turn the sky to purple. They use tracers and dynamite to turn my dear city into ruins. Already you can't recognise the central district. All those lovely houses were affected by the fire.

Sunday 24 December. A moment of calm. A delusive calm. Then we were at it again. I was there in the radio and TV district, looking for

terrorists. House after house we asked people if they'd heard any noises in the night. When we found spent cartridges in front of suspect houses we knew where the thugs were. The houses were surrounded and bullets began to ring around us. Of course, we lay down or ran away. There was nothing more we could do, so we left the soldiers to do their job.

I wasn't afraid any more. I laughed when a group of people called us irresponsible. After all, we have only one death. Compared with the tortures that people from Timisoara suffered, this was nothing. Then we stayed

at the metro station from 11am–2am, guarding it against the fighters with our bare hands. There were two of them who fired from time to time without hitting any of us. I guess pity stopped them. I can't think of any other reason.

Wednesday 27 December. Kathy, think of me, as I will think of you, on New Year's Eve. All that I wrote to you. You taught me what's freedom, you taught me to be brave. I'm not ashamed of myself any more. Better than talking is fighting for your freedom.

Happy New Year!   *Viorica*

AN AUDIENCE WITH THE PATRIARCH

Nelson Mandela was finally released from prison on 11 February. Allister Sparks had a private meeting with him.

18 February 1990
My first impression on meeting Nelson Mandela last Wednesday was of a curious blend of simplicity and stateliness.

There he was, tall and straight and quite surprisingly thin, standing in a doorway of his poky little house on Valakazi Street dressed in slacks and a pullover.

He had heard that I was outside and had sent for me to offer some warm words about my work as a journalist. They were simple words, offered without flattery, but I felt as though I had been presented with a major press award.

The gesture was typical. All through the first week of a schedule so pressured as to be nightmarish, Mandela has paused to make these little acknowledgments to people below the rank of the major activists, whose modest contributions to the anti-apartheid cause he has observed and noted on some inner personal honours list. It is part of his charisma: the omniscient leader who notices the least of his flock.

This natural leadership quality has been apparent from the moment he walked through the

gates of Victor Verster prison, looking slightly hesitant at first like someone blinking in the light after emerging from a dark room, but quickly adjusting to his new environment.

One had always wondered whether it would be possible for anyone to live up to the extraordinary image that had evolved of him, but to a remarkable extent Mandela has done so. He made a satisfactory, if not electrifying, impact on the two big rallies he addressed; he is not a rousing orator but he speaks in a dignified, senatorial style that commands attention.

The mind reels at the thought of a man who has been isolated from the world since John Kennedy and Harold Macmillan and Konrad Adenauer were in power, who went to jail before South Africa had television and had never seen a TV camera in his life before last Sunday, being pitched overnight into a leadership role of such immense responsibility and having to face the kind of barrage of media questioning that only an American president might occasionally experience.

It was a situation fraught with potholes. Yet he never put a foot wrong. It was as though he had been doing it all his life.

Many prisoners who have been in jail for far shorter periods and

come out into more normal circumstances have experienced several reorientation problems. Yet Mandela showed no signs of stress when I met him in the midst of this hurly-burly.

He had just completed nine international television interviews in a row but he looked completely relaxed. As we sat chatting on a settee in the cramped little sitting room, he came across as warm and friendly. But there is also a stillness and dignity in his bearing that keeps him slightly remote.

Mandela spoke easily of his life in prison and the exhilaration of his release. The worst thing about being in jail, he said, was the pain and guilt he felt at knowing that his family was exposed to harassment and insecurity without him being there to protect them. 'And yet I knew I had taken the right decisions in doing the things for which I was imprisoned,' he said. It was like a clinical analysis of his own emotions.

When the conversation turned to more substantive matters he was meticulous in not presuming a leadership role to which he has not yet been formally appointed. 'I am just an ordinary member of the ANC,' he said, despite the massive display of public adulation for him that shows he is unquestionably the leader of his

Crowds outside the South African Embassy in London celebrating the news of Mandela's release.
'He has scolded his people severely for their lack of discipline.'

people.

He is a patriarch with a common touch. In his speeches to the great rallies in Cape Town and Johannesburg, and in smaller asides, he identified viscerally with his people's sufferings, but he also scolded them quite severely for their lack of discipline and the soaring crime rate in black townships.

A detailed analysis of his speeches gives an indication of where things may go from here. This is not towards some kind of Lancaster House conference like the one that settled the Zimbabwe conflict in a single tough bargaining session, but rather into a series of issue-by-issue negotiations that will gradually expand into a set of understandings which together will constitute a broad area of agreement.

Both sides have their formal proposals: the De Klerk government its idea of a great *Indaba* with the ANC, Pan-Africanist Congress and the various tribal 'homeland' leaders; and the ANC with its Harare Declaration, which calls for a mixed-race interim government that will hold the ring while one-person-one-vote elections are held for a constituent assembly to negotiate the post-apartheid constitution.

Mandela told domestic reporters on Thursday the next step should be a face-to-face meeting between the government and the ANC. This meeting, he elaborated in a later interview with the state-run television service, might reach a compromise in which the government would lift the state of emergency and grant a full amnesty, while the ANC 'should simultaneously issue a statement committing itself to peace'.

The government insists it must stay in power, and the constitutional affairs minister, Dr Gerrit Viljoen, said the other day it would not agree to the election of a constituent assembly because that would establish the priciple of one-person-one-vote even before the negotiations began.

Active lobbying and campaigning is going on all the time to increase the bargaining chips, even as the bargaining itself begins. By the time any equivalent of Lancaster House takes place, the main battles will be over. Its task will be to ratify and codify the deals already struck.

The mastermind behind the process is a man who has been cut off from the world for more than half his adult life. But as Nelson Mandela told me in that conversation, the one good thing about his long years in jail with those hard-faced white warders is that it gave him an insight into the Afrikaner mind and how to deal with it.

Allister Sparks

Jane Grigson, The Observer
Magazine*'s cookery writer from
1968, 'was a real writer, not just a
recorder or inventor of recipes. And
she had a sensuous nature. She
looked, attentively at everything,
and tasted, smelled, listened and
touched with the same attitude.'
The pictures with her articles –
which appeared in the Magazine
for over 20 years – reflected her
sense of style and her insistence on
the importance of freshness, above
all, in food, and beautiful
presentation.*

Above, *photograph published in
the Magazine on 30 September
1990, after her death, as part of
The Best of Jane Grigson series. In
her recipe for Basic Seviche she
wrote, 'Choose fish for freshness
rather than superiority of status.
Tiny queen scallops are
magnificent. Quality is everything.'*

Right, *Jane's Vegetable Curry,
published 14 October 1990.*

FLAVOUR OF TRUE GOODNESS

Jane Grigson, born in 1926, died in March 1990. Here, two of her closest colleagues pay tribute to her.

The first I knew of Jane Grigson was a typescript sent to me by Anthea Joseph of Michael Joseph, my own publishers.

Her *Charcuterie and French Pork Cookery*, published in 1967, was a real novelty, and a wonderfully welcome one.

The subject had been little dealt with in English culinary textbooks, but here was a writer who could combine a delightful quote from Chaucer on the subject of a pike galantine with a careful recipe for a modern chicken and pork version of the same ancient dish, and who could do so without pedantry or hint of preciousness. Jane was always entertaining as well as informative.

Living half the year in France, the other half in their small Wiltshire farmhouse, provided her and her husband Geoffrey with unusual opportunities for driving about the country, searching out interesting food markets and small restaurants where local specialities were likely to be on offer.

The Grigsons didn't frequent expensive establishments. They couldn't afford to. Indeed, I remember Jane telling me that for many years they couldn't even afford a fridge. So, for her, fresh food and good-quality produce never lost their importance or their impact. I think that was one of the essential points which made her articles and her books on English food so worthwhile, to herself as well as to her readers. Those were truly brave undertakings, and they were handsomely rewarded.

On one occasion, after lunching with Jane, I took her back to my Pimlico shop so that she could see the glazed stoneware salting jars and rillette pots and the earthenware terrines we were at that time importing from France.

Jane found those traditional farmhouse and charcuterie preserving pots and jars as beautiful and beguiling as I did myself and of course they were very relevant to her book. We shared many tastes and convictions, so it was hardly surprising that we soon became firm friends, conducting long Sunday morning telephone conversations, corresponding on subjects of mutual interest – anything from medieval English bread laws to eighteenth-century French ice creams (only a couple of weeks ago Jane was fascinated to learn that rye bread ices were already popular in the 1770s) – and every now and again meeting for a lunch or a dinner in London.

As a writer Jane leaves an unfillable gap. As a friend she is irreplaceable.

Elizabeth David.

COOK WITH THE RECIPE OF LOVE

Jane was the best-known and best-loved cookery writer of her generation. She treated the reader as her equal. This was a novel attitude among recipe writers when she first burst upon the food world as The Observer Magazine's cookery writer in 1968. It took hard work to achieve this relationship with her readers: Jane and her helpers tested every recipe published under her name. After coming down from Cambridge she joined the publisher George Rainbird as picture researcher for a great work he was doing for Thames and Hudson, an encyclopaedia of *People, Things and Ideas*. The editor was the poet, critic and naturalist Geoffrey Grigson. He sacked everybody on the project except Jane.

For Jane it was a *coup de foudre*. She was in her mid-twenties, Geoffrey in his late forties. She had hero-worshipped him since the age of 15, when she had bought a copy of his anthology *The Poet's Eye*. They got by on very little money, but lived exactly as they chose. At first this was in London, but later at a magical farmhouse in Wiltshire and an even more magical house at Troo in central France, where the principal room was a cave and they led what Jane called a 'troglodyte existence.'

The experience of French village life was central to Jane's writing. She understood the French character, and had the unforced appreciation of their language and manners that comes from living among them. Their only child (Geoffrey had three others from earlier marriages) Sophie, was partly brought up in Troo.

Geoffrey's death in 1985, though he was aged 80, was a blow from which Jane did not really recover. Life with Geoffrey, she often told me, had been such fun, so full of interest, that she could not imagine enjoying it without him, Affable though she was, Jane approved of Geoffrey's sometime savage temperament. She could see that it was occasionally necessary to be negative, and she appreciated the gusto with which Geoffrey would square off for a critical fight. She was capable of a display of strong feeling herself, if she felt someone she loved was being threatened, or as when, in 1988, she tongue-lashed the then Agriculture minister.

Jane was at the height of her powers as a writer when she discovered that she was ill with cancer. She widened her range to confront the food issues of today. At her own suggestion, she wrote about her cancer, and, judging from her postbag, gave heart to hundreds of fellow-sufferers.

Paul Levy

HOGGART'S TRUE STORIES

25 February 1990

Dolly Parton's breasts are a perfectly normal size. There, I've said it. Naturally you don't believe it. I don't expect you to believe it, even though it's absolutely true. This is not the first time I have had this experience.

Years ago I wrote an article about holidaying in Northern Ireland. I praised the gorgeous countryside, the friendly people, the opportunities for riding, fishing and boating, and mentioned how – not surprisingly – it was wonderfully uncrowded. Sadly the *Guardian*, for which I then worked, refused to print it on the grounds that some things were so improbable that nobody would believe them even if they were endorsed by a team of notaries public headed by George Washington with his little axe.

Did you know that there are still many first-rate French restaurants in Beirut and that one of the world's greatest red wines, Château Musar, is made in the Bekaa Valley? This is also quite true, but I don't really ask you to believe it. I'm not sure I do myself.

So here, to test your suspension of disbelief, are a clutch of more perfectly true facts about other people which you may not find yourself able to credit. In life we often find ourselves in the position of *Sun* readers; we assume that *some* of what is laid before us must be factual, but have no way of knowing which.

The first concerns Miss Parton's bosom. I know about it not because I've seen it, but because I've seen her. She was sitting near me on a four-hour flight from Chicago to Vancouver. The plane was a DC-10 of United Airlines, of which a number had fallen out of the skies, so I was relieved to learn that the dozens of maintenance men who appeared on board, milling around before take-off, weren't checking the flaps, or not the ones on the plane.

Miss Parton is minuscule. I have seen bigger 10-year-old girls.

Her jeans must have been sprayed on because they don't make adult sizes that size. On top of this bird-like torso, the breasts naturally give the appearance of being enormous. On a normally built woman, they would look, well, normal.

Princess Di is actually quite bright. In fact, I suspect she is very bright. I've only met her twice, at the cocktail parties they give journalists at the start of Royal Tours, at which you have to promise you won't repeat anything they say, except of course to name-drop gloatingly to your friends, but she struck me as smart, quick, amusing and even caustic at times. She also has the famous smile, so dazzling that you could perform brain surgery by its luminescence, and which is swivelled upon anyone who has made an even mildly amusing remark, thus making them her devoted slave for life.

My impression is that her whole 'gosh-I'm-such-a-dippy-girl-don't-pay-any-attention-to-little-me' schtik is designed to make you surprised by her intelligence and to have precisely the effect it did in the above paragraph.

Bob Geldof wasn't always so generous. In the Seventies, before Band Aid but when the Boomtown Rats were one of the most successful pop groups in the world, he was in Dublin discussing with his sister Lynn a birthday present for their father. Geldof produced £10 as his contribution, muttering that the band's royalties had been slow coming in that year.

Mrs Thatcher is, on the side, a bit of a sexy baggage. Of course I don't mean she has affairs. When could she find the time? But her penchant for handsome, somewhat roué fellows like Cecil Parkinson is well known. She is also one of those people who expects others to take a pride in her appearance. A word of sycophantic flattery – 'Prime Minister, you look absolutely wonderful

tonight' – will be greeted with a crisp 'And when do I look anything else?' A friend of mine, chief aide to an American senator, told me this story. The senator had called on Mrs T in Downing Street and was getting the usual treatment: an uninterrupted exposition of her views on East-West relations, arms control, fiscal policy, and for all I know, the prospects for next year's Grand National

After a while my friend, loyal to his boss, felt he ought to break the flow. So he began to look at her, slowly, up and down, putting as much lust into his expression as any normal chap could manage. The result was gratifying. She began to stumble, thoughts ceased to glide from her tongue, she lost her place and began to return his gaze, if in less lubricious fashion. The senator leapt in, said what he had to say, and got out unscathed.

Barry Humphries is not a quiet, resigned little man at the mercy of Dame Edna. That's a pose for TV. In real life he is almost as raunchy, and occasionally savagely witty, as Edna herself.

Norman Tebbit is usually very polite. In Chingford I once watched him talk with great courtesy to a woman who complained that her son had failed to get a job because 'the law said they had to give it to a nigger.' Tebbit explained that black people had been invited to this country; now they were here they should be given every opportunity, and this sometimes would make difficulties for white people. He was sorry, but there it was. I don't believe he was talking like this because I was listening, since I wasn't, being curled up in a dead faint on the floor.

Simon Hoggart

SIMON HOGGART (b. 1946)
Joined paper from Guardian *1981;*
US correspondent 1985-9; now leader
page columnist. Books include House
of Ill Fame.

FARZAD BAZOFT

18 March 1990

Universal outrage is a fiery emotion, quick to come and quick to dissipate in further thoughts and new suspicions. It is a supreme irony that British relations in the Middle East have been torn apart by Salman Rushdie, a novelist born in India, and Farzad Bazoft, a journalist born in Iran, both of whom happened to set up shop in Britain. It is even more ironic that martyrdom to a brutal regime should come to a warm, chaotic and eager young journalist with a debt-ridden past and a prison sentence behind him.

None of this – as the Prime Minister, the Foreign Office, Dr David Owen and many others have commendably insisted – makes any difference. Farzad Bazoft was a reporter who, on an invited trip to Iraq, went to a weapons plant in pursuit of a story all his colleagues were chasing. There is no serious evidence that he was there for any other purpose. He made no secret of his intentions to his colleagues or his hosts. The Iraqi authorities produced no proof of espionage, other than 'confessions' clearly extracted from a man under in-

tolerable pressure and fear for his life. They do not stand up to even cursory inspection.

He died a horrible death without a fair trial or appeal. The MPs who have used their privileged position to give substance to Iraqi propaganda in favour of this barbarity without any proof – Mr Rupert Allason, Conservative MP for Torbay, Mr Anthony Beaumont-Dark, Conservative MP for Selly Oak, and the most despicable of all, Mr Terry Dicks, Conservative MP for Hayes and Harlington (who made a public statement the day before Farzad's execution that he 'deserved to be hanged' and thereby justified the savage act) – have demeaned their office and shamed themselves as responsible human beings. To dance on an innocent man's grave in this way beggars civilised description. The newspapers that gave credence to their views are little better.

In any other country Farzad would be alive today to proclaim his innocence, to cross-examine witnesses through a lawyer of his own choice and then to appeal against any sentence. Instead, he was denied all these rights and finally deprived of the right to life itself. Worse, in death he has had to suffer contemptible, unsupported innuendo to which he can no longer reply.

The case also raises important issues about relations between Britain and Iraq. The Government has been forthright in its condemnation and powerful in its pleas for clemency. As far as Mr Bazoft and Mrs Parish were concerned, we could not have expected more. The Foreign Office was probably right to be cautious about a total break in diplomatic relations while 2,000 British subjects are at risk. But what kind of relations do we want? Business as usual, the message from the Foreign Secretary, simply won't do. This was not just an aberration to which we must turn a blind eye. Executions and torture are a routine feature of the present regime.

The truth is that we are humouring a dictator, which is

Farzad Bazoft. 'His death has focussed world-wide attention on the barbarities of Saddam Hussein.'

rather like negotiating over hostages, which, as Mrs Thatcher keeps reminding us, never pays. Nor does it make sense to talk, as Ministers do, of the overriding imperatives of trade and exports. It is these very exports, many of them concerned with arms and military technology, which have helped to create the monster who ordered yesterday's anti-British demonstrations in Baghdad.

We should know our enemy. Since his war with Iran, in which he engaged in Nazi-style barbarities, Saddam Hussein has set out to be the regional superpower of the Middle East, gathering the technology to enable him to threaten Israel, making himself the prime protector of the PLO, sending arms to the Christians in Lebanon to upset the Syrians and forming a network of alliances with Jordan and the Gulf states in which he is the senior partner. Britain's policy of appeasement towards him has been based on the belief that he is the most useful force against Communism on the one side and Islamic fundamentalism on the other.

The execution of Farzad Bazoft provides one more illustration of the failure of this appeasement policy. Hussein cannot be controlled by words and messages, no matter how eminent and how well-meaning the senders. A man who unleashes chemical weapons against his own people is not likely to restrain his use of the same weapons against any other enemy – or nuclear warheads once he gets hold of them. The second anniversary of the massacre by gas of the Kurds of Halabja is a good time to remember this.

If Farzad Bazoft's death has achieved anything, it has been to focus world-wide attention on the barbarities of Saddam Hussein, of which Farzad himself was just the latest victim. Britain may be right to seek to retain its historic and cultural relations with the people of Iraq, but anything it does to perpetuate Saddam's regime can be measured in dead and broken bodies. Hussein is a ruler who will continue to perpetuate the most horrendous acts of cruelty against his own people as well as his guests. Morality as well as national self-interest requires us to underline the values of fair trial, fair treatment and free ex-

pression, which are not ethereal ideals but principles by which we judge ourselves and by which we have every right to judge others. Nor are they confined to this island. All over the world freedom is breaking out, even in South Africa, Latin America and Eastern Europe.

Does it really serve our long-term purposes in the Nineties to side with Saddam Hussein and lend him our money when so much of the world is crying out for help in achieving nobler aims? And is it not patronising, if not shameful, to dismiss the desires of the people of Iraq, many of whom have died and been tortured in protest at Saddam Hussein?

The Farzad who was forced to 'confess' to spying after seven weeks incommunicado, the Farzad who was hustled out of court a week ago without hearing his death sentence translated into English and who had still not been told that the sentence was confirmed when the British consul visited him on his last morning, was a fond, flawed and frightened human being. We need not apologise for the values that would grieve and rage for him.

A JOURNEY BACK INTO MY FAMILY ALBUM

27 May 1990

We had made plans, my father and I, to return to the estate. We had promised each other. Soon, we said. When we get some time. And then time ran out. He died last August and we buried him next to his mother and father and brothers in the little cemetery on the hillside in Quebec, and we stood together, our arms around each other, singing the *Viechnaya Pamyat*, the hymn of eternal memory.

Now, on a bright May afternoon, I am at last on that journey of return, without him, heading towards a little village called Kroupodernitsa, 180 kilometres south-west of Kiev. My great-grandfather built a great house in

the 1860s on the banks of the river Ross and he is buried in the crypt of the village church. I am the first member of my family to come back since February 1917.

The road has given out long ago. The car is crawling along rutted washboard tracks through vast empty fields of black soil. I cross the Kiev-Odessa railway line. It can't be far now. Somewhere along these tracks, there used to be a family station where the Moscow train would stop specially, so that the family with all the servants, baggage, tutors and nannies could be decanted into the brougham for the final ride down the pitted road to the big house. Then at the crest of the hill, in the mustard field, I see it,

the twin silver domes of great-grandfather's church. There are photographs from this viewpoint, taken by the English nanny in 1913. Nothing has changed. I am about to walk into one of her Box Brownie snaps.

In the overgrown churchyard, there is a little chapel and inside I find a sexton swabbing down a tomb with a mop. I tell him my name. He holds my hand in his and blinks in astonishment. 'Praise be to God,' he says and crosses himself. I look down at the name on the tomb. It is my uncle, the one who died of typhoid, the one whose picture my grandmother kept by her bed all her life.

In the cool darkness of the crypt, set into the red tiled floor, with a wall of icons glinting behind it, is the tomb of my great-grandfather, a black basalt slab topped with white marble. The white marble is strewn with withered daffodils and tulips and painted cardboard Easter eggs. Every time the villagers lay their wreaths at the Soviet war memorial, they also come into the church and lay flowers on my great-grandfather's tomb.

As I walk up the dusty track to the priest's house among the sheep and the barefoot children, and I peek over the picket fences into the tangled gardens, I can see that the peasant huts are exactly as they were in the photographs of 1913. Lenin once said Communism was electricity plus Soviets. It is not clear that Communism has even got them all electricity, and the wells in the courtyards tell me many of the houses don't have running water either. Many roofs are still thatched, as they were in the English nanny's photographs.

I am taking tea in the priest's house, with my back to a wall of icons, eating sausage and pickled tomatoes, when the priest himself and his son burst in. They are both wearing homburgs over a full mane of hair, and they are carrying bread and bottles of vodka from a shopping trip to the nearest town. They are big ruddy men with capacious stomachs, stained cassocks and big appetites. I hand them an envelope full of roubles and toasts are drunk to the regilding of the iconostasis.

To my amazement, they rummage about and produce a photograph of my great-grandfather, kept by one of the old peasants. I tell them that I am touched that they remember the family, but they say, 'It is normal', and in a place where time seems barely to move at all, a place so far away from perestroika and its fevers, perhaps they are right. It is normal, how things ought to be, that 70 years ago is kept alive as if it were yesterday.

Finally, I say we must see the old house. When we get there, at the top of the dusty track leading back into the village, there is no

mistake about it. The peacock fan decorations on the gables are gone, the porches have been stripped away, the white plaster work has fallen from one of the wings, exposing all the wattle-and-daub lathing. The great white gates and the ornamental gardens have vanished. But I could recognise it anywhere.

The house is now a village school. In the room where my great-grandfather died, there is the principal's desk and a picture of Mikhail Sergeyevich Gorbachov hanging on the bare white-washed walls.

It is getting dark, and I have three hours to travel back to Kiev on country roads. I embrace them all, the priest and his wife and their children and grandchildren, the school caretaker and his wife.

I promise to return again, with my brother and my wife and children. I thank them again, with my hand over my heart, for taking care of the graves of my ancestors. And then suddenly, the priest begins to sing, and they all take it up, the *Viechnaya Pamyat*, the lament I heard last on a Quebec hillside at my father's grave. All of the feeling a son will always hide from his father, all of the sorrow that we keep hidden from ourselves, finally found the place where it could be expressed.

Michael Ignatieff

MICHAEL IGNATIEFF (b. 1947) *Former fellow of King's College, Cambridge. Became editorial page columnist of* The Observer *in 1989, also working as TV presenter on BBC2's* The Late Show.

CRICKET'S MASTER CRAFTSMAN

9 September 1990

Len Hutton, who died last week aged 74, was one of the greatest and wisest of all cricketers, our first professional captain, and scorer of the highest Test innings (364) by an Englishman.

The Yorkshire club, unwontedly effusive, described him as 'every boy's hero and the cricketer every man wanted to be'.

Between 1934 and 1956, when he was knighted on his retirement, he scored 40,000 runs, including 129 centuries, at an average of 55. But, as R. C. Robertson-Glasgow warned, 'to admire Len Hutton merely for the quantity of his runs is like praising Milton for the length of *Paradise Lost*'.

The style was the man. His success was as much a triumph of character as technique. In Barbados in 1986, when England were being destroyed by the West Indies fast bowlers, I said to Peter May, the frustrated chairman of selectors: 'I doubt if *anybody* could play these people on this pitch.' He looked up sharply and said: 'Len could. He batted 10 hours on

the 1954 tour and showed us all how to do it. We were two Tests down, but we drew the series after that. It just needs one man.'

Len Hutton was that man too often. For much of his career he carried the England batting, a burden that took its toll on and caused his early retirement.

The Bishop of Liverpool, David Sheppard, a former England batsman and longtime student of Len, told me that the clue to his elusive personality was to be found in the Protestant movements of Bohemia. The Huttons, in fact, were brought up in the Moravian community at Fulneck, near Pudsey, Leeds, founded by Count Zinzerndorf, who came here from Czechoslovakia in the 1730s.

It was an austere upbringing – 'strict but caring', as he later described it. He had three devoted aunts who watched over him like guardian angels. His genius for cricket was spotted early by Herbert Sutcliffe, the great Yorkshire and England batsman, who played with Len's father and brothers at Pudsey St

Lawrence, but he also developed a talent for soccer. One day, when he had injured his knee, he arrived home to find that his aunts, all silently knitting after a family conference, had put his football boots on the fire, a burnt sacrifice to his future destiny.

His shrewd sense of cricket's inner mysteries made him successful as a captain, winning and retaining the Ashes against Australia (though, strangely, he never captained Yorkshire), and later as a Test selector and writer on the game, enlightening *Observer* readers for close on 30 years. Though usually terse and taut as his batting, his writing was often enlivened – like his conversation in his more relaxed later years – by wry flashes of deadpan understatement which got funnier the more you thought about them, and which those around him learned to treasure and share with each other as 'Lenisms'.

Asked what he thought of a once fashionable England player, he replied carefully, wrinkling his famous 'knob of garlic' nose (which, contrary to legend, was not inflicted by a demon fast bowler, but from a misdirected throw by a wicket-keeper): 'Well, he lacks something at the highest level, some quality . . . there's a word I'm seeking . . . it'll come to me in a minute . . .' Then, with a twinkle and a flattening of vowels: 'I've got it! *Ability* . . . that's what he lacks . . . that's the word I'm looking for.'

His family were a source of great pride and pleasure to this very private man. He told me that he recently enjoyed watching his grandchildren play cricket more than Test matches, though he was a faithful attender to the end. He rang only last week and arranged to come in for a cricket lunch at *The Observer*. I asked him about Gooch's 333 at Lord's. He said Gooch was always the most likely modern player to challenge his record.

He then praised young Tendulkar, who reminded him of another Indian, Gavaskar. 'They both have little feet, you see,' he added cryptically. Len had an obsession

about the size of a batsman's feet. Once, after Bradman had hit England all over the field, he went to the Australian's dressing-room and discovered the secret of his genius: 'I looked at his boots – they were the same size as Fred Astaire's!' He enjoyed expounding the theory – how seriously I could never tell – that the main reason why batsmen like Colin Cowdrey and Viv Richards were not as good as Bradman was that they had big flat feet, which meant that they couldn't drive as nimbly at the pitch of the ball and keep it down.

He also had a theory about hands, as I learned when I played golf with him. As I peppered wild shots all over Wimbledon, I suddenly heard this voice behind me: 'It's all in the hands, Donald.' He then demonstrated how great stroke-players like Cowdrey and Tom Graveney had a sure touch with the irons. Whenever I play golf now, I shall always hear that gentle Yorkshire voice of admonition: 'It's all in the hands, Donald.'

He was forced to think about hands after breaking his arm in the gym during Royal Marine training in the war. It was broken badly, in several places above the wrist, requiring a number of operations and skin grafts from his leg. When it was over, he found that his left arm, the guiding force for a right-handed batsmen, was more than two inches shorter than the other. There was a serious chance, at the age of 25, that he might never play again.

As it was, he missed six years' cricket because of the war – at his prime from the age of 23 to 29 – and returned a different player. He had to change his technique, playing with a boy's bat and eschewing shots like the hook, which limited his repertoire against fast bowling. As E. W. Swanton said: 'Given a full career without intermission or accident, who can tell what his record might have been?' Len was a man without bitterness, though I once heard him express a moment's sadness over what might have been.

Hutton: 'A triumph as much of character as of technique.'

◆

We were lunching at the Garrick and a member came over to say he'd never forgotten a brilliant innings Len had played in South Africa in 1939. 'Ah yes,' Len said, '1939 – everybody remembers 1938, but I was actually better in 1939. I was nearly as good as Bradman. After the war, of course, I was a different man. I'll never know how good I might have become in those lost years. I might not have got any better at all. The trouble is, you see, I'll never know.'

People sometimes said that he was a hard Yorkshireman, selfish and ungiving. He was certainly hard in his playing days, as he had to be. Of the old enemy he once said: 'In Australia the pitches are hard, the ball is hard, and the men are hard. You have to be harder to beat them.' When it mattered he was, and he did.

But that is not how he should be remembered. He was unfailingly courteous and modest, with a hidden reserve of humour in those wide-apart blue eyes that never missed a trick, and he had a knack of making people feel they were his friends. I am haunted, as I know he was, by an *Observer* profile of 1951 which said that he was 'not lovable', if only because he didn't greatly care whether he was loved or not. I think he did care, though he needn't have worried about it.

Donald Trelford

Citizen, Once Again, of the New Germany

Paul Oestreicher is Director of International Ministry at Coventry Cathedral. In this article he welcomes the transformation of his homeland and recalls the years since leaving as a refugee.

7 October 1990

My birthplace, Meiningen, lies just inside East Germany. Coburg lies only a few miles away in the West. When I was born the border simply separated Thuringia from Bavaria, and does so again now in one Germany. The dogs, minefields and watchtowers are already memories of a long nightmare.

For my family the nightmare started when I was two, in 1933. My father's parents were Jews from Bavaria. After Hitler's accession to power my non-Jewish mother was described as a whore, sullying German blood, by marrying a Jew. I was an officially designated *mischling* (halfcaste), by 1938 living hidden in a Berlin cellar, while my father went from consulate to consulate begging for visas. Just in time, New Zealand came to our rescue.

Today I am a citizen of New Zealand, of the United Kingdom and, once again, by right of birth, of the new Germany. My Jewish grandmother had hoped to follow us; but war made that impossible. She shared the fate of millions in the Holocaust. I could never, these last 30 years, cross the Berlin Wall without remembering the awesome gates of Buchenwald, Belsen and Auschwitz. Without that unparallelled German depravity, and all that went with it, there would never have been a Blitz to commemorate in the Coventry where I now work for peace and reconciliation. No Allied inferno incinerating 70,000 people in Dresden, no defeated and divided Germany. No 40 years of Leninist twilight for the people of Weimar, Leipzig, Rostock and Karl-Marx-Stadt, now Chemnitz once more. And no cause now for anyone to fear a reunited Germany.

Do I share those fears? I would, if reunited were the right word, if the old Reich had been reborn last week. But it is not. The new Germany is not the Germany of Bismarck, the Kaiser or of Adolf Hitler.

My experience with the Germans over 35 years began with a theological research scholarship at Bonn University. I respected and came to love my professor, Helmut Gollwitzer, a key figure in the resistance to Hitler who had just written the tale of his postwar years in Stalin's prison camps. He preached *Ostpolitik* when it was still derided in Bonn and elsewhere. I loved my professor and the few others like him. But the Germans all round me – what had they been doing when their Jewish, gipsy, Communist and gay neighbours just disappeared?

My mother's mother was still alive in Meiningen, in the Communist East. En route there, I determined to visit an anti-Nazi family in Leipzig who had sheltered my parents. I didn't get that far. The Stasi picked me up and handed me over to the Soviet security police. They thought they'd caught a spy with a false New Zealand passport. My German was too good and I lived in Bonn.

There followed a long KGB interrogation. I have never since been so afraid. My life depended on the intelligence and decency of one Russian. I prayed he would believe me – and he did. He had me put on a train for Cologne. I had been quickly cured of any potential romantic illusions about Soviet-style democracy. But I was determined not to let that experience frighten me off or embitter me. I have been back to East Germany at least once a year ever since, determined, wherever I could, to break down the insane ideological wall, as well as the physical one, between East and West.

Gradually, I began to trust the social forces shaping the new Germany and the students among whom I lived. I recoiled at much of the blatant commercialism, but I knew too that hardly anyone felt like singing 'Deutschland, Deutschland Uber Alles.' They didn't then. They don't now. And, after moving to England in 1957 I began to develop a love-hate relationship with East German society: a hatred for the system, but a love for many of its people.

It was in 1964 that my real work of bridge-building to Eastern Europe began. The British Council of Churches invited me to set up an East-West Relations Committee to help to break down the isolation of the East European churches. The hard slog of organising visits and delegations in both directions began. The outstanding leadership of the GDR's Protestant Churches was already evident. It was eventually to be a major factor in bringing down the whole Communist regime.

'Do you believe in a Communist future?' I once asked a 16-year-old girl in Potsdam. 'Only in the morning', was her witty reply. Translated: not once I get out of school. Germany's young generation in East and West are sceptical of all doctrines and healthily disrespectful of authority. They are as angry as their elders when pseudo-fascist fringe groups beat up Turkish immigrants or smash Jewish gravestones.

The cry of the hundreds of thousands in the streets of Leipzig – 'No Violence' – toppled a dictatorship; Germans today are proud of that. I know, as a Christian, that the masses can cry 'Hosanna' on one day and 'Crucify Him' on the next. With Buchenwald next to Goethe's Weimar and Belsen not far from Beethoven's Bonn, I am not given to easy illusions. But the new Germany of which the Christian humanist Richard von Weizsacker is the undisputedly popular President gives much ground for sober hope.

Paul Oestreicher

PICTURE ACKNOWLEDGEMENTS

The publishers wish to thank all past and present Observer photographers and picture editors who have kindly assisted in the compilation of this book, by giving not only photographs but also their memories or advice. In particular, Bill Barrett, Jane Bown, Bryn Campbell, Colin Jacobson, Colin Jones, Tony McGrath, June Stanier. Special thanks are also due to Tony Mancini at the Observer Picture Library, to Geoff Care, Scott Harrison at the Observer Library, and Alan Smith and all at Topham Picture Source, not only for historical material but also for Observer Magazine syndicated pictures.

Abbreviations indicate MEPL= Mary Evans Picture Library, Hulton = Hulton Picture Company, IWM= Imperial War Museum, OL= Observer Library, OM= Observer Magazine, OPL= Observer Picture Library, TPS= Topham Picture Source.

6TL: Gerry Cranham, 6TR: OPL/Neil Libbert, 6CL: Dod Miller, 6CR: OPL/Nobby Clark, 6BL: Eamonn McCabe, 6BR: OPL/Chris Smith, 11: Jane Bown, 13: TPS, 14: Mansell Collection/Bulloz, 16, 17: OL, 18: National Maritime Museum, 20: OL, 21: TPS, 22: National Portrait Gallery, 23: Hulton, 25: TPS, 26, 27: MEPL, 28-29: by gracious permission of Her Majesty the Queen, 33: National Portrait Gallery, 35: Hulton/ Bettmann Archive, 36, 37: MEPL, 39: by gracious permission of Her Majesty the Queen, 41: MEPL, 43: TPS, 44: Hulton, 46, 47: TPS, 48-49: MEPL, 50: TPS, 51: OPL, 52: TPS, 53: MEPL, 55BL: Hulton, 55R: TPS, 56: AKG, Berlin, 57: TPS, 58: Hulton, 59, 61: OL, 63: OPL, 64: OPL/IWM, 66B: Popperfoto, 66-67, 69: OPL/IWM, 70: OL, 71: OPL, 72: OL, 73, 75T: OPL, 75B: TPS, 76-77: OPL, 77L: OPL/ (c) NY Review Opera Mundi, 77R: OL, 78: TPS/AP, 79, 80: TPS, 81: OL, 82: Kobal Collection, 83: OPL, 85: Hulton, 86T: OPL. 86B: TPS, 88T: Hulton, 88B: OPL, 89: OL, 90:TPS/AP, 91TR: TPS, 91B: IWM, 92: TPS/AP, 93: OPL/©IWM, 94: IWM, 95: OPL/AP, 96: TPS, 96B, 98: TPS/©IWM, 99L: Jane Bown, 99R: OPL/Nigel Powry Photography, 101T: TPS/Novosti, 101B: TPS, 103: TPS/©IWM, 104: OL, 105: TPS/ Novosti, 106: Hulton, 107: TPS, 108: OL, 109: OPL/ Mauritius Verlag, 111T: TPS, 111B: TPS/Keystone

Tokyo, 114: TPS/AP, 117: Popperfoto, 120: OPL/ Metropolitan Museum, NY, 121: TPS/Keystone, 122, 123: Jane Bown, 124: OPL/National Film Archive, 125: OPL/Keystone, 126: Jane Bown, 128: Popperfoto, 129: OL, 130: Hulton/Bert Hardy, 131: OPL/Camera Press, 132: OL, 133, 135, 140, 142, 144: Jane Bown, 145: OPL/J.T. Goldblatt, 149: OL, 153T: TPS/PA, 153B: Jane Bown, 154: TPS/AP, 155: OPL/Ian Berry, 162-163: OPL/Don McCullin, 164: TPS, 166: OPL/ Don McCullin, 167: TPS, 171: Kobal Collection, 172: TPS, 173: Jane Bown, 177: Camera Press/Norman Parkinson, 178: OPL/Stuart Heydinger, 181: OPL, 183: Kobal Collection, 184: OPL/Don McCullin, 185: TPS, 186: OPL/PA, 187: OPL/Keystone, 190-191: Bryn Campbell, 193: OPL/Andrew Wilson, 196, 197: OPL/ David Newell Smith, 199: OL, 200: OL/United Feature Syndicate, Inc., 201: OPL/David Newell Smith, 203: Michael Peto Collection, University of Dundee, 204: Science Photo Library/NASA, 205: OPL/Magnum/Ian Berry, 206: OPL/Bryn Campbell, 209: OPL/Tony McGrath, 210T: Bryn Campbell, 210-211: Jane Bown, 212: OPL/Bryn Campbell, 213: Jane Bown, 215: OPL/Crispian Woodgate, 216, 217: OM/ TPS/Norman Eales, 218-219: Chris Smith, 221: OPL/ Gavin Young, 223: Jane Bown, 224: OPL/David Newell Smith, 225T, 225B: OM/Bryn Campbell, 227: OPL/ Doug Scott, 229: OPL/Nobby Clark, 232: Alastair Black, 235: OPL/Nobby Clark, 237: OM/Colin Jones, 238: Eamonn McCabe, 239: OPL/Gamma/Uzan, 240T, 240-241, 241T: Impact/Colin Jones, 242: Jane Bown, 245: Eamonn McCabe, 247: Eamonn McCabe, 248: OM/TPS/Bryn Campbell, 251: OPL/Keystone, 252: OM/TPS/David Steen, 253: OM/TPS, 255: TPS/PA, 256: OM/TPS/Colin Jones, 257: OPL/PA/Martin Cleaver, 260: TPS/PA, 261: Kobal Collection, 262: Jane Bown, 263: OPL/Neil Libbert, 264, 265: OM/TPS/Bill Burnside, 266: Tony McGrath, 267: Eamonn McCabe, 270: OPL/Richard Mildenhall, 272: OPL/Radek Skorski, 273: OPL, 274: Jane Bown, 276: OPL/Derek Cattani, 277: OM/TPS/David Gamble, 278: OPL/Mike King, 284: OM/TPS/David Gamble, 286: OM/Peter Lavery, 289: Bill Robinson, 291: OPL/Roger Hutchings, 293: OM/Network/Mike Goldwater, 295: TPS/PA/ Adam Butler, 296: OM/TPS/Sara Taylor, 299: OPL/ David Harden, 302: Trog (Wally Fawkes).